CLASSICAL CLOSURE

CLASSICAL CLOSURE

READING THE END IN GREEK
AND LATIN LITERATURE

Edited by Deborah H. Roberts,
Francis M. Dunn, and
Don Fowler

PRINCETON UNIVERSITY PRESS   PRINCETON, NEW JERSEY

Copyright © 1997 by Princeton University Press
Published by Princeton University Press, 41 William Street,
Princeton, New Jersey 08540
In the United Kingdom: Princeton University Press, Chichester, West
Sussex
All Rights Reserved

Library of Congress Cataloging-in-Publication Data
Classical closure : reading the end in Greek and Latin literature /
edited by Deborah H. Roberts, Francis M. Dunn, and Don Fowler.
p.   cm.
Includes bibliographical references and index.
ISBN 0-691-04452-X (alk. paper)
1. Classical literature—History and criticism—Theory, etc.
2. Narration (Rhetoric)   3. Greece—Civilization.   4. Rome—
Civilization.   5. Closure (Rhetoric)   6. Rhetoric, Ancient.
I. Roberts, Deborah H.   II. Dunn, Francis M.   III. Fowler, Don,
1955–
PA3009.C53   1997
880'.09—dc21   96-44439
                                                                                    CIP

This book has been composed in Bembo

Princeton University Press books are printed on acid-free paper
and meet the guidelines for permanence and durability of the
Committee on Production Guidelines for Book Longevity of the
Council on Library Resources

Printed in the United States of America by Princeton Academic Press

10   9   8   7   6   5   4   3   2   1

For Sophia, Andrew, Alexander, and Hannah

The common end of all *narrative*, nay of *all*, Poems
is to convert a *series* into a *Whole*: to make these
events, which in real or imagined History move on in a
strait line, assume to our Understandings a *circular*
motion—the snake with it's Tail in it's Mouth.
                              —Coleridge, *Collected Letters*

Contents

Preface   xi

Notes on the Contributors   xiii

Abbreviations   xv

Chapter 1. Second Thoughts on Closure   3
Don Fowler

Chapter 2. Equal Honor and Future Glory: The Plan of
Zeus in the *Iliad*   23
Sheila Murnaghan

Chapter 3. Odes and Ends: Closure in Greek Lyric   43
Ian Rutherford

Chapter 4. Wanton Kings, Pickled Heroes, and Gnomic
Founding Fathers: Strategies of Meaning at the End of
Herodotus's *Histories*   62
Carolyn Dewald

Chapter 5. Ends and Means in Euripides' *Heracles*   83
Francis M. Dunn

Chapter 6. Lucretian Conclusions   112
Peta Fowler

Chapter 7. Closure in Latin Epic   139
Philip Hardie

Chapter 8. Final Exit: Propertius 4.11   163
W. R. Johnson

Chapter 9. Endgames: Ovid's *Metamorphoses* 15 and *Fasti* 6   181
Alessandro Barchiesi

Chapter 10. How Novels End: Some Patterns of Closure in
Ancient Narrative   209
Massimo Fusillo

Chapter 11. Is Death the End? Closure in Plutarch's *Lives*   228

 Christopher Pelling

Chapter 12. Afterword: Ending and Aftermath, Ancient and
Modern   251

 Deborah H. Roberts

Bibliography   275

Index   303

THIS COLLECTION of essays addresses the problem of closure (variously conceived) in a broad sampling of classical texts, and in so doing hopes to alert classical scholars to the usefulness of this inquiry, while offering avenues into classical literature for scholars in other disciplines.

The study of closure has played a significant part in contemporary literary criticism, as the survey of scholarship at the end of this volume demonstrates, and is implicated in many of its concerns. Approaches to closure may address formal features of the ending, psychological or narratological aspects of reaching or searching for an end, aesthetic issues of unity or incompleteness, political and cultural constraints of order and authority, ethical issues of freedom and autonomy, and metacritical questions of interpretive authority and competence. For these reasons, a survey of scholarship on closure would range almost as widely as a survey of literary and cultural criticism, and a collection of essays on closure in classical studies might involve any number of objects and methods. In order to give this collection greater coherence, and because of our own shared interests, we have invited discussions only of literary works, and in particular of the endings or conclusions of literary works. The deliberately narrow focus of our subject (classical literary endings) will, we believe, place in relief the wide range of methods this study may employ: these endings pose many kinds of question that may be answered in very different and interesting ways. In general, the study of closure tends to coincide, sometimes explicitly and sometimes not, with the metacritical question of how to approach or interpret a text; we hope that this volume, both in the arguments of individual essays and in the variety of approaches they collectively employ, will help to frame and explore this problem.

Don Fowler introduces this collection by simultaneously surveying and deconstructing the study of closure: internal divisions and segmentation complicate the notion of an ending, intertextuality complicates the notion of a discrete work, and recent directions in criticism complicate the assumption that the nature of a work (open, closed, or indeterminate) can be separated from the act of interpretation. The essays that follow are arranged by chronological order of the authors they discuss; given the varied and overlapping approaches of these essays, this traditional format seems most convenient, although readers will find that matters of central concern cut across temporal, cultural, and generic boundaries. Several contributors offer typologies of closure for classical authors or genres (as Barbara Herrnstein Smith has done for the sonnet and other poetic forms, and Marianna

Torgovnick for a selection of novels): Ian Rutherford discusses formal and thematic devices in Pindar and other Greek lyrics, Massimo Fusillo considers narratological techniques in several Greek novels, and Christopher Pelling describes closing patterns in Plutarch's *Lives*, while Deborah Roberts discusses various forms of a single closing technique—allusion to events that follow the end. Some contributors challenge received opinion concerning defective or incomplete endings (Carolyn Dewald on Herodotus, Peta Fowler on Lucretius, Alessandro Barchiesi on Ovid's *Fasti*), while others challenge positive or positivistic readings of the endings of Euripides' *Heracles* (Francis Dunn), Propertius's last book of elegies (Ralph Johnson) and Ovid's *Metamorphoses* (Barchiesi). Generic considerations are important to several authors, who draw attention to the inconclusive endings of epic (Philip Hardie), the comforting closure of romantic fiction (Fusillo), or the "terminal generosity" of didactic biography (Pelling). A reading of closure may stress an author's resistance or challenge to the constraints of political ideology (Johnson, Barchiesi), or it may stress instead the relation between author and audience: P. Fowler, Roberts, Dewald, and Dunn discuss ancient and modern works that in various ways require the reader to construct a moral or a sequel—or leave the reader unable to do so. The delay or deferral of closure in narrative genres may likewise generate a reader's interest in the end to come (Hardie, Fusillo), or it may negotiate and maintain cultural notions of heroism and mortality, as Sheila Murnaghan argues in her discussion of the *Iliad*.

The subject of closure is endless. Even within the narrow domain of endings in classical literature, the essays assembled here can be no more than a beginning. Our own beginning was a panel on closure at the 1989 meeting of the American Philological Association; the success of that panel brought our attention to the need for, and the interest in, a collection such as this. All three editors of this volume would like to thank the readers and editors at Princeton University Press for their help and encouragement, the Faculty Research Fund at Haverford College for financial assistance, Valerie Howard at Jesus College and Dorcas Allen at Haverford College for typing parts of the book, and our contributors for their patience.

Notes on the Contributors

ALESSANDRO BARCHIESI is Professor of Latin Literature at the University of Verona, and has worked on classical scholarship and literary theory. He has written a book on Vergil and Homer (*La traccia del modello*, Pisa 1984), and one on Ovid and Augustus (*Il poeta e il principe*, Rome 1994, which is being translated for the University of California Press).

CAROLYN DEWALD is Associate Professor of Classics at the University of Southern California; she has written principally on Herodotus and Thucydides, and her interests include Greek and Roman rhetoric, literary criticism, and historiography.

FRANCIS M. DUNN teaches Classics at the University of California, Santa Barbara. He has edited two collections of essays, *Beginnings in Classical Literature* (*Yale Classical Studies* 29, 1992) and *Sophocles' Electra in Performance* (*DRAMA* 4, 1996), and is the author of *Tragedy's End: Closure and Innovation in Euripidean Drama* (Oxford 1996).

DON FOWLER is Fellow and Tutor in Classics at Jesus College, Oxford. His interests include Latin poetry, literary theory, and Hellenistic philosophy, and he is writing a book on books and reading in classical Latin poetry.

PETA FOWLER is Lecturer in Classics at St. Anne's and St. Hugh's Colleges, Oxford. Her interests include Latin poetry, Hellenistic philosophy, and ancient literary criticism.

MASSIMO FUSILLO is Associate Professor of Literary Theory in the Department of Studies in Modern Civilization at the University of Messina. He has published chiefly on Hellenistic poetry, ancient narrative, Greek theater and its modern performance, and modern reception of classical literature. His major works are *Il tempo delle Argonautiche: Un'analisi del racconto in Apollonio Rodio* (Rome 1985), *Il romanzo greco: Polifonia ed eros* (Venice 1989; as *Naissance du roman*, Paris 1991), and *La Grecia secondo Pasolini: Mito e cinema* (Florence 1996).

PHILIP HARDIE is a Fellow of New Hall, Cambridge. His books include *Virgil's "Aeneid": Cosmos and Imperium* (Oxford 1986) and *The Epic Successors of Virgil* (Cambridge 1993).

W. R. JOHNSON teaches Classics and Comparative Literature at the University of Chicago. He is the author of *Darkness Visible: A Study of Vergil's Aeneid* (Berkeley 1976) and of numerous articles on Latin poetry. His most recent book is *Horace and the Dialectic of Freedom* (Ithaca, N.Y. 1993)

SHEILA MURNAGHAN is Associate Professor of Classical Studies at the University of Pennsylvania. She is the author of *Disguise and Recognition in the Odyssey* (Princeton 1987) and of articles and reviews on Greek epic and drama and gender in classical Greece.

CHRISTOPHER PELLING is a Fellow of University College, Oxford. He is the author of a commentary on Plutarch's *Life of Antony* (Cambridge 1988); has edited volumes of essays on *Characterization and Individuality in Greek Literature* (Oxford 1990) and *Greek Tragedy and the Historian* (Oxford, forthcoming); and has published widely on Greek and Latin historiography.

DEBORAH H. ROBERTS teaches Classics and Comparative Literature at Haverford College. She has written on Greek tragedy and on Aristotle's *Poetics*, and her interests include ancient literary criticism, the classical tradition, and children's literature.

IAN RUTHERFORD is Lecturer at Reading University. His main interests are Greek lyric poetry, Greek religion, and ancient literary criticism, and he is the author of *Pindar's Paeans: A Reading of the Fragments with a Survey of the Genre* (Oxford 1997) and *Canons of Style in the Antonine Age: Idea Theory in Its Literary Context* (Oxford 1997). He is currently working on a study of pilgrimage (*theoria*) in ancient Greek religion and society.

Abbreviations

Abbreviated names of ancient authors and works follow the *Oxford Classical Dictionary*.

A&A	*Antike und Abendland*
A&R	*Atena e Roma*
AC	*L'Antiquité classique*
AClass	*Acta classica*
AFLN	*Annali della Facoltà di Lettere e Filosofia dell' Università di Napoli*
AJA	*American Journal of Archaeology*
AJAH	*American Journal of Ancient History*
AJPh	*American Journal of Philology*
ANRW	*Aufsteig und Niedergang der römischen Welt*
BICS	*Bulletin of the Institute of Classical Studies*
BMCR	*Bryn Mawr Classical Review*
C&M	*Classica et Mediaevalia*
ClAnt	*Classical Antiquity*
CPh	*Classical Philology*
CQ	*Classical Quarterly*
CR	*Classical Review*
CSCA	*California Studies in Classical Antiquity*
CW	*Classical World*
DArch	*Dialoghi di archeologia*
D-K	H. Diels and W. Kranz, eds., *Fragmente der Vorsokratiker*, 6th ed. Berlin, 1954.
FGrH	*Fragmente der griechischen Historiker*, ed. F. Jacoby. 14 vols. Berlin, 1923–1958.
G&R	*Greece & Rome*
GRBS	*Greek, Roman, and Byzantine Studies*
HSCPh	*Harvard Studies in Classical Philology*
ICS	*Illinois Classical Studies*
JHS	*Journal of Hellenic Studies*
JRS	*Journal of Roman Studies*
LCM	*Liverpool Classical Monthly*
MAL	*Memorie della Classe di Scienze morali, storiche e filologiche dell' Accademia dei Lincei*
MD	*Materiale e discussione per l'analisi dei testi classici*
M-W	R. Merkelbach and M. L. West, eds., Hesiod, *Fragmenta Selecta* in F. Solmsen, ed., Hesiod, *Theogonia, Opera et Dies, Scutum*, Oxford, 1970.

OLD	*Oxford Latin Dictionary*, ed. P.G.W. Glare. Oxford, 1982.
PCG	*Poetae Comici Graeci*, eds. R. Kassel and C. Austin. 1983–1991.
PCPhS	*Proceedings of the Cambridge Philological Society*
PLF	*Poetarum Lesbiorum fragmenta* (Lobel and Page 1955)
PLLS	*Papers of the Liverpool Latin Seminar*
PMG	*Poetae melici graeci* (Page 1962)
PMLA	*Proceedings of the Modern Language Association of America*
PVS	*Proceedings of the Virgil Society*
QS	*Quaderni di storia*
QUCC	*Quaderni urbinati di cultura classica*
RE	*Paulys Real-Encyclopaedie der classischen Altertumswissenschaft*, ed. G. Wissowa. Stuttgart, 1894–1959.
REL	*Revue des études latines*
RFIC	*Rivista di filologia e d'istruzione classica*
RhM	*Rheinisches Museum*
RPh	*Revue de philologie*
RSC	*Rivista di studi classici*
SBAW	*Sitzungsberichte der Bayerischen Akademie der Wissenschaften, Philos.-Hist. Klasse*
SH	*Supplementum Hellenisticum*, eds. H. Lloyd-Jones and P. Parsons. Berlin, 1983.
SHAW	*Sitzungsberichte der Heidelberger Akademie der Wissenschaften, Philos.-Hist. Klasse*
SIFC	*Studi italiani di filologia classica*
SMSR	*Studi e materiali di storia delle religioni*
TAPhA	*Transactions of the American Philological Association*
TLL	*Thesaurus Linguae Latinae*, Leipzig, 1900–.
TSLL	*Texas Studies in Language and Literature*
WS	*Wiener Studien*
YClS	*Yale Classical Studies*
YFS	*Yale French Studies*
ZPE	*Zeitschrift für Papyrologie und Epigraphik*

CLASSICAL CLOSURE

CHAPTER 1

Second Thoughts on Closure

DON FOWLER

> The populace cheered and danced for joy where
> they stood, and there was no discordant voice as
> young and old, rich and poor, united in
> jubilation, for though they had understood very
> little of what was said, they were able to surmise
> the facts of the matter from what had already
> transpired concerning Charikleia; or else perhaps
> they had been brought to a realization of the
> truth by the same divine force that had staged this
> whole drama and that now produced a perfect
> harmony of diametric opposites: joy and sorrow
> combined; tears mingled with laughter; the most
> hideous horror transformed to celebration; those
> who wept also laughed; those who grieved also
> rejoiced; they found those whom they had not
> sought and lost those whom they ought to have
> found; and finally the offering of human blood,
> which all had expected to see, was transformed
> into a sacrifice free of all stain.
> —*Heliodorus* Ethiopica *10.38 (trans. Morgan)*

IN FOWLER 1989b (pp. 78–79), I distinguished five senses in which the word "closure" was used in modern criticism:

1. The concluding section of a literary work;

2. The process by which the reader of a work comes to see the end as satisfyingly final;

3. The degree to which an ending is satisfyingly final;

4. The degree to which the questions posed in the work are answered, tensions released, conflicts resolved;

5. The degree to which the work allows new critical readings.[1]

---

[1] Cf. Mortimer 1985, 31–32.

But, I argued, although it may on occasions be useful to distinguish these senses, they are all intimately connected:

> Where the concluding section of a work makes the reader feel that it has closed satisfactorily by resolving all the conflicts of the work, the reader will tend to see the meaning of the work in that resolution. A work on the other hand which leaves questions unanswered will be "open" to different interpretations, and may leave the reader feeling that where the work stops is not really The End.

One of my aims in that piece was to evince a dissatisfaction with literary histories that emplotted the opposition between "open" and "closed" types of literature against time and space:

> Some have talked of "Western endings" with "a strong sense of impact and finality" and "Eastern endings" where the work "continues to develop quietly and complete itself in the reader's mind after the actual printed ending." It has been argued that openness to new interpretations is the hallmark of the classic work, in comparison to popular and ephemeral literature; and that the literary work is open while the oral work is closed, or the literary work closed but the oral work open. But the opposition is usually portrayed diachronically; the classical work is closed and complete, the Romantic open and fragmentary; modernist works are more "open" than traditional ones, postmodernist works are more radically open than modernist ones; the postmodernist work ironically achieves the closure that modernism made impossible. These varying interpretations are not detailed merely to produce scepticism; the oppositions are not the fantastic intentions of critics. Romantic, modernist, and postmodernist writers dramatize their own practice in precisely these terms. Nevertheless, without denying the value of detailed historical investigation of the swings of the pendulum, it seems to do more justice to our intuitions to see the tension between "open" and "closed" as one ever-present in the literary work. All works leave things undone as well as done; all great works have that paradox at the core of their greatness. "One greatness of the great disquieter lies in the great truths for which he clears the ground; one greatness of the great truths is the great disquieting questions which are cracked out of them"; "Attempts to characterize the fiction of a given period by its commitment to closure or open-endedness are blocked from the beginning by the impossibility of ever demonstrating whether a given narrative is closed or open."[2]

But while I am happy in one sense to stand by my distrust of the grand narratives of closure and aperture, I am embarrassed now by the lingering essentialism that replaced them with a permanent and ongoing dialectic

---

[2] The two concluding quotations are from Adams 1958, 215, and J.H. Miller 1978, 3: for further references, see Fowler 1989b, 79.

between the two. I now appreciate more clearly that whether we look for closure or aperture *or a dialectic between them* in a text is a function of our own presuppositions, not of anything "objective" about the text.[3] In the last few years, as Francis Dunn points out in chapter 5 of this volume, the fashion has swung toward an interest in closure rather than the deferral or subversion of it: particularly a closure effected, in the tradition of Foucault and the New Historicism, by the realities of power. The old game of showing that endings don't work has to some extent been replaced by the new game of showing that they do. I continue to feel that it is more satisfactory to play the two tendencies off against each other; but I am more aware now that that has to do with my own ideology, temperament, and mood rather than with the nature of the universe.

But although there has undoubtedly been a move toward a greater interest in closure, an asymmetry in the rhetoric has remained: given a simple choice of being open or closed, it is difficult for a twentieth-century person to choose to be closed. One of the great problem endings in classical literature is the concluding story of Aristaeus and Orpheus in Virgil's *Georgics*.[4] Do we stress the success of Aristaeus, as for instance Gian Biagio Conte does in a celebrated reading of the episode,[5] or is that success itself contaminated by the failure of Orpheus, as is argued by "pessimistic" readers of the *Georgics* such as David Ross and Richard Thomas?[6] Thomas Habinek has recently attempted to use the notion of Aristaeus's act as *sacrifice* (an important theme in recent work on cultural closure, to which I shall return) to argue for a reading that sees in the ending "the restoration of order in a universe riven by lust and greed":[7] "Just as the first sacrifice settled forever the place of humans in the universe, so the sacrifice performed by Aristaeus restores the order of this world, and leads to the re-creation of the swarm of bees, suggestive as they are of reborn human society." Habinek admits that even as sacrifice, Aristaeus's act "recapitulates the very ambiguities it seeks to erase,"[8] but he sees those Orphic ambiguities as eventually themselves vectored into a sense of complex success: "Aristaeus and Orpheus, or technology and art, or history and the Golden Age, although initially positioned as opponents and causes of each other's doom, become interlocked in Virgil's vision of newborn bees, clustered like grapes, rising from the carcasses of oxen slaughtered in Aristaeus' ritual

[3] Cf. Fowler 1994.

[4] For a good recent treatment of the dialectic between Orpheus the "poet" and Aristaeus the "farmer" in relation to the rest of the *Georgics*, see Perkell 1989, with my remarks in Fowler 1990, 237–38.

[5] Conte 1986, 130–40.

[6] See, e.g., Ross 1987, 214–33; Thomas 1988, ad loc.

[7] Habinek 1990, 216.

[8] Ibid., 219.

of recompense and renewal." In reply to this, Richard Thomas once more picks apart what Habinek has joined, stressing the inevitable complexities and fissures that are involved in any contextualization of the *Georgics* in relation to ancient sacrifice.[9] He presents the issue in terms above all of closure: "We have a choice: either we accept that this is an 'open' ending . . . or we can try to impose a closed ending on the poem, a natural human, but misguided and disastrous critical tendency."[10] My own sympathies here are entirely with Thomas and pessimism, but the terms in which he presents the choice are obviously not fair: although no one wants to be "closed," the choice between a reading that stresses unresolved ambiguities and one that tries to mediate and subsume them within a higher resolution is not simply one between a good liberal openness and anal-retentive boorishness.

Nor, as I say, is it simply *better* than either to hover between these alternatives. The best attempt at grounding the dialectic of ending and continuance[11] lies perhaps in the psychoanalytic reading offered by Peter Brooks in *Reading for the Plot*, with its indebtedness above all to the Empedoclean binaries of *Beyond the Pleasure Principle*, Eros and Thanatos:

> What operates in the text through repetition is the death instinct, the drive towards the end. Beyond and under the domination of the pleasure principle is this baseline of plot, its basic "pulsation," sensible or audible through the repetitions that take us back in the text. Yet repetition also retards the pleasure principle's search for the gratification of discharge, which is another forward-moving drive of the text. We have a curious situation in which two principles of forward movement operate upon one another so as to create retard, a dilatory space in which pleasure can come from postponement in the knowledge that this—in the manner of forepleasure? is a necessary approach to the true end. Both principles can indeed become dilatory, a pleasuring in and from delay, though both also in their different ways recall to us the need for end. This apparent paradox may be consubstantial with the fact that repetition can take us both backward and forward because these terms have become reversible: the end is a time before the beginning.[12]

The strength of this mediation is of course that it is not so much a dialectic between the open and the closed as a deconstruction of the opposition

---

[9] For the ambiguities of sacrifice, see below, and especially Elsner 1991, with Galinsky 1992, 474–75.

[10] Thomas 1991a, esp. 216.

[11] Cf., e.g., MacArthur 1990, 274–76, with, however, the expected leaning toward aperture. For a strong statement in favor of "closed oppositional" reading, see now Doherty 1995, 31–63.

[12] Brooks 1984, 102–3. Cf. Cave 1988, 211–19; Bowie 1987, esp. 159–63; Mitchell-Boyask 1996, 289–92.

itself that shows their mutual implicature. But as ever, the categories are as indispensable as they are imperfect. Neither ending nor continuance, neither closure nor aperture are ever inscribed in the structure of the universe, but at times we may need to come to an end or refuse one, not simply stay on the fence.[13]

One area of discourse in which both ends and beginnings are particularly urgently inscribed is that of politics. Not only is it true, as Alessandro Barchiesi remarks in this volume, that "to bring something to an end is a clear sign of power,"[14] but the continuance of power is constantly threatened by closure. The politics of closure naturally implicate both the modern critic or historian and the account that she is constructing. One of the factors in a growing distrust of the simple rhetoric of openness, especially in the United States and Great Britain, was undoubtedly the way that the communitarian values of solidarity came to position themselves in radical opposition to the self-proclaimed "open society" of Reaganite and Thatcherite liberal capitalism,[15] while the *almost* "natural" ends and beginnings of what the tee-shirts proclaimed as the "Democracy World Tour 1988" were also a blow to many people's beliefs in the ends of history. The ancient literary genres where the politics of closure have been particularly important are fifth-century tragedy and comedy and Latin epic. To what extent can the "open" revolt of the Aristophanic or Sophoclean hero against the communal values of the polis be recuperated through democracy's own inscription of communal self-questioning?[16] Contrariwise, how far do we wish to "open up" the closure of a great civic drama like the *Oresteia*?[17] How much of an Endlösung are the finales of the *Aeneid* or the *Metamorphoses* for the debates over the "Augustanism" of those poems? And how satisfactory is it to phrase critical readings always as questions?

One of the most interesting factors in the development of the way these issues have been explored in relation to Latin epic has been the use of models previously deployed in relation to fifth-century Greece:[18] it is unfortunate that this development has not been more reciprocal. I have already mentioned the use by Thomas Habinek of the ambivalent ending that sacrifice represents in relation to the *Georgics*, and the work of Girard

---

[13] Cf. Martindale 1993, esp. 18–19, on the parallel problems of beginning: "Against truth as closure we can then adopt a provisional holding still of the signifying chain for purposes of enablement. I can, in other words, decide to begin, will to begin, to renew myself."

[14] See below, p. 207.

[15] For an explicit formulation of this motivation in relation to Virgilian criticism, see especially Wiltshire 1989, esp. 139–43.

[16] For Sophocles, see above all still Knox 1964; for Aristophanes, Bowie 1993; for all "Dionysiac" drama, Goldhill 1987.

[17] Cf. Goldhill 1984a.

[18] Cf. Henderson 1991, 52–54; Hardie 1991.

has been central to recent work on tragedy, above all Helene Foley's study of Euripides.[19] It has also been used in relation to Latin epic by C. Bandera, and more extensively by Philip Hardie.[20] What is attractive to me in Hardie's work (as in Foley's) is of course in part precisely his delicate negotiation of the dialectic of opening and closure, in which he is in many ways truer to Girard than are some other followers. Seeing, for instance, the killing of Turnus as a sacrifice can be used simply to "make it all right":[21] Hardie's Girardian reading is much more poised.[22] His earlier book, *Virgil's "Aeneid": Cosmos and Imperium*, with its stress on Jupiter's ordering of the cosmos, was one of the most important works that helped move Virgilian criticism on from the "open" pessimism of the Harvard school, but his rewriting of his own work in *The Epic Successors of Virgil* mirrors the rewriting of the *Aeneid* itself in silver epic. The other distinctive feature of his work (to which I shall return) is the way in which it unites literary history and the politics of closure: the endless new beginnings of silver epic are also the endless new beginnings of the Roman empire, the hopeful yet hopeless attempts to ground both closure and continuity in the political sphere.

The other important political reading of epic teleology, again uniting formalist literary history with the structures of ideology, is that of David Quint in his comparative study of the genre from Virgil to Eisenstein, *Epic and Empire*.[23] Using the basic opposition of the "open" nature of romance and the teleology of epic, he constructs a wide-ranging political dialogue with its roots in the intertextual bifurcation of the simultaneously Iliadic and Odyssean *Aeneid*:

> One major unifying strand of the story I tell is how the *Aeneid* ascribes to political power the capacity to fashion human history into narrative; how, drawing on the two narrative models offered to it by the *Iliad* and the *Odyssey*, Virgil's poem attached political meaning to narrative form itself. To the victors belongs epic, with its linear teleology; to the losers belongs romance, with its random or circular wandering. Put another way, the victors experience history as a coherent, end-directed story told by their own power; the losers experience a contingency that they are powerless to shape to their own ends.[24]

---

[19] Girard 1977; Foley 1985. For a full bibliography on the use of Girard in Greek studies, see Mitchell 1991, 98 n. 2.

[20] Bandera 1981; Hardie 1993b, 1993d, and Chapter 7 in this volume. Cf. Fowler 1993.

[21] Cf. Renger 1985.

[22] See below, Chapter 7. There are good remarks on the application of Girard to "literature" in Mitchell 1991.

[23] Quint 1993; cf. Quint 1989.

[24] Quint 1993, 9.

So on Quint's reading, the *Aeneid* moves from the repetition and circularity of Aeneas's wanderings in the first half of the *Aeneid* to the repetition with change, the directionality and teleology of fate, in the second half; and the same polarities may be seen at work throughout the epic tradition, as the losers of history try—and fail—to produce narratives of their own. They fail, because "power makes the best poetry": "Only by bravely embracing a position of poetic, as well as political weakness, can Lucan and his successors make epic speak on behalf of the defeated."[25]

Quint's version of the history of epic is itself an exceptionally powerful narrative of literary and political closure, but like all successful narratives of binary opposition, it cries out for deconstruction. "Epic" and "Romance" are more implicated in each other than he allows, just as power demands continuation as well as the climactic focus on the present: the reign of Augustus is to be an Endzeit, but also *imperium sine fine*, a rule that transgresses the boundaries of Ocean.[26] And as he notes, resistance to the ends of empire is often also a will to power. But the teleological power play of the *Aeneid* is projected onto another opposition that has been central to modern thought about ends, that of gender. If Jupiter represents the end, Juno is hardly the mean: "From the beginning Jupiter is associated with the end. . . . The poet is already looking forward to the eventual end which Jupiter will impose on the poem, and on the anarchy of Juno who, as befits the deity of the Kalends, has dominated the beginning: her second word is 'beginning' (*incepto*, 1.37)."[27] Indeed, it has been argued that her first word is also a beginning: in *mene incepto desistere victam*, it is possible to hear the angry echo of the first word of the *Iliad*, *menin*.[28] Juno is forever starting things up again when they are about to come to a premature end, forever opening gates and wounds that should be closed. She is also mad in her attempted proliferation of narratives, setting up counterfates to what we all know is the only possible story, the master narrative that is literally in the mind of God.[29] This gendered opposition between masculine truth and closure and feminine error and powerlessness is brilliantly parodied at the end of the *Metamorphoses*, where in Ovid's version of the epic reconciliation scene, the true course of events is always already fixed in Jupiter's Big Book:

---

[25] Ibid., 209. Compare, of course, Conte 1986 on the power of the epic code.

[26] *Aeneid* 1.278–79 (significantly at the beginning of the poem), 6.791–97. Cf. Feeney 1991, 137–38; and for the politics of boundaries, Fowler 1995b.

[27] Feeney 1991, 137–38.

[28] The suggestion of Levitan (1993).

[29] I am indebted here to Debra Hershkowitz, who is working on madness in epic: see, e.g., Hershkowitz 1994 on Statius.

> sola insuperabile fatum,
> nata, movere paras? intres licet ipsa Sororum
> tecta Trium! cernes illic molimine vasto
> ex aere et solido rerum tabularia ferro,
> quae neque concussum caeli neque fulminis iram
> nec metuunt ullas tuta atque aeterna ruinas.
> invenies illic incisa adamante perenni
> fata tui generis. legi ipse animoque notavi
> et referam, ne sis etiamnum ignara futuri.

(Met. 15.807–15)

Jupiter's book is also the *Aeneid*, retrospectively figured as the epic of closure in contrast to Ovid's epic of change and continuity:[30] and as God the Father he is both male reader and male author, *himself* laying down the law once and for all, the Way Things Are.

This equation between logo- and phallocentricity, between the closure of meaning and male power, has played an important role in modern thought about gender, and in contrast feminist critics have often figured their own discursive practices as more "open." In part this is the necessary rhetoric of any group challenging existing power, but in the writings of French feminists such as Cixous and Irigaray, it takes a stronger form as a claim about the fluidity and dissemination of "women's writing." As Cixous puts it herself in a typically and significantly "lyrical" passage:

> As soon as you let yourself be led beyond codes, your body filled with fear and with joy, the words diverge, you are no longer enclosed in the maps of social constructions, you no longer walk between walls, meanings flow, the world of railways explodes, the air circulates, desires shatter images, passions are no longer chained to genealogies, life is no longer nailed down to generational time, love is no longer shunted off on the course decided upon by the administration of public alliances.[31]

Since it is a cliché that almost all ancient literature is written by men, one might suspect that such a view of textuality would be relevant only to a small range of authors like Sappho or Sulpicia. But what Cixous figures as a writing practice can also be an approach to reading, and simply to endorse male authorial control over women's voices in their texts is to acquiesce in a naive notion of the power of the author in the face of a deter-

---

[30] Cf. Fowler, forthcoming a.

[31] Cixous 1991, 49–50. Cf., e.g., Cixous 1986, 88 etc.; Gallop 1982, index s.v. "closure," esp. xiii on closure and virginity, 32 on the "feminist gesture" (perhaps) "to end with questions, not to conclude but to be open."

mined reader. Even Canidia can be given a hearing.[32] But one particular irony of this rhetoric is that traditionally women have often occupied the other pole of the opposition: their lives have been seen as cloistered or confined in contrast to the open world of the male. The dark world of the women's quarters has been set against the public space of the agora or forum, the small-scale female genres of private lyric or elegy contrasted with the wide-screen epics of masculinity.[33] This double perspective on constructions of the feminine is particularly significant for works like Ovid's *Heroides*, where the female "authors" set the small world of elegy against the open spaces of epic and in the process produce a text that "defies textual limits, purposely subverting traditional dichotomies and blurring the boundaries between the fictional and the authentic, rhetoric and poetry, narrative and speech."[34] And in general, the familiar polarity in feminist criticism of antiquity between readings that stress the totalizing power of male dominance in the ancient world and those that use the various types of "reading against the grain" to open up the *gynaikonitis* makes the issues associated with closure a particularly fertile meeting-point for modern criticism of gender.

Politics and gender are two (?) areas in which the interplay of modern concerns and the rhetoric of our constructions of antiquity is particularly marked: a third is what is happening to notions of textuality itself in the postmodern age. The fixed text in a book, read serially from beginning to end by a solitary reader, has become the marker of that "closed" textuality that is being replaced by the fluid openness of developments such as hypermedia and cyberspace, in which there are "no conventional endings, or beginnings or middles."[35] It is clear, however, that for all the excitement of the new forms that it produces and justifies, this rhetoric depends on an unacceptable simplification of what the "traditional" text is and does in the hands of a reader, and a concomitant domestication of the poststructuralist challenge to reading practices.[36] Différance and dissemination are inevitable features of language, not blueprints for the structure of hypertext docu-

---

[32] Cf. Oliensis 1991b.

[33] Cf. Fowler, forthcoming b.

[34] Kauffman 1986, 61. I am indebted here to Effie Spentzou, who is working on the instabilities of space and place in the *Heroides*.

[35] Lanham 1989, 269. Cf. Landow 1992, especially 57–59 ("Beginnings and Endings in the Open Text"), 60–64 on the "open, open-bordered text" (61), and 109–12 ("Narrative Beginnings and Endings"); Delany and Landow 1991, especially the papers by Statin and Moulthrop.

[36] Note the subtitle to Landow 1992: "The Convergence of Contemporary Critical Theory and Technology." For criticism of the view that "before the twentieth century the structure of most works of narrative fiction was based on some kind of teleology," see Szegedy-Maszak 1987, 44.

ments. The opposition of the open and the closed is in fact a common feature of the historiography of all "communications revolutions":[37] the development of language itself, of writing, of the codex, of printing, of film, of the computer. The one that is simultaneously of most interest to classicists and most central to modern thought is of course the development of writing and the contrast between orality and literacy. As ever, the opposition plays itself out in contradictory ways: writing is both orphan and surrogate/supplement, it both fixes and frees. In the Big Book of Ovid's Jupiter, the truth is written down once and for all: but when Virgil's Aeneas asks the Sibyl for revelation, he begs her to sing, not write:

> foliis tantum ne carmina manda,
> ne turbata colent rapidis ludibria ventis;
> ipsa canas oro.[38]

Similarly, in modern criticism of ancient literature, the opposition between performance and written textuality has led both to the view that the performance of a play or a recited poem can fix meaning[39] and to the view that oral performance opens out the fixed text to new possibilities.[40] These debates are familiar in relation to fifth-century tragedy, and to a lesser extent to Homeric studies:[41] again, they are becoming important also in relation to Roman poetry.[42] What is striking is that however the opposition is worked, writing tends all too often to play its familiar role of the despised second-best: either it lacks the necessary determinants of meaning that the context of performance provides, or it lacks the necessary flexibility and aperture of "real-life" textual intercourse.[43] It would seem that

[37] For the term, cf. Eisenstein 1979, still one of the most subtle and nuanced versions of the myth.

[38] *Aeneid* 6.74–76, cf. 3.445–52. Aeneas echoes [Plato] *Epist.* 2.314a–c.

[39] Cf. for Greek tragedy especially Taplin 1977, though he has developed his views considerably since then; see, e.g, Taplin 1983, 156–57. For Roman poetry, see, e.g., Cairns 1984, suggesting performance of Propertius 4.8 in the temple of Apollo on the Palatine; Wiseman 1985, 92–101 on Catullus 34 and Delos, 198–206 on 63 and the Megalesia, and more generally on performance 124–29; and McKeown 1987, 63–73 on Ovid's *Amores*: where, for instance, at the difficult junctures in *Amores* 2.9 and 3.11, "a pause, accompanied by a gesture of despair and perplexity, would be sufficient to overcome any difficulty an audience might feel in understanding the shift in Ovid's attitude" (73).

[40] Cf. Goldhill 1986, esp. 284 (performance as "a process of interpreting the text and *opening* the text to the interpretation of an audience," my emphasis), and Goldhill 1989.

[41] See especially Martin 1989.

[42] Cf. the papers in Vogt-Spina 1990, especially E. Lefèvre's introduction; and more generally Quinn 1982.

[43] Cf. Martin 1989, 7: "The text becomes simply the *flexible* springboard from which the performer continually takes off and to which he returns—it has no *rigid fixity*" (my emphasis).

classical studies still have a lot of investment in the primacy and immediacy of the word of the father.

As I say, however skeptical one may wish to feel about these big myths of closure, there is no escaping them: there is no other way to figure what we want to say about ending other than through stories like these and the oppositions that structure them. There can of course be no final conclusion. But the acceptance of the multiplicity of the stories that we can tell about our ends and our beginnings can also, for good or ill, lead to a familiar postmodern retreat back from theory to practice. There is a sense in which there is nothing of theoretical interest to say about closure, but many interesting things to say about endings. In the second half of this chapter, therefore, I want to turn to some more specific aspects of ancient closure, but before doing so, I want to make one further very general point about the issues involved. If many other aspects of literary debate can be made to look like special cases of the problematic of closure, closure itself is a special case of the question of *segmentation*, of how we divide up texts and the world they constitute;[44] and that general problematic is another way in which to think of closure is to be forced to cross the boundaries of the literary into wider cultural and political analysis. One of the most distinctive features of modern thought has been the growing realization that divisions that seem natural may yet be cultural: first in social science, and ultimately even in the hardest of physical sciences. As we have learned above all from anthropology, there is more than one way to cut up the world. The way a culture segments reality will depend on two factors: the types of boundary it recognizes, and above all its beginnings and endings, and what one might term its *segmental ontology*, what sorts of sort it acknowledges (not to mention, of course, its notions of "boundary" and "sort").

These issues are clearest in the case of infratextual closure:[45] particularly in the case of texts like the *Iliad* or *Odyssey*, where we are not confident in seeing any existing articulation as primary,[46] how we divide up the text will depend on what devices we recognize as signals of ending or beginning and what notions we have of divisions like "episode" or "scene." Because these terms are so basic to our critical vocabulary, it is difficult to defamiliarize them, but they clearly merit analysis. The problems seem less obvious at the level of individual texts, but the grouping of texts into oeuvres or genres or periods is central to our readings of them. The segmentations involved here may seem better accommodated to notions of a map or a web, in which there are multiple boundaries rather than begin-

---

[44] Cf. Fowler 1995b.
[45] Cf. Fowler 1989b, 86–97; and 114 on segmental ontology.
[46] Cf. Taplin 1992; Stanley 1993, esp. 248–96, with Schmiel 1993; Schwinge 1991.

nings and endings, but literary history of any kind inevitably imposes the linearity of plot on these relationships: one person's life work, like Virgil's ascent through the genres and his final farewell at *Aeneid* 12.952,[47] or a genre like Latin love-elegy, which on the same organic model begins, flourishes, and reaches its "end" with Ovid. And from these literary lumpings and cuts, it is an easy move to bring into our story more general aspects of cultural segmentation. The "hierarchy" of genres through which Virgil ascends from pastoral to didactic to epic is clearly a sort of *cursus honorum*; and the power of these Roman images of societal order is well demonstrated by the celebrated end (or is it?) to Manilius's *Astronomica* (5.734–45):

> utque per ingentis populus discribitur urbes,
> principiumque patres retinent et proximum equester
> ordo locum, populumque equiti populoque subire
> vulgus iners videas et iam sine nomine turbam,
> sic etiam magno quaedam res publica mundo est
> quam natura facit, quae caelo condidit urbem.
> sunt stellae procerum similes, sunt proxima primis
> sidera, suntque gradus atque omnia iusta priorum:
> maximus est populus summo qui culmine fertur;
> cui si pro numero vires natura dedisset,
> ipse suas aether flammas sufferre nequiret,
> totus et accenso mundus flagraret Olympo.

And as in great cities the inhabitants are divided into classes, whereof the senate enjoys primacy and the equestrian order importance next to this, and one may see the knights followed by the commons, the commons by the proletariat, and finally the innominate throng, so too in the mighty heavens there exists a commonwealth wrought by nature, which has founded a city in the sky. There are luminaries of princely rank and stars which come close to this highest eminence; there are all the grades and privileges of superior orders. But outnumbering all these is the populace which revolves about heaven's dome; had nature given it powers consonant with its legions, the very empyrean would be helpless before its fires, and the whole universe would become embroiled in the flames of a blazing sky.[48]

---

[47] The final *umbrae* of the *Aeneid* figure the death of its author (*indignata*) as well as of Turnus, and finally put to rest the flight from shade begun in the *Eclogues* (10.75–77, cf. *Georgics* 4.564, 567).

[48] Trans. Goold 1977: note the emphatic closure, with the whole world consumed in a total *ekpyrosis*. Compare Ulysses' famous speech at Shakespeare *Troilus and Cressida* 1.3.83ff.; and Ajax's deception speech, Soph. *Aj.* 666–76 with Jebb 1907, ad loc., and Knox 1979, 126–29.

Similarly, the annual succession of magistracies in the Greek *polis* and (especially) Republican Rome, often used by historians to structure their stories, provides another cultural model to intensify the "natural" unit of the year, as later the reigns of the emperors (which rarely achieved the harmony of democratic closure) will powerfully structure thought about the succession of events.

But the cultural poetics of segmentation, the "units of thought" of Greek and Roman antiquity, have many more ramifications. One may think, for instance, of the procession or parade: a structuring device for a number of Pindaric *epinikia*, a model ending for tragedy (the *Oresteia*) and comedy (*Lysistrata*), then at Rome, in the twin forms of the triumph and the funeral cortège,[49] a central institution in which the participants moved to a strong ending of ultimate felicity or death while the spectators viewed a succession of passing representations, painted battles, and death masks.[50] The importance of the reflection of this in epic has been well noted by David Quint:

> Epic loves a parade, perhaps because the procession that keeps its shape through both space and time resembles its own regular verse schemes—meter, rhyme, stanza—that similarly spacialise time and join the poem's beginning in interconnected sequence to its end. . . . The imperial triumph [on the shield of Aeneas] is one in a series of triumphs, itself a triumphal procession of Roman conquests that are presented in linear chronological order—"in ordine," like the "longo ordine" in which Augustus' foreign subjects file by. The triumph gives its shape not only to the political unity of the empire but also to a unified narrative that imperial conquest has conferred upon Roman history.[51]

And one route that the deconstruction of that reading might take is to see in the epic procession not just the triumph but the passage to the last rites of death. Equally, a cultural poetics of segmentation has to consider also the way in which the divisions and boundaries of literature structure the "social drama."[52] This is at its most obvious in ritualized areas such as religion, law, and politics, but it is a much more widespread phenomenon. The fact that notions like "act" and "scene" are basic not only to historiography but to history itself is sometimes used to bolster a strongly realist view of history: if the participants themselves figured, say, the Peloponnesian War as a

---

[49] One might add the marriage procession, so often intertextual with funerals but interestingly rarely figured as a triumph.

[50] And of course here the whole question of segmentation in the visual arts is relevant: see Fowler 1991 and 1996.

[51] Quint 1993, 31.

[52] The term is especially associated with the work of Victor Turner: see conveniently Turner 1981, with further references.

tragedy, that patterning might be said to be truly "there" in the historical process, not just a story told by Thucydides. But the participants in history as much as later historians are likely constantly to resegment their own experience; even "as it happens," there is always more than one story to tell, more than one possible beginning, middle, and end.

But as I say, in the second half of this paper I want to turn to some more specific aspects of closure. One aspect that has been prominent in recent criticism is the interplay between form and content that results from the thematization of notions of beginnings and endings—and indeed middles. We have already seen this in relation to the politics and gendering of closure, particularly in relation to the *Aeneid*, and again silver Latin epic provides many examples. This is especially because many of the traditional "faults" of Lucan and the Flavian epicists can be reinterpreted self-reflexively as manifestations of this thematization. The expansive, digressive nature of these epics has always been seen as one of their worse features: they do *go on* a bit, they refuse to *get down to it*. But the *morae* of these epics, their refusal to move toward their end, has in recent criticism been thematized, in various ways. For David Vessey, in the *Thebaid* "the principle of 'delay' provides the one free factor in a fixed universe":[53] more radically, in John Henderson's "alternative" reading, the poem hesitates between the teleology of power and a despairing reflection of its endless disasters:[54]

/Does Epic Narrative here re-found the authority of a teleology, the respite and retrieval of some "vision": Aristotelian "*stasis*"? (So "Eteocles"—and "Theseus.")

/Does Epic Narration founder, undecided, on the blinded despair of "Thebes" ("and Argos . . .?"): Thucydidean "*stasis*"? (So the various "Polynices"—and "Adrastus," "Creon." . . .)

Similarly, Jamie Masters has powerfully revalued Lucan's notorious longueurs:

Powerless as Lucan may be to prevent the final catastrophe, he has at least the power, as poet, of delaying it within his poem; we can conclude, then, that Lucan is anxious to display his reluctance to allow the action to proceed, and he achieves this by erecting barriers that are at once literary and artificial. But again there is more. Although Lucan is reluctant, he does yet continue the action; and in writing the poem he is allowing the civil war to be reenacted, he is reenacting the war.[55]

Just as *Waiting for Godot* is not boring but about boredom, so the tedium of delay in Roman epic may be thematized into wider stories of guilt and

---

[53] Vessey 1973, 166; cf. Feeney 1991, 339–40.
[54] Henderson 1991, 60. Cf. Henderson 1993, 182.
[55] Masters 1992, 5.

hesitation. Even the end of Lucan's poem can be read, as Masters suggests, as not so much showing by its inconclusiveness that the poet died early as "*pointing . . .* to its own inconclusiveness, *avoiding . . .* any kind of resolution" (my emphasis) and thus reflecting its central theme of "evil without alternative, contradiction without compromise, civil war without end."[56] This kind of thematization of nonclosure, in particular, is a central trope, of course, of much modern and postmodern criticism; and it is always itself open to reversal. Maybe we prefer to say simply that Lucan came to a bad end. Are the "inconsistencies . . . ambiguities . . . absurdities . . . and . . . incongruities" of Petronius's *Satyricon*, in which "episodes are not resolved; they disintegrate," in fact "integral emblems of a world-view that expresses a consistent vision of disintegration through the inter-relationship of form and content," as Froma Zeitlin argued in a celebrated article;[57] or is it just "a collection of loose strings"?[58] It is naturally usually more interesting for a modern critic to link form and content; but thematization can always be refused.

Texts, then, not only have beginnings, middles, and ends, but can often be made to talk about them, too. Another aspect of this is the various forms of Gide's "*mise-en-abyme*."[59] Internal narrators and related authorial surrogates (prophets, controlling gods, visual artists, letter-writers), in drawing their own stories to a close, will often provoke reflection on the way that the framing narration may be read. Some of the most sophisticated examples of this can be found in the convoluted nested stories found in the Greek novel, especially Heliodorus's *Ethiopica*, whose internal ends and means have received detailed scrutiny from John Winkler and John Morgan.[60] But their contrasting approaches to the *Ethiopica* reveal an inherent ambivalence in the way that the ends of individual stories within a large work can be made to reflect on that larger work. Of necessity, the closure of any included stories cannot be complete: the framing narrative has to continue. Often it will not be clear exactly how we are to relate the story to the rest of the work, and the interpretation of the stories may frequently be thematized into a more general hermeneutical problematic.[61] In the *Ethiopica*, that "the narrative is full of signs that point wrong trails" is

---

[56] Ibid., 259. It is interesting to compare this rhetoric with versions of the shattering of traditional form by modernism; cf., e.g., Kinney 1992, 165–93 on *The Waste Land* as "anti-narrative."

[57] Zeitlin 1971, 633, 655.

[58] Schmeling 1991. Schmeling does not in fact see the *Satyricon* as a flawed work, and indeed praises Petronius's "total artistic control over his narrative" (377); but he reads the game with the reader's sense of an ending as self-contained play rather than thematically reflexive.

[59] See especially Dällenbach 1989.

[60] Winkler 1982; Morgan 1989a. Cf. also Cave 1988, 17–21.

[61] Cf. Winkler 1985, 11–14, "hermeneutic entertainment."

common to both Winkler and Morgan, but whereas the former stresses how reading, seeing, and interpreting are thereby problematized, Morgan notes that we do in the end reach a conclusion, and a particularly strong one: "A classic closed ending; no questions are left to be asked, the text closes because there is nothing more that could be told."[62] There is no a priori way of resolving the dispute between these two divergent possibilities of reading the lesson of included closure, though particular features may shift individual critics in one direction or the other. Some critics may even want to combine them.[63]

Similar issues are raised by the internal narratives of Greek tragedy, especially but not only by the messenger speeches. Christina Kraus has noted how in Sophocles' *Trachiniae*, the internal stories are always incomplete:

> Before the play reaches its own *lysis*, Sophocles shows that neither endings nor meanings are ever foregone conclusions, and his characters repeatedly find either their narrative of the past or their interpretation of it radically questioned. Even long-finished events are part of a still-evolving causal chain that renders definitive interpretation impossible. These interpretative crises in the *Trachiniae* most frequently result from the revelation that a critical detail has been left out of a story. Unless every item in the chain is fully narrated, the meaning of the whole cannot be correctly read, and the missing information is invariably the locus of catastrophe.[64]

Traditional readings of tragedy have seen these unfinished stories as milestones on the road to the final end, where all is revealed and all is resolved: Kraus, however, takes the more modern line that we learn from the fate of these stories that "the ending of the play is no more fixed than the ending of each story within the play" and thus (particularly because of the uncertainties over the Oetean pyre) "the play's narrative as a whole . . . recapitulates the movement described by the narratives within it, ultimately refusing closure."[65] Sophocles more than any other ancient author has benefited from the modern trend toward opening out his endings,[66] and Kraus's reading is an attractive one supported by a wealth of detailed argument: but it, too, is vulnerable to attack by a concerted enough traditionalist, for whom however misleading the stories on the way, there is ultimately a master narrative in the mind of the play(wright).

One aspect of textual mirroring that is always present to a degree in any form of *mise-en-abyme*,[67] but that is also a broader phenomenon, is the way

---

[62] Morgan 1989a, 318; cf. Bartsch 1989.

[63] On the question of authorial control versus the power of the reader, see also Deborah Roberts, Chapter 12 in this volume.

[64] Kraus 1991, 76.

[65] Ibid., 77, 98.

[66] See especially Roberts 1988; and, e.g., Taplin 1983 on the *Oedipus*.

[67] Cf. Dällenbach 1989, 35, 111–12 on "infinite duplication."

that a division of a text may function as a microcosm of the main text. So, for instance, Karl Galinsky claimed that *Aeneid* 5 was a miniature *Aeneid*,[68] and Debra Hershkowitz has made a similar claim for *Aeneid* 3.[69] Other books of the *Aeneid* might be read in the same way. The *Odyssey* famously contains a miniature version of itself in Book 23, when Odysseus answers Penelope's attempt to make her adventures into an epic[70] with a summary of the *Odyssey* from his own point of view, with some interesting variations in order, duration, and frequency.[71] This use of a microcosmic recapitulation becomes a closural device in its own right; one can compare, for instance, the wonderfully self-conscious narration by Chaereas at the end of Chariton's novel (though this time Calirrhoe, unlike Penelope, gets the last word).[72] This tradition perhaps gives some closural force to the concluding summary in Statius's *Thebaid*; but since it is a summary of what will happen, not of what has happened, and since its series of indirect questions is rather a device of the opening,[73] we are conscious much more of unfinished business:

> non ego centena si quis mea pectora laxet
> voce deus, tot busta simul vulgique ducumque
> tot pariter gemitus dignis conatibus aequem
> *turbine quo* sese caris instraverit audax
> ignibus Evadne fulmenque in pectore magno
> quaesierit, *quo more*. . . .

(12.797–802)

A related phenomenon is where part of one work encapsulates the whole of another, as Monica Gale has argued happens with *Georgics* 3 and Lucretius's *De rerum natura*:[74] the prologue has a number of links with the prologue to the *De rerum natura* (and even more, of course, to the "proem in the middle"[75] at the opening of Book 4), while the concluding plague in echoing the Lucretian ending produces a powerful effect of false closure.[76] The *inclusion* of an earlier work in this way will naturally suggest that in

[68] Galinsky 1968.

[69] Hershkowitz 1991.

[70] Cf. her use of the *polus* motif (23.304–5)—which is of course a phenomenon of epic openings (*Iliad, Odyssey, Little Iliad*, etc.).

[71] E.g., Odysseus, unlike Homer, does not mention that he had sex with Calypso; and he falls asleep on travelers' tales of plunder.

[72] Cf. Chariton 8.7.3ff.: Chaereas tries to start at the end, but the people make him tell them all and leave nothing out (cf. 8.8.2). Calirrhoe ends the book with a prayer to Aphrodite for the shared death that at that very moment, like Rosencrantz and Guildenstern in Stoppard's play, they must inevitably suffer with the dying of the text.

[73] Cf. Hine 1981, 127–28.

[74] Gale 1991, esp. 414–15.

[75] Cf. Conte 1992.

[76] Cf. Peta Fowler, Chapter 6 in this volume.

some way the *conclusion* of the earlier work is thereby transcended and made more provisional: so the *Aeneid* includes Aeneas as an internal epic narrator telling the story of Troy known from Homer and Cyclic epic, Ennius includes a summary of Naevius, and Silius works in homage to all three of his epic predecessors in the ekphrasis of the paintings dealing with the First Punic War that Hannibal burns at Liternum.[77] Ovid's "Little *Aeneid*" in *Metamorphoses* 13 and 14 sets out more aggressively to diminish the stature of his predecessor's epic events—the exiguous blood of Priam leaves hardly a stain in the narrative (13.409)—but this is in a sense a second version even for Ovid, since, as Philip Hardie has argued, the Theban narrative earlier in the *Metamorphoses* is also a mini-*Aeneid*.[78] And all this from a man whose major work had itself already been included in summary form in his predecessor's sixth Eclogue.[79] Things very quickly get to look like that central fin-de-siècle image, the "fractal" plot of the Mandelbrot or Julia sets; as one increases the resolution of one's critical eye for an end, one sees ends and beginnings infinitely receding before one.

But this is not merely a question of Chinese boxes, of ends within ends without end. When one maps the occurrence of allusions to earlier ends in Greek and Latin literature, one soon sees that more complicated games with ends and beginnings may be constructed. As I noted before,[80] one phenomenon observed by James Zetzel is that of works that allude to ends at their beginnings and vice versa: Catullus 64 to the end of the *Argonautica*, the opening of the last book of the *Argonautica* to the first book of the *Iliad*. One effect of this is paradoxically to make an allusion to beginning a possible sign of the end; again, the prospective indirect questions of the end of the *Thebaid* come to mind. In the background, too, may be an old dream of the West, the idea of the *carmen perpetuum* that might unite all stories into one big master narrative, a truly Epic cycle linking works in a golden chain.[81] Just as historians like to play with being arranged in serial order, Xenophon after Thucydides, Livy *Ab urbe condita*, Tacitus *Ab excessu Divi Augusti*, so all writers take their beginnings from their pasts and bequeath their ends to those who come after. But there is always also an overlap between the tales, and its inevitable consequences of rivalry and contestation. Allusions to ends as to beginnings will often be found throughout a work, in a constant dialogue with the pre-existing segmentations of history and myth. Another obvious nodal point is the middle of a work, not only in the sense of Conte's "proem in the middle" and the new start that the second half often makes, but also because the bipartite struc-

[77] Cf. Fowler 1996.
[78] Cf. Hardie 1990.
[79] Cf. Knox 1986, 11–12. On Ovid's generic inclusiveness, cf. Solodow 1988.
[80] Fowler 1989b, 101 n. 93, referring to Zetzel 1983, 261 with n. 28. Cf. also Barchiesi, Chapter 9 in this volume.
[81] Cf. Calasso 1993—after Ovid.

ture that several works possess (in the wake of the *Odyssey*) means that the end of the first half may often be reflected also in the beginning of the second in an anxiety as to whether we really need a new beginning at all. The midpoint is always, as the Argonauts say in what is probably the opening book of the second half of Valerius Flaccus's *Argonautica*, the point at which the venture of the plot, and its telling *cardine summo / vertitur atque manibus nunc pendet ab unis*, is all in the hands of the reader.[82] However much the author is constrained by the plot to keep going, to bring the venture to a close, the reader can always put down the book a bit earlier and go do something useful. The presence of this possibility throughout the work produces a constant awareness of the possibility of a "premature" closure.

There seems at first sight a symmetry between ends and beginnings, in that one boundary is fixed, the other open, but in fact it is frequently easier to say where the beginning ends than where the end begins. This is particularly clear in music, where often, as one critic has remarked, "whereas the beginning has an obligatory opening period that therefore confers on it a nominal end, the ending takes over from the middle and is only retrospectively perceived as having begun."[83] Closural signals begin to accumulate toward the end of any work, and "toward the end" may be quite near the beginning: the reader may be offered any number of possible places to stop in the closing pages, as the writer finds herself gripped not simply by an inability to achieve closure but by an *embarras de richesses*. In these circumstances, there is no a priori way to distinguish between an accumulating sense of final closure, and a stronger sense of actual false closure. The *Odyssey* is here one celebrated example, where the problems of the endings are more significant than merely questions about who composed it/them; and epic provides more instances, such as the close of *Thebaid* 11, where there is a complex mixture of closural and anticlosural elements, as Philip Hardie points out in Chapter 7 of this volume.[84] The recall both of the ending of the *Oedipus Rex*—or rather, of the ending there ambiguously refused, the exile to Cithaeron—and of the end of the *Aeneid*,[85] the presence of night and departure/return, these are all closural; but the Pelasgi have embraced not death but a *dedecorem . . . vitam*, and Book 12 will open with the famous words *nondum cuncta*: that's not all folks; you ain't seen nothing yet, as Book 12 provides another microcosm of the whole epic. The more endings we get, the more we feel we are in the general area of

---

[82] 5.20–21, the prayer to Apollo to prevent the death of Tiphys.

[83] Agawu 1991, 67: see in general ch. 3 (51–79) and Agawu 1987. There has been some interesting work more generally on closure in musicology: see, e.g., Clément 1988; Robinson 1988; and Abbate 1991.

[84] Pp. 152–53.

[85] Note that the last line of the *Thebaid*, *nox favet, et grata profugos amplectitur umbra*, echoes not only the last line of the *Aeneid* but also the opening *fato profugus*, making explicit Virgil's own more discreet hint in *fugit*. Does this open things up, or close them down?

The End, but also, the less confidence we feel that the "real" end is necessarily the one for us. In fact, readers notoriously rearrange their own endings: ask a variety of people how a well-known book or film ends, and one is liable to find a variety of answers. In life, too, it can be very hard to get it right, and it can be as embarrassing to go on as to stop too soon: did King George V die with the words "How goes the empire?"—or "What's on at the Empire?"—or "Bugger Bognor"? All ending, however "good," has to be, in the end, just stopping. But equally, any stopping can be made good, if the game is played right. "Toward the end" of Yeats's play *Deirdre*, Naoise and Deirdre decide to wait for death at the hands of Conchubar, and remember the story of another king and queen:[86]

NAOISE: What do they say?
    That Lugaidh Redstripe and that wife of his
    Sat at this chess-board, waiting for their end.
    They knew that there was nothing that could save them,
    And so played chess as they had any night
    For years, and waited for the stroke of sword.
    I never heard a death so out of reach
    Of common hearts, a high and comely end.
    What need have I, that gave up all for love,
    To die like an old king out of a fable,
    Fighting and passionate? What need is there
    For all that ostentation at my setting?
    . . . .

DEIRDRE: He's in the right, though I have not been born
    Of the cold, haughty waves, my veins being hot,
    And though I have loved better than that queen,
    I'll have as quiet fingers on the board.
    O singing women, set it down in a book,
    That love is all we need, even though it is
    But the last drops we gather up like this;
    And though the drops are all we have known of life,
    For we have been most friendless—praise us for it,
    And praise the double sunset, for nought's lacking
    But a good end to the long, cloudy day.
NAOISE: Light torches there and drive the shadows out,
    For day's grey end comes up.

This is in fact neither how the play dies nor how Naoise and Deirdre come to a close: but it is as good an end as any.

---

[86] 432ff.: for the motif of playing the game at one's end, cf. Sen. *Tranq.* 14.7 on Julius Canus.

CHAPTER 2

Equal Honor and Future Glory: The Plan of Zeus in the *Iliad*

SHEILA MURNAGHAN

THE OPENING LINES of the *Iliad* give two apparent definitions of the poem's plot: the *mēnis*, "wrath," of Achilles, which, in the first line, the narrator asks the Muse to sing, and the *Dios boulē*, "plan of Zeus," which we learn in the fifth line was being accomplished through the deaths of the many Achaeans who perished as a consequence of Achilles' wrath. Both of these rather abstract formulations appear to correspond to the same specific course of events, which is set in motion in the first book of the poem: the scheme devised by Achilles and Zeus, with Thetis as their intermediary, to avenge and repair Achilles' loss of honor at the hands of Agamemnon through Trojan success in the war. This scheme or plot (in a literal sense) among the principal divine and human characters thus appears to define the plot (in a literary sense) of the poem in which it is narrated.

Though this correspondence seems clear at the outset, it eventually disappears as the *Iliad* draws out its story beyond the evident completion of that scheme. The poem continues past the point when Agamemnon realizes his error and does everything in his power to appease Achilles; past the point when Achilles no longer feels any anger toward Agamemnon or inclination to stay out of the war; and past the point when the Trojans are succeeding in the war. Both the wrath of the central hero and the plotting of the supreme Olympian god turn out to have unforeseen dimensions that are not exhausted by the enactment of that limited scheme. The poem escapes the limits of that plot in another sense as well, in that it contains long stretches of narrative, principally battle narrative, that have little to do with the Achilles plot, in which Achilles is not so much significantly absent as completely out of the picture. As the expected boundaries of its action are repeatedly dissolved, the *Iliad* explores the forces that keep its narrative going. It reaches its own conclusion only after showing how, in a world characterized by heroic anger and the plotting of Zeus, closure is systematically deferred.

The expansiveness of the plan of Zeus, which the proliferating plot of the *Iliad* dramatizes, is also indicated by the way the expression *Dios boulē* evokes a broader mythological context. A scholiast commenting on *Iliad* 1.5 connects the plan of Zeus with the entire Trojan War rather than with the single episode of Achilles' glorification at the Achaeans' expense.[1] He cites a tradition that the Trojan War, along with the other great legendary war, the Theban War, was part of a scheme devised by Zeus to relieve the earth of its burdensome excess population. This tradition was apparently found in the *Cypria*, the poem that related the outbreak of the war, and the scholiast quotes a passage of seven lines from the *Cypria*, which ends by characterizing the war with the same phrase through which the *Iliad* characterizes its own plot: *Dios d'eteleieto boulē*, "The plan of Zeus was being accomplished." This larger version of a plan of Zeus evidently provided the blueprint for the entire multipoem Trojan saga, which the *Cypria* initiated.[2]

Furthermore, as the scholium to *Iliad* 1 makes clear, the whole Trojan War should be understood as only one episode in Zeus's plan, which takes in the Theban War as well. And even this larger cosmic story encompassing both legendary wars, the story of Zeus's response to the earth's oppression by human beings, is itself only one episode in an even larger plot, in which Zeus is always and everywhere engaged in archaic mythology, and which finally transcends all specific narratives: the plot of mortality. Zeus is the paramount representative of a form of divinity that is defined through the absence of mortality: the Homeric gods are *athanatoi*, "undying." Zeus constantly reasserts his nature and his power by assuring the existence for others of what he definitively lacks, repeatedly securing the mortality of mortals.

This ongoing project divides itself into a number of episodes, contained in a variety of narratives, all of which express the plotting of Zeus and tell the same underlying story: the birth of Athena, the abduction of Persephone, the contest of Zeus and Prometheus, the marriage of Peleus and

---

[1] This is Fragment 1 of the *Cypria*. See Davies 1988, 34–36.

[2] Since the *Cypria* was almost certainly later than the *Iliad*, one cannot assume, as the scholiast did, that the precise account of the origins of the Trojan War given there would have been current at the time when the *Iliad* was composed. On the other hand, the general notion that the Trojan War was planned by Zeus as a way of taking many human lives was clearly part of the larger epic tradition and would have been familiar to the *Iliad*'s original audience. A fragment of Hesiod's *Ehoeae* (fr. 204 M–W) portrays the war as Zeus's means of eliminating the entire race of the demi-gods. The proemlike summary of an alternative *Iliad* sung by Demodocus in *Odyssey* 8 describes a quarrel between Achilles and Odysseus and concludes: *tote gar rha kulindeto pēmatos archē / Trōsi te kai Danaoisi Dios megalou dia boulas* (*Od.* 8.81–82). This conception of the Trojan War has even deeper roots in ancient Near Eastern myths of the destruction of humanity by the gods. See Kirk 1972, 79; and, for a full discussion, Scodel 1982. Another scholium on *Il.* 1.5 makes it clear that it was already debated as early as the time of Aristarchus whether the *Dios boulē* alluded to there was the plan proposed by Thetis (Aristarchus's view) or something else. Erbse 1969, 10. For yet more possibilities, see Redfield 1979, 105–8.

Thetis.[3] Archaic mythology responds to the human necessity of dying by treating it as a plot against humanity by a superior being. One mark of this sinister conception of death is that Zeus's plots not only impose death as an inevitable necessity, but intensify it, turning it into something actively sought for human beings in the form of violent death, early death, or death for the entire race.

As the master plot of archaic mythology, Zeus's imposition of death on mortals is retold numerous times. Zeus's rule is endless, and, correspondingly, there is no end to the human mortality that guarantees it. Thus the plan of Zeus is presented, in the phrase that surfaces to define the plots of both the *Iliad* and the *Cypria*, in the imperfect tense: *eteleieto*, "was being accomplished."

Yet, as a discrete narrative, each account of the accomplishment of Zeus's plan necessarily has a delimited shape and comes to some definable end. That end involves checks on Zeus's death-dealing power, which come through the assertion of those resources that allow humanity not to evade individual death, but to survive within the span of an individual lifetime and to continue as a race: technology, agriculture, sexual reproduction, and the capacity to appease the gods through sacrifice. The story of the separation of men and gods, beginning with the meal at Mecone, which is told in the *Theogony*, ends with humanity's new mortal condition mitigated by the availability of food and of fire, procured for humanity by Prometheus, and by the existence of women, although this final acquisition is presented not as a blessing from Prometheus, but as Zeus's conclusive act of malevolence. The *Hymn to Demeter* ends with death, initially imposed by Zeus in the form of Persephone's marriage to Hades, mitigated in a range of ways, all springing from the activities of Demeter: the existence of the seasons, which betoken both Persephone's periods away from the underworld and the possibility of agriculture; the fertility of the earth; the lasting fame of heroes like Demophoon; the easier version of death enjoyed by initiates into the Mysteries.

While it might seem at first, then, that these narratives move toward a defeat for Zeus and end with the limitation of his power, that is only

---

[3] For language identifying these episodes as *boulai* of Zeus, see *Hymn. Hom.* 2.9, 30, 414 (Demeter); Hesiod *Op.* 71, 79, 99; Hesiod *Th.* 534; *Cypria* 1.7. Not only do all of these narratives express Zeus's plotting, but the phrase *Dios boulē* is conventionally used in early Greek epic to refer to the plot of a narrative. See Nagy 1979, 82, 98, 100–101, 134. Aside from the prologues of the *Iliad* and the *Cypria*, places where this usage seems most explicit include *Od.* 8.82 and 11.297. This widespread emphasis on the Will of Zeus is one of the thematic links that connect our individual examples of early Greek hexameter poetry and identify them as participants in a common tradition, even as they variously interpret that tradition according to narrower generic constraints or the individual concerns of their poets. On this shared heritage, see Thalmann 1984, esp. xi–xxi.

superficially the case. Zeus also sponsors the life-sustaining remedies that constrain his imposition of mortality, for he needs the human race to continue in order that human beings, through their ever-recurring mortality, can go on affirming the immortality of the gods. Thus in the numerous Near Eastern myths of the destruction of the human race that the various versions of the *Dios boulē* echo, it is always the case that humanity is not entirely annihilated.[4]

In Greek mythology, the gods' need for human beings is explicitly expressed in the notion that they are somehow dependent on the sacrificial offerings human beings make. Yet the manifest uselessness of those offerings suggests that they symbolize a deeper symbiosis, whereby mortals benefit the gods simply by being mortal. The interest of Zeus in an outcome that appears to circumscribe his power is registered in both the Prometheus and the Demeter myths, as the existence of Pandora becomes Zeus's final countermove against humanity and as the appeasement of Demeter also becomes the occasion of her return to the Olympian circle. These myths conclude with the full implementation of a boundless continuity, in which human beings constantly die but humanity preserves itself sufficiently that the race persists and still more people die. As chapters in a story that has a beginning in the coming to power of Zeus but no ending, these narratives find closure not in the definitive resolution of any issue, but in the completed institution of an ongoing state of affairs.

As an account of the Trojan War, the *Iliad* is one chapter in this larger story and rehearses Zeus's imposition of mortality from the perspective of its own distinctive concerns, in particular a concern with warfare as experienced by heroes caught up in the quest for individual *kleos*. Through a much-admired art of synecdoche, the *Iliad* incorporates the entire history of the war into its account of the brief episode of Achilles' wrath. Accordingly, in its opening lines, it aligns the plan of Zeus with Thetis's and Achilles' project of restoring Achilles' lost honor. Though it may thus appear that the *Iliad*'s interpretation of the Trojan legend involves replacing Zeus's larger plan of wholesale destruction with this narrower plan, that appearance is misleading.[5] Rather, the *Iliad* artfully exploits its freedom to reconceive traditional material by playing the two possible referents of the *Dios boulē* off against each other and so revealing the limitations in Achilles'—and our—initial understanding of his situation.

The opening sections of the plot draw us into the illusion that the *Dios boulē* is nothing more than the plan suggested to Zeus by Thetis, which Zeus cooperatively enacts and which has as its sole aim the securing of

---

[4] Scodel 1982, 40–42.

[5] For this view, see ibid., 47; Kirk 1972, 79; and especially Slatkin 1991, 122, for the insightful formulation of the narrower plan of Zeus as a "distillation" of the larger version.

glory for Achilles. But the plan Achilles imagines himself to have initiated has unexpected consequences, and he finds himself enlisted in Zeus's prior and overriding purposes. Thus the *Iliad* contains a number of allusions that link its plot to the traditional motif of Zeus's plan to destroy a great many people, in addition to its ambiguous evocation of the *Dios boulē* at 1.5,[6] and as his story unfolds, Achilles himself comes to see the connection. He voices this recognition when he ends his quarrel with Agamemnon and returns to battle in Book 19. He now identifies Zeus as the instigator of the quarrel rather than, as he first appeared, the ally called in on Achilles' side once the quarrel was under way. If Zeus had not been behind the quarrel, he says, Agamemnon would never have stirred up Achilles' spirit and stolen his woman, *alla pothi Zeus / ethel' Achaioisin thanaton poleessi genesthai*, "But somehow Zeus wanted there to be death for many Achaeans" (*Il.* 19.273–74).

Over the course of the *Iliad*, the wrath of Achilles is revealed as another variation on Zeus's deadly master plan. It serves to forestall the inevitable victory of the militarily superior Achaeans, making room for further deaths on the Achaean side while Achilles is out of the battle, on the Trojan side after his return. Achilles serves Zeus's purposes so effectively because his wrath proves to be extendable in ways that he does not foresee or control, so that he goes on fulfilling Zeus's plan even after his own is complete. Achilles' unwitting service to Zeus is expressed in the deferred closure of the *Iliad*'s plot, with which this discussion began.[7]

Against all expectations (see Nestor at *Il.* 9.164), Achilles remains unappeased by Agamemnon's capitulation and offer of gifts in Book 9, and then his original anger at Agamemnon is transformed into a second wrath against Hector. The catalyst for this transformation is the death of Patroclus, which is for Achilles a bitter and unintended consequence of his success in enlisting Zeus's support for his own quest for glory. Like a character in a fairy tale, Achilles achieves the fulfillment of his wish only to find that it comes in an unexpected and unwelcome form that reveals the limitations of his own power. This is dramatized in Book 18 when Thetis finds Achilles deep in grief for Patroclus and asks him why he is weeping,

[6] As Kullmann has shown (1955, 1956).

[7] At *Iliad* 15.49–77 Zeus offers Hera an outline of future events, including the linked deaths of Sarpedon, Patroclus, and Hector and the ultimate destruction of Troy, and makes it clear that his promise to Thetis and Hector's consequent success are implicated in that larger scheme. At this point, right after his awakening from Hera's seduction of him in Book 14, he is exhorting her to cooperate with him and suggesting that their interests are really the same. Thus the impression he gives in Book 1 that he is acting in opposition to Hera is—like the impression that he is capitulating to Thetis and Achilles against his own will—here revealed to be false. Zeus's engagement with Achilles' wrath is expressed in his statement at 15.72 that he will not stop his own anger (*cholos*) until Hector has driven the Achaeans back to the ships.

for "that has been fulfilled / by Zeus which before you prayed for, reaching out your hands" (*Il.* 18.74–75). In his wretched response, Achilles complains that instead of protecting Patroclus, he has sat by his ships *etōsion achthos aourēs*, "a useless burden on the earth" (*Il.* 18.104), perhaps a subtle reference to Zeus's larger scheme as formulated in the account of the Trojan War that made its way into the *Cypria.*[8]

At the beginning of the *Iliad*, Achilles believes that he is set apart from Agamemnon precisely because he is able to dictate a plan to Zeus. In fact, he is unwittingly in the same position as Agamemnon when Zeus manipulates him in order to set that plan in motion. The only difference is that the poet makes Agamemnon's situation explicit from the outset. Recounting the false dream sent to Agamemnon, through which Zeus sends the Achaeans back to battle to be slaughtered, the narrator adds:

> Having said this, he was gone, and he left that man there
> imagining things in his heart that were not going to happen;
> for he thought he would take Priam's city on that day.
> Fool! He did not know what Zeus was planning (*ha rha Zeus mēdeto erga*);
> for he intended to impose yet more sufferings and groans
> upon the Trojans and the Danaans through mighty combat.
>
> (*Il.* 2.35–40)

This passage makes clear the connection between the way the human characters' limited projects are subsumed into Zeus's larger plan and the deferral of closure in the narrative structure of the *Iliad*. Agamemnon entertains hope that the story of the Trojan War will end that very day, but Zeus intends to prolong it so that more warriors will suffer and die on both sides.

Contrary to what Agamemnon supposes, he and Achilles are caught up in a plot that postpones the war's inevitable end. Such postponements occur repeatedly in the *Iliad*. Achilles' withdrawal and return to combat frame a long battle narrative structured as a series of moments in which the war is nearly brought to a conclusion, but always somehow continues. The time in which the story is set, the ninth year of the war, is a point at which both the fated ten-year time span at one level, and the willingness of the participants to continue at another level, are nearly exhausted, and the *Iliad* records the drawing out of the war just a little longer so that its destructive power can be exploited to the fullest. The threat of peace takes many forms, which are canvassed as the narrative unfolds: swift victory in battle for one or the other side, abdication by one side or the other, the construction of a truce, the decision of the conflict through a duel between representatives of each side.

---

[8] Slatkin 1991, 122 and, for the overturning of expectations for both characters and audience as a definitive feature of the *Iliad*, 49–52.

As the *Iliad* recounts occasion after occasion on which impulses toward peace are overcome, it records Zeus's ongoing success in impelling human beings to bring on their own deaths. In the process of doing so, it provides a full-scale investigation of the motivations that make human beings complicit in their own destruction. It reveals the forces that prevent the human actors from accepting moments of peaceful closure and that keep them busily extending the course of the war and, with it, the plot of the poem. In concert with Zeus, the human heroes who populate the *Iliad* respond to the necessity of dying by turning death into an active project, purposefully inflicting death on other people and courting it for themselves. They do so whether or not Zeus actively intervenes in their lives, as he does in the lives of Achilles and Agamemnon, because ceaseless human destruction is built into their system of values, which itself reflects Zeus's underlying purposes.

The warriors of the *Iliad* are committed to the repeated generation of death because they identify with a set of values—the heroic code—that enlists them in a quest for honor that is endless. For these heroes, honor is indispensable, since it is essential to their sense of self, and yet always to be sought. In the world of heroic warfare, the honor through which heroes know themselves is constantly subject to question. The aristocratic warriors who fight at Troy come to the war already heroes by virtue of their ancestry and their past deeds, and yet they are never able to rest on their laurels. Instead they are caught up in an endless attempt to distinguish themselves, which is also a quest for sufficient compensation for their efforts, for an adequate description of their deeds, and for a satisfying affirmation of who they are.

The world of combat is one of constant insecurity, in which heroes can never pause to enjoy the honor they earn. The press of battle is often too great even to allow the stripping of spoils from a defeated enemy; comrades in arms are too busy to stop and take note of one another's achievements. More subtly, friends and enemies conspire to keep warriors fighting by repeatedly questioning their identity as heroes.

Leaders keep their subordinates fighting by calling into question those features of heredity and status on which heroic identity is based. Thus Agamemnon, sending his resting troops back into battle at the beginning of Book 4, accuses Odysseus and Menestheus of enjoying the privileges of heroic status without earning them, suggesting that they are always ready to participate in feasts, but not equally ready to enter the battle (*Il.* 4.338–48). In a related tactic, he then tells Diomedes that he is not living up to the reputation of his father Tydeus (*Il.* 4.370–400), now undermining the hero's sense of inherited excellence rather than of social merit. In an intensification of this strategy, Athena urges Diomedes on once he is fighting by expressing doubt that he really is the son of his father (*Il.* 5.812–13). A hero is made to experience himself as a series of claims that are always open to question, that therefore must always be substantiated in action once again.

If a hero's allies undermine such claims, his enemies do so all the more. Opponents in battle automatically see themselves as attempting to disprove one another's claims to superiority. These claims are implicit in the act of facing the enemy, but are also regularly made explicit in the form of boasts, so that an encounter is often the testing of stated assertions by one or both participants. As James Redfield puts it, Homeric combat is "a kind of experiment which falsifies the hypothesis of one hero or the other."[9] This conception is reflected in the poem's recurrent formulations of battlefield encounters as learning experiences, as opportunities for people to find out the truth about one another (e.g., *Il.* 8.110–11; 16.242–45).

The ceaseless warfare of the *Iliad* is thus fueled by an endless supply of open questions about the merits of the participants, experienced by them as a continuous deprivation of the stable sense of identity on which they depend. The honor through which they know themselves is repeatedly lost in the climate of negative speech they inhabit,[10] and that loss always has to be made up through renewed efforts. The urge to repair loss links the quest for honor to the other motivation for fighting that Iliadic warriors most often display, revenge for fallen companions. The death of a companion is an incitement to action both as a source of dishonor to his fellow warriors and as a loss that inspires in them the attempt to repair it through further deaths.

The link between these two motivations is dramatized in the event that sparks the *Iliad*'s plot, Agamemnon's loss of Chryseis, who is both a badge of honor and someone he personally prizes; his attempt to repair that loss within his own camp turns that camp into an arena of conflict and inspires the variation on normal warfare according to which Achilles is responsible for myriad deaths among his own companions. The same connection surfaces more complexly in Achilles' return to battle in an attempt to repair the loss of Patroclus. This recurrent experience of honor as something lost is then key to the ongoing fulfillment of Zeus's plan, and also to the protraction of the *Iliad*'s extended narrative. The heroic system depends on a constant questioning of honor, and this provides the *Iliad* with its version of what David Miller calls "the narratable: the instances of disequilibrium, suspense, and general insufficiency from which a given narrative appears to rise."[11]

Warfare perpetuates itself because it provides the context for the attempt

---

[9] Redfield 1975, 129.
[10] On which see Slatkin 1988.
[11] Miller 1981, ix.

to recover lost honor, and yet also frustrates it. On the battlefield, a hero's attempts to repair past losses only invite new ones: for a hero to kill an enemy to avenge a fallen companion only turns the hero and his companions into targets for new enemy assaults; an attempt to put his achievements into words through boasting only provokes the enemy to another attack. Somewhere in this endless give-and-take, the hero is almost certain to die, losing his own life before he has a chance to experience the honor he has earned. Thus Agamemnon repeatedly holds out to his troops offers of prizes to be granted when Troy is defeated, a conclusion that seems always to be postponed and that many of them will never see.

This constant thwarting of honor during a warrior's lifetime is purportedly compensated for by honor after death, and yet that promise, too, goes largely unfulfilled for all but the greatest heroes. The press of battle leaves little room for the recovery and honoring of the dead. Even when the war is briefly suspended for that purpose, as it is by the Achaeans on the advice of Nestor in Book 7, there is no prospect of distinguishing and memorializing each individual (*Il.* 7.323–43, 433–41). Nestor suggests that some men's bones may be set aside and taken home for burial in the future, when the Achaeans return there, but then goes on to propose that they construct a single tomb, *akriton*, "indiscriminately," and that that tomb be put to use as the foundation of the Achaeans' new fortifications (which are themselves destined to disappear after the Achaeans leave; *Il.* 7.442–63, 12.3–35, cf. 23.326–33). When the Trojans take advantage of this truce to gather their dead, they find it difficult even to identify individual bodies (*Il.* 7.424).

As the story of Hector illustrates, the posthumous honor of even the greatest warrior is jeopardized by the same pressures that compromise his recognition in life. As Hector faces death in Book 22, he knows himself to be shamed in the eyes of his fellow Trojans for his unsuccessful military gamble (*Il.* 22.98–110), and he is aware that Achilles' hatred makes it unlikely that his body will be properly buried. His only hope is in *kleos* itself (*Il.* 22.304–5), the reputation that is solidified and perpetuated in heroic song, and that he and the other major heroes of the *Iliad* do achieve. Numerous other heroes do not, or do so only fleetingly as they are briefly mentioned in poetic "obituaries" and then forgotten as the poet's (and audience's) attention moves on to other things.[12] Given the importance of *kleos* through song to the character's lives and to the *Iliad*'s own value, it is striking how little and how joylessly it is actually envisioned within the poem. Hector is the character who dwells most on fantasies of his own

---

[12] For an appreciation of these "obituaries" as a valiant attempt to mark the lives and achievements of even insignificant heroes, see Griffin 1980, 140–43 and the other critics he quotes there.

future glory,[13] but those fantasies are tied to a painful vision of Andromache's future (*Il*. 6.458–63) or to the kinds of unrealistic hope to which he
is prone (*Il*. 7.87–91). The only character who refers explicitly to her
future commemoration in song is Helen, and she does so without pleasure,
presenting that future song as the cause of her present sufferings (*Il*. 6.354–
58). This is in notable contrast to the *Odyssey*, whose story of honor
achieved and enjoyed includes episodes in which the hero experiences his
own celebration in song.

Not only is the fulfillment sought by the *Iliad*'s heroes constantly deferred, but that fulfillment is always questionable, because the bargains on
which the heroic code depends are by nature unequal. Warriors who are
caught up in the instinctive drive to assert themselves do not normally
notice this inequality, but Achilles' ability to pursue honor by doing nothing gives him an opportunity to become aware of it. Achilles points to the
most extreme instance of this inequality when he declares in his speech to
the embassy in Book 9 that no number of gifts can be equated with the
loss of his life, but it is always the case that the rewards of heroic endeavor,
whether material gifts, social privileges, or poetic commemoration, come
in a currency markedly different from the expenditures of effort through
which they are earned. The search for an adequate match between a hero's
investment of energy and acceptance of risk and the honor that rewards
them is always inconclusive. The conditions that the *Iliad*'s plot illuminates
can never assure a perfect equilibrium between a hero and his public valuation, or the removal of all suspense about whether a hero will continue to
live up to his reputation, or the enjoyment of compensation sufficient to
make a hero indifferent to the loss of his life.

Both the protracted course of the war and the extended battle narrative
that fills much of the *Iliad* nonetheless have their limits, and these limits
generate the moments of temporary closure that punctuate the poem's narrative of ongoing mortality. Though heroes are caught up in a quest for
individual distinction that leads them to court death, they are also enlisted
in the preservation of their society and, to borrow A. H. Adkins's terminology, pursue cooperative virtues as well as competitive ones.[14] The forward motion of battle narrative is routinely checked as heroes pause to rest,
to participate in the rituals of feasting through which their social bonds are
renewed, to take note of what they have achieved, and to honor the dead.
At a less routine level, both the Achaeans and the Trojans take periodic
steps toward bringing the war to an early close, proposing to end the ongoing slaughter by entering into a truce.

As in the mythological paradigm the *Iliad*'s society echoes, these checks

---

[13] Martin 1989, 136–37.
[14] Adkins 1960, 7.

on the onward march of death also reinforce it, assuring that the band of warriors survives to go on fighting, killing, and dying. As in that paradigm, these closural elements are related to notions of natural regeneration, in both the human and the agricultural spheres. Often, pauses in the flow of combat are motivated by human needs for food and sleep and are tied to the cyclical rhythms of nature, as when an episode of fighting ends despite the unfinished business that remains because of the need, as a recurrent formula expresses it, *nukti peisesthai*, "to obey the night." The need for such pauses is underscored in Book 19, when Odysseus insists, despite Achilles' rage for battle, that the army stop to eat and sleep, stressing that this is essential if they are to continue to fight (*Il.* 19.154–83, 215–37). Achilles absorbs this message and repeats it with characteristic concision in his exhortation to Agamemnon, "Now go to your meal, so that we may bring on Ares" (*Il.* 19.275).

The transitory quality of such pauses is related to society's dependence on the muting of competition, on a certain blurring of distinctions that fosters social harmony and yet also threatens to undermine it. As members of a society unite, they give up something of their individual claims and so accept another form of unequal bargain, one in which unlike things are equated, in which individuals who differ in their abilities and achievements are treated as if they are more nearly equal than—from their own perspectives—they really are. The typical heroic hostility to equation is well illustrated by the response of Sthenelus to the speech, cited above, in which Agamemnon provocatively accuses Diomedes of falling short of his father Tydeus. Sthenelus bursts out that he and Diomedes are in fact superior to their fathers: "So do not ever hold our fathers in like honor [*homoiē . . . timē*]" (*Il.* 4.410). The countervailing tendency of heroic society to gloss over distinctions is well illustrated in the language of Nestor as he tries to salvage Achaean harmony by making peace between Achilles and Agamemnon in Book 1. Even while he asserts to Achilles the higher authority of Agamemnon, he uses rhyming terms and balanced phrases that make the two seem equal.

> If you are stronger (*karteros*), and a goddess mother bore you,
> Yet he is mightier (*pherteros*), since he rules over more people.
>
> (*Il.* 1.280–81)

Nestor follows this statement with advice to each hero to yield to the other. The failure of this advice shows how much this equalizing pressure is at odds with the heroic passion for distinction evinced by both Achilles and Agamemnon. That quest for distinction has a strong antisocial dimension, which is expressed in the fantasy Achilles voices as he sends Patroclus into battle (*Il.* 16.97–100). In that vision, all of the competing claims on both sides of the war have finally been played out, and only Achilles and

Patroclus remain to take Troy and triumph over all. This fantasy places Achilles decisively at the top of the warrior hierarchy, but at the cost of any survivors who might recognize and honor his achievement. Normally, societies keep themselves going and thus preserve a context for honor, however imperfect, by keeping those claims untested among their members and channeling heroic energies toward competition with external enemies. This process lies behind the assumption expressed in *Iliad* 19 that the preservation of Achaean society is linked to continued hostilities toward Troy.

Those externally directed competitive energies assure that in the *Iliad* the two opposing sides cooperate in keeping the war alive. There are, of course, moments in the *Iliad*'s plot when the combatants do seem willing to suspend the war, entering into the kinds of unequal bargain that peace depends upon. Thus in Book 3 both the Trojans and the Achaeans are willing to conclude a truce according to which for one side the loss of Helen would go effectively uncompensated. But that truce is broken when an individual Trojan, Pandarus, is unable to resist the opportunity to distinguish himself by taking a shot at Menelaus (*Il.* 4.86–104).

The fragility of such truces is further underscored by the similar episode in Book 7, in which the general fighting stops for a single combat between Hector and Ajax. Planned from the outset by the gods as simply a day-long pause in the war (*Il.* 7.29–32), this ceremonious encounter enacts a combination of civility and equality that assures the resumption of hostilities. Both Hector and Ajax's Achaean supporters have hopes that the duel will be decisive (*Il.* 7.74–91, 202–5), but it leads instead to what the Achaeans present as their second-best hope, that Zeus will grant *isēn amphoteroisi biēn kai kudos*, "equal strength and glory to both" (7.205).[15] Thus it is inevitable that, as the two combatants agree to break off in deference to nightfall and exchange gifts, Hector looks forward to a future occasion when they will fight "until the god / distinguishes us and gives victory to one or the other" (*Il.* 7.291–92).[16]

As in the mythological scheme of the *Dios boulē*, so in the warrior society that enacts that scheme, the continuity of a stable situation comes at the cost of human individuals. If heroes are not actively courting death, they are systematically devalued through active shaming or through the quieter loss of status that comes with social accommodation. Inevitable death and participation in social life are united in their power to erode the sense of distinction that is always a component of human motivation, but is the

---

[15] Note the difference between the two imagined bits of *kleos* quoted by Hector at 89–90 and 301–2.

[16] For a widely influential discussion of the destabilizing effect of lack of differentiation among individuals within a community, see Girard 1977.

mainspring of heroic existence. This double assault on human particularity is expressed by Achilles in his speech to the embassy in Book 9 through the notion of *iē timē,* "a single honor," a refinement of Sthenelus's *homoiē . . . timē,* "like honor," that, as a number of commentators have pointed out, is inherently paradoxical.[17]

> There is an equal portion for the one who hangs back, and in the case of one
>   who fights hard.
> The coward and the brave man are held in a single honor.
> The man who does nothing and the man who does much die the same.
>
> (Il. 9.318–20)

Here Achilles formulates his complaint that all human distinctions are rendered meaningless by the equal subjection of everyone to death in terms borrowed from his complaint about Achaean society, which is that unequal contributions are met with equal rewards. And though Achilles believes, possibly with some justice, that he has a particular grievance against Agamemnon as a leader, the loss of distinction is, as we have seen, a constituent feature of all social life. Achilles describes this threat to individual distinction by playing on a certain slipperiness in the idea of equation. The central ritual of heroic social life, the *dais eisē,* "the equal feast," is an occasion when distinctions are properly maintained, and the feast is understood to be equal in the sense that each participant is given a portion that equates to his distinctive merit.[18] Yet the inclusion of everyone in the feast necessarily limits the distinction that can be conveyed by participation in it, and the concept of equality is all too easily transferred, as it is here by Achilles, to situations in which everyone is equally honored.

This is the same limitation that Achilles finds in the universality of death: heroic endeavor, however distinguished, is not efficacious enough to overcome death; a heroic death, however distinguished, is not ultimately different from any other death. Achilles uncovers the common element in these two seemingly opposed aspects of the heroic system, detecting the same leveling effect both in the social arrangements that preserve warrior society and in the death on which that society is purposefully bent.

If the story of Achilles' wrath as the fulfillment of Zeus's plan continues far longer than expected, pressing on beyond a number of points of likely conclusion, it does finally come to a close. The time arrives at which Achilles can no longer evade the violent, early death that he invites by playing out his role as agent of destruction. And the larger theme of the Trojan War also has its limit in the eventual Achaean victory. Zeus's purposes may be infinite, but they depend on working through human agents,

---

[17] See Schein 1984, 105–6, building on the suggestion of Parry (1964).
[18] Motto and Clark 1969, 118–19.

who have their inevitable ends. The *Iliad* is notable, however, for not narrating either of the conclusive events toward which its plot moves, the death of Achilles and the fall of Troy. Instead, it stops after recounting an event, the death of Hector, in which both of those outcomes are implicit: as Thetis tells him, Achilles' death is fated to follow Hector's (*Il.* 18.95–96), and it is clear that Troy can no longer stand without its greatest defender.

Not only does Hector's death represent within the *Iliad* the end of Achilles' life and the end of the Trojan War, but the ransoming of Hector's body also brings a sense of closure to the poem. Hector's funeral aligns the final lines of the *Iliad* with a natural moment of closure in the rhythm of human experience; Achilles' accession to Priam's request concludes his extended wrath; and the language and events of Book 24 echo and invert the language and events of Book 1 so as to create a strong formal close.[19] But by displacing the more finally conclusive events of Achilles' death and the fall of Troy onto the death and ransoming of Hector, the *Iliad* does nonetheless mute the finality of its ending, and this accords with the *Iliad*'s role as one more chapter in Zeus's endless scheme.

The more cosmic versions of the *Dios boulē* discussed above end when the conditions of human life, with its ineluctable individual mortality and its strategies of communal survival, have been established as an ever ongoing state of affairs. The *Iliad* recounts the *Dios boulē* as experienced by individual mortals and shows how their actions serve to make that state of affairs unending, and so it is fitting that it should end at a point when the war is still ongoing (as *Il.* 24.667 reminds us) and when Achilles, for all that his fate has been decided, is still caught up in the complex of motivations that turns heroic society into a mechanism for constant and accelerated mortality. While effectively concluding the wrath of Achilles, the ransoming of Hector still captures the inherent inconclusiveness of the larger story that the *Iliad* tells through the episode of the Wrath.

The ransoming of Hector is clearly marked as the fulfillment of Zeus's planning through the negotiation between Zeus and Thetis that brings it about. Zeus summons Thetis to Olympus, requires her acquiescence in Achilles' surrender of the body, and sends her as a messenger to Achilles to impress the necessity of it upon him (*Il.* 24.77–140). This action contributes to the poem's effect of formal closure by inverting the initial negotiation between Zeus and Thetis at the end of Book 1 and signals that the surprisingly extensive plan they devised then has finally run its course.

The significance of Thetis's acquiescence in the return of Hector's body has recently been clarified by Laura Slatkin, who has investigated the my-

---

[19] Macleod 1982, 32–35.

thology concerning Thetis that lies behind the plot of the *Iliad*.[20] Thetis's history is another episode in the story of Zeus's preservation of his own immortality through the imposition of mortality on human beings. Zeus initially desires to marry Thetis, but abandons that plan when it is revealed that she will bear a son who will usurp his father. Zeus escapes mortality— of which the replacement of father by son is a hallmark—by avoiding this marriage for himself and imposing it on a mortal, Peleus, with the consequence that Peleus's son Achilles is also mortal. In this myth, then, there is a direct causal link between the continuous immortality of Zeus and the death of the mortal Achilles. The marriage of Peleus and Thetis fulfills Zeus's plan in two ways. First, it is the occasion of the discord that leads to the Trojan War with its myriad deaths, and thus it provides the first event in the *Cypria*'s account of the *Dios boulē* in the form of a scheme to relieve the earth of human population. Second, it leads to the mortality of the paradigmatic human hero Achilles and thus underlies the *Iliad*'s account of the *Dios boulē* in the form of Achilles' quest for honor.

Thetis's agreement to the limitation on Achilles' powers involved in his giving up Hector's body thus represents, in displaced form, her acceptance of his mortality.[21] Her joining of the Olympian circle, which is marked by a shared meal, recalls the ending of another version of the *Dios boulē*, the *Hymn to Demeter*, which concludes with Demeter returning to Olympus after bringing about a range of outcomes, all involving the mitigation of death, including the intermittent immortality of her daughter Persephone and the everlasting honor of her mortal nursling Demophoon. Thetis's role in the *Iliad* echoes Demeter's in a more focused form, and her yielding to Zeus marks her achievement of one particular goal, the securing of honor for Achilles.

The significance of Achilles' action in releasing Hector's body is further illuminated by an exchange between Zeus and Hera, in which the quarrel sparked by Zeus's initial agreement with Thetis is patched up. Hera objects to the idea that Achilles should return the body, because she feels his doing so will obliterate the distinction between him and Hector. She protests to Apollo, who has proposed the idea, on the grounds that it would involve giving *homē timē*, "like honor," to both Achilles and Hector (*Il.* 24.57). Zeus, however, reassures her on this point. He declares that *ou men gar timē de mi' essetai*, "There will not be a single honor" (*Il.* 24.66), but he goes on to add that Hector has won the gods' love through the many sacrifices he has offered to them.

The opposed perspectives of Zeus and Hera are resolved in a situation that is defined as an unequal bargain—as the treating of unlike things as

[20] Slatkin 1991.
[21] Ibid., 105.

like—but that is colored by a promise of future distinction. This final episode of the poem thus enacts heroic society's characteristic combination of the promise of distinction in the future with the striking of unequal bargains in the present. Achilles' acceptance of ransom for the body of Hector, which for him is freighted with the lost life of Patroclus, represents a final resolution to the issue of the unequal bargain that has surfaced repeatedly at key junctures in the *Iliad*'s plot, beginning with Agamemnon's rejection of Chryses' ransom for his daughter Chryseis, which Achilles' action here obliquely corrects.

Agamemnon rejects the offer of ransom for Chryseis because he does not see the gifts her father offers as commensurate to her; as he explains to the assembled Achaeans, he likes her and does not feel that the gifts he is offered can compensate him for her loss (*Il.* 1.109–15). The outcome of this episode reveals that he would have done well to accept the ransom, despite its inadequacy, because in the event he loses her anyway—and now without compensation. Agamemnon's refusal is echoed in Achilles' rejection of his gifts during the embassy in Book 9, where the same issues surface again and are addressed more explicitly. Achilles, like Agamemnon, rejects what he perceives as an unequal bargain, declaring that Agamemnon's gifts cannot make up for what he has lost in the past, the honor bound up with his possession of Briseis, or for what he must lose in the future, the rest of his life.

Achilles' rejection meets with two responses from his former companions, both of which amount to defenses of the unequal bargains of social life. One is Phoenix's account of Meleager, who similarly rejected material gifts as an inducement to fight, but ended up fighting anyway out of concern for his community, at which point those gifts were no longer available. Phoenix's message, which is borne out by Achilles subsequent experience, is that there are other reasons for fighting besides the gifts to be won; since these other reasons will lure him back anyway, he might as well accept whatever rewards are offered in exchange for his likely loss of life, however incommensurate. Soon afterwards, Ajax condemns Achilles by referring to the institution of the blood price, pointing out that people are willing to accept the inadequate material settlement that is the only available recompense for irrecoverable lost relatives.

> For even from the killer of his brother someone
> will accept a price, or for a dead child.
> And the killer stays there in the country, having paid much,
> and the heart of the other is held in check and the strong spirit,
> once he has received the price.
>
> (*Il.* 9.632–36)

Achilles is deaf to the message directed at him by his fellow Achaeans in Book 9, and he remains indifferent to the imperfect exchanges of communal life as he returns to battle bent on revenge for the death of Patroclus. He accepts Agamemnon's gifts on his return to the Achaean army in Book 19, but it is clear that they mean nothing to him. And, in his encounter with Lycaon at the beginning of Book 21, he refuses to enter into an arrangement to ransom Lycaon such as he had engaged in regularly in the past. His holding on to Hector's body is his final, futile act of resistance against the substitutions and approximations that compromise the satisfaction offered by his world. His continued assault on Hector represents a repeated effort to recover what is lost through revenge, an attempt to undo Patroclus's death by overcoming his killer, as Hecuba seems to understand when she later comments that, despite his mistreatment of Hector's body, Achilles could not bring Patroclus back to life (*Il.* 24.756).

This sequence of rejected bargains is finally broken when Achilles enters into a bargain with Priam, taking material gifts in exchange for Hector's body. The compensation he receives is notably incommensurate with the intense attachment to Patroclus that Hector's body represents for him, and yet it is the only compensation there is. The *Iliad* brings to a close its exploration of the reasons why human beings in the end do willingly enter into unequal bargains by depicting two interlocked experiences of the relinquishing of grief, an emotional transition that entails letting go of the hope that what has been lost can be exactly recovered. This is an experience of closure that is also the precondition of future action, as Achilles acknowledges when he tells Priam that nothing is accomplished by mourning: *ou gar tis prēxis peletai krueroio gooio* (*Il.* 24.524). The truce that is constructed by Achilles and Priam is, like the other truces recorded in the *Iliad*, a temporary pause that facilitates the continuation of the war—the final manifestation of the pattern of incomplete closure that pervades the poem. This quality is captured in the lines in which Priam proposes the terms of the truce, where the return to battle becomes the concluding event of a rounded twelve-day sequence.

> For nine days we will lament him in the hall,
> on the tenth we will bury him, and the people will feast,
> on the eleventh we will build a mound over him,
> on the twelfth we will fight, if that is what must be.
>
> (*Il.* 24.664–67)

Like the other truces of the *Iliad*, the compact between Achilles and Priam depends on the equation of unequal things. This structure is registered in the *Iliad*'s final episode in a variety of ways, not only in the equation of Hector's body with the ransom Priam offers for it, but also in the substitutions—of Priam for Peleus, of Achilles for Hector—that turn the encounter of Achilles and Priam into a simulation of the two reunions of father and son that will now never take place. Whatever future distinction is to be secured for Achilles by the *Iliad* or by other forms of commemoration, such as the magnificent funeral recounted in the *Odyssey*, the poem ends with an enactment of equal honor. However singular the achievements recorded by the poem as a whole, Achilles shares the narrative focus of the final book with the living Priam, from whose perspective the story of the ransoming is told and whose action is presented as an extraordinary heroic exploit, and with the dead Hector, whose achievements are honored in the final sections of the poem.

And, like all the truces of the *Iliad*, the compact of Priam and Achilles is limited by the continuing investment of human beings in the search for complete distinction. This limitation is reflected in the contradictory quality of Achilles' statements, which preclude any reading of his condition at the end of the poem as one of detached transcendence of the conflicting impulses that animate his society. While it seems from his sober statement about the uselessness of grief that he accepts Priam's ransom with a full awareness of how little it matches what he has lost, he is not at ease with his bargain. He feels a need to defend it to Patroclus and addresses a speech to him in which he assures Patroclus of the value of the gifts he receives.

> Do not be angry with me, Patroclus, if you should learn
> even though you are in Hades, that I ransomed shining Hector
> for his dear father, since he gave me gifts that are not inadequate (*aeikeia*),
> and I will share with you a fitting portion of them.
>
> (*Il.* 24.592–95)

Here Achilles expresses an ability to settle for less: he is willing to treat the ransom as adequate compensation, and he is willing to have his own honor diminished through sharing that ransom with Patroclus. On the other hand, his fantasy of a future transaction between them shows that he still seems to think, and to need to think, that he can somehow get Patroclus back.

Furthermore, Achilles is not really reconciled to the equalizing of honor involved in his bargain with Priam. Readers of the poem often find the implicit link between Priam's request that Achilles remember his own father and Achilles' willingness to give up Hector's body to be the most significant and compelling aspect of this episode: if Achilles' respect for Priam's paternal concerns springs from thoughts about his own father, his gesture becomes a moving acknowledgment of the common condition of humanity. And yet this is something Achilles himself refuses to admit. Whatever we may feel has happened between them, it is necessary to Achilles to deny that Priam's appeal has inspired his own action.

Do not provoke me, old man. I have on my own decided
to ransom Hector for you. There came as a messenger to me from Zeus
my mother, who bore me, the daughter of the old man of the sea.
And I recognize about you, Priam, and it does not escape my notice,
that one of the gods has led you to the swift ships of the Achaeans.

(Il. 24.560–64)

This passage, which cannot easily be assimilated to accounts of Achilles as the exponent of a common humanity, reveals how fully caught up he remains in the idea of individual distinction.[22] He continues to stress what separates him from other mortals, his divine mother and his special connection to Zeus, rather than the connection to other mortals he inherits from his mortal father Peleus, the connection to which Priam has alluded with results that Achilles will not acknowledge.

While Achilles distances himself from Priam's appeal in this way, he does also himself make a point of the shared experience of Priam and Peleus. He does register the connection on which Priam's appeal is based, but in a displaced form, which is also an account of Zeus's role in shaping human affairs. Seeking to impress on Priam the uselessness of mourning, he points out that the best that mortals can hope for from Zeus is a mixture of good and bad, and he describes the two jars from which Zeus dispenses variously blessings and hardships *(Il.* 24.527–33). Through this image, Achilles conveys the ambiguity of Zeus's plan, which incorporates both the pressures that induce human beings to invite their own deaths and the blessings that mitigate the hardships of mortal life. He illustrates this mixture by instancing both Peleus and Priam (linked explicitly with the words *kai se* at *Il.* 24.543), both of whom have experienced a life of initial prosperity darkened by the painful loss of a beloved son. Both men thus exemplify the way Zeus causes human beings to suffer more than they have to: both suffer a loss that reverses the natural order of things through the purposeful, premature death brought about by warfare.

Before the story of the *Iliad* begins, Zeus masters the challenge posed by Thetis by making Achilles mortal. The *Iliad* shows how Achilles, in common with the other mortals who make up his society, responds to his mortal state by intensifying it, actively bringing on the deaths of many others and finally his own death. It shows how he and his fellow warriors become active promoters of Zeus's purposes, engaged in a constant project of mutual destruction that never ceases for long and that will continue after the events of the *Iliad* are over. The examples of Priam and Peleus point up how differently Zeus and his mortal agents experience the fulfillment of

---

[22] Macleod suggests that Achilles evokes Zeus's will in order to keep himself in check since his anger could easily flare up again: Macleod 1982, 136. That residual capacity for anger is, of course, itself a sign of his continued investment in the motivations that fuel heroic warfare.

his plan. Zeus's success involves seeing Achilles, the man who would have been his son, die; in this way, he protects himself against the challenge of a son who could be his rival and so maintains his immortality. His victory is accomplished by imposing the same experience on mortal fathers, and to them it brings the mortal condition in a cruelly intensified form. Though Peleus and Priam are only two of the many mortals who exemplify this pattern, they do also have a closer tie, to which Achilles' speech implicitly alludes. Both suffer through the actions of Achilles himself in his role not as the instigator but as the agent of Zeus's plan, a role he plays equally for his hated enemy and for his beloved father—both in his glorious achievements as the killer of Priam's sons and in his own early death.[23]

[23] Versions of this paper were delivered at Harvard University on March 18, 1993, and at the Center for Hellenic Studies on February 2, 1995. I am especially grateful to the graduate students of the Harvard Department of the Classics for inviting me to speak and for forming part of a lively and receptive audience. My thanks also to the editors and referees of this volume and to Joseph Russo for their helpful comments on an earlier draft.

CHAPTER 3

Odes and Ends: Closure in Greek Lyric

IAN RUTHERFORD

THIS CHAPTER aims to survey closural techniques in Greek lyric poetry. At the outset, one has to face up to the fact that the number of complete songs that survive is small; it is only slightly augmented by a few disconnected endings transmitted in papyri. Worse, the sample that has come down to us is far from being representative: most of what survives comes from the fifth century B.C.E.; for the influential lyric poetry of the late archaic period (seventh to sixth centuries B.C.E.), we have little evidence. Furthermore, most of the extant songs belong to one genre, the *epinikion* or victory song; besides *epinikia*, all that survive are a few *dithuramboi* (narrative songs, originally associated with Dionysus) by Bacchylides and some *paianes* (hymns to Apollo, roughly) by Pindar.

An additional set of problems is posed by uncertainties about performance context. A reasonable assumption for the classical period is that the primary purpose of the composition of songs was performance, and not the display or circulation of a written text (although it is likely that the poets envisaged their songs being read at a later stage). In many cases, we can be reasonably certain what the performance context was—a festival, for example, or some other celebration, or a symposium. But even then, many uncertainties remain. Would the performance frame have given the audience a good idea of when the song was going to end, as for example in the case of a song performed by a chorus processing along a certain route, which might have been expected to stop when it reached its destination? Again, in some cases the performance of a song would not have been an isolated event, but would have taken place as part of a sequence of performances of ritual and song, and the question arises how events that followed the performance of the song have affected the issue of closure. Another problematic issue is whether pauses between formal segments, such as triads, would have been such as to encourage the illusion that the ending of a segment was the ending of the whole song.[1]

---

[1] Performance and display/circulation of written texts will be discussed in Rutherford 1997; ending of song coinciding with arrival at destination, performance of song followed by further performances, and infratextual closure are discussed below.

Despite such uncertainties, and the deficiencies inherent in our sources, the subject of closure in Greek lyric poetry merits study. The endings that do survive show a high degree of sophistication, and it is clear that by the fifth century, poets had developed a wide repertoire of closural techniques. To illustrate these, I have selected a number of types of technique and theme: requests, framing devices, themes of reception, themes relating to limits, and myths. At the end of the chapter, I also consider quasi-closural features within songs: cases in which a division between two triads—the major formal segments in fifth-century lyric—is marked by an accumulation of closural features, and cases where a cluster of features so placed seems to give a deceptive impression that the song is coming to an end ("false closure").

LAST REQUESTS

Writing in the second century C.E., Aelius Aristides noted that *dithuramboi* and *paianes* usually ended with prayers.[2] Certainly, prayer is a common closural motif in surviving classical lyric.[3] In the *epinikia*, closural prayers request continued prosperity for the victor and his family or polis (*Ol.* 6, *Ol.* 8, *Ol.* 13), and sometimes further victories (*Pyth.* 5, *Isthm.* 7). In other cases, the singer prays on his own behalf (*Pyth.* 2, *Nem.* 9). In *paianes*, final prayers can also be for prosperity and success (*Pa.* I, *Pa.* II), or they can request that Apollo accept the singer or his song (*Pa.* V, VI). One *paian* ended with the exhortation "act very justly" (*Pa.* VIId): μάλα πρᾶξον [δι]καίως, which seems to be directed at men rather than gods.[4]

The reasons for ending with a prayer are complex. First, the structure could be seen as reflecting the cletic hymn structure: invocation, sanction, request; the prayer comes at the end because it has to be preceded by the parts of the song that please the deity (in *do ut des*, *des* comes after *do*).[5] Second, final prayers naturally come last because they relate to the future. They point beyond the end of the song, requiring a response from the deity. One might also argue that the final position is particularly sensitive:

Texts used in this chapter are Snell and Maehler 1987–89 (Pindar) and Maehler 1970 (Bacchylides); the translations are my own.

[2] *Or.* 26 (*Regarding Rome*), 108: κράτιστον οὖν, ὥσπερ οἱ τῶν διθυράμβων τε καὶ τῶν παιάνων ποιηταί, εὐχήν τινα προσθέντα οὕτω κατακλεῖσαι τὸν λόγον ("So it is best, just like the poets of *dithuramboi* and *paianes*, to finish my speech by adding a prayer").

[3] The closural prayer seems to be a constant across cultures: ancient Egyptian hymns ended with prayers (Assmann 1975, 19).

[4] All of the Hellenistic *paians* on stone collected by Powell (1926) conclude with prayers for prosperity, not for reception by the deity.

[5] On the structure of cletic hymns, see Ausfeld 1903; Bowra 1964, 200.

this is the last thing the (divine) audience will hear, and their impression will be formed on this basis; it is a position as sensitive as the beginning. That's how I would interpret a fragment from the beginning of a *prosodion* (processional song) composed for the Aeginetans in honor of Artemis Aphaea (fr. 89a):

> τί κάλλιον ἀρχομένοις[ιν] ἢ καταπαυομένοισιν
> ἢ βαθύζωνόν τε Λατώ
> καὶ θοὰν ἵππων ἐλάτειραν ἀεῖσαι

What is better for us beginning or ending than to sing of Leto with her deep girdle and the driver of swift horses?

Thus, Pindar *Olympian* 8 and 13, and *Nemean* 9, end conspicuously with a reference to Zeus, which seems to correspond to the more common pattern of "beginning with Zeus," familiar from the opening of Hesiod's *Works and Days*.[6]

As might be expected, closural prayers contain themes that are in themselves closural. *Olympian* 13 concludes with a prayer to Zeus under the epithet *Teleios*, which means primarily "authoritative," but also suggests the meaning "associated with an ending."[7] Again, *Paian* II ends with a prayer to the hero Abderus for victory in a "final war" over the Thracians (line 106), and here the refrain, which occurs at the end of each of the three triads, reinforces the effect of the final prayer.[8] In other final prayers, the construction seems to suggest ideas like "completeness" and "unity," as in *Olympian* 8:

> εὔχομαι ἀμφὶ καλῶν μοίρᾳ Νέμεσιν διχόβουλον μὴ θέμεν·
> ἀλλ' ἀπήμαντον ἄγων βίοτον
> αὐτούς τ' ἀέξοι καὶ πόλιν |||

I pray that, for the sake of the share of good things, [Zeus] may not cause Nemesis to be divided in counsel, but may bring a painless life, and thus increase to themselves and their city.

The idea of an undivided Nemesis emphasizes the idea of unity, and the detail "and their city" adds a sense of totality.[9] So the famous prayer at the

---

[6] This pattern is found in Pindar at *Nem.* 2.1–3, 5.25–27; *Pa.* VI.1; also at Alcman, *PMG* 29 (= 89Cal.), Aratus *Phaen.* 1–16, Aristides 43 (εἰς Δία), 31. I am grateful to Carolyn Dewald for this observation.

[7] See further below.

[8] In general the refrain can be a problem for closure, as is shown by Smith (1968, 59–63).

[9] Alcaeus, *PLF* 42, begins with the destruction of Troy, then recounts the marriage of Peleus and Thetis, and ends by recapitulating Troy's destruction: οἰ δ' ἀπώλοντ' ἀμφ' Ἐ[λένᾳ Φρύγες τε] καὶ πόλις αὔτων ||| ("They perished around Helen—the Phrygians

end of *Pythian* 8 is directly addressed to Aegina, but includes her husband Zeus and three generations of their progeny.

> Αἴγινα φίλα μᾶτερ, ἐλευθέρῳ στόλῳ
> πόλιν τάνδε κόμιζε Δὶ καὶ κρέοντι σὺν Αἰακῷ ῳ
> Πηλεῖ τε κἀγαθῷ Τελαμῶνι σύν τ' 'Αχιλλεῖ. |||

> Dear mother Aegina, convey this city in a free voyage together with Zeus, ruler Aiakos, Peleus, good Telamon, and with Achilles!

The most important figures of Aeginetan mythology are arranged in an encompassing frame that surrounds both the prayer and the idea of the city.

FRAMES AND SEALS

Songs may also conclude with references to poetry. Such references provide a frame, surrounding the message—the narrative—with statements that draw attention to the medium. Some songs end with self-identifications on the part of the poet—in classical poetry never explicit, but conveyed via reference to his native land, as in *Isthmian* 6 and *Pythian* 4 (so Bacchylides *Ode* 3). Another common pattern is an exhortation to deliver the song to the victor (*Ol.* 6; *Isthm.* 2 and *Isthm.* 5). Other songs end with an exhortation that the song be delivered to a dead relative in the underworld: in *Olympian* 8 the messenger is Angelia, daughter of Hermes; in *Olympian* 14 it is Echo, an effective choice, because an echo is what would naturally be left after the sound of the song stops reverberating, and because an echo, being an imitation of a real utterance, is also in some sense dead.[10]

A special function of references to poetry at the end of a song is to assert the value and excellence of the song—by highlighting the skill of the poet, the tradition behind him, or the prestigious origin of the genre. It has become conventional to refer to passages performing such validating speech-acts as *sphragides*, because the word *sphragis* ("seal") seems to be used by ancient poets with a similar force, and because the concept of a "seal" seems to be a good metaphor for the mechanism.[11] *Sphragides* are not confined to the ends of songs, but this is a good place for them, since one naturally sets the seal after the letter has been written, or the product has

---

and their city"). For "totality" as a closural topos, see Smith 1968, 182–86; Schrijvers 1973, 152.

[10] On echo, see Hollander 1981, 13 n. 5. On the figure in general, see Segal 1985. Compare Fusillo's discussion of paratextual references in the Greek novel (chapter 10 in this volume).

[11] See the full discussion in Kranz 1961; Schrijvers 1973, 149–50; Cerri (1991) warns that the original poetic sense of *sphragis* may have been more literal.

been made ready to sell (though from the point of view of the receiver or consumer, the seal ought to come at the beginning).

In most Pindaric examples, the "validating" function of the closural *sphragis* is only implied. The closest we come to explicit recognition of it is in a fragmentary cult-song, probably a *prosodion*, that ended with reflections about the value of wisdom and the dangers of "swift judgment," using the metaphor of the final mark that is placed on gold after it is tested. The function of the ending—to reassure the listener or reader that the song is a high-quality product—is directly analogous to the function of the seal of approval placed on the gold in the image.[12]

Sometimes, Pindar guarantees the value of his song by linking it to the virtue of the patron (which is undisputed, at least as far as the patron is concerned). This happens at the end of *Olympian* 1 (Pindar and Hieron), and in the closing "Z" section[13] of *Olympian* 6 (Pindar and Hagesias are linked by the tradition that a nymph from Stymphalus was the mother of Thebe, the eponymous nymph of Thebes). Interestingly, there is an antecedent for linkage of a poet's excellence to that of his patron in the ending of the so-called Polycrates Ode of Ibycus (*PMG* 282). Probably, this relationship is reciprocal: the song is validated by the excellence of the patron, but it is also implied that the patron's victory or virtue depends on validation in song.[14]

Another type of closural *sphragis* comprises references to songs and their origins. Consider the end of *Nemean* 8:

> ἦν γε μὰν ἐπικώμιος ὕμνος
> δὴ πάλαι καὶ πρὶν γενέσθαι
> τὰν Ἀδράστου τάν τε Καδμείων ἔριν |||

But indeed there was a song of praise in ancient times, and before the strife of Adrastus and the Cadmeians began.

The thought that there were victory songs even before the expedition of the Seven against Thebes implies the genre is as old as the Nemean Games, or even older. A second example of this pattern would be Bacchylides *Ode* 14 ("Io"), where the narrative of the wanderings of Io is traced in the final lines to the birth of Dionysus and the origin of the *dithurambos*. Comparable, I think, is the conclusion of Bacchylides *Ode* 17, which ends with young men and women performing *paianes* and crying *"ololuge"* when

---

[12] This fragment is discussed further in Rutherford 1992.

[13] The "Z" section is the part of a song that follows the mythological narrative (= the "Y" section). The part before the narrative is the "X" section. I borrow these terms from Hamilton (1974), who observes (65–67) that the "Z" section shows much less consistency than the "X" and "Y" sections of the epinician; the only thing that can be generally said about it is that it contains praise.

[14] A good discussion of the relation between patron and poet is found in Kurke 1991, 140.

Theseus surfaces after his adventure under the sea. Since Ode 17 is probably itself a *paian* performed on Delos by a chorus from Ceos, the performance described at the end of the myth should probably be seen as a back-projection providing a mythical antecedent for its own performance and genre.[15]

An analogy exists between songs that end with reference to poetry and three songs that end with references to trainers. *Nemean* 6 ends with a reference to Melesias; *Isthmian* 4 closes with mention of the trainer Orseas, whom the poet promises to praise along with the victor; and *Nemean* 4 ends with a comparison of a hypothetical epinician-poet to a wrestler:

> οἷον αἰνέων κε Μελησίαν ἔριδα στρέφοι,
> ῥήματα πλέκων, ἀπάλαιστος ἐν λόγῳ ἕλκειν,
> μαλακὰ μὲν φρονέων ἐσλοῖς
> τραχὺς δὲ παλιγκότοις ἔφεδρος. |||

How would he praise Melesias and twist in strife, weaving words, impossible to out-wrestle in speech, thinking gentle thoughts to those who are good, but rough to leap on those who fight back.

The role of Melesias here is ambiguous: he could be the object of the praise, or the model that the wrestler-poet follows, or both.[16] The modern reader, even if she or he is familiar with Pindar's general closural practice, will probably find these endings lacking in force, because a trainer does not seem an important enough figure for the final position, but not so a contemporary audience, for whom the trainer's key role would have been self-evident. I would suggest that we might think of such endings as examples of a type of inverted closural *sphragis*, where the trainer's name, appended like a trademark at the end of the song, underwrites the skill of the victor and advertises the trainer's contribution to the victory.

THEMES OF RECEPTION

Many endings are underscored by themes that have to do with reaching the end of the action. The earliest surviving example of this is a spectacular one: in Archilochus's Cologne Epode (196aW), the narrator reaches another natural end point—orgasm—in the final lines.[17] In *epinikia*, winning

---

[15] Other examples of themes relating to song often come at the end of narratives: the dirge that the Muses sing over the dead Achilles in *Isthm.* 8, which provides a neat transition to the idea of a song sung in honor of a dead relative of the victor; in *Ol.* 10 the narrative of the first Olympics is followed by a description of the victory celebration, which concludes with song (lines 76–77).

[16] On this dual role, see Bernadini 1983, 117–18.

[17] Compare the fart let loose by the statue of Priapus in the final lines of Horace *Sat.* 1.8.

a race might be expected to have asserted itself as a closural theme; in fact, the only example is *Pythian* 9, which ends with a secondary myth, occupying the fifth and final triad: Alexidamos, one of the ancestors of Telesicrates, had competed in a race to win the hand of the daughter of Antaeos, ruler of Irasa, whose father had placed her at the end of the racetrack to be a literal goal. Unsurprisingly, Alexidamos came in first, and the song ends with an image of him being pelted with leaves and crowns.

A related theme is returning home. *Pythian* 4 illustrates its use both on the level of myth (the Argonauts return to Greece) and on the level of politics (Pindar encourages Arcesilas to readmit the exile Damophilus). In *epinikia*, the return of the triumphant victor is often the end point anticipated, particularly in the context of a *komos* or revel (*Ol.* 9, *Nem.* 5, *Isthm.* 5).[18] This form of ending is at its most elaborate in *Olympian* 6.98, dedicated to Hagesias, an inhabitant of Syracuse, but originally from Stymphalus in Arcadia, so that Pindar can claim that his victorious return to Syracuse represents movement from one home to another.

Another complex case is *Nemean* 2, which ends with the poet appealing for a successful return for Timodemus, presenting the hero's homecoming as a sort of beginning, and assimilating the song to a *prooimion* or prelude sung by the Homeridai. Just as such a prelude precedes and points toward the performance of a rhapsody, so the song precedes both (in the remoter future) further victories by Timodemus and (in the immediate future) a celebration (line 25: ἀδυμελεῖ δ' ἐξάρχετε φωνᾳ, "Lead off with sweet voice").[19] The idea of the song as a proem to a celebration is perhaps also already present in Sappho, *PLF* 30, a *komos*-song that ends with an exhortation to someone to wake up and come to his comrades in order to take part in a nocturnal celebration: ἀλλ' ἐγέρθεις, ἤϊθε[ε . . . | στεῖχε σοὶς ὑμάλικ[ας . . . | ἤπερ ὄσσον ἀ λιγύφω[νος | ὕπνον [ἴ]δωμεν ||| ("But, having woken up . . . go to your comrades . . . [so that] we see less sleep than the sweet-voiced bird").

A theme that deserves a special notice is the idea of crowning, whether crowning the head of the victor (*Ol.* 14.24; *Pyth.* 9.124–25; *Isthm.* 7.51) or crowning an altar at home (*Ol.* 9.12; *Nem.* 5.54). A crown can also be a metaphor for general success (*Pyth.* 1.100). According to Athenaeus, Aristotle in his *Symposium* argued that crowns are appropriate in the worship of the gods because offerings to the gods should be complete and whole, because fullness is completeness, and because crowning implies fullness. For the last step, Aristotle cited the Homeric use of the verb ἐπιστέφεσθαι in

---

[18] The specialized idea of receiving a *komos* accompanying a victor in the games is dealt with by Heath (1988). For the theme of "return" in Pindar in general, see the discussion of Kurke 1991, pt. 1.

[19] On *Nem.* 2 a good study is Krischer 1965; also Kurke 1991, 42–43. Hardie (chapter 7 in this volume) discusses the description of celebration in the final lines of Statius *Thebaid*.

the sense of "fill a cup with wine" (*Od.* 8.170). Aristotle's idea that crowning implies completeness is suggestive in view of the common occurrence of the theme of crowning at the end of songs.

A processional song can end with the idea of the chorus reaching the sanctuary and being welcomed there, for example *Paian* V.45. Another closural possibility for a cult song is illustrated by Sappho, *PLF* 43: this seems to have described a celebration at night, and it ends with the singer implying that she or he has to end the song because dawn approaches (ἄγχι γὰρ ἀμέρα |||, "For day is near"). This closural technique was not continued by Pindar or Bacchylides, at least not in the extant genres.[20]

As a secondary phenomenon, a motif of reception becomes associated with endings, even when this sort of "celebratory reception" is not involved—for example, at the end of *Isthmian* 8 (Epidauros has received Kleandros) or *Nemean* 1 (Heracles received Hebe).[21] Finally, a motif of reception is also found at the end of infratextual segments as a way of reinforcing the impression of closure. Thus, the myth of *Nemean* 5 relates the attempted seduction of Peleus by Hippolyte, in reward for which Zeus presents Peleus with Thetis; the myth could well end there (as in *Nem.* 4), but the new triad begins unexpectedly with the sense: "(Zeus gave him Thetis) . . . having persuaded Poseidon, who often comes to the Isthmus, where crowds receive him with music and compete in the games." Poseidon's regular journey to the Isthmus is of no relevance to the myth, but it provides a transition to the catalogue of victories that follows, and, against this background, the idea of his being received at a festival provides an effective closure for the narrative.[22] One might compare Homer's practice of ending sections of the *Odyssey* with the idea of a deity arriving at a festival or religious center, as at the end of the song of Demodocus at *Odyssey* 8.361–66, where Ares departs for Thrace, while Aphrodite is received in Paphos.[23]

---

[20] See Fowler (1989b, 102), who cites Curtius (1953, 89–91), for parallels.

[21] The reception motif is found in final position also in *Pyth.* 1 (see below) and Anacreon, *PMG* 357. A later example is Callimachus *Iambus* 2, which consisted of an Aesopian fable accounting for human loquacity, ending with a short speech frame: ταῦτα δ' Αἴσωπος | ὁ Σαρδιηνὸς εἶπεν, ὅντιν' οἱ Δελφοί | ᾄδοντα μῦθον οὐ καλῶς ἐδέξαντο ||| ("So spoke Aesop of Sardis, whom the Delphians did not receive well when he recited his tale")—a sinister adaptation of the motif.

[22] Pindar resorts to a similar closural theme in *Ol.* 8.48–51 from twenty years later, where Poseidon carries Aiakos back from Troy to the Isthmus, and the ridge of Corinth is described as δαιτικλυτάν, which suggests that Poseidon is returning to a feast, another feature regularly found in endings. On this transition, and the one in *Nem.* 5, see Carey 1989. Other examples of the reception motif: the narrative of *Ol.* 13, dealt with below; *Pyth.* 9.73: Cyrene receives Telesicrates when he returns from Delphi; *Isthm.* 1.51: receiving song; *Pyth.* 4.23.

[23] Also *Ol.* 6.41–42, where Athena departs from Scheria for Olympus; and *Ol.* 7.87, where Athena goes to Athens.

KNOWING YOUR LIMITATIONS

In some *epinikia*, the achievement or excellence of the victor is symbolized by the superhuman accomplishment of a hero, who transcends mortal limits. Thus, at the end of *Olympian* 14, the beauty of the hero is compared to that of Ganymede, and at the end of *Isthmian* 1 there is an implicit comparison between the virtue of the hero and that of Heracles, who made it to Olympus.

More usually, *epinikia* end with a narrower vision of limits: the hero has achieved the ultimate, and he should go no further, and neither should the song. The idea occurs in a minimal form in certain closural *gnomai* or morals that advise moderation, for example in the final two lines of *Nemean* 11: one should pursue a measure of gain; the madness of unapproachable desire is too intense. Related, too, are closural *gnomai* that draw attention to the variability of fate. Thus, in the closing lines of *Olympian* 7, an assertion that the whole of Rhodes celebrates the victory of Diagoras is immediately followed by a pessimistic warning: within a single period of time the winds can change, and the force of this qualification is to check any temptation to believe that the present success will last forever.[24] There is a precedent for this form of ending in Solon's *Prayer to the Muses* (13W), the extant text of which ends with a description of *atē*, which, he says, one man has at one time and another at another, when Zeus sends it to punish mankind. The theme of mutability is used with a more oblique closural application in *Olympian* 4, which ends with the athletic victory of Erginus, who won despite his comparatively advanced age. "Grey hair often grows in young men and in violation of the fitting time of life."[25]

A more complex example of an ending on the theme of "limitations" is provided by *Isthmian* 7, contrasting just and unjust aims. Pindar begins with the unjust aim: it is best to accept the "natural" limit of life, and if one sets one's aim too high, one will incur the fate of Bellerophon. The contrasting idea of a just aim is illustrated in the final three lines of the song, which consist of a short prayer for a Pythian victory for Strepsiades:

τὰ μακρὰ δ' εἴ τις
παπταίνει, βραχὺς ἐξικέσθαι χαλκόπεδον θεῶν
ἕδραν· ὅ τοι πτερόεις ἔρριψε Πάγασος
δεσπόταν ἐθέλοντ' ἐς οὐρανοῦ σταθμούς
ἐλθεῖν μεθ' ὁμάγυριν Βελλεροφόνταν

[24] Other examples are *Pyth.* 12; *Ol.* 5; *Pyth.* 7; *Isthm.* 3.

[25] Compare also Euripides *IT* 1150–51; Horace *Odes* 2.11. Hair is a closural feature in a couple of earlier poems: Sappho, *PLF* 120 (F6), closes with a reference to a black beard, the thought being that a certain man has married young, before his beard turned black. Esser 1976, 94 (see the review of R.G.M. Nisbet, *CR* 29 [1979]:148–49). The closural associations of hair and crowns are discussed by Oliensis (1991a).

Ζηνός. τὸ δὲ πὰρ δίκαν
γλυκὺ πικ⌐ροτάτα μένει τελευτά.
ἄμμι δ', ὦ χρυσέα κόμα θάλλων, πόρε, Λοξία,
τεαῖσιν ἀμίλλαισιν
εὐανθέα καὶ Πυθοῖ στέφανον. ⫼

(*Isthm.* 7.42–51)

But if anyone gazes at what is distant, he is too short to reach the seat of heaven with its bronze floor; for the winged Pegasus threw Bellerophon, his master, when he wanted to go to the homes of heaven in pursuit of the gathering of Zeus. A bitter end awaits pleasure that is unjust. But O Loxias, who are glorious with your golden hair, grant us a crown of fairest flowers from your own contest and from Pytho.

From the thematic point of view, the song could have ended well at line 48 with a pessimistic meditation of human limitations; but in this case Pindar has chosen to cap the song with a more upbeat closing prayer. A similar contrast between just and unjust aims is found at the end of *Pythian* 2, which concludes a long meditation on the need for political moderation. The unjust aim is illustrated by the envious, who stretch the measuring rope beyond its proper length, but this strategy backfires, and the measuring rope recoils and kills them. The just aim, which in this case is the aim of the average man rather than the dedicatee, is to put up with the yoke of authority, and to consort with good men.

In endings of other songs, the limits involved are partly or wholly poetic. At the end of *Nemean* 7, Pindar reasserts that he has not defamed Neoptolemus, but that ploughing the same ground thrice or four times is as vain as saying to children, "Corinth, the city of Zeus"; Pindar had encountered criticism because of his insensitive treatment of Neoptolemus in *Paians* VI, and the alternative version of the myth of Neoptolemus here was meant as a corrective. The ending of *Olympian* 3 breaks down into three elements: a priamel (if water and gold are excellent, Theron has gone as far as the pillars of Heracles in respect of virtue), a *gnomē* (journeying beyond is neither for the wise nor for those lacking in wisdom), and a personal statement (I will not pursue it—I would be a fool). The song ends there—endorsing, as it were, Pindar's decision not to pursue virtue any further. *Olympian* 2, also addressed to Theron of Acragas, ends with a similar statement of the necessity for limiting the length of an *epinikion*, even if the virtues of the dedicatee are unlimited.

ἀλλ' αἶνον ἐπέβα κόρος
οὐ δίκᾳ συναντόμενος, ἀλλὰ μάργων ὑπ' ἀνδρῶν,
τὸ λαλαγῆσαι θέλον κρυφὸν τιθέμεν ἐσθλῶν καλοῖς
ἔργοις, ἐπεὶ ψάμμος ἀριθμὸν περιπέφευγεν,

καὶ κεῖνος ὅσα χάρματ' ἄλλοις ἔθηκεν,
τίς ἂν φράσαι δύναιτο; |||

But praise encounters surfeit, surfeit that accompanies it not justly but comes from greedy men, chattering that wants to impose secrecy on good men's noble deeds. For sand defies enumeration, and how many joys that man brought others, who could say?

As E. L. Bundy argued, κόρος here is the disapproval felt toward poets who praise at excessive length. But avoiding that is only one motive for ending the song; Pindar adds that it is impossible to count the virtues of Theron.[26]

ENDING WITH MYTH

Myth can be part of an ending in two ways. To begin with, a song can end with a brief mythological paradigm, which purports to remind the hearer of a myth she or he already knows. In the last section we saw how Pindar *Nemean* 8 ends with an allusion to the myth of the Seven against Thebes. Pindar *Olympian* 10 ends with a reference to the victor, who, Pindar says, is graced with beauty "that once warded off death from Ganymede." Bacchylides *Ode* 15 (*Antenoridai*) ends with a speech by Menelaus, to the effect that Zeus is not responsible for the evils that befall men, but rather *hubris*, which destroyed the powerful Giants. An earlier example of the same technique may be Semonides' *Poem on Women*, the transmitted text of which ends with a claim that women have been a problem for men ever since Hades received those who fought over Helen at Troy (lines 114–18):

Ζεὺς γὰρ μέγιστον τοῦτ' ἐποίησεν κακόν,
καὶ δεσμὸν ἀμφέθηκεν ἀρρήκτον πέδης,
ἐξ οὗ τε τοὺς μὲν Ἀίδης ἐδέξατο
γυναικὸς εἴνεκ' ἀμφιδηριωμένους.

Zeus made this the greatest evil, and put the fetter of an unbreakable bond around us, ever since Hades received the men who fought for the sake of a woman.

But . . . can this really be the end? The syntax (the unanswered μὲν and τε) seems to point against it, unless perhaps the poet is aiming at a deliberate effect of incompleteness.[27]

In other songs, the mythological narrative continues right to the end, so

---

[26] Bundy 1972, 88–91; see also Race 1979, 260–61. Cf. the *praeteritio* at the end of Statius *Thebaid* 12.797–809, discussed by Hardie (chapter 7, this volume).

[27] Of modern editors, only Campbell (1967) thinks that it might be complete.

that there is no "Z" section. In such cases, the song can end with a monologue delivered by one of the characters in the myth. Thus, Erginus is
speaking at the end of the short *Olympian* 4; Euxantius may well be speaking at the end of *Paian* IV; and in *Nemean* 1, the prophecy of Teiresias
continues to the end of the song, where it concludes with the thought that
Heracles will marry Hebe and praise the law of Zeus—a very satisfactory
end point for the narrative.[28] As we have seen, Menelaus is speaking at the
end of Bacchylides *Ode* 15. There may be precedents: an iambic poem,
probably to be attributed to Archilochus, ended in monologue, without a
speech frame.[29]

Rather different closural problems are raised by *Nemean* 10, the second
half of which is taken up by the myth of Castor and Pollux. Pollux begs
Zeus to restore Castor to life, and Zeus grants that both brothers spend half
their lives above ground and half below; the song ends with a speech frame
and a statement that Zeus carried out his promise:

ὣς ἄρ' αὐδάσαντος οὐ γνώμᾳ διπλόαν θέτο βουλάν,
ἀνὰ δ' ἔλυσεν μὲν ὀφθαλμόν, ἔπειτα δὲ φωνὰν χαλκομίτρα Κάστορος |||

> When he said this, he did not make his counsel double in respect of his
> thought, but released the eye, and then the voice of Castor with his bronze
> girdle.

This is as much a beginning as an end. The idea of Zeus granting the
prayer of Pollux concludes the mortal part of the story of the Dioskouroi,
but it also initiates the immortal part of their story, and ending with the
implication that Castor started to speak makes the reader curious about
what he was going to say, which is surely anticlosural.

An example of a mythological ending without any direct speech is Bacchylides *Ode* 16 ("Heracles"), a short song, consisting of a single triad, that
relates key events in the story of Heracles and Deianeira in reverse order: it
begins in the antistrophe with Heracles' death, and ends with the observation that the catastrophe had been inevitable ever since Deianeira had received (note the reception motif!) from Nessus the drug, described in the
final words as a supernatural portent (δαιμόνιον τέρας), as if it predicted
the death of Heracles rather than caused it. So again this is an open and
allusive ending.[30]

Even mythological narratives that do not continue to the end of the
song can end in an open and allusive way. In *Olympian* 9, for example, the

---

[28] The reference to "the law of Zeus" at the end of this poem perhaps suggests the beginning of fr. 169a: νόμος ὁ πάντων βασιλεύς. For closing references to the beginning of
works, see Fowler 1989b, 101 n. 93. So the end of *Ol.* 3 seems to allude to the start *Ol.* 1.

[29] Fr. 23W, on which see Clay 1986; also Burnett 1983, 70–71; West fr. 24 seems to end
with a first-person statement also (see Burnett 1983, 44–45).

[30] On this poem, see now the excellent article of Platter (1994).

myth relates the early history of Locris and the birth of the hero Opous. Opous honored all immigrants, including Menoetius, father of Patroclus, who was to prove his valor to Achilles when they fought Telephus (76–79):

ἐξ οὗ Θέτιος γόνος οὐλίῳ νιν ἐν Ἄρει

ἐπ.γ' παραγορεῖτο μή ποτε

σφετέρας ἄτερθε ταξιοῦσθαι

δαμασιμβρότου αἰχμᾶς

From that time the son of Thetis urged him never in deadly war to post himself far from his own man-subduing spear.

Here the epithet δαμασιμβρότου is probably meant to allude to the fatal consequences for Patroclus of his friendship with Achilles, and in particular his use of Achilles' armor.[31]

The comparative frequency (two out of eight) of myth endings in Bacchylides' *Dithuramboi* raises the possibility that this form of closure might have been part of the technique of that genre. However, the lack of evidence for the *dithurambos* before the fifth century makes this impossible to prove. It is equally likely that ending in mid-myth is something that classical lyric poets inherited from Lesbian lyric, since the quasi-epic narrative song of Sappho describing the wedding of Hector and Andromache (*PLF* 44.33–36) ends in mid-myth without any sort of frame. (Here again there is a resonant mythical allusion: the *paianes* sung by the wedding guests in the closing lines can be taken as an ominous allusion to the *paianes* sung over the dead Hector in *Il.* 22.391–94[32]).

INFRATEXTUAL CLOSURE AND THE TRIAD

Every triad end has a certain closural force in virtue of its formal properties, and quite often Pindar makes the end of major thematic sections correspond to the end of formal divisions, to maximize the sense of closure, or makes a climax come at a formal break. However, this is not his consistent practice: he can sometimes go to the other extreme and avoid it com-

---

[31] There may be a reminiscence of the use of the epithet ἀνδρόφονος for the hands of Achilles at *Il.* 18.318. At Bacchylides 5.175, a narrative ends with the ghost of Meleager telling Heracles about his sister Deianeira; he says she is still ignorant of Aphrodite, to whom he applies the epithet θελξιμβρότου, which suggests that the charms of Aphrodite need not always be benign. In *Ol.* 9.79 the reference to the spear is also noteworthy: spears or weapons often figure at the end of formal or thematic units: see Race 1989, 198 n. 11 (= 1990, 48).

[32] Nagy 1974, 137–38; Garner (1990) suggests that allusion at the end of a song is particularly common.

pletely, as he does in *Olympian* 9, for example, where no triad end corresponds even to a major break in punctuation, let alone to a thematic division.

For an example of a strong effect of infratextual closure at the end of a triad, I return to *Nemean* 8. We have already seen that the song ends with a statement that epinician poetry existed before the War of the Seven. This balances the equally potent statement at the end of the second triad that wraps up the narrative whose focus is the unfair contest over the arms of Achilles and the suicide of Ajax:[33]

> ἐχθρὰ δ' ἄρα πάρφασις ἦν καὶ πάλαι
> αἱμύλων μύθων ὁμόφοιτος, δολοφραδής, κακοποιὸν ὄνειδος·
> ἃ τὸ μὲν λαμπρὸν βιᾶται,
> τῶν δ' ἀφάντων κῦδος ἀντείνει σαθρόν.

There was after all hateful seduction even in ancient times, seduction that accompanies flattering speeches, deceitful, a destructive shame. It does violence to the brilliant, and raises up the ill-founded glory of those who are insignificant.

The μὲν . . . δὲ construction seems to have a closural force all its own (there is a parallel to the antithetical final epigrams in sonnets whose closural properties have been analyzed by Barbara Herrnstein Smith).[34] The antithetical thought is tailored to the metrical contours, with the μὲν clause covered by the first "E-," and the δὲ clause by "E x e."

Olympian 13 is an *epinikion* that shows a particularly subtle and inventive use of infratextual closure. The "Z" section begins with a transition on a poetic theme, and quickly moves into a catalogue of the victories of the Oligaithidai, the victor's family.

> καὶ πᾶσαν κατὰ
> Ἑλλάδ' εὑρήσεις ἐρευνῶν μάσσον' ἢ ὡς ἰδέμεν.
> ἄνα, κούφοισιν ἐκνεῦσαι ποσίν·
> Ζεῦ τέλει', αἰδῶ δίδοι καὶ τύχαν τερπνῶν γλυκεῖαν |||

Searching throughout all of Greece, you will find more than you can see. Up and swim off with light feet! Authoritative Zeus, may you give a sense of shame and a share in sweet delights.

---

[33] For aspects of these lines, see Köhnken 1971, 33–34.

[34] *Nem.* 4.95–96; *Pyth.* 9.123–25, 12.31–32; at the end of narratives: *Pyth.* 2.48; *Isthm.* 1.30–31. Other examples are Gorgias's *Encomium of Helen*, c. 23: Ἑλένης μὲν ἐγκώμιον, ἐμὸν δὲ παίγνιον ("Praise of Helen on the one hand, my joke on the other"), and Agathon's speech at Plato *Symp.* 179d; Alcaeus, *PLF* 70, ends with a statement that a god has stirred up strife, sending the people into delusion and giving glory to Pittacus, and the μὲν . . . δὲ structure provides a sense of closure. For the epigrammatic endings of sonnets, see Smith 1968, 50–56.

Many features here belong to types commonly found in Pindaric endings: the idea of a limit ("more than one can see"); the reference to poetry (implied in ἐκνεῦσαι, "swim out!"); the final prayer for prosperity (there are no further victories to wish for). One can also add the epithet τέλειος under which Zeus is invoked, which, as I suggested earlier, implies a reference to the end.[35]

To move to infratextual closure, the coordination of triad end with catalogue end also occurs earlier; the antistrophe and epode of the second triad contain a catalogue of victories by Xenophon and his family, which ends like this:[36]

> ὅσσα τ' ἐν Δελφοῖσιν ἀριστεύσατε
> ἠδὲ χόρτοις ἐν λέοντος, δηρίομαι πολέσιν
> περὶ πλήθει καλῶν, ὡς μὰν σαφὲς
> οὐκ ἂν εἰδείην λέγειν ποντιᾶν ψάφων ἀριθμόν. ‖

As many victories as you won among the Delphians or on the lawns of the lion, I quarrel with many over the number of excellences, since I could not state the number of the pebbles of the sea clearly.

The thought of the last sentence is an instance of a theme connected with limits in a closural position. The first triad also ends with a sort of catalogue—a list of inventions and virtues of the Corinthians. The deployment of a catalogue in an epode is quite common. We find it, for example, in *Nemean* 6, where each of the three epodes contains a catalogue of victories: the first, those of Alcidamas's grandfather Praxidamas and his brothers (this one spills over into the second strophe); the second, other relatives of Alcidamas, ending with the Nemean victory of Creontidas, whom "the food of the lion once crowned when he won under the shady primeval mountains of Phlious"; and the third, the victories of Alcidamas himself (including an Olympic victory that he failed to get because of an adverse lot), which conclude the triad, ending with a reference to the trainer Melesias.[37]

To return to *Olympian* 13, the third and fourth triads narrate the myth

---

[35] A similar reference is perhaps present in *Pyth.* 1.67, the only other occurrence of this epithet in Pindar, where the reference would be to the result of a series of conflicts. For the sense of τέλειος, see Waanders 1983, 202. There is an analogous play on the sense of τέλος at *Pyth.* 8.24–25: τελέαν δ' ἔχει δόξαν ἄπ' ἀρχᾶς ("It has perfect glory from the beginning"). Compare Barchiesi (this volume, chapter 9, note 6) on Ovid's use of the word *finis*.

[36] Bowra (1964, 342) suggests that we think of the two catalogues as the same one, interrupted by the myth to produce a varied structure.

[37] See above. Another example of catalogue being confined to the epodes is *Pyth.* 8, where the second epode lists the victories of the uncles of Aristomenes (leading into the myth of the Seven against Thebes), while the fourth epode mentions the comparatively modest victories of Aristomenes.

of Bellerophon and Pegasus. The conclusion of the myth comes at the end
of the fourth triad, with a comparison of the fates of Perseus and Bellerophon (lines 91–92):

> διασωπάσομαι οἱ μόρον ἐγώ·
> τὸν δ' ἐν Οὐλύμπῳ φάτναι Ζηνὸς ἀρχαῖαι δέκονται. ‖

I will pass over his death in silence; but the other one the ancient mangers of
Zeus on Olympus receive.

The themes of "death" and "reception" contribute to the sense of closure.
In fact, the closural force of this ending is a good deal stronger than that of
the end of the whole song. The end of the third triad comes in mid-
narrative, when Pallas appears to Bellerophon in a dream and tells him to
receive (δέκευ) a magic bridle and show it (δεῖξον) to Poseidon by sacrificing it (lines 68–69):

> ἄγε φίλτρον τόδ' ἵππειον δέκευ,
> καὶ Δαμαίῳ νιν θύων ταῦρον ἀργᾶντα πατρὶ δεῖξον ‖

Come, receive this horse charm, and, sacrificing a shining bull, show it to
father Damaios.

As elsewhere, end of triad coincides with end of speech.[38] But what stands
out is the reception motif, which in this case seems to be reinforced by a
folk etymology linking δέκομαι ("receive") with δείκνυμι ("show").

Olympian 13 is unusual, then, in that the ends of each of the five triads
correspond either to a formal break or to a climax within a formal segment. I suggest that it should be interpreted as an experiment in closure.[39]

FALSE CLOSURE

False closure comes about when closural features occuring at the end of
a triad or other formal segment (of the sort I looked at in the previous
section) conspire to create the impression that the song is ending, when in
fact it continues.[40] What makes lyric poetry particularly susceptible to giving the impression of false closure is that transitions in songs use the same
themes (*gnomai*, references to poetry, first-person statements) as endings.

[38] Führer 1967, 69.
[39] It is a metrical experiment also: the start of the strophe is in aeolic, which modulates to
dactylo-epitrite at the end of the strophe and throughout the epode, the epode ending with
a heavily iambic clausula.
[40] See Fowler 1989b, 97–101.

The sort of ambiguity between transition and ending that can occur is illustrated vividly by the problem of the unity of "*Isthmian* 3" and "*Isthmian* 4." These two songs have the same metrical structure, the first comprising a single triad, the second four triads. "*Isthmian* 3" ends with an exhortation for permanence: "Things change, but the sons of the gods are unwounded by them"; "*Isthmian* 4" begins: "There are countless paths open to me on every side." It is still debated whether the apparent ending of "*Isthmian* 3" is in fact an ending at all, and not rather a transition to another section of the same song. Most scholars now believe that the songs are independent, but the fact that there has been a debate at all shows that the difference between transition and ending is not always clear-cut.[41]

However, genuine cases of false closure seem to be found in some of Pindar's most celebrated *epinikia*. *Pythian* 1 begins with a description of an eagle (str. a–ant. a), then moves to the famous portrayal of Typhon under Tartarus (ep. a–str. b). The second triad concludes with prayers to Zeus and Apollo for the safety of the new city of Aetna. There seems to be a new beginning at the start of the third triad, which leads via a string of *gnomai* to references to Hieron's intervention against the Etruscans in Italy, and a brief mythological allusion to Philoctetes; then a transition to Deinomenes and the foundation of Aetna under Dorian principles (str. d). After that follow prayers to Zeus for continued success in war, which culminates with a short priamel in praise of Hieron and Deinomenes:[42]

ἀρέομαι
πὰρ μὲν Σαλαμῖνος, Ἀθηναίων χάριν,
μισθόν, ἐν Σπάρτᾳ δ' ἐρέω τὰν πρὸ Κιθαιρῶνος μάχαν,
ταῖσι Μήδειοι κάμον ἀγκυλότοξοι,
παρὰ δὲ τὰν εὔυδρον ἀκτὰν Ἱμέρα παίδεσσιν ὕμνον Δεινομένευς
    τελέσαις,
τὸν ἐδέξαντ' ἀμφ' ἀρετᾷ, πολεμίων ἀνδρῶν καμόντων. ‖

From Salamis I shall take as my reward the favor of the Athenians, and in Sparta, I shall tell of the battle in front of Kithairon—places where the Medes with their crooked bows were defeated. But by the well-watered bank of the Himeras, I shall win a reward by paying a song of praise to the sons of Deinomenes, the song that they received through their valor, when their enemies were defeated.

---

[41] See Krummen 1990, 33 n. 2. Another contribution is Lidov 1974, arguing that these are distinct songs performed on the same occasion one after the other.

[42] The point of this priamel is presumably to distract attention from the political criticism that Herodotus levels at the Sicilians: that they did not take part in the war against the Persians.

The song could end here. Four triads is long enough, and a priamel can make an effective ending (as in *Ol.* 3.42–45). The position of these lines as the climax of a long prayer (starting in line 67, reestablished in line 71) also makes them appropriate for an ending (particularly since the prayer begins by invoking Zeus under the epithet *Téleios*, which, as in *Ol.* 13, seems to cue the reader for an ending). Reinforcement of the sense of an ending is provided by the reference to poetry, and the reception motif. However, the structure is augmented with a fifth and final triad, which broadens the focus beyond war with the Carthaginians and Etruscans to a level of generalized advice, ending with a comparison of the reputations of Croesus and Phalaris, and a *gnomē*.[43]

More complex is the use of false closure in *Nemean* 7. The narrative of the death of Neoptolemus extends over the second and third triads. The crucial moment of his death comes at the end of the second triad, and the narrative continues into the strophe of the next triad, with a short frame that gives a positive "spin" to his death. This is followed by an address to Aegina, which turns out to be a transition to a series of *gnomai*: one can have too much even of good things (a somewhat closural *gnomē*); men differ, and, though no man can be completely happy, Thearion is fortunate. The third triad ends with these lines:

ξεῖνός εἰμι· σκοτεινὸν ἀπέχων ψόγον,
ὕδατος ὥτε ῥοὰς φίλον ἐς ἄνδρ᾽ ἄγων
κλέος ἐτήτυμον αἰνέσω· ποτίφορος δ᾽ ἀγαθοῖσι μισθὸς οὗτος. ‖

I am a guest-friend. Holding away dark blame, and bringing true glory to a friendly man like streams of water, I will praise him. This is suitable payment for good men.

The end of the triad coincides with the end of a clause, satisfying the first condition of false closure. Considered on thematic terms, the reference to poetry and the *gnomē* would provide a satisfactory ending, if not a resounding one, and the effect is somewhat reinforced by the *gnomē* about excess and limit in the lines immediately preceding. If (by some strange quirk of textual transmission) the final two triads had been lost to us, the ending of the third triad would have been accepted as the ending of the song. What the fourth and fifth triads add is development of the earlier section by way

---

[43] Notice the unique double instance of the reception motif here: οὐδέ νιν φόρμιγγες ὑπωρόφιαι κοινωνίαν μαλθακὰν παίδων ὀάροισι δέκονται. τὸ δὲ παθεῖν εὖ πρῶτον ἄθλων· εὖ δ᾽ ἀκούειν δευτέρα μοῖρ᾽· ἀμφοτέροισι δ᾽ ἀνήρ | ὃς ἂν ἐγκύρσῃ, καὶ ἕλῃ, στέφανον ὕψιστον δέδεκται. ‖‖ ("Nor do *phorminges* beneath the roof receive him into soft fellowship with the chatter of boys. Success is the first prize; second is to have a good reputation. But the man who finds both, and takes them, the crown he has received is the highest").

of new and contrasting themes, and metapoetical comment. The fourth triad begins with an apology for inappropriate language (lines 64–71), then makes a fresh beginning (cf. line 77), starting with Zeus, god of Nemea, moving to Aiakos, and then, unexpectedly, to Heracles, whose shrine seems to have adjoined the home of Sogenes, and whom he addresses with a prayer. The theme of Heracles serves the purpose of offsetting the story of Neoptolemus, which, however it is presented, is not a wholly positive paradigm, by providing a more suitable role model for the young Sogenes. In the final lines (which we considered earlier), Pindar reasserts that he has not defamed Neoptolemus, and he expresses the futility of repeating himself with the *gnomē* that ploughing the same ground several times is useless. It is the broader scope of the fourth and fifth triads that transforms *Nemean* 7 from a run-of-the-mill *epinikion* to a complex artefact that threatens to consume itself; but in the very fact that the latter section of the song transcends the narrow limits of generic function, I find corroboration of my hypothesis that the first three triads could be interpreted as constituting a complete song, albeit a much simpler one.

I have tried to present a typology of closural techniques used by ancient Greek lyric poets, insofar as these can be established on the basis of the surviving evidence. In the fifth century there were differences in closural practice between genres: themes relating to limits tend to be more popular in *epinikia*; ending with the myth seems to be more common in narrative *dithuramboi*; *paianes* sometimes ended with the idea of being received by Apollo. What remains of the archaic period suggests that the main forms of lyric closure were already established in that period: one difference is suggested by the song of Sappho that ended with the idea that a celebration must end at dawn; there is no parallel for this in extant fifth-century lyric. Of all the areas I have covered, I would suggest that Pindar's deployment of closural techniques at triad end, with or without the intention of creating the false impression that the song is about to end, is a particularly rich one, and one in which further progress could be made. There are also a number of related issues that I have not had space to cover in this chapter, but that nevertheless invite further investigation. These include the endings of choral odes and other lyric poems in drama, and the reception of the closural practice of Greek lyric poetry by later lyric poets, for example Horace.[44]

[44] I'd like to thank the editors of the volume and the anonymous readers for helpful advice in the preparation of this paper.

CHAPTER 4

Wanton Kings, Pickled Heroes, and Gnomic Founding Fathers: Strategies of Meaning at the End of Herodotus's *Histories*

CAROLYN DEWALD

> It is obvious, or should be, that the present
> conclusion was not intended by the author.
> Herodotus might conceivably have wanted to
> conclude with the capture of Sestos; yet he could
> not have done so with the story of the pickled
> hero Protesilaos and with an anecdote from the
> time of Cyrus. Most importantly, no book is
> finished which has no end, but breaks off; that of
> Herodotus, however, has its introduction and
> organization, and intends to be a work of art.
> —*U. von Wilamowitz,* Aristoteles und Athen
>
> Is it irony, or has Herodotus lost his mind?
> —*F. Jacoby, "Herodotus" (on 9.122)*

HERODOTUS is often called the first historian, the father of history. When we read his text, we are reading the first extant Greek work that set out to do many of the things history-writing does: in this case, as he tells us in his first sentence, to record great and wonderful deeds of Greeks and barbarians, both other matters and *di' hēn aitiēn epolemēsan allēloisi*, "why they made war on one another."[1] In doing so, he also provides our most important source for late archaic and early classical Greek history; our historical narratives of the Mediterranean world of the sixth and fifth centuries B.C.E. could not have been achieved without his narrative at their base.[2] But his

---

[1] For Herodotus as the first historian, see Cicero *Leg.* 1.1.5; Dionysius of Halicarnassus *Thuc.* 5; Momigliano 1958; Schadewaldt 1982; Fornara 1983, 29–32; Hartog 1988, xviii–xxii; Lateiner 1989, 6–10. See also Latte 1956 and the discussion in Marg 1982a, 122–36.

[2] See Strasburger 1956, 131–33; the index entry "Herodotus" for Jeffery, *Archaic Greece: The City-States c. 700–500 B.C.* (New York, 1976) reads simply *passim.* See Finley 1985,

very primacy as our first historian and our most important source for a crucial period of ancient history can also mislead us. When we undertake to read the work of someone like Herodotus, a *prōtos heuretēs*, or first inventor, there is a peculiar danger that we will read him too easily, through the lens of the fully developed genre that his work began.[3] For Herodotus's text, though in many ways it resembles later historical narratives, is also in numerous ways anomalous. One of its anomalies is its "sense of an ending."

History is about process, and change over time. A historical narrative has to have an ending—despite the best efforts of a Diodorus, a Gibbon, or the Durants, it can't indefinitely continue—but the particular ending chosen is always problematic. There are no real beginnings and endings in history itself, and the historical writer, imposing shape and coherence on his or her chosen subject, must intervene to make an end, and to make what is in real life at best a momentary caesura into a lasting and significant literary silence.[4] As we shall see, however, Herodotus's text refuses this strategy. It does not seem to have a real conclusion; at its end, no literary signals are given us as readers that anything particular has happened, or has finished. Here I want to explore how that is so, and argue that, nonetheless, the end of the *Histories* is, historiographically, a real choice. The way Herodotus chose to write his ending suggests important connections for us to make about Herodotus's understanding of the nature of power, the nature of historical epochs, and the relation of knowledge to historical narrative.

Looking closely at the problems of the *Histories*' ending entails first looking briefly at the shape, the narrative emplotment, of the work as a whole. It is a long narrative—in our current standard edition, 800 pages of Greek prose, divided into nine books.[5] It is structured throughout as a series of loosely connected and approximately sequential, semi-discrete narratives that trace the growth of Persian power from the reign of Cyrus in about 550 B.C.E., through the reigns of Cambyses and Darius, down to the detailed narrative of Xerxes' massive invasion of Greece in 481–479 B.C.E. A great deal of information about sixth-century Greek politics, wars, and migrations is in the early books parenthetically introduced. As the

---

10–11 and 17 for the primacy of narrative in ancient history and, more generally, Veyne 1984, 93 and n. 5: "History is narration; it is not determination nor is it explanation"; see also Mink 1987, 182–203 ("Narrative Form as a Cognitive Instrument") and White 1987, esp. 1–57. The Herodotus text used in this chapter is How and Wells 1928; the translations are my own.

[3] See Saïd 1975, 32; cf. Erbse 1956a, 211, for Herodotus's ambitious sense of his own accomplishment. Herodotus himself put a lot of importance on firsts—cf. van Groningen 1953 and Kleingünther 1933.

[4] See Pelling, Chapter 11 in this volume, note 1.

[5] For the significance of the book divisions in Herodotus, see Immerwahr 1966, 79 n. 2, and for a more general discussion of the closural power of ancient book divisions, D. Fowler 1989b, 88–93.

focus narrows to issues of Greco-Persian confrontation from Book 5 onward, Herodotus concentrates on following two narrative threads that intertwine: a Persian thread, as the Persians resubdue Ionia in the 490s and then mount a full-scale invasion of Greece; and a Greek thread, which traces the self-serving disunity of the leaders of the Ionian revolt and, shortly thereafter, the remarkable political will shown by Athens, Sparta, and other mainland states threatened by Xerxes' invasion.[6] A sequence of four major battles defines the Persian Wars proper as Herodotus narrates them in Books 7 through 9: Thermopylae, Salamis, Plataea, and Mycale. Herodotus brings events just past the battle of Mycale and there, to our taste, lets the narrative drift to a stop with three rather unconnected and oddly focused wrap-up episodes and a final tacked-on pendant, an anecdote about a conversation between Cyrus the Great and the ancestor of one of the Persians caught in the events of 479.

Formal closure is a conspicuous part of Herodotus's narrative technique from the very beginning of the work. Each new stage of the narrative, whether it lasts for dozens of pages or half a page, is presented as a largely self-contained whole, set off from what has come before by an introductory sentence and, in most cases, brought to a definite end, whether by a formulaic end sentence, a gnomic aphorism, an authorial reflection, or a brief summary of the preceding narrative. In Book 1 alone we encounter the following sentences ending narrative sections:

> This is the way it was concerning the rule of Croesus and the first conquest of Ionia. (1.92.1)
> The Lydians, then, were enslaved by the Persians. (1.94.7)
> Thus, then, being born and raised did Cyrus rule and later overthrow Croesus who had begun the injustice, as I earlier said, and, having subdued him, thus he ruled all of Asia. (1.130)
> But the Milesians, as I earlier said, taking an oath with Cyrus himself, kept quiet. Then in this fashion for the second time was Ionia enslaved. (1.169)
> Thus was Babylon captured for the first time. (1.191.6)
> Now concerning the end of the life of Cyrus, although many stories are told, this one has been narrated by me as the most credible. (1.214.5)

Sometimes the introductory sentence of the next narrative unit links such an ending formula explicitly to what has gone before; sometimes Herodotus tacitly assumes that we can make the connection ourselves.[7]

---

[6] Immerwahr 1966, 34–45 and 233–37. The Greek thread only begins to provide the major narrative frame after 8.40, as the Greeks seize control of the war (256). See more generally Jacoby 1913, 333–41.

[7] See Immerwahr 1966, 46ff., and esp. 52 for Herodotean parataxis and formulaic ending sentences; and Munson 1983, 121ff. for a detailed account of the transitional sentences in Book 1. Both Munson (123) and Immerwahr (47) note that the introductory and conclud-

In the last third of the *Histories*, although the small and semi-discrete accounts loosely linked to one another are more clearly coordinated to be part of an ongoing single story, the Persian invasion of Greece, individual units of action continue to be structured much as they have been throughout the previous books. But there is no grand and particularly emphatic finale at the end of Book 9; there is not even a formulaic end sentence of the type to which we have become accustomed at the endings of narrative sections. The *Histories* simply stops at the end of the anecdote about Cyrus the Great: "So, seeing what he meant, the Persians got up and went away, worsted in their reasoning with Cyrus, and they chose to rule living in a barren land rather than, sowing plains, to serve others in slavery" (9.122.4). Although this sentence has something of an aphoristic flavor, nothing in its formal structure or in the structure or content of the anecdotal flashback to which it is attached prepares us to think that Herodotus's massive narrative has come to a close.

The problem does not lie only in the last sentence's formal construction. In the work as a whole, one finds what Hayden White calls "terminating motifs"—thematic resolutions certainly more striking than those found in the *Histories*' last pages—clustered in the account of Plataea.[8] Three vignettes recounted as part of that battle vividly summarize a contrast between Greeks and Persians and leave us seeing what it means that Greeks have won the war. Pausanias, the Greek victor, returns a courtesan in the Persian camp to her Greek family on Cos (9.76); he explains to an Aeginetan why Greeks do not humiliate their enemies after death (9.79); finally, he laughs at the disparity between a skimpy Spartan dinner and an opulent Persian one (9.82). These scenes indicate that after Plataea, Greeks and Greek values are again to prevail on the Greek mainland; they also highlight, for most interpreters, some of the dominant themes of the *Histories*—Greek simplicity, freedom and respect for the individual, versus Persian hierarchical autocracy and luxury—much more sharply than anything that transpires on the *Histories*' last twenty pages.[9]

The final nine pages of the *Histories* consist of a sequence of discrete and partial accounts, each of which suggests another facet of the last stages of

---

ing sentences that mark short narrative passages are indistinguishable from those marking major new narrative units, a hallmark of the paratactic style. For infratextual closure and segmentation in general, see D. Fowler, chapter 1 in this volume.

[8] White 1973, 5–6: "A terminating motif indicates the apparent end or resolution of a process or situation of tension."

[9] Cf., for instance, the summary of basic Herodotean themes in Usher (1985, 22), or in Immerwahr (1966, 306–7). Von Fritz (1967, 272–79) interprets the contrast between the luxurious Persian dinner of 9.82 and the simplicity Cyrus advocates in 9.122 as part of a more complex pattern of oppositions between Greeks and barbarians. The basic contrast between Greeks and Persians sketched by Herodotus is the subject of Konstan 1987.

the war. The account of the last major battle, Mycale, ends by emphasizing the fateful way in which the Ionians in the Persian army abandon their allies in favor of their Greek kinsmen: "Thus indeed for the second time Ionia revolted from the Persians" (9.104). This formal recognition of an epoch's conclusion, though brief, would not have been out of place if it had been positioned at the end of the entire narrative; we would have considered it a typically Herodotean formulaic end sentence signaling not only the conclusion of the episode of Mycale but also the final re-separation of Ionia from Persia, the subject upon which Herodotus had focused in the *Histories'* first pages. But the account of Mycale is followed by four further episodes; whatever formal end the *Histories* possesses lies in these four passages. Let us look first at the variety of discrete closural moves they separately contain.

9.105–7: This typically Herodotean assessment of Greek and Persian actions after a major battle is rather discursive, but it does once more demonstrate the basic weaknesses of how each side conducts its politics and warfare. Contingents from the Greek cities argue for different courses of action by dividing along ethnic and geographical lines and cannot decide on a single plan, while Persian grandees responsible for the loss at Mycale insult each other, and the brother of the king takes the defeat personally as an insult against "the house of the king." Disunity among the Greeks and dynastic autocracy on the Persian side are not new themes in the *Histories*; both sides here behave predictably and, indeed, almost as clichés of themselves.

9.108–13: Masistes, Xerxes' brother and one of the Persian generals at Mycale, has just been shouting at his fellow general Artayntes for being "worse than a woman" (9.107)—but in the meantime Xerxes is back at Sardis trying to seduce Masistes' own womenfolk. This second episode formally brings the Persian narrative line to a close by showing the rot at the center of the enormous Persian empire: Xerxes, waiting for his returning army at Sardis, keeps busy, first by trying to seduce Masistes' wife, and then, when he is unsuccessful, by marrying Masistes' daughter to his own son and then seducing her. Xerxes tries at the end to rescue Masistes from the debacle his own royal behavior has created, but Masistes revolts and Xerxes is forced to destroy him and his family; this is the last picture we have of Xerxes and the Persian royal house. A formulaic sentence brings the episode to a close without overt interpretive comment from Herodotus: "Now about the love of Xerxes and the death of Masistes such things occurred"; the moral thrust of the episode as a whole, however, is clear and very strong.[10]

9.114–21: The Persian narrative line has now been finished, and on a negative note; the third episode picks up the end of the Greek narrative

---

[10] For its echoes of themes found at the beginning of the *Histories*, see below, note 17.

thread, tracing the account of how the Athenians stay on in the region of the Hellespont to subdue Sestos after the Peloponnesian contingent goes home. In sharp contrast to the portrait just drawn of Xerxes' behavior at Sardis, the interpretation of this Greek episode is left ambiguous; the only moral value placed on action in it is voiced by a Persian villain for self-serving reasons. The closural power of 9.114–21 comes from the presence in the episode of two highly charged symbolic objects: bridge cables and a corpse.[11] For after they finally take Sestos, the Athenians capture Oeobazus, the Persian possessing the ropes that had tied together Xerxes' boat of bridges spanning Asia and Europe; they also capture Artayctes, the clever and wicked Persian governor of Sestos. Herodotus tells us that Oeobazus is tortured to death by Thracians and the ropes are taken by the Greeks, recalling with the ropes the beginning of Xerxes' invasion (7.25, 34–37, 54–57). The fate of Artayctes is even more symbolically significant, as Herodotus portrays it. Artayctes had outraged the temple of the Greek hero Protesilaus at Elaeus and so is punished by crucifixion, and his son by stoning, perhaps at the very spot where Xerxes first led his army into Europe. The mention of Protesilaus and his *temenos* reminds us, in good ring-composition style, of the brief discussion of the Trojan War at the beginning of the *Histories* (1.3–5), but it also creates a referential loop that goes back further still, to the beginning of Greek literature and history in the *Iliad* and to Protesilaus's role as the first Greek ashore at Troy.[12] This is closure with a vengeance, as it were, but Herodotus immediately modifies its dramatic force by appending a sentence about Greek dedication of the spoils, including the ropes, and a dry annalistic summary: "And in this year nothing more than these things happened."[13]

9.122: The last episode does not focus at all on the end of the Persian War, but it, too, contains some elements of closure. Its form is that of a pendant attached to the Sestos narrative. Ending a narrative with a tenuously attached anecdote is a procedure that Herodotus has used at earlier points in the *Histories*;[14] here the pendant consists of a flashback, a conversation between Artem-

---

[11] For objects highly charged as symbols in Herodotus, see Dewald 1993; for the multiple resonances of the episode as a whole, see Boedeker 1988.

[12] See Boedeker 1988 for the hero Protesilaus, the themes of boundary transgression, retribution, and divine vengeance, and the strong terminating motifs implicit in the Protesilaus and Artayctes stories. Vandiver (1991, 223–29) largely follows Boedeker.

[13] Cf. 6.42.1 and, to a lesser extent, 9.41.1 and 9.107.3 for similarly formulaic expressions; for other expressions suggesting that Herodotus paid attention to the campaigning season as a structuring device, cf. 6.31.1, 7.37.1, 8.130.1, 8.131.1. Lipsius (1902, 195), followed by Jacoby (1913, 375) and Pohlenz (1937, 164), believed that the last sentence of 9.121 showed that Herodotus intended the work to continue; Macan (1908, 828) and Powell (1939, 80) believed it to be an interpolation by someone who had read Thucydides. Immerwahr (1966, 145 n. 188) does not think it a problem. For the relative lateness of Greek annalistic writing, see Fornara 1983, 16–23; for the larger question of Herodotus's general use of chronology to organize his text, see Lateiner 1989, 117–25 and, on this passage, 119 n. 30.

[14] See Immerwahr 1966, 61–62 and 145 for Herodotus's habit of placing parenthetical

bares, an ancestor of Artayctes the wicked governor of Sestos, and Cyrus the Great. Cyrus convinces the Persians, against the opinion of Artayctes' ancestor, that they should choose "to rule living in a barren land rather than, sowing plains, to serve others in slavery." "Slavery" is the last word of the *Histories*, and the episode as a whole anecdotally and epigrammatically explores connections linking the political will of a people to the issues of freedom and empire.[15] Its plot line turns on the intersection of two basic narrative modes on which Herodotus has relied throughout the *Histories*: ethnographic descriptions, and detailed accounts of political activity and decision-making. Here Herodotus shows Cyrus *persuading* the Persians that they should continue to live, as they always have done, in rugged poverty—and the Persians at the end agreeing with Cyrus. Thus Persian customs are shown to be dependent on a moment in Persian political decision-making, a nice point on which to conclude for an author who has generally tended to alternate between passages of ethnographic description and straightforward political narratives.[16]

The last four narrative segments in the *Histories*, taken together, raise issues that tie them closely to the work as a whole. First, Eastern royal domestic tension is connected with the theme of political subversion. Right at the beginning of the *Histories*, a king, Candaules, overlooks his wife's capacity to harm him and dies in consequence, his dynasty supplanted by that of the queen's new husband. Xerxes' preoccupation with the same narrowly private, sexual sphere at Sardis in 9.108–13, and the way he is there finally dominated by his own wife, Amestris, produce, in respect of this paired political and domestic theme, the effect of ring composition for the *Histories* as a whole.[17] Thematically and morally we are left

---

material in a pause between logoi; cf. 4.144. For genealogical narrative links in Herodotus, cf. note 39 below.

[15] Other ways of integrating the Cyrus episode into the larger thematic structure of the *Histories* are explored by Bischoff (1932, 78–83), who views it as the final contribution to the theme of the "warning fate" of oriental kings, the "Grundidee des Geschichtsschreibers" (82), and by Lateiner (1989, 49), who links 9.122 to earlier passages analyzing Persians and the theme of oriental expansion. See also Immerwahr 1966, 146 n. 191.

[16] See Stein 1882, 219 for the similarity between 9.122 and the Hippocratic *Airs, Waters, Places* 23–24; cf. Bornitz (1968, 198), who thinks character in the anecdote is connected with hard living conditions, not climate. For the importance of custom (*nomos*) in Herodotus, see Evans 1965; Immerwahr 1966, 319–22; Humphreys 1987; Gould 1989, 94–109; Lateiner 1989, 126–35, 137 n. 28 and 145–62. This way of thinking about custom has a strong sophistic flavor; for other examples of it in the *Histories*, see 1.82.7–8, 1.146.3, 1.157.2, 1.196.6, 5.88.2.

[17] According to Wolff (1964, 58), the Gyges story might have been shaped by Herodotus deliberately to correspond to the Masistes story, which may well have been historical and related by Halicarnassan informants. Wolff notes that Herodotus, by ending the narrative with the events of 479, does not narrate Xerxes' reign to its end, but Xerxes' treatment of his

in no doubt that Xerxes the King of Persia is on his way down. The interlocking themes of Eastern sexual misbehavior and dynastic instability are closely allied to the more general themes of the Persian treatment of women and the difficulty Persians have in distinguishing what is theirs from what is not. The Greek general Pausanias, as we have already noted, frees one of the Greek concubines of the defeated Persian army at Plataea and restores her to her family on Cos (9.76). In the last pages of the *Histories*, however, Persians, both at the level of the king himself and at the level of the local official, are depicted once more seeking to ignore or transgress the limits customarily set on sexual, domestic, and political behavior. The confusion of what is his and what is not demonstrated by Xerxes at the center of the realm is copied at its periphery by Artayctes, the Persian governor at Sestos (9.116, cf. 7.33).[18] Finally, and most importantly, in the last pages of the narrative, boundary transgression and its rectification are also presented as larger, geopolitical issues.[19] The *Histories* begins with Croesus and Cyrus conquering and taxing Ionians; they end with the Persians attacked and defeated in Asia, the island Ionians free, and an ambiguous political portent for the future: Athenian troops willing to stay all fall in the region of the Hellespont to help Xanthippus (the father of Pericles) subdue Sestos.[20] The last, gnomic anecdote about Cyrus makes reflections concerning people, their lands, and their political choices that are generally applicable to both Persians and Greeks in 479 B.C.E.

What are our real problems, then, with the ending of the *Histories* as Herodotus has written it? We can analyze the entire final sequence in retrospect, as I have just done, as highly relevant to our readerly understanding of the end of the war and the end of Herodotus's *Histories*—but this is our learned interpretive achievement as re-readers rather than an immediate response to the text when we first meet it.[21] The problem is

---

son's wife and her family points ahead for the alert reader to Xerxes' death in 465. The first and last reigns that structure the *Histories* as a whole are depicted as *Harems-Liebesgeschichten*. Herington (1991) discusses other kinds of thematic ring composition that might be in operation at the end of the *Histories*.

[18] See Immerwahr 1966, 308–14 and 322–26; and Lateiner 1989, 141–44.

[19] Gyges' adjuration in 1.8.4 to "look to one's own" is thematically relevant here both to the sexual motif and to the geopolitical one. The two spheres seem to be interchangeable when government is dynastic.

[20] For the importance of the Thracian Chersonese to Athens, see Davies 1978, 58–59. Meyer's arguments (1899, 217–18) that Herodotus chose to end his narrative with Athenian activity at Sestos are now generally accepted; see further Burn 1984, 552–57. For objections, see Jacoby 1913, 376–78. Aly (1921, 194–95) astutely distinguishes the general problem of incompleteness (including unfulfilled promises in the *Histories*), the problem of the appropriate place for an ending, and the problem of an appropriate form for an ending.

[21] See Iser 1989, 10 and, more generally, 1978, 30–38, for the (real and implied) reader's roles in constituting a text.

this: a reader who comes to the end of the *Histories* unprepared has no way of judging that it is really the end, except for the presence of a blank space following the Cyrus episode. At the end of the anecdote about Cyrus and Artayctes' grandfather, no formal and definitive statement of closure occurs; instead, the narrative simply recounts the fact that the Persians decided to stay in their barren ancestral lands. Moreover, what closural moves we might find in the four last episodes are ambiguous as signals of ending because, from our experience of reading the *Histories* as a whole, we have been educated by Herodotus into thinking that the closural gestures at the end of one episode are also markers indicating the beginning of another. Until the very end of the Cyrus episode in 9.122, closure has always provided a bridge linking one narrative unit to the next; paradoxically, it has been a sign of continuity as well as an ending. If we did not already know that 9.122 was the last episode, we would not be at all surprised at its end to discover that Herodotus had decided to go on narrating the events of the next campaign season instead, by taking up the threads of what happened to the Greeks, perhaps at Byzantium. To assure us that this really was *the* end, he also could have constructed an emphatic conclusion, perhaps with authorial reflection, or at least a collection of striking symbolic terminating motifs. But he has chosen instead a very subdued and indeterminate ending for the whole, given the rules that his own text seems previously to have established for how narrative works.

A basic interpretive imbalance also pervades these pages and makes them a disconcerting end for the *Histories*. As the above summary of the narrative structure should make clear, after Mycale Herodotus develops the moral implications of the Persian story line very clearly, but leaves his account of Greek actions ambiguous. Our final view of contemporary Persia is the story of Xerxes destroying Masistes, his loyal brother, by attempting to seduce Masistes' wife, successfully seducing his daughter (married to Xerxes' own son), and finally being forced, through his own wife's machinations, to destroy the whole family. As an anecdote, this sums up the "harem politics" that have dogged Persian royal government throughout. But when we turn to the next episode, the last narrative about the Greeks, nothing equally pointed and definitive appears. The Athenians, we are told, subdue Sestos, because the Athenian commanders maintain such discipline over their troops that they stay at Sestos through the fall (9.117). Is this perhaps an ominous (or inspiring?) sign of what is to come in the Pentekontaetia? Herodotus does not say. The only named Athenian commander is Xanthippus, the father of Pericles, a relationship mentioned not here but earlier in the *Histories* (6.131). But Herodotus does not develop the figure of Xanthippus at all, although he is a potentially significant character to balance against Xerxes and of considerable interest in the light of the role the Athenians (and his own son) will play in Greek international politics after 479. Other elements in this last anecdote about the Greek side also fall flat. The divine portent that Xanthippus's captive, Artayctes, claims to see in the fish hopping about in the frying pan is, as Wilamowitz implies, mildly comical, and the narrative does not support Artayctes' own desperately self-interested claims to have seen a portent.[22] There are no lofty speeches or restatements of Greek ideals; Herodotus makes it clear that Xanthippus has Artayctes crucified because the local population wants him dead.[23]

Both Artayctes and his son die overlooking the spot where Xerxes' armies first marched into Greece. As we have seen, this is a vivid image with lots of closural resonance, since the mention of Protesilaus alludes back to two beginnings: the beginning of the Trojan expedition (itself defined as the beginning of Greek history), and the beginning of the text of the *Histories*, where it had also been mentioned. But the narrative at the end of Book 9 gives no hint of whether Xanthippus's crucifixion of Artayctes was a good thing. Especially given Herodotus's emphasis on the magnanimity, modesty, and moderation shown by Pausanias shortly before, in the narrative of Plataea, the repeated contrasts drawn in the Plataean account between Greek and Persian ways of life, and the inspiring religious portents occurring at both Salamis and Plataea, one would have liked at least a sentence from Herodotus summarizing and characterizing the Athenian behavior at Sestos with which the Greek narrative thread of the *Histories* ends. But Herodotus does not put a value, positive or negative, on any of the Athenian actions; instead, one encounters the bald statement that nothing further happened in that year.

Our interpretive difficulties become still more acute as the scene changes from the Sestos narrative to the brief anecdote about Cyrus and Artembares at the very end of Herodotus's long narrative (9.122). Even when

---

[22] Wilamowitz 1893, 26, quoted at the head of this essay. Darbo-Peschanski (1987, 57) comments: "L'inquêteur laisse à Artayctès lui-même la responsabilité d'interpréter son sort comme une vengeance des dieux." Herodotus elsewhere presents the personal manifestation of the power of gods or heroes more seriously; cf. his treatment of two local heroes at Delphi (8.38–39), or the unequivocal weight he puts on the role of Demeter protecting her sanctuaries in the narratives of Salamis, Plataea, and Mycale (8.65, 9.65.2, 9.101.1) or the role of Poseidon at Pallene (8.129.3). (Boedeker has suggested to me, however, that the oddness of the Protesilaus episode may have more to do with differences in the way Greeks perceived gods and heroes than with a desire on Herodotus's part to downplay Protesilaus's role in the narrative.) Ceccarelli (forthcoming, sec. 3.2) argues for an implicit connection between the fish story that Cyrus tells the Ionians in 1.141 and the leaping fish of 9.120. The Ionians, as "fish," are in Book 9 no longer netted and dancing, but dancing free: "Les ponts sont rompus, les poissons revivent." The theme of "beau territoire" occurs in each context, too, just after Cyrus's *ainos* in Book 1, as part of his final *ainos* in 9.122.

[23] Schmid (1934, 591 and 597, following Jacoby 1913, 466) points out that the whole narrative of Athenian actions at the end of the *Histories* does not include the kind of detailed information that Herodotus would have received from Athenian sources.

analyzed as an independent segment unconnected to the rest of the *Histories*, the Cyrus anecdote is puzzling.[24] It is not without merit and interest; as I have noted, it has a certain structural elegance, because its plot line consists of the intersection of two basic narrative modes on which Herodotus has relied throughout the *Histories*: ethnographic descriptions, and detailed accounts of political activity and decision-making. In 9.122 the Persians are shown making a deliberate decision about their customs and way of life; they choose to remain strong and rugged, by living in their rugged land. What the Persians choose here, however, seems paradoxical: in order to remain free, they must choose to rule. But in order to rule they have to stay rugged. Thus, it appears, rulers of empires must refuse to enjoy the fruits of their labors, in order to survive as rulers.

This is, however, a much more subtle picture of empire than that presented in Book 1's version of the story of Cyrus and the beginning of Persian empire. There Herodotus shows the same Cyrus initially motivating the Persians to attack the Medes. Cyrus sets the Persians a day of clearing weeds and a day of banqueting. Asked which they like better, the Persians choose the banquet, and so muster the will to fight the Medes (1.125). Cyrus in Book 1 is portrayed as a typical conqueror, urging conquest of wealthy neighbors, while in Book 9 he is rather a "warner," a wise man urging the Persians to retain their own primitive simplicity.[25] The two episodes, each prominently positioned at a key place in the narrative, hold what Immerwahr calls "nearly contradictory" meanings. Of the two, the version in Book 1 more clearly reflects what happens in the rest of Herodotus's narrative. The larger implicit meaning of the final anecdote— the Persians happily stayed in their stony homeland—is not one borne out by the version of Greco-Persian confrontation found in the rest of the *Histories*. By the time we have reached the Cyrus anecdote of Book 9, we have just finished reading about a war of conquest in which the would-be conquerors, most vividly at Plataea, are depicted as luxury-lovers. Their king has spinelessly fled; the last story of him in the *Histories* has just focused on his attempt to seduce his own brother's wife and daughter. The

---

[24] Legrand (1968, 76–77) suggests it is not Herodotean at all, but the work of an enthusiastic annotator, perhaps a follower of Hippocrates from Cos, Halicarnassus's nearest island neighbor. Glaser (1935) thinks that Herodotus wrote it, but that it is an expression of "cultural pessimism" on Herodotus's part, with both Hippocratic and sophistic influences behind it. For motifs in the anecdote that Greeks might have recognized as closural, cf. Rutherford, chapter 3 in this volume, on "returning home" and "knowing your limitations" as closural themes in Pindar.

[25] Immerwahr (1966, 146 n. 190) believes that the apparent contradiction is not a problem: "The two anecdotes . . . illuminate a single problem from two different points of view, a method altogether characteristic of Herodotus." On the general principle of finding unity in diversity and even contradiction between one passage and another, see Fornara 1971, 9. For other interpretations of the episode, see note 15 above.

Persians of Books 7 through 9, especially at the highest levels, are not the Persians portrayed in 9.122.

This fact, coupled with the paratacticity of Herodotus's customary narrative style and the uncertainty of the interpretive valence of the preceding Sestos episode, leaves important parts of the meaning of the Cyrus anecdote highly uncertain. What does it have to say about Persians, about Greeks, and about the troubled relations between them sketched in the narrative of the war just concluded? Herodotus does not tell us directly. We are left as readers to interpret this aspect of the Cyrus episode for ourselves; the interpretation we will make will depend entirely on the kinds of connections we choose to draw between this anecdote and all that has gone before, connections that are all to a certain extent arbitrary choices on our part. The effect is perilously close to that of some modern "interactional" computer games—Herodotus sets it up so that we, the readers, must write the very end of the *Histories* ourselves.

Three different interpretations are often advanced for the way the Cyrus episode reflects on Greeks, on Persians, and on the implicit contrasts and comparisons of their political identities:

> *The Hero Gives Good Advice.* Cyrus, the father of the Persians, saves them by reminding them of their roots in their hard land, the source of their strength. If we read the episode simply at its face value, both Cyrus and the Persians are to be interpreted positively.[26] There is some justification for this reading in the fact that the Persians were still the most powerful people in the Mediterranean world in the second half of the fifth century, when Herodotus wrote. In this interpretation, if the story is meant to apply at all to the Greeks, it is as a positive analogy: the implication is that the good advice Cyrus the hero gave sixth-century Persians continues to be useful for fifth-century Greeks.[27] This version of the ending of the *Histories* requires the smallest amount of implicit connection with other narratives in the *Histories* to sustain its meaning.
>
> *Persians Lose, Greeks Win.* If we insist on connecting the Cyrus anecdote to the story of the Greek victories of 480 and 479 narrated in the immediately preceding pages, however, its interpretation becomes more ambiguous. Artembares, Cyrus's interlocutor in the anecdote, is identified as the ancestor,

[26] Burn (1984, 61) thinks 9.122 might be an anecdote that originally commemorated Cyrus's real decision not to move his capital to Babylon but to stay at Pasargadai (cf. Bornitz 1968, 196). As such, it conveyed a truth about sixth-century Persia.

[27] Krischer (1974) emphasizes that the Persians in 9.122 are presented positively, as worthy fifth-century opponents to the Greeks; Cobet (1971, 175–76) and Gould (1989, 59–60) read the episode more generally as one with a gnomic thrust: Herodotus's own final meditation on the connection between luxury and power, put into Cyrus's mouth. Cobet (174) stresses the connection in the anecdote between the primitiveness and the strength of a people, a concept important for the *Histories* as a whole.

after all, of Artayctes, the clever and wicked governor of Sestos crucified in 479 for decadent behavior, in particular for using the sanctuary of Protesilaus for sexual activity. If we read the genealogical connection between the two narratives as an important key to the meaning of the plot line, and also recall the thematic ties that reach back to the immediately preceding narrative of Xerxes' self-indulgent behavior at Sardis, it is not clear that Herodotus wants us to limit our reading of the Cyrus anecdote to its interest as an ethnological observation and its surface stress on good advice taken by sixth-century Persians. If we read it rather in the narrative context afforded by Greek victory in the Persian Wars, the Cyrus anecdote suggests that not analogy but polarity dominates the implicit narrative connection being established between Greeks and Persians in 9.122. For (although Herodotus does not say so explicitly in the anecdote) the Persians as he has described them for the preceding three books of narrative seem to have changed, and to have forgotten Cyrus's advice—in this reading, the unexpressed implication is that therefore they have been conquered by their more primitive and stronger opponents, the Greeks. For a fifth-century Greek (and especially Athenian) audience, this would provide 9.122 as a happy ending for the work as a whole. The Persians over time forgot Cyrus's advice; the Greeks, on the other hand, seem to have retained their hardy freedom and to have won the Persian Wars in consequence. This is the reading later Greek audiences and many modern ones assumed Herodotus meant us to make.[28]

The Persians Forgot and Perhaps the Greeks (or at least Athenians) Will Too. A third interpretive possibility requires a still more complicated set of connections to be drawn between this narrative and that of the preceding Persian and Greek narrative threads. Granted that the Persians of 479 do not seem to have followed Cyrus's advice; perhaps the implication is that the Greeks, and in particular the imperialistic Athenians with whom the contemporary narrative of events has ended, are also likely to forget their simple roots and come to grief. In this interpretation, the most important narrative connection is not a contrast between Persian failure and Greek success, but an implicit parallel between the (ironic?) interpretive vagueness in the immediately preceding Sestos episode, and the (ironic?) portrait of hardy Persians listening to Cyrus here. That is, if we read the Sestos episode and its lack of articulated values as

[28] Dionysius of Halicarnassus *Pomp.* 3.8: "[Herodotus] begins with the reasons why the barbarians injured the Greeks in the first place, and proceeds until he has described the punishment and the retribution which befell them: at which point he ends" (trans. Usher 1985). Macan (1908, 831) comments on the Cyrus story: "It is at once the rationale of the Greek success, and a call to future expansion. . . . What the Persians had done in the days of Kyros, why should not the Greeks do in the days of Kimon, or of Perikles?" Both Jacoby and Pohlenz expected Herodotus to emphasize Persian failure and Greek success, but could not convince themselves that 9.122 as it stands struck the proper note; see notes 31 and 32 below.

a tacit lack of enthusiasm for Athens's leadership and Xanthippus's decision to crucify Artayctes, the connection between the last two narratives in the *Histories* is again analogical rather than polar: Greeks again resemble Persians rather than acting as their opposites. Where the analogy in the first interpretation advanced above was positive, however, the analogy is now a negative one. Perhaps Herodotus is implying that the Athenians are at Sestos already on their way to becoming like the Persians, so that they, too, will fail to remain simple and hardy, and thus deserving of empire. For Herodotus, writing in the late 430s and perhaps into the 420s, the Athenians have not yet been brought low, but given the fact that "small becomes big and big small," it might well happen.[29]

Other aspects of the end of the *Histories* lead to uncertainty in understanding the meaning of the ending, but it is the Cyrus story that presents interpreters of Herodotus with the most serious problems, because, depending on what elements in the preceding narrative one wants to stress, and how one links them up, the political import of the Cyrus anecdote can be interpreted in so many different and even mutually contradictory ways.[30] This fact has dismayed a number of the scholars who first convincingly articulated the overall logic of the work and many of its major themes. Both Felix Jacoby and Max Pohlenz, two otherwise very dissimilar interpreters of Herodotus, conceded that the narrative of Sestos was a logical place for Herodotus to stop, but both dismissed the text of the ending as we have it as inadequately developed. Jacoby and Pohlenz assumed that Herodotus must have intended a reading in which Greek success was to be contrasted with Persian failure, but they came to the conclusion that Herodotus was somehow prevented from finishing it, perhaps dying in the midst of his final revisions. That is why Jacoby asked of the Cyrus anecdote, "Is it irony . . . or has Herodotus lost his mind?" He thought it especially odd that the end of the *Histories* contains no mention of the role of Athens, in a positive light, as the prime mover in the struggle for Greek

[29] As in fact it did, in 404—see the end of this chapter. Aly (1921, 195), Schmid, (1934, 597), Glaser (1935, 18–20), and Cobet (1971, 175–76) think the warning is aimed directly at Athens. How and Wells (1928, 337) see a veiled warning to "the conquerors," presumably the Greeks, in the Cyrus anecdote. See Fornara 1971, 56 and 80–86 for a general discussion of Herodotus's ambivalence toward Athens.

[30] White (1973, 7–11) claims that four possible emplotments typically characterize historical narratives. Following Northrop Frye, he labels them romance, comedy, tragedy, and satire (though I prefer his alternative term, irony, for satire). Without here entering the debate about the validity or inclusiveness of such typologizing, we can note the odd fact that the various ways I advance here for reading the Cyrus story at the end of Book 9 can be neatly fit into White's four plots. "The Hero Gives Good Advice" is romance, "Persians Lose, Greeks Win" is comedy, "Persians Forgot and Greeks Will Too" is tragedy, and the various polyvalent readings I discuss thereafter are irony. But cf. Gossman 1990, 285–324, esp. 309, for a subtle critique of the purely "narrativist" view of history for which White argues.

freedom.[31] Pohlenz, ordinarily a less judgmental reader than Jacoby, on the whole concurred, although what he missed particularly was a global restatement of the great theme of the Greek struggle for freedom against the barbarians. Pohlenz pointed out that at numerous other points in the *Histories*, Herodotus effortlessly achieves the effect of forceful closure, and he asked: "Why is there lacking to the whole the formal conclusion that he considers necessary for all the parts?"[32] What such readers (and they are among Herodotus's best) miss at the end of the *Histories* is not just the expected formal marker of ending; they are asking also for some sense of pattern completed and unambiguous interpretation given, both of which Herodotus seems to withhold.

At the beginning of this chapter I said that Herodotus was in many respects an anomalous historian. Part of the response of Wilamowitz, Jacoby, and Pohlenz to the *Histories'* end has to do with our customary expectations, as nineteenth- and twentienth-century readers, concerning what endings in historical narrative normally mean. As I suggested at the outset, a particular historical narrative, with its delimited subject matter, its beginning and its end, is by definition an arbitrary and highly selective slice of the larger continuum of human experience over time. A narrative claiming to be the examination of a particular set of real events—say, the French Revolution, or the Persian Wars—has many options for its beginning and end, and its different options emphasize different combinations of data, and different meanings as inherent in them. The historian's choice of ending is crucial to our overall interpretation of the work, because it is (as in any narrative) the ending that sets the capstone on the plot and so determines the final shape of a history's story line. It is the historian's choice of an ending (and thus of a plot) that sets the reader some basic limits on the meanings the historian sees in the plethora of data belonging within the chosen limits of his or her investigation, and it is for this reason a particularly important pointer to the patterns and underlying coherence of the work and to the individual and idiosyncratic understanding of the historian who wrote it.[33] In this context, the question of Wilamowitz, Jacoby, and Pohlenz is still pertinent: when Herodotus clearly knew how to write a real climax at the end of a given episode, why did he choose to end his

---

[31] "Soll das Ironie sein (was niemand glaubt, auch Gomperz nicht), oder hat H. den Verstand verloren?" (Jacoby 1913, 375). He goes on to say: "Am Schluss eines Werkes, das uns zeigen soll, wie die Macht dieses Reiches zerschellt ist an dem Nationalgefühl und der Macht Athens . . . wäre diese Anekdote nicht bloss unpassend, sondern unmöglich und eines denkenden Menschen unwürdig. Also ist das Werk unvollendet" (376).

[32] "Warum fehlt dem Ganzen die formelle Abrundung, die er bei jedem Teile für notwendig hält?" (Pohlenz 1937, 165)

[33] See Mink 1987, 23–26, 48, 60, and for "retrospective intelligibility," 136–37. See also Pelling, chapter 11 in this volume, note 1.

Histories with a series of anecdotes not obviously advancing a coherent interpretation of Persians and their relation to Greeks, or at least a final anecdote with an unequivocal meaning of its own? Why end with the Persians persuaded by Cyrus to limit their homesteading ambitions to the skimpy soil of Persia, when we have just spent 800 pages reading that they did not stay there, or stay simple and hardy?

It is important not to overstate the problem for Herodotus. As we have seen, if we look closely at the narrative of events after Mycale, in the largest sense he does bring the *Histories* as a whole to a close. Xerxes not only has left Greece, but also has fallen, and has fallen in ways that point toward his own death at the hands of his son some fifteen years later. The bridge cables are in Greek hands, while the contemner of Protesilaus and outrager of Greek territory and women is crucified overlooking the straits where Xerxes first crossed into Europe, leaving the Athenians in charge of Sestos. These moves are deliberate enough that we can reasonably argue with Wilamowitz and say that what we have was probably the ending of the *Histories* Herodotus chose to write. But it is an ambiguous ending, and we are entitled to look for reasons why Herodotus wrote it as he did.

One set of answers clusters around the possibility that ambiguity itself did not mean to Herodotus what it does to us, looking back through the lens of nineteenth- and earlier twentieth-century historiography. Certainly the majority of contemporary scholars are more comfortable than Wila-mowitz, Jacoby, or Pohlenz were in accepting a certain amount of Herodo-tean open-endedness in the context of our changed understanding of early Greek literary history in the last fifty years or so.[34] In particular, we are more interested in the existence of archaic oral narrative. Oral narratives traditionally are supposed to tolerate a much looser formal organization than does a written text, because they can rely on the physical connections between narrator and audience to supply much of the audience's sense of a given performance's form and shape. Herodotus is the author (in many respects a very self-conscious one) of a written work—but much in the way that Herodotus's text is put together clearly comes from his familiarity with and borrowing from oral storytelling conventions.[35]

[34] Fränkel in 1924 already saw open-endedness as a quality of Herodotus's prose; for ex-cerpts, see Fränkel 1982, 746. Van Groningen points out that typically works of archaic or early classical literature are shaped as long chains of discrete narrative segments, rather cur-sorily linked together. Quite often, the elements in such a sequence are not fully worked into the integrative schema of an overarching whole, and the finish is quite abrupt: "On cesse quand on a traité le dernier morceau de la série, quand on n'a plus rien de nouveau à dire." Van Groningen comments on Herodotus 9.122 in particular that "la dernière phrase . . . est la fin de l'anecdote, rien d'autre"; hence any attempt to interpret it produces "hy-pothèses non fondées" (1960, 70).

[35] For Herodotus and oral techniques generally, see Murray 1987 and Evans 1980 and 1991, 89–146. Some chunks of narrative that underlie the *Histories*' parts can be distin-

One has only to look at some of the basic compositional habits of the *Histories* to see how much Herodotus's ways of structuring his material resemble traditional oral patterns of thought and speech.[36] Herodotus himself emphasizes his dependence on oral epichoric or local sources: he makes it clear that logoi that the Athenians say, or the Corinthians, Spartans, Persians, and so on, form the basis of his own narrative.[37] As typically in oral versions of a people's accounts of their collective past, some of the deepest structures in Herodotus's text are genealogical. Even the basic structure of the *Histories* is a dynastic one: Herodotus organizes his whole narrative around a sequence shaped by the reigns of one Lydian king, Croesus, and four Persian kings, Cyrus, Cambyses, Darius, and Xerxes.[38] People's family connections are sometimes brought in, moreover, to explain anomalous behavior, like that of Cleisthenes, archon of Athens and architect of its democratic political structures, but to Herodotus more pertinently the grandson of the tyrant of Sicyon (5.67.1). Both the beginning and end of the *Histories* emphasize intergenerational genealogical links: Gyges/Croesus at the beginning, Artembares/Artayctes at the end.[39]

I have already mentioned Herodotus's use of parataxis, but many of the other specifics of his literary style—clear, simple sentence structure, continuous use of summary participles and even whole summary sentences, obvious and even formulaic markers of the beginnings and ends of episodes, and a preference for short, discrete interpretive units often organized into annular or ring-like patterns—all these are techniques often used by oral narrators to facilitate an aural audience's ease of comprehension. Herodotus frequently uses extended parentheses to supply background and context for a given story—what one might call, when overutilized, the Scheherazade structure. Finally, an oral, epichoric background might explain Herodotus's frequent reliance on variant versions of events that do not agree with one another. It is quite possible that the interpretive openness of the ending of the *Histories* as we have it seemed reasonable both to him and to his audiences because it recognizably fit a tradition to which

---

guished that originally might have been self-contained oral performances or even written manuscripts, like the narratives of Croesus and Cyrus, Egypt, Darius in Scythia, Ionia at war, and Xerxes' disastrous invasion of Greece. For further discussion of closure in an oral text, see in this volume D. Fowler, chapter 1, and Fusillo, chapter 10. See also Fowler 1989b, 79–80.

[36] Aly 1921. See also Lang 1984; Cobet 1988; and Evans 1991.

[37] Darbo-Peschanski 1985.

[38] Focke 1927, 24–25; and White 1969, 42. The fullest exploration of this underlying organizing structure is that of Cobet 1971, 158–71.

[39] Herodotus recounts parenthetical stories about relatives of actors in the main narrative, as in 6.125–31 or in 9.93–94, the notorious excursus on Evenius, the father of Deiphonus. See Focke 1927, 22–23; and Schmid 1934, 597 n. 5. Cf. Lateiner (1989, 119–22), who downplays genealogy and even chronology as Herodotean organizing principles.

Greeks of his generation were accustomed—perhaps one that Herodotus had himself used to end discrete oral performances of his own for a number of years before writing down the *Histories* as a whole.

Oral conventions may indeed have created the conditions under which an ending like Herodotus's might have been regarded as acceptable by his fifth-century audiences; what they do not explain is why this author thought this ending a suitable one for his text. One could, entirely hypothetically but as plausibly, advance an interpretation relying on authorial intentionality: perhaps Herodotus saw that a work with as many interpretive directions and formal structures as his *Histories* has could not be given a conventional ending that relied on the marks of closure used to end the individual narrative episodes. It is certainly true that the work as we have it is so big and so multifaceted that any particular application of closure at the very end would have limited the meanings of the whole.[40] Perhaps what Herodotus felt needed doing at the very end of his work, given its length, interpretive polyvalence, and the variety of its narrative voices and techniques, was to end it arbitrarily and by doing so to leave it free, with the Cyrus anecdote acting as the knotted fringe of the fabric, still capable of being untied at any moment and continued.

This kind of answer could be adapted to late twentieth-century poststructuralist modes of interpretation by arguing a reading of the final Cyrus episode that is self-consciously and ironically polyvalent on Herodotus's part. That is, perhaps Herodotus has constructed an ending that deliberately sustains three different and even contradictory interpretations because he did not think there was any one authoritative version of who the Greeks were at the end of the Persian Wars. There is no doubt some truth here: Herodotus was acutely aware, especially as he traveled around the Greek-speaking world, that different parts of the near past were viewed very differently by different communities. His last anecdote about Cyrus might well have been constructed so that it could be received very differently by different Greeks—read as a happy ending by the Athenians, as a bitterly ambiguous one by other Greeks.[41] If this attributes too much political cynicism to Herodotus, perhaps more abstractly he was, like postmodern critics today, aware of the eternal slippage of signifiers over signifieds, and the hopelessness of assigning determinate meanings when language by its very nature is about the play of difference, the perpetual de-centering of what just a moment ago was thought to be known and understood.[42] These are answers to the problem of Herodotus's ending that

[40] Focke 1927, 23.

[41] Cf. what Barchiesi, Chapter 9 in this volume, calls "the politics of closure" (207). See, however, Evans 1991, 92, for Herodotus as an uncomfortable, honest observer.

[42] For ways in which Greek texts can include a postmodern indeterminacy at their core, see Murnaghan's reading of the *Iliad* and Dunn's reading of Euripides' *Heracles*, chapters 2

are in some ways tempting in their contemporaneity, and in their recognition of Herodotus's own awareness of multiple voices and multiple viewpoints they are certainly correct.[43]

The arguments advanced up to this point for the ambiguities of the *Histories'* end have placed a positive value on ambiguity for its own sake. But I would like to suggest a further interpretive possibility, one that is tempting, even if not compelling, because it draws on one of the most profound and pervasive authorial stances Herodotus takes throughout his long work as an interpreter of events. It is possible, that is, that Herodotus chose an ambiguous ending not because ambiguity was a good thing in itself, but because it allowed him to express in practice some basic truths about his understanding of how the world of *ta anthrōpeia* works, in particular, the right relationship between knowledge and action. It is certainly suggestive that as a narrator, at the end of the *Histories*, he observes the same rules that he portrays as constraining the most intelligent actors inside his narrative. Repeatedly, individual narrative plots in the *Histories* trace a vital connection between the existence of a phenomenal world full of hard realities that need to be recognized, and a corresponding need on the part of actors in events to understand both the necessity of knowledge and the limits of one's own knowledge if one is to take effective action.[44] In general, genuine knowledge in the *Histories* is portrayed as hard to come by, and very few individuals in the narrative apply it usefully to their own circumstances. Those who do understand are often powerless; the observation of the anonymous Persian in Book 9 reads like a cri de coeur: "The most horrible pain of those among men is this, having thought for many things, to control nothing" (9.16).

Herodotus concludes the proem of his *Histories* proclaiming that "because big becomes small and small big, and knowing that human happiness never stays long in the same place, I shall recount both alike." History did not separate the Persian Wars tidily from the fifty-year period of Athenian dominance that followed. Writing for readers farther into the future than himself, Herodotus has left it for us to look back and fit the Athenian presence at Sestos in 479 into what happened afterward, in his own generation and later, and to pick out the connections that later remained relevant from the series of small narrative units that formed the end of his *Histories*.[45] Just as at the *Histories'* beginning Herodotus shrugs and proceeds to Croesus from the stories of mythic rapes, without choosing among them (lost as they are in the mists of the irretrievable past)—so here, at the

---

and 5 in this volume. For a more extreme example, see Goldhill's deconstructionist reading of Greek tragedy (1986) and the critique of this method by Clark and Csapo (1991).

[43] Meier 1987, 45.

[44] See, for instance, Bischoff 1932; Marg 1982b; and Dewald 1993.

[45] Lateiner 1989, 50 and 213.

Histories' end, by finishing with a reversion to Cyrus, a paradigmatic figure from Book 1, and an ambiguous anecdote about him, Herodotus leaves us with the fact of the apparent interpretive uncertainties of the contemporary world of the Pentekontaetia.[46] He also provides us with a practical example of his own interpretive canniness and modesty—a modesty that we should appreciate at its full intellectual worth, if we have been astute readers of how the world portrayed in his *Histories* works. Like the most successful characters in the *Histories*, Herodotus knows where the limits to his own knowledge lie.

If this is why Herodotus has written the end of the *Histories* as he did, he has in this respect written with considerable historiographical sophistication.[47] For the disturbing indeterminacy and polyvalence of the final ending leaves us with a concrete demonstration of a particular relation established between the world and the act of interpretation, since it provides an instance in practice of Herodotus's tacit acknowledgment of his own intellectual limits. As narrator, he refuses to commit himself to the interpretation of the new narrative thread that appears in his story as the Persian expedition to the Greek mainland draws to a close. Herodotus has early in the *Histories* taught us to "look to the end" to understand meaning, and to resist speculating on meaning when the end is not yet clear (1.32.9). Like Solon in his conversation with Croesus, at the end of his own *Histories* Herodotus does not judge the Athenian military presence in the Thraceward regions in 479 because it relies for its meaning on a story whose outcome was still in doubt at the time that he wrote. Neither Athenians nor Peloponnesians had yet won what Thucydides was to call the Peloponnesian War.

Was the contemporary Athenian empire a good thing or a bad thing? Herodotus's *Histories* does not tell us. But everything else we have seen about the *Histories* shows us that Herodotus expected that the real connections between the Sardis, Sestos, and Cyrus episodes would be revealed in time. The *Histories* is silent on this score not because Herodotus thought there was no answer, or because he didn't want to offend someone, or because the answer didn't matter, but because at the time of his writing this part of the pattern had not yet emerged. If so, he has constructed an ending in accordance with this reality, and one that forces us his readers to supply the meaning of the Cyrus episode that we can look back on from our vantage point in the future and say best fits the evidence. It is often said that all history is contemporary history. Herodotus forces us to see an

---

[46] See Pelliccia 1992, 78, for the false-start *recusatio* at the beginning of the *Histories*.

[47] See Appleby, Hunt, and Jacob 1994, ch. 7, "Truth and Objectivity," for what they call "practical realism," that is, how a working historian might try in practice to negotiate the uncertainties of language and the difficulties of ascertaining fact.

equally important truth—meaningful contemporary history can never be written, since its significant patterns do not come clear to the mortals who need to understand it except by the passage of time, as they look back and retroactively make the sense of the past that it is impossible for a contemporary viewer to see. This is the point that Croesus finally got on his pyre, as he cried out, "Solon, Solon, Solon!"

The insignificant roadstead, Aigospotamoi, where Artayctes the wicked governor of Sestos was captured in 479, was three-quarters of a century later, in 404, to be the scene of the final defeat of the Athenian fleet, and the end of fifth-century Athenian empire (Xen. *Hell.* 2.21–28). Herodotus almost certainly did not live to know this fact (or at any rate does not show us that he had it in mind when he wrote up 9.119), but it might have given him great pleasure to reflect upon it. For Herodotus, the patterns formed by events were not something he, as a narrator, imposed upon them, or created. He seems to have believed that, by being attentive, one can hope to read historical patterns out of the facts—but also that a historical interpretation succeeds only by acknowledging and respecting as well the reality of the interstices, the blank spaces that the historian himself cannot fill in yet from his own narrative present.[48]

[48] I would like to thank Deborah Boedeker, John Gould, Donald Lateiner, Greg Thalmann, and the editors of this volume for their helpful comments.

CHAPTER 5

Ends and Means in Euripides' *Heracles*

FRANCIS M. DUNN

> CLOV: The end is terrific!
> HAMM: I prefer the middle.
> —Samuel Beckett, *Endgame*

WHAT is closure? Is it something in the text or the plot: the manner in which events come to an end that may be happy or sad, surprising or predictable, final or uncertain? Is it something in our response: an expectation of unity or coherence or ambiguity by which we judge what we see and read? Is it something in the culture: a system of values or an exercise of power that makes the text do its work? As the various essays in this collection demonstrate, the study of closure is interesting because it asks about the establishment of order in many different ways. In my reading of Euripides' *Heracles* I hope to show how these various constructions of order depend on one another, and also how the play's persistent evasions of order resist familiar approaches to closure.

I begin, in a very traditional way, with a problem—the long-standing question of unity. On this count, *Heracles* has come in for harsh criticism, most notoriously in Swinburne's description of the play as a "grotesque abortion";[1] and if continuing debate on the unity of the play seems by now a bit tiresome, the problem is a real one. The drama consists not of a single, unified plot but of two or three separate, independent actions: the suppliant drama of Megara and Amphitryon, who are besieged by the upstart Lycus and rescued from death at the last minute by Heracles; the startling epiphany of Iris and Lyssa, who cause Heracles to murder the family he has just rescued from Lycus; and the final debate, in which Theseus persuades Heracles to live and to accompany him to Athens. This episodic or "broken-backed" structure of the play has caused critics such as Murray and Norwood to condemn it as inartistic; others, such as Conacher and Kamerbeek, have argued around the problem by showing that despite the disjointed action, there are important continuities in theme and imagery; and Arrowsmith and Michelini go further, finding a positive virtue in the

---

[1] Quoted by Verrall (1905, 136).

play's surprising reversals.[2] As we shall see, there are also readings of *Heracles* that avoid this problem by looking for a coherence (whether religious, political, or cultural) that stands outside the plot; but is there a reading that will make sense of this episodic plot, and somehow find a method in the sudden entrance of Iris and Lyssa, and the unmotivated arrival of Theseus? It is a valid question—but also a loaded one.

By posing this question, we make an assumption that may or may not be valid. In Aristotelian terms, we are looking for a plot that is complete and whole, with each part following by necessity or probability from what precedes; and by conducting this search, we imply that a unified plot is better than one that is not. We might not go as far as Norwood, who concludes that because the play falls into two parts, "we cannot view it as a single piece of art"; but we are doomed to special pleading, excusing an inferior plot by invoking other qualities that redeem it—a continuity of imagery, for example, or a "conversion" of the plot.[3] I begin with a reading of *Heracles* that entertains different assumptions. If the critic thinks of plot in Aristotelian terms as an organic body or a plastic whole, then the play indeed falls into two or three separate parts, leaving the problem of explaining how they fit together. But we may choose to read events of the plot with a view to their effect upon the spectator; rather than searching for a shapely whole, we can ask about the rhetorical effect of sharp transitions from one scene to the next. In these terms, the plot of *Heracles* negotiates a series of endings: the spectator is implicated in a play with expectations of closure, time after time reaching an apparent end, only to find it is part of a larger, unfinished story. This rhetorical reading of the play will then pose further questions about closure and the construction of order.

NARRATIVE ENDS

When *Heracles* begins, the end is already at hand. In other plays of Euripides, the prologue allows a god or mortal to hint or speculate at where events will lead; the nurse, for example, fears that Medea will harm her children (*Medea* 36–39), and Dionysus threatens to prove his divinity to Pentheus by force (*Bacchant Women* 50–52). But in this play, no anticipa-

---

[2] The play is "broken-backed": Murray 1946, 112; compare Norwood 1954, 47. Separate parts convey "a single theme": Conacher 1967, 83; compare Kamerbeek 1966, 5–10. Contradictions produce "a dramatic mutation": Arrowsmith 1956, 50; compare Michelini 1987, 276.

[3] Norwood 1920, 229. On continuity of imagery, see esp. Sheppard 1916. In speaking of "conversion" of the plot, Arrowsmith (1956, 50–51) argues that the world described in the first half of the play is replaced "point for point" by the opposite world portrayed in the second.

tion is necessary. As Amphitryon explains in his prologue speech, all is finished: Heracles has not returned from Hades and must be presumed dead; the tyrant Lycus has seized power; and he plans to consolidate his power by killing all the members of Heracles' family, including Amphitryon himself. In desperation, they have taken refuge at the altar of Zeus the Savior, but as Amphitryon describes the situation, this is clearly the end:[4]

> Here we keep watch utterly destitute, without
> food or drink or clothing, resting our bodies
> on the bare earth; we are sealed out of the house
> and lie here with no chance of rescue (ἀπορίᾳ σωτηρίας).
>
> (51–54)

What suspense can this endgame possibly hold? Megara, like Amphitryon, concludes that there is no hope or chance of rescue (80), and as the play gets under way, the only source of interest is the old man's greater willingness to wait and hope for the best (an abject faith in hope that he paradoxically describes as a virtue, 105–6). This modest impasse is quickly broken in the following scene by the entrance of Lycus, who will make good on his threats even if this means murdering suppliants at the altar. The tyrant's violence persuades Amphitryon that Megara was right, and together they make a virtue out of necessity by asking to die before the children, and by obtaining permission to dress them in proper funeral clothing. Before we come to the first choral ode (348–441), the end announced in the prologue has been reached; and no sooner is the ode finished than this end is decked out in the visual spectacle of a family dressed for death (442–50) and in the verbal trappings of sacrificial rite: "Where is the priest? Who will sacrifice these unfortunates? The sacrificial victims are ready to lead to Hades" (451–53).

This premature end is not entirely satisfying. It is false insofar as the spectator knows that the play cannot possibly end so soon, and it is anticlimactic insofar as this apparent end comes so easily, at the price of so little dramatic conflict; but it is also disappointing because it is not the end we want. In Greek drama the gesture of the suppliant must succeed; it is the moral high ground of those who are unfairly treated, sanctioned by the gods and ignored by mortals at their peril, and in this case the pious gesture is directed to none other than Zeus Soter, the Savior (48).[5] Tragedy, of course, is not afraid to stage violent threats against the suppliant, threats averted at the last minute by the prophetess in *Ion*, for example, or by Theseus in *Oedipus at Colonus*. What makes *Heracles* unique is that the

---

[4] Translations are my own, following the text of Diggle 1981.

[5] For a general discussion of suppliancy, see Gould 1973.

threat apparently succeeds and is followed by an enactment of the failure of supplication: mother, children, and grandfather abandon the altar and prepare themselves for death in a spectacular and shocking perversion of propriety. Finally, this end is unsatisfactory in that the spectators (unlike Megara, Amphitryon, and the chorus) know that Heracles should complete this famous labor and return from Hades with Cerberus.[6] So if the plot has already reached its end, one that is confirmed with the visual and verbal trappings of death, it is also clear that somehow this cannot be the end.

Just as the cast prepares to make its final exit, Heracles suddenly appears. He quickly prepares a happier ending, vowing not only to protect his family from death, but to kill Lycus, give his head to the dogs, and slaughter all hostile Thebans (566–73). The drama of despair and death quickly becomes one of victory and revenge; an ode of celebration anticipates the tyrant's return, and in one of the shortest episodes in Greek tragedy (701–33), Lycus is lured inside the palace and is killed by Heracles. This second ending seems much more effective than the first: the suppliants are saved, the labors of Heracles are complete, and there is order in the world. "Hooray!" the chorus exclaims, "Justice and the fate of the gods return," ἰώ / δίκα καὶ θεῶν παλίρρους πότμος (738–39).[7] The happy end demonstrates the greatness of the hero, allowing the chorus in two consecutive odes to celebrate him as a triumphant victor (καλλίνικον, 681, 789).

This second ending seems more effective than the first; the suppliant drama is now complete, and Heracles' victory is crowned with song. But what does the hero himself think of this happy end? After returning to save his children from death, and even before killing Lycus, he rejects the glory of victory; he has discovered what it means to be a father, and he therefore disowns his labors, his heroic stature, and the title of victor:

> To hell with my labors!
> I was a fool to perform them, and ignore [my children];
> in fact I ought to die protecting them, since they
> would have died for their father. Can I say
> it is right to battle with a hydra and a lion in

---

[6] Bringing the dog back from Hades is the only labor specified in Homer (*Il.* 8.367–69; *Od.* 11.623–25). Megara's ignorance of the outcome and Lycus's violence explain her decision to leave the altar; there is no indication that this is an act of impiety, *pace* Burnett (1971, 161–62). Compare Knox 1979, 339.

[7] This celebration of the death of Lycus as a change from evil (μεταβολὰ κακῶν, 735) and a resurgence of justice (δίκα καὶ θεῶν παλίρρους πότμος, 739) echoes the celebration of the death of Clytemnestra in Euripides' *Electra* (ἀμοιβαὶ κακῶν, 1147; παλίρρους δὲ τάνδ' ὑπάγεται δίκα, 1155, likewise in dochmiacs). The echo of that climactic (if morally ambiguous) revenge reinforces the (apparently) conclusive nature of this scene in *Heracles*.

Eurystheus's service, and not labor against the death
of my children? I shall not be called my former
name, Heracles the Victorious (ὁ καλλίνικος)!

(575–82)

Heracles rejects his role as a triumphant hero who turns failure into success, and prefers to play the part of a father who loves his family; instead of
the exceptional figure who battles monsters and slays the tyrant, this will
be a common man bound by the needs and clinging fingers of his children:

> Whoa! They don't let go but cling to my clothes
> even more. Were you so close to danger?
> I'll take these dinghies (ἐφολκίδας) by the hands
> and haul them like a ship; I won't refuse to
> take care of children. All people are equal:
> the better sorts love their children, and so do
> those who are nothing.

(629–35)

There is a surprising gap between this ordinary man and the hero celebrated by the chorus as son of Zeus (802–6); the chorus may sing of a
victorious finale, but Heracles is more interested in a new and better beginning with his family.

Before we have a chance to sort out this conflict, the happy end is
suddenly overturned. Striking terror into the chorus (815–21), Iris and
Lyssa appear above the building and announce their plan, at Hera's command, to drive Heracles mad and make him murder the children he has
just rescued. Nothing has prepared the audience for this reversal,[8] which is
realized step by shocking step: Iris announces Hera's plan to crush Heracles
(822–42), Lyssa describes the onset of madness in excited trochees (858–
73), the chorus accompanies Amphitryon's cries of horror with frantic
dochmiacs (875–909), and the murder of Megara and the children is finally
reported in grisly detail by a messenger from within (922–1015). But the
unfolding of this end is only complete with the visual spectacle that
emerges from the palace; the chorus exclaims: "Look at the poor children
lying before their wretched father, look at him sleeping a hideous sleep
after murdering his children—the body of Heracles propped around with
bonds and knotted nooses, tied to the courtyard's stone columns" (1032–
38). We last saw Heracles towing his children with metaphorical strings;
now he is lashed to a pillar of his fallen house. And the earlier spectacle of
Megara and the children dressed for death is repeated and made final: now

---

[8] After only 800 lines the viewer could be confident that more was to come, but nothing
in the play so far prepares for the turn of events that will follow. If anything, the viewer will
expect an elaboration of the conflict between the triumphant and the domestic Heracles.

they are really dead, and their would-be savior lies bloody and unconscious among them.

Surely this time the narrative has reached its end; nothing can undo this catastrophe, and nothing can make it more complete. The bloody spectacle, like the stage littered with corpses at the end of *Hamlet*, seems to leave room for nothing else—nothing, that is, except a brief coda: like Agave in *Bacchant Women*, Heracles can still wake up and realize what he has done; and like Sophocles' *Ajax*, he can deal with the horror of this recognition by taking his own life. He gradually awakes, learns from his father what has happened, and knows there is only one thing to do:

> Ah! How can I spare my own life now
> that I am the murderer of my dear children?
> I'll go and leap from some smooth rock,
> or plunge the sword into my spleen
> and so avenge my children's blood,
> or burn my flesh in fire to drive away
> the wretched life that waits for me.

(1146–52)

The act of suicide will bring the catastrophe to its natural conclusion—but how is this possible? The Heracles of legend was no suicide. The hero's end had been told many times in many ways (taking him to Hades or Olympus or both), but never with this final gesture of shame and despair.[9] Once again the narrative reaches a natural and inevitable end, yet one that in some respect cannot be right (this bind is reflected in the phrasing of Heracles' decision to take his life as a series of rhetorical questions, οὐκ εἶμι . . . ἀπώσομαι βίου; 1148–52).

No sooner does Heracles announce his deadly plan than he is foiled by the entrance of Theseus (ἀλλ' ἐμποδών μοι θανασίμων βουλευμάτων, 1153). This intervention is poorly timed and apparently useless: Theseus was on his way to save Heracles' family from Lycus (1163–68), and as the pile of corpses makes clear, he is far too late for that. Yet as he learns what has happened, Theseus becomes not simply an awkward obstacle to suicide, but a friend who will encourage Heracles and promise him refuge in Athens. The end that seemed so final is replaced by another, as the epiphany of Iris and Lyssa is replaced by that of Theseus. This brings us to the last of the plot's many endings—the last and the least conclusive.

---

[9] In the earliest reference to the end of Heracles, his death proves to Achilles that all men are mortal (*Il.* 18.117–19). In the *Odyssey* his shade is in the underworld while he is in Olympus (11.601–3), and in the *Catalogue of Women* he dies and goes to Hades before joining the immortals (Hesiod fr. 25.24–28 M-W). The lines of the *Catalogue* describing his apotheosis are obelized in the papyrus, and this part of the legend seems relatively late; see March 1987, 58.

The final scene promises a clear and emphatic ending by bringing on Theseus in the role of deus ex machina. This overt gesture of closure is a familiar device in Euripides: nine of the extant plays end with a deus, and three more (*Medea*, *Children of Heracles*, and *Hecuba*) end with a mortal who takes on the superhuman powers of a deus. *Heracles* is unique in presenting such an ambiguous figure: Theseus plays the part of a deus, but he never has the power or authority that this role requires. Our "deus" has all the formal trappings of a god on the machine: he appears for the first time in the final scene; he intervenes with a command, foretells the future, and announces that shrines will be named for Heracles (even using the formulaic language of such aetiologies, ταῦτ' ἐπωνομασμένα / σέθεν τὸ λοιπὸν ἐκ βροτῶν κεκλήσεται, 1329–30); he intervenes to resolve an impasse, and his dispensations are accepted by the characters onstage.[10] But in other respects, Theseus is only the shadow of a deus. He is not a god, but a mortal, and a mortal, furthermore, who lacks the power and authority of the person he has come to save (we are constantly reminded in the latter part of the play that Heracles had earlier rescued Theseus from Hades, 619, 1222, 1235, 1336, 1415); he has no divine power to rescue Heracles from death and must rely instead upon argument and persuasion, and the most he has to offer is not divine salvation but a safe place of exile. Perhaps like a deus he issues a command ("So leave Thebes, as the law requires, and follow with me to Athens," 1322–23), but this, in context, is no more than one friend's attempt to persuade another. He seems able to foretell the future (1331–33), but his words can just as readily mean that after promising gifts and land on his own behalf (1326–31), he is making a further promise on behalf of the city ("After you die and go to Hades, all the city of Athens will honor you with sacrifices and heaps of stone," 1331–33).[11] And perhaps, like a god, he can point to the contemporary world of the audience ("These sanctuaries shall be named for you in the future by mortals," 1329–30), but his words actually describe the immediate future, while Heracles is still alive (ζῶντος, 1331).

If the powers of Theseus are dubious, so, too, is the respect they earn. Usually, the authority of a deus ex machina is explicitly confirmed by the human characters, who promise to do as the god commands. When Athena orders a treaty and ritual dedications at the end of *Suppliant Women*, for example, the king ratifies this arrangement by announcing: "My Lady Athena, I will obey your words; you set me straight so I will not err" (1227–28). Likewise in *Orestes*, the surprising settlement imposed by

---

[10] On the formal trappings of the deus, see Dunn 1996, ch. 3. On the diminished stature of this deus, compare Dunn 1996, 116–19.

[11] The latter reading is favored by later tradition, which attributes the gift both of τεμένη (Philochorus *FGrH* 328 F18.3 = Plut. *Theseus* 35) and of a βωμός (Aelian *VH* 4.5) to Theseus himself.

Apollo from the machine is formally endorsed by Orestes and Menelaus (1679–81).[12] But when Heracles finally decides to live, he makes a point of casting this decision not as an acceptance of Theseus's advice but as a rebuttal, dismissing Theseus's arguments as irrelevant (πάρεργα <γὰρ> τάδ' ἔστ' ἐμῶν κακῶν, 1340). Each time Theseus offers help, Heracles is reluctant: "Stand up. No more tears."—"I cannot, my limbs are frozen" (1394–95); "Enough. Give your hand to a friend."—"I won't wipe blood on your clothes" (1398–99). At last he tacitly acknowledges his dependence on the king ("Put your hand round my neck and I'll lead you."— "A friendly pairing, with one in misfortune," 1402–3), but immediately reneges and turns back to embrace his father and the bodies of his children (1406, 1408). And when Theseus tries to shame him into submission ("No one who sees you playing the woman will approve," 1412), Heracles turns the tables on his benefactor by asking who saved Theseus from Hades: "Am I so lowly (ταπεινός)? I don't think I was back then" (1413). By the time they leave the stage a few lines later, Theseus's magnanimous gesture has been emptied of all authority, and reduced to the bickering between friends.

Our deus is no deus, and our protagonist at the end remains in limbo. Is Heracles defeated, crushed by Hera's revenge? Is he victorious, having survived her anger? Or is he neither, having done nothing more than decide not to commit suicide? What about his future? Is it bleak, exiled from Thebes and Argos with the blood of his wife and children on his hands? Is it promising, with the prospect of honors from Theseus and the Athenians? Is it banal in the extreme, the uneventful life of a hero with no more dragons to slay? Or is it a cipher, an unknown quantity, since the story of Heracles' exile in Athens had never before been written?[13] As we come to the end of the play, there is no convincing deus to help us make sense of what has happened. And after a series of incomplete endings, the plot and its protagonist remain neither at an end nor at a beginning.

I should add that if the play as it stands lacks an effective ending, critics do not hestitate to create one for it. Textual critics have done so by removing or transposing the final exchange between Heracles and Theseus,

---

[12] Compare *Hippolytus* 1442–43, *Andromache* 1276–77, *Iphigenia Among the Taurians* 1475–76, *Ion* 1606–8, *Helen* 1680–81. Such explicit and formal endorsements may well entail ambiguity or irony (as I believe is the case in *Orestes*); in *Heracles*, however, there is no such endorsement, but a reluctant bickering instead.

[13] There was a shrine of the god Heracles at Marathon in 490 (Herodotus 6.108 and 116), and the tradition of his initiation at Eleusis may be as old; see Boardman 1975. But the story of Theseus giving him land in Athens is probably Euripides' invention: see F. Jacoby on Philochorus 328 F18 (*FGrH* IIIB, supp. 1, 307–8). The story of Heracles' retirement to Athens is almost certainly his invention, otherwise unattested and contradicting his apotheosis in Locris.

thinking that the closing scene will be more "edifying" without their bickering.[14] Others are more ambitious, smuggling into the play a more resounding conclusion. Burnett laments that Heracles' happy ending is "painfully absent" and invents a glorious sequel acted out in the imaginations of the spectators, as Heracles becomes a god, marries Hebe, and banquets among the Olympians. From Theseus's vague mention of honors in Athens, Foley extrapolates a sequel in which Heracles is integrated into the life of the city and is worshiped as a hero. And from Heracles' failure to commit suicide, Barlow constructs a more satisfying conclusion, a "positive decision" to embrace life and a new form of heroism.[15] These are effective endings, but they are not the ending Euripides gives us.

CLOSURE AND ANTICLOSURE

So far, my discussion of the play is a complete little story, with a beginning, middle, and end. We began with a problem, a drama lacking unity; then we followed the course of the plot, not looking for a single action but noting a series of crises and premature endings; and we concluded that the play has its own logic of confronting a series of apparent ends, only to find that in each case the ending is a false one, and the action somehow continues. As *Heracles* takes us through one finale after another, it reverses familiar expectations, leading not from a beginning to the end, but from ends to means: the coherence of the action (if there is such a thing) consists in the process of overturning ends and beginning again, and the outcome of the plot (if it has one) consists of a scene and a protagonist that cannot be evaluated because the next chapter and the new character have yet to be written.

One lesson of this story is that by setting aside the search for an Aristotelian unity of plot, and by following a complex engagement with the viewer's expectations of closure, we can make more sense of a problem play. But the lesson does not necessarily apply to other texts: it is in an atypical and broken-backed play, after all, that we find the sequence of enacted events less intelligible as an organic body than as a rhetorical game. And our conclusion raises questions of its own. First, what do we make of

[14] Wecklein would delete from 1404 to 1428, Diggle (1981) does not believe lines 1410–17 are genuine, and Bond would transpose the latter to follow 1253, arguing that the lines are not "edifying" and therefore do not belong at the end: Bond 1981, 417.

[15] Imagined sequel: Burnett 1971, 181–82; contrast Silk 1985, 16: "Euripides, therefore, does what Sophocles had never done, and negates Heracles' apotheosis altogether." Civic integration: Foley 1985, 165–67; compare Gregory 1991, 148–49. New heroism: Barlow 1981, 112 and 126; compare notes 24 and 35 below. On the critical tenor of this final scene, which, rather than affirming humane values, questions the honor of suicide, see Romilly 1980.

this rhetorical game? If the drama replaces ends with means, do we view this reversal in negative terms as a rejection of familiar notions of order, overturning or deconstructing our need for ends and for closure? Or do we view it more positively as discovering a new aesthetic, an interest not in the catastrophic end of tragedy, but in something closer to the continuous process of everyday life? This is not a trivial question, and to answer it will require looking more closely at some of the other ways in which this play subverts or refashions a sense of order. A more general question follows from the first. In reading the plot and the way in which it negotiates various ends, must we assume that it is somehow engaged in constructing or demolishing a sense of order? Or do we need and can we find a model that presupposes neither a revised notion of closure nor a gesture of anti-closure? Finally, we might ask whether we are asking the right questions at all. Criticism has recently shifted its attention from texts to contexts, and in the process from anticlosure to closure. Whereas poststructuralists, in rejecting the aesthetic unity of New Criticism, celebrated various subversions of unity, authority, and ideology, cultural criticism tends to find a new, overriding order in the cultural system that shapes and determines literary production. So perhaps, instead of trying to explain reversals in the narrative, we should be looking for a larger order that shapes the text from without. In the sections that follow, I attempt to open up a critical "middle" by turning to notions of order that are more dependent upon the play's social and cultural context. In so doing, I hope to describe more fully the problems of closure that are posed in *Heracles*, and I shall examine some critical approaches that address these problems in useful ways.

DIVINE ENDS

In the last scene of *Heracles*, as the final end of suicide is overturned, the hero must learn to make his way without the benefit of familiar ends or goals. And the lack of known precedents for his career in Athens creates for the spectators a correlative uncertainty or lack of bearings. But it does not follow that an end or purpose is entirely absent. It may be that mortal affairs acquire coherence only when seen from a privileged vantage, and that our mortal hero simply lacks access to the larger divine ends that govern his life. As we shall see, divine ends give explicit direction to the action of this play—without providing a greater sense of coherence.

Traditionally, the story of Heracles is watched over by two gods and by two conflicting divine purposes. Zeus, the father of Heracles by Alcmene, favors his success and rewards his son with the divine end of apotheosis.[16]

---

[16] Zeus often felt concern for Heracles, and sent Athena to help him (*Il.* 8.362–65); and in

Hera, on the other hand, hates this illegitimate child and makes every effort to harm or destroy him. As the story is usually told, the two designs are naturally subordinated one to the other: Heracles' long and painful suffering at the hands of Hera is eventually rewarded with his father's gift of apotheosis. But in Euripides' version there is no such logic.[17] The reward comes first with the deliverance of Heracles from Hades and his family from Lycus, and this happy end is then wiped out by the madness sent from Hera; one plan is canceled out by the other. In this version, the happy end sanctioned by Zeus is not apotheosis but deliverance from danger and death, yet Euripides takes pains to portray it as a similar demonstration of Zeus's favor toward his son. In the prologue, Amphitryon, Megara, and the children take refuge at the altar of Zeus the Savior, testing the god's readiness to help the family of his son, and reminding us that the altar was dedicated by Heracles himself (48–50). The challenge issued by this ritual gesture is repeated in words as Amphitryon denounces Zeus as an unworthy father of Heracles and as a foolish and unjust god if he will not protect them (341–47). He later repeats the challenge: "I call on you, Zeus, throwing my hands to heaven—if you mean to help these children at all, protect them now. Soon you won't be able" (498–500). And when Heracles returns in safety and rescues his family, this proves that he is indeed the son of Zeus (696, 804) and that the justice of the gods has been realized (737–39, 772–73). It is this happy end clearly portrayed as the design of Zeus that is then overturned by the design of Hera; as Iris says:

> At first, before he finished his bitter labors,
> necessity saved him, and his father Zeus
> never allowed me or Hera to do him harm.
> But now he's performed the tasks of Eurystheus,
> Hera wants to taint him with new blood,
> with the murder of his children, and I do too.

> (827–32)

In the prologue, Amphitryon described Heracles' labors as sufferings inflicted by Hera or necessity (20–21)—sufferings that will only be relieved with the help of Zeus Soter. But now, as the design of Zeus is overturned, Iris describes the same labors as a temporary reprieve offered by Zeus from the sufferings that Hera will inflict (828–29). Elsewhere the subordination of Hera's designs to those of Zeus gives a belated purpose to his sufferings, but here the overthrow of Zeus's plan by Hera's has the opposite effect.

---

vase painting, when Heracles reaches Olympus, Zeus receives him: see, for example, plate 26 in March 1987.

[17] On Euripides' probable reversal of the order of labors and madness, see Bond 1981, xxviii–xxx. Commentators often note a different effect of this reversal, namely the heightened pathos and "tragic senselessness" of Hera's revenge; thus Arrowsmith 1956, 47.

After one god has had her way with the man, which god will then be waiting his turn? The uncertainty is driven home by Lyssa's explicit reminder that Hera's punishment of Heracles is not deserved (849–54).

But the play does not simply leave us with one divine end upstaged by its opposite; it leaves us with several competing purposes. Most intriguing is that of Athena, who according to the messenger saved Amphitryon and put an end to Heracles' madness: "But an image appeared, looking like Athena and brandishing a spear; she threw a rock against Heracles' chest, which checked his frenzied slaughter and sent him to sleep" (1002–6).[18] This intervention is appropriate for a goddess who often assisted Heracles in his labors;[19] and it seems to hint at another divine plan, a personal protection that will guarantee Heracles' eventual success, just as Athena guarantees the favorable outcome of the *Odyssey*. The part she plays here, however, fails to suggest a larger purpose. First, the messenger cannot be sure he really saw Athena: "An image arrived that looked like Pallas," he reports, ἀλλ᾽ ἦλθεν εἰκών, ὡς ὁρᾶν ἐφαίνετο / Παλλάς (1002–3). And her intentions remain obscure. There is no preparation for her entrance, no explanation of her action, and no hint of a larger design; she hits him with a rock and he falls asleep. After this sudden and enigmatic intervention, Athena is not heard of again.[20]

A succession of unpredictable and conflicting designs has little to commend it over the workings of chance. In fact, these various divine ends share pride of place with τύχη or chance, which plays an important role in *Heracles*.[21] Amphitryon places a high value on not being anchored to chance (μὴ 'κ τύχης ὡρμισμένον, 203); it is chance that destroyed Amphitryon (509), and chance reversals that may alter at any moment the fortunes of Lycus (216), Megara (480), or the people of Thebes (766). Chance in general is not the active and pernicious force that we find personified in the fourth century and later; it is instead an unpredictability, an absence of coherence that in this play is hard to distinguish from the de-

---

[18] I omit from translation the corrupt ἐπὶ λόφῳ κέαρ in 1003.

[19] According to Homer, Athena helped Heracles in his labors (*Il.* 8.362–63) and escorted him back from Hades with Cerberus (*Od.* 11.626). She is shown helping him in metopes of the Temple of Zeus at Olympia, and in vase painting regularly accompanies the hero to Olympus; see Mingazzini 1925.

[20] There may be an earlier allusion to the same episode at 907–8. Either Amphitryon or the chorus addresses either Heracles or Athena (ὦ Διὸς παῖ); if Heracles, his slaughter of his family is compared to Athena's famous defeat of Enceladus (Παλλάς, third person); if Athena, she is now causing an unspecified confusion (τάραγμα ταρτάρειον) as she did against Enceladus (Παλλάς, vocative), a confusion not specified until 1002–6.

[21] It is mentioned more often in this play (15 times) than in any extant play except *Helen* (24 times), *Ion* (18 times), and *Hippolytus* (16 times). It occurs 15 times also in *Iphigenia Among the Taurians*.

signs of the gods.[22] Is Heracles a subject of Hera's plans for revenge, or is he instead a slave to chance (τῇ τύχῃ δουλευτέον, 1357)? Did Hera's anger destroy the hero, or was it chance (καὶ τοὺς σθένοντας γὰρ κα-θαιροῦσιν τύχαι, 1396)? Or are the two somehow, paradoxically, the same (πάντες ἐξολώλαμεν / Ἥρας μιᾷ πληγέντες ἄθλιοι τύχῃ, "Wretches, we are all destroyed, struck by a single blow of chance from Hera," 1392–93)?

If we look to the divine realm for a larger perspective that will make sense of the action, we find instead a confusion of ends, a multiplicity of purposes that fails to form a coherent whole. This experience is shared by the play's protagonists. In the opening scenes, as Heracles' family faces almost certain death, Amphitryon denounces Zeus for failing to uphold justice: "In virtue I, a mortal, defeat you, a mighty god" (342), "You are either an ignorant god or born unjust" (347). After Heracles' victorious return, however, the chorus happily proclaims that the justice of the gods prevails (737–79, 772–73). And after the murder of his family, when Theseus invokes the example of the gods, Heracles emphatically rejects their example:

> I don't believe the gods love forbidden
> beds and fasten chains to their hands;
> I never did and never will suppose
> that one god is another's master.
> God, if he is truly god, needs nothing;
> those are the worthless words of poets.
>
> (1341–46)

There is of course a contradiction: if stories of divine incest and violence are untrue, how can we believe the story of Zeus's adultery with Alcmene? The contradiction is only heightened by repeated reminders of the active role Hera has played (1253, 1263–64, 1266–68, 1303–10, 1311–12, 1393) and of the adultery that aroused her jealousy (1263–64, 1268, 1309). But contradiction at this point has its own logic.[23] At the end of this disastrous and inscrutable story, we are left not with the vehement rejections of Amphitryon nor with the facile celebrations of the chorus, but with a divide between the way things are and the way they ought to be. Various attempts have been made to remove these inconsistencies, either by restoring a simple divine scheme or by removing it entirely. Burnett argues that the plot is an ironic version of traditional theodicy, in which the spectators (but not the characters) recognize the hybris of Megara and the divine honors ac-

---

[22] On τύχη in Euripides, see Meuss 1899, 10–14.
[23] On the importance of this contradiction, see Halleran 1986.

corded to Heracles. Others have argued that a divine scheme is abandoned, and is replaced by a mortal world and humane values.[24] But it seems to me that *Heracles* leaves us in a much more complicated middle, where familiar ends lack authority, but new ends are not available to take their place.

HEROIC ENDS

Heracles, more than any other extant play of Euripides, is about the hero; it focuses upon a single exemplary hero and his exploits, and it asks how and why he is special. So if ends are inconclusive in the mortal narrative and the divine superplot, perhaps we can find them instead in the heroic ideal, in cultural values that the drama reflects or interprets. In this play there are three ways in which this ideal is most clearly embodied: in the hero's weapon, in his birth, and in his death.

In art and in drama, there are three visual props or icons that regularly identify Heracles and represent his labors: his club, his lion skin, and his bow. In this play only the bow is important. This enhances dramatic economy, and identifies the hero more closely with the various labors he performed with the bow; but it also marks him with a dubious emblem. The bow conventionally distinguished cowardly Persians from Greek soldiers (Aeschylus *Persians* 146–49) and Scythian slaves from Athenian citizens (Aristophanes *Acharnians* 707). And in epic it regularly denotes the antihero: Odysseus, who preferred cunning survival to the heroism of Achilles, was a bowman, and so, too, was the infamous Paris, whom Diomedes denounces in the *Iliad*: "Archer, scoundrel glorying in your bow, philanderer, if you and your weapons were put to the test that bow would do you no good, nor a host of arrows" (11.385–87).[25] In *Women of Trachis* Sophocles emphasized the heroic stature of Heracles by making little mention of the bow;[26] but Euripides revels in the problem. Early in the play, the bow becomes a subject of debate as Lycus denounces Heracles for using a coward's weapon:

> And [he is] especially cowardly
> because he never wore a shield on his left arm
> or came near a spear, but holding his bow

[24] Ironic theodicy: Burnett 1971, 157–82. Rejection of the traditional divine scheme: Conacher 1967, 88–90. The divine sphere and divine parentage replaced by the mortal world: Gregory 1977. A traditional contract with the gods replaced by a more humane and moral one: Yunis 1988, 139–71.

[25] Aeneas likewise taunts Pandarus the bowman, who curses his bow (*Il.* 5.171–78, 204–16); compare Hera taunting Artemis the archer (*Il.* 21.483, 491).

[26] The bow is mentioned only twice (266, 512–17), and emphasis is placed instead on Heracles' hands (488, 517, 1047, 1089, 1102, 1133).

(that worthless weapon) stood ready to flee.
A bow is no test of a man's courage—
but one who stands and looks unflinching
at the spear's swift furrow and holds his rank.

(158–64)

Real heroes face off with spears, standing their ground and looking one another in the eye. The hero, of course, is a cultural construct, and in Lycus's criticism we see an interesting slippage from the distinctly aristocratic point of view represented in Homer (where princes in heavy armor fear and disdain extras who need only bows and arrows) to the more egalitarian viewpont of the hoplite (the armored infantryman in close formation who fears and despises the more mobile bowman). But in each case the bowman is an outsider, a suspect opportunist who subscribes neither to the rules of gentlemanly warfare nor to the hoplite's civic loyalties.[27] When Amphitryon answers Lycus, defending Heracles and his use of the bow, he makes no attempt to rehabilitate his weapon, but openly praises the crass expedience of one who uses it: "He stands far off and holds the enemy at bay by wounding them with weapons they cannot see; he never shows his body to those who face him, but remains well-guarded. This is wisdom in battle" (τοῦτο δ' ἐν μάχῃ / σοφὸν μάλιστα, 198–202). Long before Heracles enters onstage, we find that the emblem that sets him apart represents cowardice and expedience as much as any positive virtue.

The actions performed by the bow are equally problematic. Heracles' labors, of course, are described in positive terms, and these great deeds are repeatedly described as the work of his bow (366, 367, 392, 423). But so, too, is the bloody and perhaps excessive revenge he vows against the Thebans ("I'll handle them with this victorious weapon and fill all Ismenus with slaughtered corpses, tearing them apart with winged arrows," 570–72). And so is the murder of his family. The messenger tells with chilling emphasis how Heracles called for his bow (942), readied his quiver and bow against his children (969–70), took aim at the first son and hit him by the liver (978–79), crushed the second with his club because he was too close for the bow (991), and finally killed the third and Megara with a single arrow (1000). The grisly narrative empties the weapon of any positive, heroic associations. Finally, at the end of the play, as the hero prepares

---

[27] If Lycus endorses the civic solidarity of hoplites, it does not follow that Heracles embodies an opposing set of values. Foley, for example, wants Heracles' bow to represent an older, individualistic heroism, while Michelini wants it to represent a newer, sophistic heroism (see Foley 1985, 167–75; and Michelini 1987, 242–46). Neither is correct. Odysseus's personal and domestic vendetta against the suitors is hardly an archetype of heroic warfare, while the sophistic tone of Amphitryon's debate with Lycus does not necessarily characterize Heracles himself. Otherwise, both have good observations on the bow and its connotations, as does Hamilton (1985).

to leave for Athens, he ponders whether or not to take his bow. Can he bear to take it with him, since it is now a sign that speaks of his hideous murder? (And it literally speaks, as Heracles imagines it saying, "Wearing us, you wear your children's killer," 1380–81.) Can he possibly leave it behind, stripping himself of this mark of his greatness (1382–83)? He does neither, keeping it reluctantly not as a mark of his past achievement nor to perform future exploits, but simply as a means of self-defense (1384–85), concluding ἀθλίως δὲ σωστέον, "In wretched manner it must be preserved" (1385). The bow has been emptied of meaning, and the man has been shorn of heroic distinction.

Heroic stature presumes heroic beginnings, and Heracles' greatness is also defined by his birth. A central concern of the play is the hero's parentage, and the problem of establishing whether Amphitryon or Zeus was his father. The question is a familiar one: Greek kings and princes regularly traced their lineage back to the gods, and based their privileged position upon this authority. Achilles, as the son of a goddess, began with a privilege that he parlays into special honors at Troy. And because Achilles is by birth half mortal and half immortal, son of Peleus and Thetis, he has been given the further privilege of choosing between the two, living a long but mortal life or pursuing immortal glory (*Il.* 9.410–16).[28] Heracles also has a choice between mortal and immortal parentage, but he must choose between the competing claims of different fathers, Amphitryon and Zeus.[29] The play dwells on this paradox in order to present Heracles' choice not as the pursuit of his privileged or more common pedigree, but as a crisis about his very identity. Is he, like Achilles, part mortal and part divine, or is he entirely mortal? Can he, as the son of Zeus and Alcmene, aspire to a privileged end, or must he, as the son of Amphitryon and Alcmene, accept his common humanity? The problem is framed in the opening words of the play, where Amphitryon describes himself both as the father of Heracles (πατέρα τόνδ' Ἡρακλέους, 3) and as one who shared his marriage bed with Zeus (τὸν Διὸς σύλλεκτρον, 1). At the height of Heracles' success, after Lycus has been killed, the chorus finds it easy to decide: "Your ancient marriage, Zeus, has unexpectedly been proven true, and time has shown the glorious strength of Heracles" (801–6). And in the depth of Heracles' despair, as he explains to Theseus why he has nothing to live for, a different answer will seem obvious: "Zeus, whoever Zeus is, fathered me as an enemy for Hera—but don't be angry, old man: I consider you and not Zeus my father" (1263–65). Stories associated with Her-

---

[28] Of course, the special stature of Achilles (divine mother, explicit choice of lives) embodies values and aspirations shared by all the princes at Troy. On heroic ideology more generally, see Murnaghan, Chapter 2 in this volume.

[29] On the theme of dual parentage, see esp. Gregory 1977.

acles include a number of intriguing ambiguities (hunter/warrior, hero/buffoon, even male/female),[30] but it is his contradictory parentage to which this play most clearly draws attention. In the final scene, this conflict is restated but not resolved: Heracles will regard Amphitryon as his father (ἡγοῦμαι, 1265) although he knows that Zeus fathered him (ἐγείνατο, 1263)—whoever Zeus is (ὅστις ὁ Ζεύς, 1263)!

The hero has a privileged beginning and a distinctive emblem, but he is defined above all by his end; the way in which a man chooses to end his life is central to the heroic ideal. The archetypal hero is Achilles in the *Iliad*, who makes a choice between two ends, a long and uneventful life at home or an early but glorious death at Troy; the way in which Achilles makes and lives out this choice secures his heroic stature. The choice is not open to everyone. Common soldiers die common deaths; their ends are not interesting. But a prince like Hector or Achilles may end his life in a way that secures immortal fame. Wealthy and noble athletes like Cleobis and Biton likewise earned heroic honors by dying at the height of their glory (Hdt. 1.31). And the "heroic temper" in Sophoclean drama presupposes a noble figure who chooses a brief and self-destructive career: the heroic death of Antigone, for example, rather than the banal survival of Ismene.[31] The antihero also has his place, and the archetype here is Odysseus the cunning survivor, who chooses a long life instead of glory (compare *Od.* 11.487–91) and family instead of immortality (compare 5.215–20); but he is a foil to the self-destructive hero who holds a privileged place in Greek culture and drama. Sophocles' Ajax, for example, after slaughtering the animals in his madness, realizes that the only way to salvage what remains of his heroic stature is to choose death by suicide:

> It's cowardly for a man to want long life
> when he has no end of troubles;
> when day after day (παρ' ἦμαρ ἡμέρα) brings him closer to
> death, then inches him back—what pleasure in that?
> I don't give a fig for the man who
> warms himself with empty hopes (κεναῖσιν ἐλπίσιν);
> a noble man must either live with honor or die
> with honor. There's nothing more to say.
>
> (*Ajax* 473–80)

The hero has no interest in the continuing troubles of life day after day, παρ' ἦμαρ ἡμέρα. His task is to secure the best possible end.[32]

---

[30] On Heracles' liminal qualities, compare Silk 1985. On male/female ambivalence, see Loraux 1990.

[31] Cleobis and Biton were endowed with the triad of good birth, sufficient wealth, and bodily strength (Hdt. 1.31.2). On the Sophoclean hero, see Knox 1964.

[32] Sophocles' play goes on to examine in a critical way the traditional values that Ajax

Heracles begins with just such a choice—one that faces not an Achilles or an Ajax, but the helpless members of Heracles' family, his wife and his frail father. Facing certain death at the hands of Lycus, what should they do? Megara, worn down by the day-after-day, eaten away by the painful time in between (ὁ δ' ἐν μέσῳ γε λυπρὸς ὢν δάκνει χρόνος, 94), prefers to imitate her husband's virtue (294) and choose a noble death (307–8). Amphitryon, on the other hand, clings to hope (καὶ φιλῶ τὰς ἐλπίδας, 91) in the faith that since all things change, they will change for the better (101–4). When Lycus prepares to kill them at the altar, Megara finally convinces her father-in-law to choose a heroic death. Yet this end is paradoxical: first, because the woman, not the man, chooses the more heroic course; and second, because Megara's noble gesture consists in accepting the sacrilegious murder of suppliants. The familiar problem of choosing a heroic end is now a difficult and uncertain affair.[33]

The ambivalence of this choice is reinforced by the return of Heracles, whose victorious entrance vindicates not the noble gesture of his wife but the craven hopes of his father. Yet his return also upstages this problem by turning attention to revenge against Lycus. After Heracles kills the tyrant, the chorus sings his praises and calls upon Thebes and the Muses to honor the victorious Heracles (τὸν Ἡρακλέους / καλλίνικον ἀγῶνα, 781–97). Yet here we come to a more serious paradox, for the hero who has saved his family, overthrown the tyrant, and delivered his city, who has completed his labors and guaranteed his fame, will have nothing to do with the heroic ideal. He disowns his labors, renounces the title of Victor, and values not deeds that set him apart from other men, but simple concerns that he shares with them all ("All people are equal: the better sorts love their children, and so do those who are nothing," 633–35); he turns from public deeds and heroic acclaim to the private and everyday concern of looking after his family and raising children (θεράπευμα τέκνων, 633), from slaying monsters to changing diapers. As he departs offstage, this conflict between heroic stature and common aspirations remains unresolved.

The next time we see Heracles, as he awakes after murdering his family, he must choose, like Ajax, between an honorable death and a life of shame. But unlike Ajax, he eventually renounces suicide. The decision is played out in a debate between Heracles and Theseus that reenacts the opening debate between Megara and Amphityron: one argues for salvaging some

---

embodies; see Murnaghan 1989. On Sophocles' version of the story as a rehabilitation of Ajax, see March 1991–93. Whereas in Sophocles such values are both reconstructed and reaffirmed, in Euripides they are not.

[33] The paradox is emphasized by Amphitryon's perversion of heroic values: "That man is best who always trusts in hope," οὗτος δ' ἀνὴρ ἄριστος ὅστις ἐλπίσιν / πέποιθεν αἰεί (105–6); compare Bond 1981, ad loc.

shred of honor by meeting death voluntarily; the other paradoxically argues that honor consists in accepting calamity. The similarity between the scenes is reinforced by a double echo, as the end of Theseus's first speech repeats the morals that conclude each of Amphitryon's speeches (1223–25 and 55–59 on the inconstancy of friends; 1227–28 and 105–6 on the nobility of endurance). And the paradox is heightened as Theseus, the young and vigorous king, argues for patience and endurance—and does so by appealing to Heracles' heroic stature: "Does Heracles of the many labors say that?" (1250), "Is this the great friend and benefactor of men?" (1252), "Have you so little memory of your labors?" (1410), "Where now is that famous Heracles?" (1414).[34] The mighty hero is summoned to the ordinary task of living and getting by, while the heroic gesture of suicide is rejected as common:

> THESEUS: So what will you do? Where will passion carry you?
> HERACLES: To die, and go where I came from, beneath the earth.
> THESEUS: Those are the words of an ordinary man (ἐπιτυχόντος ἀνθρώπου).
>
> (1246–48)

Heroic values have been inverted, and now the simple task of living is greater than all of Heracles' labors (1411).

Where does this leave us? The choice of a heroic end is constantly questioned, but so, too, is the alternative; Heracles may reject the end of the hero, but he does not adopt the antiheroic values of the wily Odysseus or the long-suffering Amphitryon. Somehow, Heracles rejects the heroic gesture of suicide without proclaiming or adopting a different set of values; with his family dead, his values discredited, his world in ruins, he nevertheless decides to live. What is he living for? We don't know, and perhaps neither does he. All he has is the friendship of Theseus, and that is not an end, a goal, or a purpose; it is simply a very ordinary means of getting by, a modest but valuable aid in the struggle, the process of life. Many critics have exalted this acceptance into a new virtue, a new goal that offers consolation amid despair and gives meaning to a shattered world.[35] But there is no redemption in this play, in what Ajax calls the endless trouble of day after day; just a challenge to which Heracles responds with ordinary courage. If meeting this challenge will eventually define new, more humane values, that must be another story; this hero and what he represents are completely destroyed (πανώλεις, 1424).

---

[34] A loose translation of the received text: ὁ κλεινὸς Ἡρακλῆς ποῦ κεῖνος ὤν; Wilamowitz's emendation (οὐκ εἶ νοσῶν) gives clearer but more prosaic sense.

[35] On the theme of friendship, see discussion below, with note 46. On new, humane values, see Chalk 1962; on nobility emerging from catastrophe, see Shelton 1979.

CIVIC ENDS

As Heracles lingers on the threshold, poised between catastrophic past and unknown future, we at least know his destination. And as the spectators turn from the horrors of the drama to their everyday lives in Athens, it is surely appropriate that Heracles makes his way to the same city. Is this the end we have been looking for—a civic closure that lurks at the edges of the drama?[36] Will Heracles leave behind the play's terrible reversals, and find order and coherence in the political and religious institutions of Athens? This is an important question, and it brings us back to the role of Theseus.

Theseus, as surrogate deus ex machina, promises to give an effective end to the narrative; and as representative of Athens, he likewise presents the city as a literal and metaphorical end to the hero's career. His second, political role is a familiar one. When Theseus arrives with an army, when he shows concern for the polluted and exiled Heracles, when he offers him a place of refuge and promises to settle him on Athenian soil, he is the statesman who embodies Athenian values by protecting suppliants. When the children in *Children of Heracles* want to escape unlawful persecution by Eurystheus and the Argives, the sons of Theseus offer them protection in Athens. When the suppliants in *Suppliant Women* want to guard the bodies of the Seven from Theban sacrilege, it is Theseus in Athens who offers them protection and support. And when Oedipus at Colonus is threatened with violence by Creon and the Thebans, it is Theseus again who offers him refuge and military protection. Even Medea, contemplating exile from Corinth, turns to Aegeus, the father of Theseus, for a place of refuge in Athens. Medea looks forward to a reception that stands outside the action (and that she will betray by plotting against Theseus), but in the other plays, the act of receiving and defending suppliants is successfully performed in an Athenian setting, at Marathon, Eleusis, or Colonus. And the generous actions of Theseus and his sons, and the civic righteousness they represent, are commemorated in the resulting burials of Eurystheus, the Seven against Thebes, and Oedipus, in Athenian soil. When Theseus offers help to the outcast Heracles, he promises a similar happy end of protection in Athens and commemoration after death (1331–33).

Yet if Theseus's role as deus is ambiguous, so, too, is his role as civic ambassador. Most telling is the fact that Theseus has no official, political authority. In other plays he and his son are invested with the authority of general or king, an authority that derives from the sovereign powers of the

---

[36] On the play's patriotic resolution, see Parmentier 1959, 8–9; for a more subtle account of its patriotism, see Tarkow 1977.

city.[37] In this play he comes to Heracles not as ambassador of the city, but simply as a kinsman and a friend (Θησεὺς ὅδ' ἕρπει συγγενὴς φίλος τ' ἐμός, 1154). In other plays, Theseus or Demophon offers refuge because both divine law and the reputation of the city require it (*Children of Heracles* 236–46, *Suppliant Women* 301–31; compare *Oedipus at Colonus* 913–14, 921–23), and in *Suppliant Women* this gesture is explicitly approved by the demos (355, 394) and is defended in debate by invoking Athenian democratic values (399–455). In *Heracles*, when Theseus helps Heracles he is acting as a private citizen, and returning the private favor that Heracles performed by rescuing him from Hades. Even the concrete offers he makes to Heracles are private rather than public ones: houses, money, and gifts that Theseus will give to his friend (1325–28).[38] In other plays the Athenian setting is decisive. The suppliants arrive at Marathon, Eleusis, or Colonus, where they are protected by the moral authority and the weapons of the Athenians, and where burial in Attic soil will bear witness to the city's virtuous deeds. In *Heracles*, on the other hand, Athens is a general destination—not a setting in which the crisis is resolved, but the venue for an unknown future. Nor is it a privileged site of burial; after death, the hero will be honored in Athens (1331–33), but there is no suggestion that he will be buried there.[39]

Theseus as ambassador of the city is no more effective than Theseus as deus ex machina. The most important difference between his role here and in other plays is that civic resolution remains a promise for the future rather than an end realized by the drama. So what does that future hold? An obvious parallel is Ion, who is told that he will be adopted into the royal family and will become the leading citizen of Athens. Yet even this most generous promise is not without its drawbacks. When Ion considers his place as a foreigner, and the jealousy he will arouse in his new household and new city, he decides it would be better not to go (*Ion* 585–647). In *Heracles*, however, there are no such promises and no such questions. We have no idea what role Heracles the foreigner and murderer can or will

---

[37] Authority: ἄναξ, *Children of Heracles* 114, *Suppliant Women* 113, 164, 367; προστάτης, *Children of Heracles* 206; ἀλκιμώτατον κάρα, *Suppliant Women* 163; compare *Oedipus at Colonus* 67, 549. Sovereign powers: ἐλευθέρα, *Children of Heracles* 62, 113, 198, etc., *Suppliant Women* 405, 477; self-government, *Children of Heracles* 423–24, *Suppliant Women* 403–8; compare *Oedipus at Colonus* 557–58.

[38] The honors bestowed by the city (1331–33), on the other hand, remain promises of what will happen after Heracles dies; compare note 11 above and discussion below. It is often assumed without argument that Theseus represents the city; thus Tarkow 1977, 28, and Foley 1985, 165.

[39] Compare *Medea*, where Aegeus enters not as a king but as a friend, and where Athens remains a future destination. An important difference is that the story of Medea's exile in Athens, unlike that of Heracles, was apparently known to the audience; see, e.g., Gantz 1993, 255–56.

play in the life of the city. The hero's future remains uncertain, a tabula rasa for which legend offers no precedent.[40]

Theseus does not have clear political authority, and he does not offer a political or civic resolution. The same is true for ritual closure. Theseus on his own behalf promises to purify the hands of Heracles (χέρας σὰς ἁγνίσας μιάσματος, 1324, with no mention of a god who will authorize this rite, as Apollo does in *Eumenides*); and he promises that after Heracles' death the whole city will honor him with festivals and shrines (θυσίαισι λαΐνοισί τ' ἐξογκώμασιν / τίμιον ἀνάξει πᾶσ' 'Αθηναίων πόλις, 1332–33). But the promise is not anchored in the specifics of cult. In *Suppliant Women* the particular act of securing burial for the Seven is commemorated both with tripod and knife guaranteeing friendship between Athens and Argos, and with a shrine marking where the bodies were cremated. In *Heracles*, on the other hand, there is no such reciprocity. Heracles will be honored in Athens, but not, as far as we are told, in a particular way, at a particular place, or for a particular reason.[41] Members of the audience may recognize a reference to various local Heracleia, but the allusion does not invest them with much significance: the festivals are unnamed (θυσίαισι), and the shrines are only heaps of rock (λαΐνοισί τ' ἐξογκώμασιν, 1332).

I suggested above that the false ends of the narrative are reprised by the deus who is no deus. And it seems to me that the empty or unrealized promise of civic closure likewise reprises an uncertain relation to public values and ideology. *Heracles* is not overtly political or topical, but it engages in a dialectic on civic values in at least three ways. First let us return to Heracles and his bow. We noted above how Lycus mocked Heracles by contrasting the bowman's cowardice with the honor of those who fight with the spear. But this leaves him open, at least before an Athenian audience, to an obvious rejoinder dismissing the spearman's sneer as aristocratic and undemocratic. In a similar debate in Sophocles' *Ajax*, this is exactly how Teucer responds; when Menelaus attacks him as a cowardly bowman, Teucer turns the jibe to his own advantage:

MENELAUS:	The archer seems to put on airs.
TEUCER:	This is no menial craft I've learned.
MENELAUS:	You could truly boast if you carried a shield.
TEUCER:	Even without one I'm a match for you fully armed.

[40] Walker (1994, 134) notes the "marginal" place Heracles will occupy in Athens, but generally (132–35) subscribes to the view that the hero is integrated into the city; compare note 15 above.

[41] There were altars and sanctuaries of Heracles throughout Attica, as detailed in Woodford 1971; but if Euripides "plants his Heracles solidly in the soil and national history of Athens" (Mikalson 1986, 98), he does so in a curiously vague and generic manner.

MENELAUS: What awesome courage your tongue begets!
TEUCER: He who is right may put on airs.

(Ajax 1120–25)

But Amphitryon makes no such reply to Lycus. Instead of defending the humble honor of the bowman, he mocks the spearman's dependence upon close, disciplined ranks (190–94), praises the bowman's ability to inflict harm while staying out of reach (195–201), and finds wisdom in saving one's skin: "In battle this is most wise, to harm your enemies and preserve your body, and not depend on chance" (201–3). It may be, as some have argued, that recent battles had shown the advantages of light infantry over heavily armed hoplites,[42] but that is not the line Amphitryon takes; he is not talking strategy but explicitly praising the expedience that Lycus denounced. And if he appropriates traditional attitudes toward harming enemies, his refutation of Lycus issues in a sophistic challenge to the solidarity that was essential in war, both in facing the shock of battle and in framing public policy.[43] Amphitryon's rejoinder does little to defend the honor of Heracles, and it indirectly challenges the civic solidarity that was an essential feature of Athenian ideology; as Pericles says in Thucydides, "We are equally concerned with our own affairs and with those of the city; . . . when a man takes no part in affairs of the city, we alone say, not that he causes no trouble, but that he is good for nothing" (2.40).

Civic and political issues are raised more directly by Lycus, who embodies the evils of tyranny just as Theseus traditionally embodies the virtues of democracy. As Amphitryon tells us in the prologue, Lycus is a foreigner who took power by exploiting civil unrest and by murdering the rightful ruler (32–4). As we soon learn, he has no respect for suppliants, threatening to murder them at the altar, and he has no respect for family ties, planning to murder the helpless father, wife, and children of Heracles. This arrogance is crowned with violent threats against the chorus of bystanders:

> As for you, old men, who oppose
> my will, you won't be wailing just
> for Heracles' children but for the fate of
> your house; I'll teach you to remember that
> you are slaves to my tyranny (τῆς ἐμῆς τυραννίδος).

(247–51)

Heracles, who murders the tyrant and liberates the city, ought to embody the opposite qualities of moderation and respect for the claims of suppliants

---

[42] See Parmentier 1959, 11–13; and Bowra 1944, 53–54.

[43] Sophistic associations are reinforced by πάνσοφον δ' εὕρημα (188) and σοφὸν μάλιστα (202); compare Michelini 1987, 245.

and dependants. And to some extent he does, especially in his newfound love for children. But he is also Lycus's double, performing the very same acts of lawless violence. He will even the score with Lycus by cutting off his head and throwing it to the dogs (566–68); he will attack the Thebans almost indiscriminately, not only punishing those who showed ingratitude (Καδμείων δ᾽ ὅσους, 568–70) but slaughtering many innocent people besides ("And others [τοὺς δὲ] I will tear apart with winged arrows, filling all Ismenus with slaughtered corpses, and the clear stream of Dirce will flow with blood," 571–73); and in his madness he acts out the crimes of Lycus, taking revenge on Eurystheus by dishonoring his suppliant father and murdering his helpless children: "Thinking [Amphitryon] was the father of Eurystheus, he pushed him away as he anxiously tried to grasp his hand in supplication (προταρβοῦνθ᾽ ἱκέσιον ψαύειν χερός), and readied his quiver and bow against his own children, thinking he was murdering the sons of Eurystheus" (967–71). In Heracles and his madness the familiar contrast between tyranny and democracy becomes confused.

A third negotiation of civic values involves the great ode celebrating the labors of Heracles (348–441). As Bond observes (on 359ff.), the traditionally Peloponnesian emphasis of these exploits has been shifted to represent the world at large: northern and southern Greece, the distant East and distant West. The effect, however, is not just to downplay the hero's mainland, Dorian connections, but to suggest instead Athenian naval enterprise throughout the Mediterranean. In particular, Heracles' task of pacifying the world is recast as an extension of Athenian imperial power. The labor involving the mares of Diomedes is no longer vaguely located in Thrace (compare *Alcestis* 491–98) but is now situated "beyond the banks of Hebrus that flow with silver," πέραν / δ᾽ ἀργυρορρύτων Ἕβρου / . . . ὄχθων (386–88), alluding to the silver mines that were an important source of revenue for Athens. The minor story of the Amazon's girdle introduces Heracles sailing "around Maiotis of many rivers and across the swell of the Euxine sea," Μαιῶτιν ἀμφὶ πολυπόταμον / ἔβα δι᾽ Εὔξεινον οἶδμα λίμνας (409–10)[44]—in other words, on the north shore of the Black Sea where Athenian settlements were established to support the vital grain trade. And a new labor altogether is added, one that strongly suggests Athenian success in policing the Mediterranean: "And he entered all the corners of the sea, establishing calm for mortal oars" (ποντίας θ᾽ ἁλὸς μυχοὺς / εἰσέβαινε, θνατοῖς / γαλανείας τιθεὶς ἐρετμοῖς, 400–402). The language is strikingly similar to that used by Pericles in the Funeral Oration: "But we have forced every sea and every land to give access to our ventures" (ἀλλὰ πᾶσαν μὲν θάλασσαν καὶ γῆν ἐσβατὸν

---

[44] I give the received text in 410; Diggle prints Markland's emendation ἄξεινον.

τῇ ἡμετέρᾳ τόλμῃ καταναγκάσαντες γενέσθαι, 2.41).[45] It is no surprise that Athenians celebrated their imperial achievements, but there is something strange about Heracles, the Dorian hero, carrying the banner of the Athenian empire. The ode confuses opposing ideologies, and shortly thereafter the Dorian paragon and his naval achievements are overturned by Heracles himself, who returns from Hades and renounces his labors (574–82). This anticipates the personal and apolitical Heracles of the epilogue, who will complement the personal and apolitical Theseus. But it does so in a manner that we might better call antipolitical, as the choral ode's celebration of imperial success is renounced, and each hero is stripped of his civic identity.

Civic ends are as elusive as narrative, divine, or heroic ends. In the course of the play, Heracles' political status is confused and weakened, and in the epilogue, Theseus is an unconvincing ambassador of Athenian values. Heracles and Theseus become not symbols of opposing cities and ideologies, but individuals motivated by a personal bond of friendship. This raises a familiar question of closure and anticlosure. Is the emphasis of the play essentially negative, abandoning coherent structure and rejecting familiar divine, heroic, and civic ends? Or is it more positive, creating a new form and describing new mortal, common, and personal values? I have argued in general for a negative interpretation: the catastrophe is complete, and there are no new ends to replace what is lost. Spectators leave the theater with a clear sense of loss, as do members of the chorus: "We go in grief, with much lament; we have lost the greatest of friends" (στείχομεν οἰκτροὶ καὶ πολύκλαυτοι, / τὰ μέγιστα φίλων ὀλέσαντες, 1427–28). On the other hand, it is because Theseus fails as a deus that he is able to approach Heracles as one man to another; and it is because he fails as a statesman that he is able to be a friend. Amid the rubble of familiar values and familiar notions of order, this friendship somehow helps Heracles survive; the hero does not reach an end or a beginning, but does at least have a means of keeping on.[46]

ENDS AND MEANS

Is this the end? As spectators and chorus struggle to make sense of the drama, how do we as critics respond? Overturning familiar ends, yet failing to define new beginnings, *Heracles* explores the unpredictable process of living—one that is governed, if at all, not by divine ends but by vagaries of

---

[45] Compare Bond 1981, xxvi–xxvii; note the similar tenor of Lyssa's praise of Heracles: ἄβατον δὲ χώραν καὶ θάλασσαν ἀγρίαν / ἐξημερώσας (851–52).

[46] On the importance of φιλία in *Heracles*, see Conacher 1967, 85–88.

chance, and that speaks to the humble and unheroic experience of private, not public, individuals. It is the curse and the blessing of everyday, ordinary people (1248) to live their lives in the time in-between (ὁ δ’ ἐν μέσῳ . . . χρόνος, 94). How does criticism approach this middle? Do we have models not just for closure and anticlosure, but for more ordinary means?

There are two models that I have found useful, both of which attempt to explain in general terms the novel's concern with mundane or ordinary experience. The first of these is Frank Kermode's discussion in *The Sense of an Ending* of what he calls "life in the middest."[47] Kermode begins by contrasting the apocalyptic end of Christianity, which promises an end that will annihilate time, with the mundane experience of life "in the middest," in the never-ending sequence of day after day. The central place of the novel in Western culture he explains as resulting from religious crisis: when the apocalyptic end no longer commanded belief, narrative fiction attempted to recapture that end within the medium or the means of everyday, secular experience. Novelistic closure is in many ways an oxymoron, and as Henry James observed, the novelist must conjure ends from the perpetual muddle of human affairs: "Really, universally, relations stop nowhere, and the exquisite problem of the artist is eternally but to draw, by a geometry of his own, the circle within which they shall happily *appear* to do so."[48] Kermode locates this peculiar failure of a peculiarly Western genre in the replacement of apocalyptic by secular time; in doing so he leans too heavily on a sense of nostalgia, arguing that narrative belatedly tries to recover the atemporal connectedness or closure of religious belief. Yet precisely because such closure is no longer possible, his argument is predisposed neither to search for closure nor to celebrate anticlosure, but to acknowledge instead the interminable muddle of life in between.

Bakhtin gives a different diagnosis of the same syndrome. In his essays on the genre of the novel, and in particular in "Epic and Novel,"[49] he describes a similar openness and uncertainty in narrative fiction, but locates this not in a fall from grace but in the forward march of literary history, which leaves behind the "closed" form of epic and discovers in the novel a new literary world. Novelistic form, which mirrors the openness and undecidedness of everyday lives, is largely characterized by contrast with epic. Whereas epic tends to portray a distant and traditional past, a national and monumental story whose outcome is already known, the novel tends to describe a contemporary present, an ordinary story that remains incomplete, a world-in-the-making where multiple futures are possible. These contrasting paradigms are both broad and relative; Bakhtin himself in-

---

[47] Kermode 1967.
[48] James 1934, 5.
[49] Bakhtin 1981, 3–40.

cluded Socratic dialogues among early examples of the novel, while Homeric epic might well be divided, in Bakhtin's terms, into the "epic" *Iliad* and the "novelistic" *Odyssey*. Yet this approach, because of its ethical emphasis, is powerful, positive—and to some extent, parochial. As we live our own lives, Bakhtin argues, our ends are never known or determined— and this is good, because we are then free to make choices and decisions; the special virtue of the novel is that its openness reenacts this freedom by portraying events as unfinalizable, giving agents in the narrative room to choose their own ends. Aeneas must labor under the shadow of a known end, the foundation and empire of Rome; Oedipus must labor to uncover an end already known to Teiresias and the audience; but the protagonist in Tolstoy or Dostoevsky lives entirely in a present whose ends are subject to constant revision.[50] The openness of the novel is a liberation from the tyranny of known ends.

Heracles is a perfect Bakhtinian hero. All known ends have been stripped away, and his final decision not to commit suicide, instead of determining what will follow, leaves both his future and his identity profoundly unclear because it commits him to the total uncertainty and total freedom of living in the present. Yet *Heracles* is not a Bakhtinian plot. For Bakhtin, the novel is characterized by what we might call systematic openness (or "aperture," to use Saul Morson's term):[51] the narrative represents characters as free at any moment to make choices and decisions just as we do in everyday life. The action of *Heracles* is the opposite. It is overdetermined, constantly overshadowed by impending ends—even if these ends turn out to be false leads. Only at a single point in the action, only at the moment the play ends, do we have a sense of aperture as the hero lingers on the threshold between a deconstructed past and an unknown future. Only at the end do we truly encounter life in the middle.

One might conclude (and it is an intriguing suggestion) that this unconventional play gives a fleeting glimpse of a completely new, novelistic impulse. But what does Greek drama of the late fifth century B.C.E. have to do with the relatively recent Western novel? The end of *Heracles* may have a similar interest in openness and undecidedness, but does this mean that it derives from the same impulse or shares the same concerns? Just as closure and anticlosure carry different ideological baggage at different times and places, so, too, does aperture; and I conclude by briefly (if somewhat reductively) setting Bakhtin and *Heracles* in their respective contexts in order to suggest some of the baggage they carry.

Bakhtin's reading of the novel is also a reading of late nineteenth- and early twentieth-century Europe. He lived in a world that seemed increas-

---

[50] On the open and unfinalizable narrative of *War and Peace*, see Morson 1987, 158–69.

[51] On "aperture," see Morson 1993, 213–16; on ethical freedom, compare Rubino 1993.

ingly governed by impersonal forces and mechanisms: the theories of Darwin, Freud, and Marx claimed in various ways that the end was determined, that laws spelled out how an individual, a species, or a society would change and develop.[52] Bakhtin's openness or unfinalizability tried to reclaim for the individual control over her or his own ends, and tried to salvage an ethical freedom and responsibility that seemed in danger of extinction. In fifth-century Athens, however, the prevailing ideology was one of civic voluntarism, a belief that members of the city could achieve whatever ends they wanted. The Periclean enlightenment did not subordinate human will to larger, impersonal forces; it did the very opposite, laying claim to an unprecedented degree of control over the future. But it claimed this freedom not in the name of the individual but in the name of his city. As Pericles says (in a passage quoted more briefly above):

> Great are the signs [of our achievement] and well known is the power we display, so that people today and in the future will marvel at us. We do not need Homer to praise us . . . but we have forced every sea and every land to give access to our ventures, and we have established everywhere eternal memorials of our favor and our vengeance. (2.41)

Toward the end of the century, this confidence was challenged more and more severely by military defeats, by civic dissension, and by the sophists' deconstruction of the teleology of progress.[53] In the rubble of this optimistic ideology, *Heracles* begins the search for new ends and new notions of order, turning from the larger public sphere to a personal and private one. But there is no celebration here of individual freedom, no proud assertion of responsibility and independence. The openness that Heracles discovers at the end allows him to choose limitations, frees him to pursue not expressions of collective will but recognition of the bonds that tie him to family and friends:

> I've destroyed my house with my shameful deeds
> and utterly ruined, I'll follow Theseus like a dinghy (ἐφολκίδες).
> No one in his right mind would rather have
> wealth or strength than good friends.
>
> (1423–26)

EPILOGUE

I will leave our hero here, poised on the threshold and freed by his sufferings to decide for the first time who he will be. But what of his critics?

---

[52] Compare Rubino 1993, 150–52, on the certainties of the natural sciences.
[53] See Cole 1990.

Does a reading of the play suggest (possible) future destinations, opening up new approaches in the study of closure? That is more than I intend to do in this chapter, although I truly hope that these essays together will suggest new ways of thinking about this subject. But what of Bakhtin: will he be of special use as we try to chart a course ahead? I pointed out that his interest in the undecidable present, and in the ethical freedom of living in this present, is a useful alternative to approaches that demand or champion closure or anticlosure of various stripes—even if the implications of "ethical freedom" for Euripides' contemporaries were radically different from those entertained by contemporaries of Tolstoy or Dostoevsky. But perhaps I overstated the case. Just as Heracles reaches his final moment of freedom and openness only after a series of ends have been overturned, ethical freedom implies a liberation from the tyranny of determinism. Yet the banner of liberation can be waved in many different causes. It is no coincidence that two critics cited above, who have argued persuasively for the ethical dimension of narrative openness or unfinalizability in Bakhtin, have opposing ideas of what this freedom entails. Carl Rubino argues that this freedom requires us, as critics, to throw off the shackles of a stifling critical tradition and open up the discipline of Classics to a multitude of voices and approaches. Saul Morson, on the other hand, argues that it requires us to remove the shackles of political correctness and challenge the prevailing modes of literary criticism. Bakhtinian freedom tends, in the end, to articulate versions of anticlosure, substituting different tyrants in more recent readings for the original straw man of epic closure. We as readers need to be aware of the ethical, as well as the aesthetic, ideological and cultural dimensions of closure; with a critical attitude that is alive to the different ways in which order is constructed, and to the various ways in which a given work and its readers and critics may challenge that construction, we can take our own places on the threshold.[54]

---

[54] I would like to express thanks and acknowledge obligation to audiences that heard and responded to portions of this paper (at the annual meeting of the Classical Association of the Middle West and South, and at Rice University, Wheaton College, Loyola University Chicago and the University of California, Santa Barbara), as well as to readers who commented on the longer written version (Deborah Roberts, Michael Halleran, Don Fowler), even if on some points we must agree to disagree.

CHAPTER 6

Lucretian Conclusions

PETA FOWLER

THE "ENDING" of Lucretius's *De rerum natura* is a traditional scholarly problem. Critics like Bignone and Kenney[1] have argued that the poem is incomplete and would have ended differently had the poet lived. In ending with the grim events of the plague at Athens, Lucretius, it is alleged, fatally undercuts the message of the poem, which is that mankind can be spiritually saved by conversion to Epicurean beliefs. In a work essentially optimistic in its promise of an improvement in the condition of mankind, the present ending is seen as dominated by a tone of gloomy pessimism and thereby self-evidently misplaced. In a work whose scope is general enough to include the universe and everything within it, the transition from our *mundus* to a narrowly localized geographical place within the cosmos, and indeed from general meteorological phenomena to a specific historical event, limited in time and space, seems to narrow the vision of the reader and direct it from the sublime (the *ipsa . . . maiestas cognita rerum*, 5.7) to the messiness and ugliness of human existence. There is also, however, a smaller philological problem: are the final lines that we are given in the manuscripts the original conclusion? It is this smaller problem that I want to examine here, but inevitably it will transpire that this problem in textual criticism also involves the wider issues of the ending as a whole, and indeed of the entire poem.

In the manuscripts, the *De rerum natura* ends with a description of the distraught relatives fighting to bury those who have died in the plague (1282–86):

> multaque <res> subita et paupertas horrida suasit.
> namque suos consanguineos aliena rogorum
> insuper extructa ingenti clamore locabant
> subdebantque faces, multo cum sanguine saepe
> rixantes potius quam corpora desererentur.

Sudden need also and poverty persuaded to many dreadful expedients: for they would lay their own kindred amidst loud lamentation upon piles of

[1] Bignone 1945, 318–22; Kenney 1977, 22–33.

wood not their own, and would set light to the fire, often brawling with much shedding of blood rather than abandon the bodies.[2]

These lines correspond to the last lines of Thucydides' section on burial (2.52.4):

καὶ πολλοὶ ἐς ἀναισχύντους θήκας ἐτράποντο σπάνει τῶν ἐπιτηδείων διὰ τὸ συχνοὺς ἤδη προτεθνάναι σφίσιν· ἐπὶ πυρὰς γὰρ ἀλλοτρίας φθάσαντες τοὺς νήσαντας οἱ μὲν ἐπιθέντες τὸν ἑαυτῶν νεκρὸν ὑφῆπτον, οἱ δὲ καομένου ἄλλου ἐπιβαλόντες ἄνωθεν ὃν φέροιεν ἀπῇσαν.

Many people, lacking the necessary means of burial because so many deaths had already occurred in their households, adopted the most shameless methods. They would arrive first at a funeral pyre that had been made by others, put their own dead upon it and set it alight; or, finding another pyre burning, they would throw the corpse that they were carrying on top of the other one and go away.

The second half of the passage in Thucydides is translated, however, in a section of the poem that the manuscripts place earlier, at 1247–51:

> inque aliis alium, populum sepelire suorum
> certantes: lacrimis lassi luctuque redibant;
> inde bonam partem in lectum maerore dabantur.
> nec poterat quisquam reperiri, quem neque morbus
> nec mors nec luctus temptaret tempore tali.

. . . And one upon others, fighting to bury the multitude of their dead; weary with weeping and grief they returned, then for the greater part took to their beds from grief. Nor could anyone be found whom neither disease had assailed nor death nor mourning at such a time.

These lines are not connected either grammatically or in terms of subject matter with their surrounding context in the manuscripts, and they clearly refer to events after 1282–86, which are indeed bathetic if they come later than the firm generalization of 1247–51. The correspondence with Thucydides[3] merely confirms that 1247–51 ought to follow 1282–86. Such transpositions are not uncommon in the text of the *De rerum natura*, and the ending of a work is notoriously liable to suffer textual corruption: another example in the immediate vicinity is the isolated line 1225, *incom-*

---

[2] All translations from Lucretius, unless otherwise noted, are from Smith 1992: other translations are taken from the Loeb Classical Library editions, except where these are unsuitable. The translations from Thucydides are from Warner 1954.

[3] Most notably *redibant* with ἀπῇσαν and *inque aliis alium* (with a suitable verb supplied in a preceding lacuna) with καομένου ἄλλου ἐπιβαλόντες ἄνωθεν. I argue below that the former is especially significant.

itata rapi certabant funera vasta, "Without mourners the lonely funerals competed with one another in being rushed through," which again has no
connection with its surrounding context and may well belong after 1281.
It is surprising, therefore, that the transposition of 1247–51 was first proposed only in the nineteenth century by Bockemueller,[4] and it has been
taken up amongst modern editors only by Martin (ironically elsewhere the
most conservative of editors).[5] I shall argue here that the transposition not
only makes better sense, but also gives us a worthy ending to the poem as a
whole. My argument will be based on the closural conventions seen in the
lines, a comparison with the other book ends of the *De rerum natura*, and
an examination of some of the principal intertexts. I shall then attempt to
look more broadly at the end of the *De rerum natura* in relation to the
Epicureanism of the poem.

THE CLOSURAL NATURE OF 1247–51

Signals of Closure

Four aspects in particular of the transposed lines are features commonly
used to signal closure. With the transposition of 1247–51, the last action
described in the *De rerum natura* is that of the mourners returning to their
homes (*redibant*). The return from a funeral is often marked as the concluding part of the ritual,[6] but the closural device of the return home is of
wider significance. It is most notably represented by the end of the *Iliad,*
which I discuss below, but it is widespread in literature, particularly in the
heroic sagas of the *nostoi* of the heroes. The *Odyssey,* the *nostos* poem par
excellence, reiterates a related but variant version of the homecoming of its
central character at the end of the poem.[7] Similarly, throughout Apollonius's *Argonautica* it is reiterated that glory is only won if the expedition
not only achieves its goal of securing the Golden Fleece but also arrives
safely home.[8] More generally, departures are amongst the most familiar of

---

[4] Bockemueller 1873, ad loc.

[5] Cf. also Bright 1971.

[6] The departure of the bereaved was the fifth and final stage of the Athenian ceremony of
public burial for the war dead, and was signaled in the closing words of the funeral speech
that constituted the fourth stage. Cf. ἄπιτε in Thuc. 2.46.2 (with a variant ἀποχωρεῖτε),
picking up ἀπέρχονται in 2.36.6–7, where Thucydides describes the ceremony; Plato
Menex. 249c; [Dem.] 60.37; Kakridis 1961, 106; Ziolkowski 1981, 164–73; Hornblower
1991, 315–16.

[7] Cf. Heubeck, West, and Hainsworth 1988–92, 1:58, 171, 194; *Od.* 24.470–71 (Eu-
peithes), 528. Cf. Thuc. 7.87.6, invoking the unusual epic word ἀπενόστησαν (cf. Hornblower 1987, 114–15) with irony at the end of the Sicilian Expedition.

[8] Cf. Hunter 1988, 440, on the "single obsessive end" of the *Argonautica.* Although the
poem actually ends with εἰσαπέβητε—the return home is viewed as arrival—ἀνερχο-

all devices of closural allusion. As Carolyn Dewald shows in chapter 4 of this volume, a departure brings the whole of Herodotus's *Histories* to a close, although as in Lucretius it is not an obviously significant one, but simply marks the end of the exemplary story, itself an external analepsis looking back to the chronological period of Book 1 and the beginning of the Persian Empire. Nevertheless, it is full of resonance for the whole work. As we shall see later, there is a similar kind of ring composition and sense of return to a starting place in Lucretius. Plato similarly often ends his dialogues with a dispersal of the characters involved in the discussion and signals closure with a simple verb for going or related compounds.[9] The ending is not constituted by the conclusions drawn from the argument—that is, it is not an "internal ending"—but rather it is one imposed by the fictitious social framework within which the discussion takes place. The departure of the characters after a discussion is an "external ending," motivated by factors extrinsic to the main issues of the dialogue. In fact, Herodotus, Plato, and Lucretius all share this "skewed" kind of ending, which does not conclude the main work as we define it but a minor part of it, the exemplary story within the main narrative in Herodotus, the digression in Lucretius, and the dramatic framework in Plato.

The return of the mourners is followed by a generalizing reflection on the sad progress of the disease (1250–51):

> nec poterat quisquam reperiri, quem neque morbus
> nec mors nec luctus temptaret tempore tali.

Nor could anyone be found whom neither disease had assailed nor death nor mourning at such a time.

The note of authority created by a general categorical reflection of this nature is another familar closural device.[10] The summarizing function of the lines has already been remarked upon by Bright,[11] who points also to the recurrence of the key thematic words, *morbus*, *mors*, and *luctus*, which encapsulate the whole experience of the plague. This function would disappear if the manuscripts' ordering of the lines were retained. The plague in its personified form has figured in the passage preceding 1247–51, at 1224 (*vis morbida*) and 1236 (*avidi contagia morbi*), whereas specific descriptions of the dead (as opposed to the physiological process of dying of

---

μένοισιν occurs at 4.1777. The scholion (ad loc.) interprets this as meaning "as they returned" (= ἀναχωρήσασιν).

[9] Cf. the end of the *Apology* (Socrates "going home" to the gods, μετοίκησις; cf. 40c, *Phd.* 117c); *Euthphr.* 15e, 42e; *Symp.* 223d; *Phdr.* 279c; *Cra.* 440d–e; *Tht.* 210d; *La.* 201c; *Lysis.* 223a–b; *Prt.* 362; *Menex.* 100b; [Plat.] *Ax.* 372a.

[10] Cf. Smith 1968, 166–71.

[11] Bright 1971, 622–23.

plague) and of grief follow the manuscripts' placement of the lines. Without the transposition, *mors* would carry less weight in 1251 because it
would not yet have been vividly personified as a powerful force heaping up
its victims (1262–63, 1272–73). And *luctus* is more striking in context if
the lines are moved because words for grief (not simply sadness) are concentrated in the section on burial, which naturally focuses on the distress of
the bereaved survivors (*dolor*, 1277; *maestus*, 1281) and their futile and excessive devotion to the dead (1286). It is after the completion of the funeral rites that we expect to see the mourners collapse from grief and
exhaustion. With the transposition of 1247–51 and 1225, all three subjects,
plague, death, and grief, recur in the sequence in which they unfold in the
account.

More specifically, the generalizing statement found in 1250–51 is a form
of the closural device that ancient rhetoricians called an *epiphonema*.[12] It is
most often found at the end of arguments or descriptions, marking off a
section of the text as a paragraph with a self-contained concluding *gnome*.
It typically contains such words as *(usque) adeo, tantus*, and *talis*: the classic
examples are *De rerum natura* 1.101 (*tantum religio potuit suadere malorum*)
and Virgil *Aeneid* 1.33 (*tantae molis erat Romanam condere gentem*, cited as an
example by Quintilian in *Inst.* 8.5.11).[13] Though common to internal closure, it is also found at the end of complete works.[14] Many *epiphonemata* are
characterized by a nominalized form of expression: abstract nouns desig-
nating emotions and qualities are employed instead of personal subjects,
adjectives, and verbs. This mode of locution has the function of detaching
the reference of the statement to individuals and particular circumstances
and conveying the point in an apparently objective and authoritative manner.[15] In Lucretius's Book 6, this abstract form of expression is particularly
apt in that the hypostasis of the three key terms is a natural extension of
the idiom used so far, and it is the accumulation of the three subjects in the
same phrase that brings this usage to a close. Nevertheless, although related
to the context,[16] lines 1249–51 have the air of a general truth: at times like
these, no one can escape these potent forces, which are introduced as unqualified absolutes.

Finally, the transposed lines can be seen as contributing to the ring com-

---

[12] Cf. Quint. 8.5.11, Lausberg 1960, 1:434, 879; Volkmann 1885, 455–56; Fowler 1989b,
103–5.

[13] Cf. *Aen.* 1.11: *tantaene animis caelestibus irae?* Quint. 1.12.7: *adeo facilius est multa facere
quam diu*; and in Greek, e.g., Dem. 6.27, 6.120.

[14] Cf. Sall. *Cat.* 61.9: *ita varie per omnem exercitum laetitia, maeror, luctus atque gaudia agitabantur*; Cic. *Phil.* 6.19: *aliae nationes servitutem pati possunt, populi Romani est propria libertas.*

[15] Cf. *De rerum natura* (here abbreviated *DRN*)1.101, 6.1250–51; Sall. *Cat.* 61.9; Cic. *Phil.*
6.19; Dem. 6.27.

[16] Cf. Bonner 1966, 261; Quint. 8.5.6–15.

position of the *De rerum natura*, whereby the concluding description of the plague corresponds to or "balances" the opening springtime address to Venus. Critics have often noted[17] that the opening of the poem with its emphasis on Venus's generative role and the procreation of the species is counterbalanced at the end by the destructiveness of the plague. If one sees one function of the poem, in G. Müller's terms,[18] as the overcoming of our natural terror at our own individual ends and the end of our world through an insight into the eternal law of growth and decline, then it is natural to find this theme being developed in two of the most important positions in the poem, at the beginning and at the end. Their stark isolation belies the fact that the two processes are necessarily complementary, that is, that one cannot take place without the other.[19] This does not mean, however, that the reader cannot mentally reestablish the links. She is helped to do so partly by the close similarity in phrasing between 1.22–23, which focuses on the far-reaching extent of Venus's power (*nec sine te quicquam dias in luminis oras / exoritur neque fit laetum neque amabile quicquam*) and 6.1250–51 (*nec poterat quisquam reperiri, quem neque morbus / nec mors nec luctus temptaret tempore tali*). The litotes created by the negative formulation and the generality of *quicquam/quisquam* perfectly express the ubiquity of plague and creation.

Tragic Patterns of Closure

Lines 2.576–80, which relate the processes of coming into being and passing away, are similarly phrased in the negative:

> miscetur funere vagor
> quem pueri tollunt visentes luminis oras;
> *nec* nox ulla diem *neque* noctem aurora secutast
> quae *non* audierit mixtos vagitibus aegris
> ploratus mortis comites et funeris atri.

With the funeral dirge is mingled the wail that children raise when they first see the borders of light; and no night ever followed day, or dawn followed night, that has not heard mingled with their sickly wailings the lamentations that attend upon death and the black funeral.

Those lines, however, raise a familar problem in Lucretian studies, in that although they formally balance birth and death, the formulation of birth in

---

[17] Müller 1975, 291–93; 1978, 218; P. Fowler 1983, 244; and cf. Bignone 1945, 318–22.
[18] Müller 1959, 25ff.
[19] Cf. 1.56–57, 263–64; 2.62–79, 294–307, 569–80; 6.769–72, 1093–96.

terms of the *vagitibus aegris* of the newly born seems to tip the balance toward a darker view of the human condition. The finality and categorical nature of 6.1250–51 might similarly be seen as emphasizing more death and pain than life and pleasure. This is accentuated by the resemblance of the lines to the "pessimistic" conclusions of Greek tragedy, such as Euripides *Heracles* 1427–8, "We go in wretchedness with loud lament, having lost the greatest of friends,"[20] and the coda that appears at the end of four of Euripides' tragedies, *Alcestis, Andromache, Helen,* and *Bacchae,* where the gnomic utterance is followed by the application to the circumstances in question, in the manner of *tali* in Lucretius:

> Many are the shapes divinities take,
> much that's unanticipated the gods accomplish;
> what we expect goes unfulfilled,
> and the god finds a way for the unexpected.
> Such was the outcome of this matter.[21]

The invoking of tragic conventions is extended by the resemblance of 1250–51 to the pessimistic assertions about the mortal condition frequently voiced in Greek plays.[22] In particular, Cicero's translation of some lines of Euripides' *Hypsipyle*[23] is remarkably similar to Lucretius 6.1250–51: *mortalis nemo est quem non adtingit dolor / morbusque.* This statement, however, is not really pessimistic, but part of a *consolatio* on the natural cycle of birth and decay: it is the human lot to experience the death of loved ones, and therefore we should not grieve over the inevitable. In a sense this is the message that is often felt to be missing at the end of the *De rerum natura*; no *consolation* is offered. Epicurus, by contrast, had explicitly condemned tragic pessimism in *Letter to Menoeceus* 126–27:

> Yet much worse still is the man who says it is good not to be born, but "once born make haste to pass the gates of Death." For if he says this from conviction why does he not pass away out of life?[24]

Euripides fragment 449 N. (from his *Cresphontes*) comes particularly close to *De rerum natura* 2.576–80:

---

[20] Cf. Roberts 1987, 52 and Dunn 1996, 13–25.

[21] Cf. ibid., esp. 58: "Codas that set a seal on the past do so either by including brief lamentations or by placing an emphasis on the finality or authority of what has happened."

[22] Cf. the (spurious?) tail-piece to Soph. *OT* 1528–30; Eur. *Andr.* 100–102; Aesch. *Ag.* 928; Soph. *Trach.* 1–3.

[23] Fr. 60.90–91 Bond, quoted in Cic. *Tusc.* 3.59 (= fr. 42 Buchner), and discussed by Segal (1990, 64–65).

[24] Cf. Theognis 425–28 West, with the scholion on Soph. *OC* 1225.

ἐχρῆν γὰρ ἡμᾶς σύλλογον ποιουμένους
τὸν φύντα θρηνεῖν εἰς ὅσ’ ἔρχεται κακά,
τὸν δ’ αὖ θανόντα καὶ πόνων πεπαυμένον
χαίροντας εὐφημοῦντας ἐκπέμπειν δόμων

For we should gather to lament the child who has been born for the evils he
is entering upon, and escort from home with joy and reverence the person
who has died and ceased from pain.

The initial reckoning of the disadvantages that await the newly born
throughout its life and a lament for its condition seem to be endorsed by
Lucretius in 5.222–34, in a passage that again emphasizes the negative
aspects of our world as a part of the argument that there is no divine
providence: the human baby at birth "fills all around with doleful wailings—as is but just, seeing that so much trouble awaits him in life to pass
through." Lucretius is at this point invoking a well-known truth found
frequently in Greek poetry, and especially tragedy, for the purposes of
demonstrating that human beings do not occupy a privileged position
among the species of the world. Yet, the image of the shipwrecked baby
and the implied conception of stepmother nature seem to reinforce the
poetic tradition with its insistence on the fragility of human life and the
instability of happiness.

As these other passages suggest, however, it is not an objection to the
final placement of 6.1250–51 that they end on a note of excessive pessimism: their tone is amply paralleled throughout. The "solutions" to this
"problem" offered by critics are various, and the ramifications of the issue
many: I shall return to some of them later. For the moment, I merely note
that if we consider the ring composition not of the whole work but of
Book 6 within it, the transposed lines themselves may be taken as pointing
to a way out for readers oppressed by the apparent tragic helplessness of the
plague. First, the phrase *tempore tali* points us back to the prologue of Book
6, where precisely such "hard times" brought about by natural forces have
been discussed, along with Epicurus's discovery of strategies for coping
with them when they occur (6.29–32):

> [sc. monstravit]
> quidve mali foret in rebus mortalibu’ passim,
> quod fieret naturali varieque volaret
> seu casu seu vi, quod sic natura parasset,
> et quibus e portis occurri cuique deceret

[He showed] what evil there was everywhere in human affairs, which comes
about and flies about in different ways, whether by natural chance or force,

because nature had so provided, and from what sally-ports each ought to be countered.

Second, *poterat* in 6.1250 stresses the status of the plague as a past event in history: it does not have to be repeated in exactly the same form. Book 6 opens and closes with Athens: we already know that at a subsequent time the redeeming and life-giving message of Epicurus was to be born and to change the course of history. In a reversal of the normal sequence, the problem follows the remedy. By this arrangement, Lucretius is in effect testing the readers' responses to the Epicurean "message" of the poem.[25] What at first appears to be a false closure, disappointing the readers' expectations, turns out on closer inspection to be a successful one in that this "surprise ending provides a perspective point from which the reader can now appreciate a significant pattern, principle, or motive not grasped before."[26]

BOOK ENDINGS IN THE *DE RERUM NATURA*

Two of the other book endings in the *De rerum natura* are particularly significant for the closure of Book 6. Books 1 and 5 both end with *epiphonemata* in which a *sic*[27] clause is followed by a *nam* clause in a four-line block:

> Haec *sic* pernosces parva perductus opella;
> *namque alid ex alio clarescet* nec tibi caeca
> nox iter eripiet quin ultima naturai
> pervideas: *ita* res accendent lumina rebus.

So you will gain a thorough understanding of these matters, led on with very little effort; for one thing will become clear by another, and blind night will not steal your path and prevent you from seeing all the uttermost recesses of nature: so clearly will truths kindle light for truths.

(1.1114–17)

> *sic* unumquicquid paulatim protrahit aetas
> in medium ratioque in luminis erigit oras.

[25] Cf. Clay 1983, 250–66.

[26] Smith 1968, 212.

[27] The manuscripts have *sic* in 1.1114, but Munro adopted the reading *sei* (*si*) from L, together with a lacuna of one line after 1114. This reading is supported by Empedocles 110DK, 100 Wright, where a future conditional clause is used in a similar context. Moreover, some scholars regard the Empedoclean lines as a concluding statement and place them either at the end of *On Nature* (Bollack) or near the end (Wright). However, although the Empedoclean model makes Munro's suggestion tempting, the parallel with Book 5 pulls the other way.

> *namque alid ex alio clarescere corde videbant,*
> artibus ad summum donec venere cacumen.

So by degrees time brings up before us every single thing, and reason lifts it into the precincts of light. For they saw one thing after another grow clear in their minds, until they attained the highest pinnacle of the arts.

(5.1454–57)

These two passages are clearly related: apart from verbal resemblances, we have the hypostasis of night, time, and reason, a common concern with concealment and discovery, and a reference to extreme points. In relational terms, *ultima* and *summum cacumen* are diametrically opposed. The latter suggests visibility on all sides and a prominence that stands out from the low-lying surrounding area. The former implies precious secrets hidden away in underground recesses, deep within the universe. This sense is conveyed by the connections of both passages with 1.407–9:

> *sic alid ex alio per te tute ipse videre*
> *talibus in rebus poteris* caecasque latebras
> insinuare omnis et verum *protrahere* inde.

So you will be able for yourself to see one thing after another in such matters as these, and to penetrate all unseen hiding-places, and draw forth the truth from them.

The idea of succession in the phrase "one thing after another" is common to all three passages—here; at the end of Book 1, of a philosophical chain of reasoning in which the basic principles of Epicureanism are discovered; and in Book 5, of the concepts of the technologies that enhance the living conditions of mankind. *Protrahere* is used again at 5.1454, *protrahit*, as is *videre*. The same images of light and dark and language of concealment and discovery occur.

The metaphor of "unseen hiding places" helps to explain the nuance of *ultima naturai* in 1.1116. Smith aptly translates this phrase as "the uttermost recesses of nature," Brown in his commentary as "nature's last secrets." The *per-* prefix in *pernosces, perductus,* and *pervideas* suggests the penetration of an inner sanctum or places shrouded in mystery; the verbs function similarly to *insinuare* in 1.409. Indeed, "natural philosophy" was known in Latin as *res occultae* or *res abditae,*[28] rendering Greek τὰ ἄδηλα; this usage is reflected in the *De rerum natura.*[29] Variant expressions in Cicero convey the qualities of concealment and mystical shrouding associated with the subject (e.g., *Brut.* 44 [*reconditis abstrusisque rebus*], *Acad.* 1.15 [*a rebus occultis et ab ipsa natura involutis*]). Thus it is natural for Lucretius to use the language of

---

[28] Cf. Reid 1885 on Cic. *Acad.* 1.19 (*de natura et rebus occultis*), Epicurus *Ep. Hdt.* 38, 80.
[29] 1.145, 933 (= 4.8).

unveiling and revelation to describe philosophical enlightenment in the prologue to Book 3. It is expressed in terms of nature's secrets being opened up and revealed to all: *sic natura tua vi / tam manifesta patens ex omni parte retecta est* (3.29–30). The influence of the Mysteries here is unmistakable.[30]

The movement in the Book 5 passage is antithetical to that at the end of Book 1: instead of piercing the central mystery, we find a gradual emergence and gaining of a peak. In fact, the opening of Book 2 showed how one movement can paradoxically lead to the other: the philosopher's *arx* of security and mental calm soars high above the plains on which struggling humanity dwells (2.7–13). Yet the *ratio* of 5.1455 is not the *ratio* of Epicureanism. The language used to describe the invention of the arts is a mixture of revealing what is hidden (*protrahit*) and of bringing to birth (*in luminis . . . oras*), perhaps reflecting the complex nature of Lucretius's account of technological inventions as a combination of imitation of nature and rational experimentation.[31] Although the development of civilization is not seen as uniformly positive and Lucretius's version highlights various setbacks and moral flaws that come about under the pressure of changes in the external environment, it is interesting to note that *ratio*, even this lower-order kind that is not to be identified with true rationality, is inextricably linked with bringing light out of darkness. The way in which the description of technological/artistic inventiveness and philosophical reasoning are assimilated to each other reveal that the activities are not so very different. Indeed, the discoveries of Epicureanism and of Lucretius himself are temporally located in the diachronic account of civilization at 5.335–37 and, more specifically, after men reach the summit of achievement in the arts at 6.5. In all of these passages there is an affirmative tone that emphasizes men's agency in sorting out their own problems, be they philosophical or technological/artistic.[32]

How do lines 6.1250–51 stand in relation to these passages and, in par-

---

[30] The culminating events in the initiation ceremony were the opening of the doors of the *telesterion* amid a blaze of light and the unveiling of the *orgia*: cf. Plut. *De prof. virt.* 81d–e, fr. 178 Sandbach; Hippol. *Haer.* 5.8.164.62ff. DS; Richardson 1974, 26; Mylonas 1961, 273, 306; Burkert 1983, 276–77. The *epopteia*, or final vision, was accompanied by a reaction of awe, well conveyed in Lucretius's *divina voluptas /—atque horror*. The language of the Mysteries had very early on been appropriated by philosophers to describe the progress from ignorance to intellectual enlightenment, and the Empedocles passage that may lie behind Lucretius's 1.1114–17 employs mystical language (110.2DK). Lucretius's language at the end of Book 1 by its similarity to the prologue of Book 3 suggests the poet in the role of hierophant, showing the way, and the reader in the part of the initiand, being led by the torches of philosophy.

[31] Cf. Epicurus *Ep. Hdt.* 75–76; Manuwald 1980, 18–30.

[32] Cf. 1.407: *per te tute ipse*; 1.1114ff.: *pernosces . . . , nec tibi. . . . eripiet quin . . . / pervideas*; 5.1456: *clarescere corde videbant*. Epicurus himself was *tali cum corde repertum* (6.5).

ticular, to the book endings of 1 and 5 ? In Book 5, human beings are at the summit of achievement, in the bright light, while in Book 6, they are at the nadir of failure, in the darkness of death. The *cor*, the seat of the mind, is no longer an area where reason operates, but where despair has taken hold (6.1151–53, 1233). No effort is made by the plague-stricken to exert themselves, but they collapse in a state of passivity (6.1249, 1250), in contrast to the agency emphasized in the other passages. The only experimentation is carried on by disease, death, and grief.[33] The powerful contrast between these antithetical pictures is strengthened by the fact that Books 5 and 6 cohere as a pair within the overall structure of the poem. They both crucially present the condition of mankind before the advent of Epicureanism:[34] there is a strong sense of continuation between Books 5 and 6 as Athens in the prologue to Book 6 clearly represents the "peaking" of civilization[35] in the birth of Epicurus. Yet this Athens is also the location for the historical plague of 430 B.C.E., and its much-vaunted civilized values and social norms disintegrate when put to the test. The creativity of the abstracts "time" and "reason" in Book 5 is undermined by the destructive experimentation of the abstracts "disease," "death" and "grief" in Book 6.

The relationship of the end of Book 6 to that of Book 1 may be read in a similar fashion, as an undermining of the rationalist optimism of the earlier passage. But we may also read the closing lines of Book 1 as already anticipating the later shock of the final end. The phrase *ultima naturai* may also be read metapoetically as looking to the end of the work, and the darkness of death in the account of the plague as already foreseen in the blind night of Book 1. From this point of view, what the reader meets with at the end of Book 6 is what she has been prepared for all along by the unbroken thread or chain of arguments that the work has offered. The plague is one more example of nature's opacity, its power to surprise and perplex. In the gloom generated by this natural disaster, the reader seems to have been abandoned by the didactic poet, but in effect a beacon light shines out from the end of Book 1 over the intervening space of five books with its promise of aid. The reader has to act on his or her own resources with the poem as a support (cf. 1.407ff.). Whether the *res*, "truth" or "facts," reinforced by Epicurus's torch (3.1), will kindle the light of truth against the smoky glare from the ignited pyres (*accendent* significantly varies *subdebantque faces* at 6.1285) remains to be seen, but the reader is invited to make the attempt.

---

[33] Cf. Verg. *G.* 4.328, *omnia temptanti* of Aristaeus. The great inventors in Book 5 were those *ingenio qui praestabant et corde vigebant*.

[34] Cf. P. G. Fowler 1983, 338–40, on *DRN* 6.2; Clay 1983, 257–59.

[35] Cf. P. G. Fowler 1983, 13–15; Segal 1990, 231–32.

INTERTEXTUALITIES I: EPIC, DIDACTIC, TRAGEDY

One of the factors that make the ending of the *De rerum natura* particularly "open" is the lack of any formal coda. Although it is difficult to make confident assertions, especially about the earliest texts, this is arguably a feature that associates the poem with epic rather than with didactic.[36] Presumably, the texts known by Lucretius and his first readers would have been published at least in some form with our present endings. We have lost the "bird-omens" section at the end of *Works and Days*, but we know that Apollonius of Rhodes athetized them. If that athetesis is accepted, the final lines of the poem possess a degree of generality, and a confidence about the future success of a man imbued with the knowledge imparted by the poem, that give them a closural force. Within 822–28, lines 826–28 constitute a makarismos-type ending:[37]

τάων εὐδαίμων τε καὶ ὄλβιος ὃ τάδε πάντα
εἰδὼς ἐργάζηται ἀναίτιος ἀθανάτοισιν,
ὄρνιθας κρίνων καὶ ὑπερβασίας ἀλεείνων

That man is happy and lucky in them [days] who knows all these things and does his work without offending the deathless gods, who discerns the omens of birds and avoids transgression.

τάων refers to the days and ἐργάζηται to the works that together form the subject of the poem. Thus the key terms figure in the conclusion. More importantly, the pupil is promised success and happiness if he masters the advice provided by the poem. Various endings speculatively proposed for Empedocles' *On Nature* carry similar predictions about the future capabilities of the pupil: 110 DK, the choice of Bollack and placed in penultimate position by Wright, has already been cited as bearing a close resemblance to the end of Lucretius's Book 1 (1114–17). In context, the end of *De rerum natura* Book 1 refers to the ensuing reading of the rest of the poem, but divorced from its context and placed at the end of the whole work, it would read like a characteristic promise of complete mastery of the subject and a thorough understanding of nature. Even Empedocles' lines envisage future meditation on the ideas of the poem by Pausanias after its close.[38] Aratus makes lower-level and consequently less exciting claims, as befits his "slight, finely wrought" (λεπτόν) poem, and promises simply accuracy in weather forecasting rather than larger-scale claims of complete

---

[36] Cf. van Groningen 1960, 70–77.

[37] Cf. Richardson 1974, 313ff.

[38] For this anticipation of future study, cf. Epicurus *Ep. Men.* 135, *Ep. Pyth.* 116, with *Ep. Hdt.* 83, echoed in *DRN* 1.398–417 (note the future *poteris*), which is in turn related to 1.1114–17 (note the futures *pernosces, clarescet, eripiet, accendent*).

knowledge and perfect happiness: but then it is difficult to see how either of these results could be brought about by a didactic poem on weather signs:

τῶν ἄμυδις πάντων ἐσκεμμένος εἰς ἐνιαυτὸν
οὐδέποτε σχεδίως κεν ἐπ' αἰθέρι τεκμήραιο.

(Phaen. 1153–54)

Study all the signs together throughout the year and never shall your forecast of the weather be a random guess.

Again the result is specified in terms that relate only to the ostensible aim of the work. A modest potential optative is used instead of the bold future indicative.

The form of Hesiod's *Theogony*, as we possess it, was probably shaped by the Alexandrians, who separated it off from a *Catalogue of Women* (not the extant one). Thus it possesses a somewhat puzzling, if very influential, four-line ending (1019–22), of which the first two lines contain a summarizing recapitulation of the section on goddesses, and the following two invoke the Muses to sing about women. West thinks that the ending would have been 1020 and that lines 1021–22 belonged to the opening of the poem following in the papyrus roll, which later got incorporated into the text. Callimachus's *Aitia* ends in a similar manner, looking forward to the poem that follows in the published edition, the *Iambi*:

χαῖρε σὺν εὐεστοῖ δ' ἔρχεο λωϊτέρῃ.
χαῖρε, Ζεῦ, μέγα καὶ σύ, σάω δ' [ὅλο]ν οἶκον ἀνάκτων·
αὐτὰρ ἐγὼ Μουσέων πεζὸν [ἔ]πειμι νομόν.

Fare well and return with great prosperity. Hail greatly, thou too, Zeus, and save all the house of kings. But I will pass on to the prose pasture of the Muses.

This ending clearly conforms to the closing formulas of the Homeric Hymns, which bid farewell and often promise a future return to the subject.[39] Callimachus, then, cleverly adapts an archaic closural technique, in which an open-ended commitment to return to the theme is expressed, to the exigencies of the published book, so that the position of the poem in the ordering of his works is brought to the reader's attention, in an extreme example of self-reflexivity. This type of ending, known to moderns as the *sphragis*,[40] continued to be popular in didactic verse, appearing twice

---

[39] Cf. *Hymm. Hom.* 2.495 (Demeter); 3.166, 177–78 (Delian Apollo); 3.545–46 (Pythian Apollo); 4.579–80 (Hermes); etc. *Hymn. Hom.* 9.7–9 is very close to the end of the *Aetia*. On the χαῖρε, cf. Hopkinson 1988 on Callim. *Hymns* 6.134.

[40] Cf. Kranz 1961.

in Nicander and once in Virgil.[41] Amongst other extant didactic works, those of Manilius and Grattius both have textual problems at the end of the extant text, though the end of Manilius, at least, may well be original (and imitate Lucretius).[42] Oppian's *Cynegetica* has no formal closure, but the *Halieutica* of his namesake ends with a prayer for the well-being of the reigning emperor, whichever Antoninus he may be (5.675–80).[43]

Although the evidence is not unanimous, there is clearly a tendency for didactic works to end with a formal conclusion—a *quod erat demonstrandum* or injunction to further study. On both the manuscripts and the transposed endings, the *De rerum natura* lacks this, although the deictic *tempore tali* marks a slight gesture toward a summation. We should not be surprised, however, to find the poem associating itself more with epic, as there has been a constant dialectic between the two genres throughout the work.[44] The relationship to the model for the epic genre, the *Iliad*, goes much further than merely the absence of a coda, however. Both works end with funeral rites, perhaps the most familiar form of social closure, "an expression of order and solidarity in a world of sometimes uncontrollable conflict":[45] in the *Iliad*, this function is related to the central themes of the poem, in that, as C. W. Macleod points out, the funeral "represents civilisation maintained in the midst of war, as the ransom represented it maintained against rage and revenge."[46] With the transposition of 1247–51, however, there is a further element of resemblance between the *Iliad* and the *De rerum natura*, in that in both cases the return home of the mourners is mentioned. In the *Iliad*, the ceremony, properly conducted, acts as a therapeutic experience, bringing a release to the emotions and a final resolution to the strife of the poem. The mourners return home to take part in a banquet:

χεύαντες δὲ τὸ σῆμα πάλιν κίον· αὐτὰρ ἔπειτα
εὖ συναγειρόμενοι δαίνυντ' ἐρικυδέα δαῖτα
δώμασιν ἐν Πριάμοιο, διοτρεφέος βασιλῆος.
ὣς οἵ γ' ἀμφίεπον τάφον Ἕκτορος ἱπποδάμοιο.

(*Il.* 24.801–4)

---

[41] Nicander *Theriaca* 957–58, *Alexipharmaca* 629–30; Vergil G. 4.559–66.

[42] Cf. D. Fowler 1995b with bibliography and his piece in this volume.

[43] Note also, however, the strikingly Lucretian conclusion to the preceding section on the death of fishermen (672–74), "And they in sorrow speedily leave those waters and their mournful labour and return to land, weeping over the remains of their unhappy comrade." The resemblances point to the *Iliad* as a shared intertext (so earlier lines 323ff. clearly point to *Il.* 22.369ff. on Hector's death): the presence of the coda points the difference from Lucretius.

[44] Cf. Conte 1994.

[45] Seaford 1989, 93; cf. Seaford 1994, 159–64.

[46] Macleod 1982, 45–46. On "funeral and antifuneral" in the *Iliad*, cf. Redfield 1975, 167–71.

> And once they'd heaped the mound,
> they turned back home to Troy, and gathering once again
> they shared a splendid funeral feast in Hector's honor,
> held in the house of Priam, king by will of Zeus.
> And so the Trojans buried Hector breaker of horses.[47]

In the *De rerum natura*, by contrast, the bereaved on their return cannot reintegrate themselves into normal life in this way, but instead yield completely to their emotions. The inversion of ritual is already present in the Thucydidean model (and the Homeric manner of Thucydides' closural devices has often been noted[48]), but the placing of the funerals and return home at the end of the poem points directly to the *Iliad*. Lucretius's attitude to ritual practices is radically different from that of Thucydides. While we observe little regard for religion in Thucydides, the failure to carry out burial rites properly is treated as a sign of the collapse of social mores and civilized life. Lucretius, however, argues against a belief in the need for burial in Book 3 (870–93) and attacks most of the rituals associated with religious worship, especially sacrifice.[49] The plague simply exposes the vacuity of meaning that Epicureans ascribe to these practices even in "normal," everyday existence, untroubled by war or plague. People still pathetically cling to their cherished beliefs even when the ritual is so hopelessly travestied that it cannot achieve its normalizing function. The gods of popular conception are implicated in the horror by appearing to allow sacrilegious behavior (1272–77). In Lucretius, then, the ritual of burial or sacrifice admits neither of a normative expression nor of an improper one.[50]

This is accentuated by the detail of the fighting among the mourners, which spans the final lines of the manuscripts and the transposed ending. This is not in Thucydides, but is another epic trait. Shedding blood over the disposal of corpses seems to be a pointless exercise, and yet this peculiarly desperate form of fighting had formed the central subject of *Iliad* Books 16, 17, and 18, while the disposal of Hector's and Patroclus's bodies dominates Books 22–24. The struggles here have a heroic aspect: the characters see themselves not as fighting over mere corpses but as establishing the *kleos*, the reputation, of the dead heroes. Eternal fame does not attach itself to a corpse that is hacked about and thrown to the dogs, as Agamemnon in the underworld makes only too plain.[51] Renown is only ensured when the hero dies nobly and is safely buried with honors that befit his status. Lucretius shares a number of details with the battles in the *Iliad*

---

[47] Trans. Fagles 1990.

[48] Cf. Hornblower 1987, 115–16 with n. 32: see especially *Il.* 24.1 and Thuc. 2.47.1 (cf. *Il.* 24.2 with 23.257, and Macleod [1982] on 24.801).

[49] Cf. 1.80–101, 2.352–66, 3.50–54, 4.1233–39, 5.1198–1203.

[50] There is a tacit reference to the custom of *conclamatio*: cf. 3.467–69 with Kenney 1971, ad loc; Servius on *Aen.* 6.218.

[51] *Od.* 24.93–97.

(fighting over the dead in appalling strife, spilling blood, a terrible accompanying noise or din, refusal to give up the corpse, and the theme of return[52]) but goes out of his way to remove any element of heroism. He presents the fighting as taking place within a polis, where concern for burial was strong, but by using the verb *rixantes* and by making the pun on "spilling blood" on behalf of those "related by blood," he undercuts the ideals of the *Iliad* and presents a travesty of the events of Books 16 to 18. Displaced from its cultural context in the *Iliad*, in which reputation, *kleos*, is the substitute for immortality of the soul, this fighting looks like a meaningless squabble. Concern for the burial of the dead, an abiding interest in Homer, is dismissed in Epicureanism as an aberration of the irrational mind.[53]

Thus the ending of the *De rerum natura* parallels the strife over the corpses in Books 16 and 17 of the *Iliad*, and the success that some achieve in disposing of the bodies and returning home from the funeral in part corresponds to Books 23 and 24. While these later books are occupied with rituals, the therapeutic effect of which is felt by all concerned, the funerals in the *De rerum natura* mark no such limit to grief or misunderstanding. In this imitation of the *Iliad* there seems to be a tacit comment that the ending there was somehow falsely optimistic, that grief and anger are not so easily overcome. The mourners bear a stronger resemblance to the striving masses of Books 16 and 17 than to the exceptional and enlightened pair of Priam and Achilles in Book 24, who both learn from their suffering. Ironically, Lucretius's mourners repeat in a travestied form (and in ring composition) the heroic actions of the new kind of hero, the philosopher with the military-sounding name, Epicurus, who in the prologue to Book 1 takes his stand over the prone bodies of mankind and challenges the threatening gods to a duel.[54]

The *Iliad* is also perhaps relevant to one final detail, specifically from the transposed ending, the retirement of the mourners to bed (*in lectum maerore*

[52] DRN 6.1286; with *Il.* 16.622, 756, 17.384–85, 397–98, 412–13, 543–45, 733–34, 18.242 (strife over the dead); *DRN* 6.1285 with *Il.* 17.360–63 (blood); *DRN* 6.1284 with *Il.* 16.565, 17.756, 759 (din); *DRN* 6.1286 with *Il.* 17.357–59, 634, 669–72 (refusal to abandon corpse); *DRN* 6.1248 with *Il.* 17.406, 636, 18.238, 330 (return).

[53] Significantly it is the contemptuous attitude toward death as expressed in Achilles' speech to Lycaon that Lucretius appropriates as the true kind of *consolatio* (3.1024–52, based upon *Il.* 21.99–113). Achilles then goes on to fling Lycaon's body into the river to ensure that it will not receive burial. Although Achilles' action is not condemned within the cultural domain of the *Iliad*, nevertheless Lycaon's fate is such that within its system of values it is contemplated with horror. Even the modern-day reader, whatever her beliefs, is sympathetic for the duration of the poem to the conventional attitude. Epicureanism, conversely, would demand indifference as a response.

[54] Cf. 1.67, *est . . . ausus primus . . . obsistere contra*; Conte 1994, esp. 1–2. One of the parallels from the *Iliad* noted by Conte in the prologue to the *De rerum natura*, 17.166–68, significantly belongs to the section where the warriors are striving to regain their dead. Glaukos is exhorting Hector to take his stand against Ajax in order to capture Patroclus's body so that the Trojans can exchange it for Sarpedon.

dabantur). The reference to bed is not entirely certain (*in lectum* is Marullus's correction of the manuscripts' *iniectum*, and is not the only possibility[55]), and the detail may seem a banal development, inappropriate to the heightened style and emphatic position occupied by the final lines. The action in itself seems domestic and familiar, and lexically *lectus* does not belong to the high style.[56] Nevertheless, the action is not without significance. In the *Iliad*, the mourners retire to bed after Patroclus's funeral (23.58), picking up a common closural device seen elsewhere in epic.[57] In Lucretius, *in lectum* contains a hint of a different sort of bed, the funeral bier. There is a sinister suggestion that the mourners, by giving way to their grief, are in effect consigning themselves to the funeral bier and bringing on their own deaths. Retiring to bed or lying prostrate is clearly seen as a sign, on the part of the mourner, of withdrawal from life. In contrast, the normal practice in Homeric epic or Greece in general was for mourners to attend a feast or wake after the funeral. Achilles' refusal to eat before and after the funeral of Patroclus, which is harshly criticized by Apollo, is part of his generally anomalous behavior.[58] The matching funeral of Hector, by contrast, is not marred by any such departure from the norm. After the Trojans return to Troy, they gather in Priam's palace and conduct a banquet: everything is done as it should be. No such positive comment is made at the close of the *De rerum natura*: here the retiring to bed contrasts with the proper conduct of the Trojans. The funeral meal signals the reintegration of the mourners into the life of the community: in Lucretius, there is no community to rejoin.

Epic and tragedy are always mutually implicated in Greek and Latin literature, and as in epic, many Greek tragedies end with funeral processions.[59] The resemblance of the transposed lines to a tragic coda has already been noticed, but there is perhaps a further tragic element in them. The funeral processions of tragedy form part of the aftermath of a *pathos*, a

[55] R.G.M. Nisbet has suggested to me *in letum* to give a stronger ending, but the normal phrase is *leto dare* (*Thesaurus linguae Latinae* 7.2.1189.40ff.; Thielmann 1882, index s.v. *letum*). *Lectus* without an epithet in the sense "sick-bed" is certainly a little odd, but *dare in* with the accusative in the sense of *imponere* is attested (Ovid *Met.* 7.608ff., *Ars Am.* 1.638, *Her.* 14.26).

[56] So, for instance, the one occurrence in the *Aeneid* (4.496) is in a technical term for the marriage bed (*lectus iugalis*); and the homely force of the word is to the point in Catullus 31.7–10.

[57] Cf. *Il.* 1.609, and of course the famous alternative end to the *Odyssey*, 23.295–96. On *Il.* 23.58, see Taplin 1992, 293, arguing for the end to a major division of the poem at that point.

[58] For the funeral meal, cf. Burkert 1983, 48–58; Kurtz and Boardman 1971, 146ff.; Andronikos 1968, 15–18; Toynbee 1971, 50ff.; and cf. Segal 1971, 66ff., and Taplin 1992, 276ff., on the importance of the shared meal of Priam and Achilles; and Sourvinou-Inwood 1981, 28 n. 47, on the importance of the location of the banquet in *Iliad* 23 by the tomb of Patroclus.

[59] Cf. Aeschylus *Septem* (on any version of the ending); Sophocles *Antigone, Ajax, Trachiniae, Oedipus Coloneus* (a special version of the motif); Euripides *Medea, Heracles, Bacchae, Supplices, Andromache,* and *Hecuba*.

destructive deed or an experience of intense suffering by one or several characters in the play. Plays in which such acts of violence are prominent generally close with scenes in which the "debris"[60] (that is, the dead bodies) is displayed in order to intensify the emotional reaction of the audience, especially as the horrific act itself is generally related in a messenger speech rather than enacted on stage. Unlike epic narrative, where the closing stages of the funeral can be presented,[61] Greek tragedy is concerned only with initiating the ceremony. The actors and chorus have to leave the stage at the end of the play,[62] and the funeral procession provides a suitable motive for clearing the orchestra.

Clearly, meaning can be generated by the manner in which this departure is made: whether everyone leaves the stage together or moves off in separate groups in opposite directions.[63] If everyone departs together with the same goal in view, then the funeral ceremony can become a powerful symbol of the assertion of communal values at the end of the play. P. E. Easterling argues for such an ending to Sophocles' *Trachiniae*, suggesting that the last four lines are an address by the chorus leader to other members of the chorus not to be left behind but to hurry and join the funeral procession.[64] In the *Ajax*, the mere fact that the funeral is allowed to take place marks the completion of the recuperation of Ajax, whose *timē*, honor, temporarily damaged by his madness, is now restored. The body whose presence onstage dominates the second half of the action is carried off by family and friends, but significantly Odysseus is excluded from the rites because the hostility of the dead man toward him is thought to continue. The ending of the *Bacchae* is particularly susceptible to different interpretations. Easterling sees a positive value in the return to the norms of social behaviour on the part of the Thebans after the devastating irruption of Bacchic frenzy.[65] But although Agave performs her proper function as chief mourner, there are several features in the reconstructed ending that might prompt us to modify a wholly normative reading. First, we know that Agave's lament was so poignant that considerable pity was roused on behalf of Pentheus. Second, the reassembling or piecing together of Pentheus's body can be interpreted as a travesty of the ritual laying-out, *prothesis*, of the body on the bier. Finally, Agave departs in the opposite direction from the corpse, excluded from the funeral, like Heracles, on account

---

[60] Cf. Dingel 1967, 106ff.; Taplin 1977, 163ff.

[61] Cf. also Pindar *Pyth.* 3.100ff., which ends with Achilles' blazing pyre.

[62] For words for departure, cf. Aesch. *Sept.* 916, 1059; Soph. *Trach.* 1275, *Aj.* 1402ff., 1414; Eur. *Andr.* 1263ff., *Bacch.* 1368ff, 1371, 1381.

[63] Cf. Taplin 1983.

[64] Easterling 1982 on *Trach.* 1275ff.; 1981, 69–72 (cf. Lloyd-Jones and Wilson 1990, 177–78).

[65] Easterling 1987.

of her pollution. The imperfect and incomplete nature of the funereal arrangement leaves in doubt society's capacity to restructure itself after the Dionysiac explosion. The tragic precedents, therefore, not only provide evidence of the socially integrative function of funerals that Lucretius is subverting, but also contain the seeds themselves of unease and disquiet at the success of such closure.[66] As modern scholarship on tragedy has often stressed, the cortège that leaves the stage at the end of a play may not be heading for any greater contentment than Lucretius's mourners, who take to their beds in unending grief.

INTERTEXTUALITIES II: THE LUCRETIAN ENDING

The use of Lucretius's ending in later texts can be as significant for its interpretation as its own incorporation of earlier texts. The *De rerum natura* becomes one model for the "problematic" ending, in which the comfort of closure is emphatically refused. In rewriting the *Iliad*, Lucretius emphasizes not the resolution of Achilles' anger and the reconciliation between enemies, but the renewal of war on the following day and the death and destruction that will follow. The power of that rewriting was in turn recognized in Virgil's *Aeneid*, which similarly ends abruptly on a ritual action, Aeneas's sacrifice (*immolat*, 12.949) of Turnus, that contains internal contradictions: a final resolution to the conflict of the second half of the poem and a foundational act for the New Rome, but also a perversion of ritual that casts doubt on the validity of civilized norms. The absence of a funeral at the end of the *Aeneid* is as strongly marked as its presence at the end of the *De rerum natura*. Ovid integrates Lucretius's ending into the final part of the *Metamorphoses*, and the juxtaposition of words from the beginning and end of Lucretius's plague account[67] provides additional confirmation for our argument about the end in Lucretius. It is not, however, a "Lucretian ending" in the sense in which that phrase is being defined here. Nor exactly is the end of Statius's *Thebaid*. This is not abrupt in the Lucretian sense, as it has a formal epilogue. It also bears the appearance of an Iliadic (and tragic) ending in that it closes with the funerals of the dead heroes and a cessation of hostilities. But an unresolved Lucretian (and tragic) note creeps in with the emphasis on the unending quality of the grief, which obviously bodes badly for the future: it is this grief that drives the sons of the Seven back to Thebes in the next generation, when they succeed in destroying the city.[68]

The two most important intertexts for the question of the transposition

---

[66] Cf. Francis Dunn, Chapter 5 in this volume, and Roberts 1993.

[67] Cf. 15.626, *quondam*, and 628–29, *funeribus fessi* and *temptamenta*, with Barchiesi, Chapter 9 in this volume.

[68] Cf. Ahl 1986, 2817–22; Henderson 1991; Hardie, Chapter 7 in this volume.

of 1247–51, however, are the endings to Virgil *Georgics* 3[69] and Sallust's *Catiline*. The end of Virgil's Noric plague contains a number of echoes of the transposed lines:

> nam neque erat coriis usus, nec viscera quisquam
> aut undis abolere potest aut vincere flamma;
> ne tondere quidem morbo inluvieque peresa
> vellera nec telas possunt attingere putris;
> verum etiam invisos si quis temptaret amictus,
> ardentes papulae atque immundus olentia sudor
> membra sequebatur, nec longo deinde moranti
> tempore contactos artus sacer ignis edebat.

(3.559–66)

>   The hide was no good, and no man
> Could cleanse the carcass in water or burn it up with fire:
> You could not even shear the fleece, it was so corroded
> With the foul pus, or work that rotten wool in the loom:
> But if you were so foolhardy as to wear the hideous garment,
> Inflamed pustules and a noxious-smelling sweat appeared
> All over your limbs: not long then
> Before the fiery curse ate up your tettered frame.[70]

The structure and generalization of *De rerum natura* 6.1250–51 are recalled by *Georgics* 3.559–60,[71] *temptaret* of Lucretius 6.1251 by *temptarat* of *Georgics* 3.563, *tempore tali* of Lucretius 6.1251 by *Georgics* 3.565–66 (*nec longo . . . / tempore*), and the sequence of verbs in the imperfect tense, *redibant, dabantur, temptaret* in Lucretius, by *sequebatur* and *edebat* in *Georgics* 3.565–66, marking a radical switch in Virgil from the descriptive present that dominates the passage from 515 to 558. The first alternative (559–62), the non-use of skins, opens with an imperfect tense, *erat*, at 559, but then switches to the present; but in the second alternative, the use of skins (563–66), there is a decisive shift to the imperfect as in the last lines of Lucretius—it has been the dominant tense in Lucretius. The gradual wearing down or chipping away of the plague is perfectly conveyed in the concluding lines of both poems: Lucretius 6.1250–51 (*morbus / . . . temptaret*) and *Georgics* 3.566 (*sacer ignis edebat*). The sound and structure of the final lines is also similar, with alliteration of *s* and *t* and pronounced enjambement: "*quem neque morbus / nec mors nec luctus temptaret tempore tali,*" "*nec longo deinde*

---

[69] Cf. Klingner 1964; and Gale (1991), who sees *Georgics* 3 as a microcosm of the *De rerum natura*.

[70] Trans. Day Lewis 1966.

[71] The opening of the final eight-line sequence: *nam neque erat . . . usus, nec . . . quisquam / aut . . . potest aut.*

moranti / tempore contactos artus sacer ignis edebat." *Sacer ignis* is Lucretian; it comes from 6.1167. It is emphatically closural for *Georgics* Book 3 because all of the natural disasters have arisen from an imbalance of the four elements and an excess of fire.[72] The invisible operation of fire in the *Georgics* is behind the maddening activities of the gadfly, the sexual energies of the human and animal kingdoms, the rage of the snakes, and the plague. Of course, it is significant that this is not the final ending in the *Georgics*, and some would see the darkness of the plague capped or transcended by the successful sacrifice at the end of *Georgics* 4; others would tend rather to assimilate that, too, to the problematic "Lucretian" closure.[73] The arguments mirror the more celebrated ones over the end of the *Aeneid*.

Also relevant to the textual problem at the end of the *De rerum natura* is the end of Sallust's *Catiline*:

> multi autem, qui e castris visundi aut spoliandi gratia
> processerant, volventes hostilia cadavera amicum alii, pars
> hospitem aut cognatum reperiebant; fuere item qui inimicos
> suos cognoscerent. Ita varie per omnem exercitum laetitia
> maeror, luctus atque gaudia agitabantur.

Many, too, who had gone from the camp to visit the field or to pillage, on turning over the bodies of the rebels found now a friend, now a guest or kinsman; some also recognized their personal enemies. Thus the whole army was variously affected with sorrow and grief, rejoicing and lamentation.

Like the *De rerum natura*, the *Catiline* ends with tantalizing abruptness and in descriptive mode. Chapters 59–60 give an account of the battle between government forces and Catiline's armed band, whereas the final chapter, 61, gives a vivid description of the scene of the battlefield in the aftermath of the fighting. This section is introduced by an *occupatio*, an address in the potential mood, *tum vero cerneres* (61.1), inviting the reader to contemplate the vividness or *enargeia* of the description. Lucretius issues similar invitations at 6.1259 and 1268. The scenes toward which the reader's gaze is directed are virtually the same in both works: heaps of corpses strewn over a wide area providing evidence of the intensity of the struggle in the process of dying, be it in armed struggle as in Sallust or in a frenzied state of mind as in Lucretius. The context in both is that of the polis or state.[74] The correlation extends to the focus on the emotional reactions of the living, of the would-be voyeurs and looters from the army camp in Sallust as they

---

[72] Cf. Ross 1987, 66–74, 149–87.

[73] Contrast Habinek 1990 and Thomas 1991a: and see Don Fowler's piece, chapter 1 in this volume.

[74] *Cat.* 61.7: *exercitus populi Romani*; DRN 6.1279: *quo prius hic populus semper consuerat humari*; 1247: *inque aliis alium, populum sepelire suorum / certantes.*

roll the bodies over to identify them, of the bereaved in Lucretius as they collapse in bed. Crucially, the ending is funereal and ritually impure: in the *Catiline* the bodies are left unburied where they have fallen, and in the *De rerum natura* the funeral is a makeshift affair.

Apart from these thematic and contextual links, there are also formal and lexical connections between the endings. There is a bipartite division between two groups of people, in Lucretius, the relatives who throw bodies onto empty pyres and those who hurl them onto pyres already occupied, in Sallust, the onlookers, *alii*, *pars*, who mourn the dead, and those, *fuere item qui*, who rejoiced at the death of their enemies. The paradox is that the bodies of public enemies, *hostilia cadavera*, can be distinguished as *amici*, *hospites*, and *cognati* by one group, and as *inimici*, private enemies by another. Personal relations become confused in a civil war.

Both works conclude with *epiphonemata* (*ita* in Sallust and *tali* in Lucretius), in which emotions are hypostatized as abstract subjects of verbs. The two words for "grief" both occur in Lucretius, although only *luctus* is a subject. The verbs *agitabantur* in Sallust and *temptaret* in Lucretius have a similar form and meaning; both frequentatives express persistent emotional arousal or attack. The emphasis is on the communal nature of the experience.[75] All of these features are strongly closural.[76]

The *Catiline* is open-ended and looks forward to the continuation of civil strife; failure to complete the account of the Catilinarian conspiracy reflects the failure of the Roman Republic to bring its *furor* to an end. Once again, the narrative technique reflexively mirrors its subject:[77] as McGushin notes (ad loc.), "The inconclusiveness of Sallust's decription is meant to underlie the inconclusiveness of fratricidal strife, the shadow of which lay over Rome at the time of writing." The *De rerum natura* is open-ended and "inconclusive" also, though not in the same way as Sallust. It leaves open the question of the possible continuance of strife, but whereas Sallust's work implies later historical developments, the question implicitly raised in the *De rerum natura* is not susceptible to historical enquiry: it cannot be answered at the historical or political level, but only at the level of each individual, and then by and for that individual alone. Sallust was vigorously opposed to the Epicurean ideal of individual *otium*,[78]

---

[75] Cf. *Cat.* 61.9: *per omnem exercitum*; *DRN* 6.1250: *nec poterat quisquam reperiri, quem.*

[76] Vretska (1976, ad loc.) notes that Sallust completes the work with an archaic exaggeration and without falling into empty pathos: the model is the *De rerum natura*. The phrase *in tali tempore* is actually used of the Catilinarian Conspiracy at 48.5 and is applied elsewhere to political upheavals; cf. Verg. *Aen.* 11.303, *non tempore tali*, of the Italian/Trojan War, and Livy 22.35.7.

[77] Cf. Cairns 1972, 163 n. 6; Lieberg 1982, 5–45; and Masters 1992, 6–10, with Don Fowler, chapter 1 in this volume.

[78] Cf. *Cat.* 1.1–4; *Jug.* 1.4.

yet his analysis of the causes of political decline brought him closer to Lucretius and those ancient moralists who attributed it to *otium*, peace, and the attendant luxury and idleness, not as in Thucydides to the indigent circumstances created by the harsh taskmaster, war.[79] Lucretius sees war and its attendants as simply exacerbating an already morbid mental condition (3.41ff.). It is not insignificant that Sallust takes up in the *Catiline* the metaphor of plague for moral corruption.[80] It does not figure in literature before Lucretius as prominently as the simple disease metaphor, and it carries connotations not available to the commoner image, of a collective crisis and of contagion.[81] The historical discussion of social mores or behavior of the populace en masse is thus a suitable, and common, context for the metaphor. The attraction of the *De rerum natura* to a writer like Sallust is that in no other text prior to it had the metaphor been developed for such a sustained stretch. Both doctors agree on the diagnosis of the sick patient, society, and on the failure of current techniques of therapy, notably politics; but they differ about the cure.

TENTATIVE CONCLUSIONS

The consideration of Bockemueller's transposition has already involved many of the wider issues of the poem's end, and in this final section I should like to look at some of these in more detail. At the beginning of the *De rerum natura*, the poet's composition of the literary text had been assimilated to the creative processes in the world.[82] Just as the poem created itself and its message at the beginning, so now at the end (with the transposition) it enacts its own dissolution as the words break down into their constituent syllables (*consanguineos* into *cum sanguine*, 6.1283–85; *morbus* into *mors*, 1250–51; *temptaret* into *tempore*, 1251). The poem itself is no exception to the law that all compound bodies (with the possible exception of the gods) decompose. The poem is frequently set up as a model for the arrangements of the atoms in the formation of larger structures by the analogy between letters and atoms.[83] A rearrangement of atoms leads to the creation of a different compound in the same way as a change in the order of letters in a word changes that word into a new one with a different

---

[79] Cf. *Cat.* 51.13ff.; Nisbet and Hubbard on Hor. *Carm.* 2.16.5.

[80] Cf. *Cat.* 10.6, 36.5; *Hist.* 1.77.9 K, 4.46. For some other allusions to the *DRN*, cf. Fowler 1989a, 138–39.

[81] Cf. Commager 1957; Schrijvers 1970, 312–24.

[82] Cf. 1.25 (*pangere*), 20 (*propagent*), 42 (*propago*), with Clay 1969, 37; more generally, see Schiesaro 1994.

[83] Cf. 1.197, 823–29, 912–14; 2.1013–18.

meaning.[84] Metaphors of weaving and unraveling are applied to both the literary and atomic processes.[85] The weaving metaphor is apt for the composition of a philosophical poem that has to lay out the interconnected propositions in an orderly manner, exhibiting its own system or *ratio* in a way that reflects the *ratio* of nature. The philosophical poet can fruitfully "imitate" nature; with his limited number of words, he can produce a vast number of different patterns. Only through the process of weaving will the *ratio* of the poem have its *species*, beautiful appearance, and the unseen processes be made visible. The word for "unraveling" is not applied to the poetic process: it is easy to extend the analogy to this stage, but difficult to see how it would work in practice, because if the analogy were properly followed through, the poem would end with a meaningless jumble of letters individually placed to mirror the disintegration of the compound into constituent atoms. If a meaningful structure is to be preserved to the very end, the most we can expect is a sense of a partial breakdown at the level of syllables (and molecules), which is, in effect, the case. Even if on the formal level the breakdown is muted, at the semantic level it is strikingly prominent. The word *temptaret* is prominently placed at the very end: it is one of the words subject to the unraveling process, and it contrasts with *pangere* at the beginning of the poem. It has by this stage become the *vox propria* for the attack of disease on the organism, occurring three times in the preceding paragraph on the *ratio* of the plague. More generally, it designates the stage before the collapse of any compound body.[86] At the end of the *De rerum natura*, the link between *temptaret* and *tempore* suggests that the process is like time in wearing down things or people.

The *De rerum natura*, then, establishes itself as a perishable construct, a composite of elements joined together in a linguistic system that can unravel and be rearranged to produce different words, arguments, books, etc. Ovid recognizes its status and, instead of promising it immortality, foresees its demise at the moment of the world's destruction:[87]

> carmina sublimis tunc sunt peritura Lucreti,
> exitio terras cum dabit una dies.

The verses of sublime Lucretius will perish only then when a single day shall give the earth to doom.

---

[84] As, e.g., in *ligna* and *ignis* (1.912–14). Cf. Friedländer 1969; Snyder 1980.

[85] Cf. 1.418: *sed nunc ut repetam coeptum pertexere dictis*; 6.42: *quo magis inceptum pergam pertexere dictis*; and on the atomic level, e.g., 1.242–43, 247, 3.209, 4.88, 5.94, *retexo* in 1.528. *Primordia, ordia prima, exordia* are all terms for the first "threads." On cosmic weaving, cf. now Scheid and Svenbro 1994, 172–77.

[86] Cf., e.g., 1.530, *temptata labare*, in conjunction with *retexi* in the preceding line; 537, *temptata labascit*; 580 in connection with *aeternum tempus* in 578 and 582.

[87] *Am.* 1.15.23–24. The language of doom appropriately comes from Lucretius (5.95: *una dies dabit exitio*; 1000: *una dies dabat exitio*; 3.898–99: *omnia ademit / una dies*).

Lucretius does not promise himself the "eternal crown" that Ennius so boastfully claims.[88] The highest praise that can be given to the godlike Epicurus is modestly restrained: his words are "most worthy of eternal life" (3.13). How, then, does the poem play itself out? To a degree, its measured self-reflexivity has been demonstrated already in the breaking up of the words in the closing lines, in the concentration of words for destruction, and in the closural devices. But in no area does it so evidently self-destruct as in that of its "message."

The "solution" for the psychological problems of human beings is a recognition that all of us, and everything else in the world as well, are subject to decay. But what is more worrying is that the representation of the fear of death is so powerfully emotive that it appears to undermine in a radical manner the radiant message of Lucretius's faith—that Epicureanism has arrived to save mankind.[89] The problem is created by the false rhetoric of closure. The generalization/*epiphonema* of 1250–51 is so packed with closural features that it is hard for the reader to step back and distance herself from the pessimism created by it. As far as the overall didactic function of the poem is concerned, this is a false closure, an unexpected one: it fails to sum up the Epicurean arguments and give them the ringing endorsement that the reader expects to carry away with her. Since the poem ends with a description, the addressivity of the language, normally so prominent in the didactic genre, is muted to its lowest point. A refusal to draw conclusions at the end of a work is not typical of an ancient moral philosopher,[90] and this avoidance of an explicit message at the end destabilizes the reader's interpretation of the whole work. Why does this happen? Why is the reader presented with a problem at the end, not an answer?

One approach is to consider the generic nature of the poem. A didactic poem presents a set of *praecepta*. The poet has the dual function of poet and teacher: a corollary of this is that the reader has the dual function of reader and pupil. In other words, both poet and reader are actively engaged in a process that carries implications for the spiritual welfare of the reader. Throughout the poem Lucretius as narrator has stressed the reader's capacity to formulate arguments for herself. Knowledge of Epicureanism is constituted not simply by a knowledge of certain facts, but by an ability to formulate new arguments in support of Epicurean axioms. Lucretius sometimes refuses to embark on further arguments and leaves it to the pupil (Memmius plays this role for the reader) to fashion new ones (1.402–17) or think up other examples (6.1080–83). This pedagogic method may bear on the ending of the poem. There are certain arguments and conclusions

---

[88] Cf. *DNR* 1.118, *perenni fronde coronam*; 121, *aeternis . . . versibus.*

[89] Cf. 1.62–79, 3.1–30, 5.1–54, 6.1–42.

[90] One exception is obviously Plato, and the aporetic endings to some dialogues, most notably the *Republic*: cf., e.g., Annas 1982.

at which pupils have to arrive by themselves. For them to be given the final and complete answer would be an abnegation of duty on the part of the teacher. Thus the plague passage can be seen as a kind of test for the reader to see if she has absorbed the message of Epicureanism.[91]

The poem on this view is "open-ended" in that the readers "write" their own "conclusions,"[92] but this open-endedness is only partial. The reader who wants to make a "success" of the poem must read the ending in the spirit of an Epicurean convert: as a provisional one, to be balanced and supplemented by the mental argument that the plague of Athens was a historical event, that subsequently Epicurus has come to save us, and that there are always corresponding creative processes to compensate for the destructive motions, at least on the level of the universe, if not of our world. To read the ending more pessimistically is an option available to the reader, and one that as we have seen, leaves its traces very clearly in the later history of the "Lucretian ending"; but it is an option that inevitably makes the poem a failure. This stark polarity has of course been with the reader from the beginning of the poem, and it is generated by the strongly positivist and solifidianist nature of Epicureanism. There is only one way to be saved, only one right way of looking at the world: Epicureanism cannot be just one philosophy amongst many, one possible model, but has to offer *the* nature of things. *Aporia* can only be a temporary state on the way to enlightenment. For the Epicurean, traveling hopefully and philosophizing well is not enough: one has to make it to the end. The reader at the end of the *De rerum natura* has to decide for herself whether she has made it, whether the poem "works." The strength of the poem is that the very power with which the more pessimistic side is presented makes more secure the enlightenment of the reader who *has* managed to accept this darkness and incorporate it into the Epicurean vision of tranquility.

[91] Cf. Clay 1983, 250–66.
[92] Cf. Fowler 1989b, 78.

CHAPTER 7

Closure in Latin Epic

PHILIP HARDIE

EPIC, at the summit of the ancient hierarchy of genres, is obsessed with power, structures of control, and ends that justify their means (Homerically, the capture of a city or the reinstatement of the head of a household). But ancient epics have a way of being strangely uncertain about their endings. To begin with, there is the brute fact that both the Homeric epics have alternative endings, in the case of the *Iliad* a matter of a variant of the last two feet of the last line plus an extra line, and in the case of the *Odyssey* a book and a bit after the line (23.296) recognized by some Alexandrian scholars as the *peras* or *telos* of the poem. The *Iliad*'s extra line, "And there came an Amazon, the daughter of great-hearted man-slaying Ares," reveals as a more profound root of this inconclusiveness than the disagreements of ancient editors the expectation in an oral tradition that an epic narrative will be continued (the arrival of the Amazon Penthesilea leads us into the next epic in the cycle, the *Aithiopis*). The prooemial mechanisms of early Greek epic are well developed, even top-heavy, making the absence of a formal coda or epilogue the more striking.[1] Thus at the very beginning of the Western tradition, we find a genre displaying an "openness" often associated with modernist texts.[2] To the extent that "secondary" Hellenistic and Roman epic is composed with a scholarly self-awareness of the closural problems in the archaic models, this uncertainty about endings is likely to remain as a defining feature of the genre; for example, the last line of Apollonius of Rhodes's *Argonautica*, by alluding to *Odyssey* 23.296, reveals the poet's awareness of the scholarly debate.[3]

A still more radical incompletion marks some of the Roman texts. Of the seven surviving epics of the first centuries B.C.E. and C.E., three (probably) remained unfinished at the author's death (Virgil's *Aeneid*,[4] Lucan's *Bellum civile*, Statius's *Achilleid*) and one, Valerius Flaccus's *Argonautica*, breaks off in the manuscript tradition in the course of what was probably

---

[1] Van Groningen 1960, ch. 6.

[2] Fowler 1989b, 79.

[3] See Livrea 1973, ad loc.

[4] Although it will become apparent that I do not believe that the ending of the *Aeneid* as we have it is one of the points of incompletion; for a contrary view, see note 26 below.

the last book. Only Ovid's *Metamorphoses*, Statius's *Thebaid*, and Silius Italicus's *Punica* have any claim to represent the considered and polished last thoughts of their authors.[5] These facts might be regarded as the trivial accidents of literary history were it not that the biographical contingencies attending the composition of the first in the series, the *Aeneid*, passed from life into literature to become a part of the normative expectations of the epic genre after Virgil. This is most apparent in the case of Ovid, who potently fictionalized his own "death through exile" as a repetition of the death of Virgil, teasing his audience with the consequences for our reading of both the *Metamorphoses* and the *Fasti* (an elegiac poem but with strongly epic qualities).[6] The impossibility of deciding whether the unfinished state of the *Fasti* is the result of an accident of transmission or of authorial suspension would no doubt have amused Ovid (if he did not indeed engineer the quandary). The "poetics of the fragmentary text," as it might be labeled, come to be central for Lucan;[7] much later, the inability of Petrarch to complete his *Africa* seems to be as much a self-fashioning ploy as the result of an enforced submission to external necessity.[8]

Within the Roman tradition, the epic figure of authority, Ennius, also fails to provide a model for a definitive ending. The *Annals* was originally written in fifteen books ending conclusively with the triumph of Ennius's patron M. Fulvius Nobilior in 187 B.C.E., but a further three books were added later as a continuation.[9] While this extension beyond an ending is analogous to, and perhaps licensed by, the continuability of the oral epic, it is determined specifically by the nature of the subject matter of an annalistic epic that takes the story down to the poet's own day: the constant flow of time renders the previous narrative incomplete and demands a new ending, which in turn is doomed to obsolescence. The Ennian epic is deprived of the satisfying sense of explanatory completion available to the aetiological or ktistic epic that narrates events in the remote past as a kind of "charter myth" for the institutions of the present day. Instead, closure as an artistic device imposing completed form on a segment of formless time is sabotaged by the "real-life" refusal of time to stand still.[10] Virgil comments implicitly on this aspect of the uncompletability of the Ennian epic in the

[5] Though some have doubted the completedness of the *Punica*, dismayed by the unusual total of books, seventeen, and have suggested that an ailing and tiring Silius brought his narrative to its predestined conclusion with the triumph of Scipio in a more compendious manner than originally planned.

[6] See Hinds 1985; Barchiesi, Chapter 9 in this volume.

[7] Masters 1992, passim.

[8] See Hardie 1993a.

[9] Skutsch 1985, 553, 563–65. The Ennian pattern was imitated by Horace when he added a fourth book of *Odes* to the enduring and self-sufficient monument of *Odes* 1–3: see Hardie 1993b.

[10] On literary closure and time, see Smith 1968, 117, 120–21; Kermode 1967 passim.

two set-pieces of historical prophecy in the *Aeneid*, the Parade of Heroes in Book 6 and the Shield of Aeneas in Book 8, both of which use Ennian allusion as both opening and closural signals[11] but in so doing draw attention to the fact that Ennius was unable to write his story to its close through nothing but the temporal limit of the biological individual.[12] Virgil was hardly unaware that as an epicist of Roman history he was subject to the same iron law. The tensions were even more acute for the poet of Augustus, a ruler who sought to legitimate his power largely through what one might call an "ideology of timelessness": the claim to have ended once and for all the interminable sequence of civil wars, to have brought about a return to the stable social and moral values of a mythical Roman past, in short, to have introduced in the present a Golden Age, that dream of a state of perfection before history, before time. In Virgil the literary question of narrative closure is inextricably linked with the Roman emperor's problem, as stage manager of history, of bringing down the curtain on the turmoil of the past.[13]

In the rest of this chapter I examine in detail the endings of three Latin epics whose narratives are brought to a conclusion, the *Aeneid*, the *Thebaid*, and the *Punica*.[14] The last two, not surprisingly, display an intensive concern with the closural devices of the by now canonical Virgilian model. In all three works, we can see a self-conscious interest in the ending as problem: this is partly in terms of the formal (Aristotelian) management of the last stages of a plot to bring it to a satisfactory point of rest, partly in terms of the pressure in epic to look to a continuation. The equivocation on endings that are also beginnings becomes something of a mannerism in epic of the first century C.E. Closure is further complicated by the possibility of more than one ending: a legendary or historical narrative has different endings from the point of view of the hero, the city, the race. Latin epic poets play with alternative endings in a way almost reminiscent of some

---

[11] The meeting of Aeneas with the shade of Anchises at *Aen.* 6.679–702 is modeled on Ennius's dream encounter with the phantom of Homer at the beginning of the *Annals*; the last line of the parade proper (846) is a virtual transcription of Ennius *Ann.* 363 Skutsch. Servius comments on the first scene of the Shield, that of the infants Romulus and Remus, *sane totus hic locus Ennianus est*; on the probable Ennian model for the concluding scene, see below.

[12] In Scipio's vision of Homer in the underworld at *Pun.* 13.778–97 Silius combines allusion to Alexander the Great's regret that he had no Homer to celebrate his achievements with allusion to the Virgilian vision of the doomed Marcellus at the end of *Aeneid* 6; the effect is to hint that Homer's mortality tragically deprived him of the chance to sing of the greater epic matter of Roman history: see Hardie 1993c, 115.

[13] For discussion of imperial epic from this point of view, see Hardie 1993c ch. 1. Hardie 1992 uses the theme of metamorphosis to look at issues of narrative and historical closure in the *Aeneid*, suggesting a close link with the concerns of Ovid's *Metamorphoses*.

[14] On the ending of the *Metamorphoses*, see Barchiesi, Chapter 9 in this volume.

recent fiction. The boundlessness of epic, always a hyperbolical genre, is also thematized, in psychological terms with regard to the unlimited nature of the passions of anger and grief, in political terms with regard to the unlimited expansion of Roman power.

THE *AENEID*

The actual ending of the *Aeneid* of course sidesteps the question of Augustus and history by narrating a final event in a much earlier story, the war in Italy between Aeneas and Turnus. The *Aeneid*'s primary narrative of the wanderings and battles of Aeneas contains prolepses of and allusions to the events of much later Roman history:[15] the question of an ending is thus complicated by the presence within the poem of more than one ending. One answer to the notorious problem of the killing of Turnus as the final scene of the epic would be to say that it is not an ending in any important sense; the real ending to the story of Rome is found instead in the survey of Roman history on the Shield of Aeneas at the end of Book 8, whose climax is the sealing of the *pax Augusta* in the triple triumph of Octavian/Augustus of 29 B.C.E. This view would stress the fact that the abrupt conclusion to the narrative of war in Italy by its very suddenness functions as a series of dots inviting the reader to continue the story, in the way that an oral epic is left open to continuation. Thus the *Aeneid* would be merely the first in a Roman epic cycle, the cues for whose continuation and completion may be found scattered over the poem. The relationship between this epic and the other poems in the cycle would then be analogous to the relationship between separate books of the *Aeneid*.[16]

But it is of course *that* ending, the finale to the last book, that sticks in the mind as the end of the *Aeneid*. It is not difficult to find in the alternative endings of the poem something approaching the radical choice of two (or more) mutually exclusive endings of some modern fiction. Before we reach that point, however, we can respond to the tension between the gloomy violence of the end of Book 12 and the joyous victory celebrations of the end of Book 8. This is the first of many points where Virgilian closure is to be read against the Homeric models.[17] Prolepsis, both direct and figurative, is a central device in particular of the *Iliad*: the Sack of Troy is the *telos* of the action of the epic taken widely as the war at Troy, and it is previewed in prophecy and image (above all in the lamentation at the

---

[15] On prolepsis, see Genette 1980, 67–78.

[16] On "Bookends," see Fowler 1989b, 88–97. Cf. the sensitive analysis of the "liminal" balance of closure and continuation in the last four lines of *Aeneid* 2 by Nagle (1982–83); on similar phenomena at the end of Book 5, see Barchiesi 1979.

[17] Fowler 1989b, 100–101.

death of Hector in Book 22). The contrast between the further limit of the action, the Greek destruction of the Trojan city and race, and the immediate ending of the poem, the temporary reconciliation between the Greek Achilles and the Trojan Priam over the body of Hector, is inverted in the Virgilian contrast between measured ritual celebration in the remote future and furious violence in the last recorded moment of the epic present.

The disorientation provoked by the co-presence of a number of "endings" within the *Aeneid* is aroused in a more intense form by the way that the last scene both stresses its own finality and provocatively fails to meet expectations of a proper ending. This irresolution operates both at the level of the value systems dramatized in the epic (above all in the often noticed clash between competing claims on Aeneas's *pietas*, respect for his opponent's aged father and duty to the slain Pallas), and at the level of formal and generic features.[18] The contrast between the killing of Turnus and the triumph of Augustus is heightened by intertextual comparison, this time with Ennius. Book 15 of the *Annals* (originally the last book) probably ended with an account of the Aetolian triumph of M. Fulvius Nobilior in 187 B.C.E. and the subsequent founding of the temple Herculis Musarum to house statues of the Muses brought from Greece by the triumphing general.[19] These are events with strong closural effect: triumph as ritual confirming the successful conclusion of war, and the erection of a physical monument memorializing the victory. Triumph and a new temple that is both victory monument and house for a divinity of poetry (the Palatine temple of Apollo) mark the end of Roman history as recorded on the Shield of Aeneas. Virgil had exploited the same Ennian combination of triumph and temple in his preview of the future completion of an epic project at the beginning of the third Georgic (an epilogue in a proem in the middle).[20]

For contrast, turn to the end of *Aeneid* 12: a final death-blow and the naked physical reality of a victorious killing.[21] The absence of any closing ritual also departs from the Homeric models (in their canonical form): the *Iliad* ends with ritual after death, the funeral of Hector, and the *Odyssey*

[18] The *Aeneid* conforms well enough to R. M. Adams's (1958, 13) definition of open form as "literary form . . . which includes a major unresolved conflict with the intent of displaying its unresolvedness."

[19] Skutsch 1968, 19; on the problem of the exact date of Fulvius's temple-founding, see Skutsch 1985, 144 n. 3. On the likely significance of the temple, see above all Martina 1981. It was built with a frontage to the Circus Flaminius, the staging ground for triumphal processions; in *Aeneid* 8 Augustus watches his triumphal procession from the threshold of the temple of Apollo, i.e., looking out over the Circus Maximus.

[20] See Conte 1992, 150–52. Ovid probably also alludes to the ending of *Annals* 15 in his reference to the temple Herculis Musarum at the end of *Fasti* 6: see Barchiesi, Chapter 9 in this volume.

[21] Farron (1982) points to the rarity of violent endings in ancient works of literature.

with ritual designed to prevent further killing, the oaths administered to Odysseus and the families of the suitors by a disguised Athena. In *Aeneid* 12 a counterpart to the Odyssean truce is found in the elaborate *foedus* struck by Aeneas and Latinus near the beginning of the book to regulate the duel between Aeneas and Turnus, where the most solemn religious language and symbolism is employed to confirm and ratify—but all to no avail. This ritual proves to be a false ending.[22] Thus the killing of Turnus inverts the expected sequence of violence followed by ritual, with respect both to the structure of the last book of the poem and to the remoter "ending" of the Shield of Aeneas in Book 8. It is hardly surprising that the most successful of the Renaissance attempts to provide an ending for Virgil's "unfinished" epic, Maffeo Vegio's thirteenth book, is largely made up of ritual actions: the funeral of Turnus and the wedding of Aeneas and Lavinia.[23]

Let us now turn from what is not there at the end to what is there. The last sentence, *ast illi solvuntur frigore membra / vitaque cum gemitu fugit indignata sub umbras*, is undoubtedly an ending, replete with "closural allusions":[24] the epic ends with the end of a life, the loosening of limbs (as a translation of the Homeric λύτο γούνατα, hinting perhaps at an Aristotelian λύσις?), with a last word (or at least a last groan), with a movement of departure (*fugit*), with the suggestion of a descent (into the underworld), and with darkness.[25] Much of this is in contrast to the continuation that the reader is now in a position to supply, the future story of Aeneas and his descendants: arrival in Italy confirmed and the end of the *fuga* theme, the fulfillment of the "journey to the stars" that has so often been foretold, all culminating in the brilliantly lit scene of Octavian's triumph staged before the temple of the sun-god Apollo. The implicit contrast between the endings of the stories of winner and loser may be compared with the proem to *Georgics* 3, where images of the victorious family of the *princeps* are followed by the picture of Envy confined in the underworld (3.37–39). The last word of Virgil's last book, *umbras*, has strong closural associations within the poet's oeuvre: it had been used to close the first poem of the major works, *Eclogue* 1.83 (*maioresque cadunt altis de montibus umbrae*), and also to mark the

---

[22] The Iliadic model is the broken terms of the truce of *Iliad* 3, which provided for the duel between Menelaus and Paris, a truce that within the economy of the *Iliad* must be rendered null if the epic is not to be prematurely brought to a conclusion. As well as the problem of how to end an epic, the poet has to find ways of keeping his lumbering narrative going.

[23] On Vegio's thirteenth book, see Kallendorf 1989, ch. 5.

[24] The term is that of Smith 1968, 172–82.

[25] Parallels at book endings: the last lines of Books 4 and 10 tell of the end of a life, and a death also occupies a closing position in 3, 5, and 6; verbs of departure occur in the last lines of 2 and 4; a voice falls silent in the last line of 3.

end of the *Eclogues* book (10.75–76), there in connection with a continuation in the form of a "rising" from one kind of poetry, pastoral, to another. By contrast, the use of *umbras* at the end of the *Aeneid* seems also to mark the end of Virgil's poetic activity altogether (we obviously do not expect that the epic poet will write out the continuation left open at this point).[26]

The last action of the poem is also marked as an ending by its place within a complex of structural patterning; it is the completion of structures both within the last book taken as a self-contained unit and within the poem as a whole. Ultimately the killing of Turnus is an act that, in important ways, makes retrospective sense of the poem as a whole, even if it is a sense that disturbs. I will first analyze the way in which the sequence of events in Book 12 thematizes the problem of how to end, before turning to structural patterns such as ring composition that are not strictly subject to temporal linearity. The question of closure cannot be separated from the analysis of the structure of the whole; my decisions on where to limit my discussions of the endings of epics are of course arbitrary.

Turnus's first words in Book 12 introduce the theme of a search for an ending (11–12): *nulla mora in Turno; nihil est quod dicta retractent / ignavi Aeneadae*. *Mora*, "delay," and the verb *morari* are keywords of the book, occurring nine times (*mora*: 11, 74, 431, 541, 565, 699, 889; *morari*: 676, 874).[27] But, despite the eagerness of both Turnus and Aeneas,[28] the destined final encounter of the two is deferred for nearly 800 lines, first by a scene in which the parents of Lavinia attempt to dissuade Turnus from his fixed intention, second by the elaborate account of the *foedus*, designed to expedite the duel but in fact allowing time for Juturna to exploit Italian unease in order to disrupt the truce and provoke a renewal of all-out war, which then rages unchecked for nearly 400 lines.

Delay had always been an important generator of the epic plot: the *Odyssey* is nothing but the tale of the obstacles that delay the hero's homecoming, and then of the deceptions by which the hero himself defers the final recognition; whereas the *Iliad* narrates an episode toward the end of the ten years' delay between the Achaean arrival at Troy and their taking of the city.[29] *Mora* becomes an even more pervasively explicit generator of

---

[26] Petrarch saw in the last line an all-too-literal self-referentiality, apostrophizing Virgil in the margin of his copy of the *Aeneid* against the last line, "You were too sure a prophet of your own death: for with such words on your lips life fled you."

[27] Cf. *Ecl.* 3.52–53: *in me mora non erit ulla, / nec quemquam fugio* (in a poem that succeeds in postponing for some time the climactic singing contest between Damoetas and Palaemon).

[28] An often rash hastiness is in any case typical of Turnus: e.g., 10.308–9, *nec Turnum segnis retinet mora, sed rapit acer / totam aciem in Teucros.*

[29] Cf. the language of *Aen.* 11.288–90: *quidquid apud durae cessatum est moenia Troiae, / Hectoris Aeneaeque manu victoria Graium / haesit et in decimum vestigia rettulit annum.*

epic length in Lucan's *Bellum civile* and Statius's *Thebaid*; in the former work it also becomes an index of the narrator's reluctance to progress with his unspeakable subject-matter.[30] The whole of the last half of the *Aeneid* is a tale of divinely engineered delay to Jupiter's plan that Trojans and Italians should live in peace together: recognizing the inevitability of the final outcome, Juno seeks *trahere atque moras tantis . . . addere rebus* (7.315). Book 12 thus functions as a concentrated encapsulation of the motif, repeating the initial alliance between Trojans and Latins in Book 7 and its ensuing disruption.[31] This "microcosmic recapitulation" is itself a closural device, a restatement of earlier themes with a quickening of tempo, leading to a resolution that had earlier been deferred.

Finally, at 723–24 Turnus and Aeneas come together for the single combat that had been envisaged all along—but not finally, for when the sword that Turnus had snatched up in error splinters, he takes to his heels, and the two only come face to face for the last time at 887ff., when Aeneas ironically (and unwittingly) repeats the terms in which Turnus initially expressed his eagerness for the end (889; cf. 11): *quae nunc deinde _morast_? aut quid iam, Turne, _retractas_?* But even at this stage Virgil will not allow us to proceed to a quick ending. The last paragraph of the narrative opens with a line framed by verbs of delay and eagerness: *_cunctanti_ telum Aeneas fatale _coruscat_* (919 cf. 916, *cunctatur*). Turnus's narcoleptic hesitation meets Aeneas's quivering energy, which unleashes a thunderbolt of a spear throw, a blow to end all blows—but which yet fails to deliver a quietus to its victim. The Iliadic model of the death of Hector leads us to expect a final verbal exchange, but Virgil swerves from Homer in making the spear wound not fatal, thus allowing for a final uncertainty about the choice of an ending. The crucial moments come with the last words of Turnus and the seconds that follow (12.936–42):

> "vicisti et victum tendere palmas
> Ausonii videre; tua est Lavinia coniunx,
> ulterius ne tende odiis." stetit acer in armis
> Aeneas volvens oculos dextramque repressit;
> et iam iamque magis cunctantem flectere sermo
> coeperat, infelix umero cum apparuit alto
> balteus.

---

[30] On Lucan, see Masters 1992, index s.v. "delay (*mora*) of narrative"; on Statius, see Vessey 1973, index s.v. *morae*; Feeney 1991, 339–40.

[31] The combination within *Aeneid* 12 of allusion both to the abortive duel between Menelaus and Paris at the beginning of the Iliadic battle narrative and to the final duel between Achilles and Hector at the end also makes of the book a "microcosmic recapitulation" of the whole of the *Iliad*.

With a terminal clarity Turnus states the simple truth that it is all over: active *vicisti* and passive *victum* present the perfected reality of victory, duly witnessed, and the winner takes the woman.[32] His last four words more explicitly call for a limit, and one of a very specifically epic kind: *odiis* refers us to the wrath that fuels both the *Iliad* (the wrath of Achilles) and the *Odyssey* (the wrath of Poseidon and the wrath of Odysseus against the suitors).[33] An end to anger is an end to a wrath epic. The problem is that the emotion of anger is inherently unbounded; it does not know how or where to stop.[34]

The immoderateness of epic emotion becomes an even greater stumbling-block to closure in the epics of Lucan and Statius. In Lucan it is combined with the other kind of limitlessness that surfaces in the *Aeneid*, the limitlessness of Roman imperial power (*imperium sine fine*, 1.279; the *non enarrabile textum* of the Shield, 8.625),[35] perverted in the *Bellum civile* through its protagonists' misappropriation of the unstoppable manpower of the city to the ends of their own furious and unbounded ambition. Statius exploits the limitations, in terms of wealth and geographical reach, of the power of his legendary actors in order to emphasize their psychological immoderation (*Theb.* 1.142–64): the key question is addressed to the brothers at 155–56, *quo tenditis iras, / a miseri? quis furor?* and *quis modus?* are insistent questions in Latin epic.[36]

But Turnus's words do seem to have the power to halt the narrative

---

[32] Finality is again marked by ring composition, as 937 picks up Turnus's initial formulation of the terms of the *foedus* (17): *aut habeat victos, cedat Lavinia coniunx.*

[33] The primary model is Iliadic, but Turnus's appeal also echoes the last words of direct speech in the *Odyssey*, Athena's appeal to Odysseus (24.542–44): διογενὲς Λαερτιάδη, πολυμήχαν' Ὀδυσσεῦ, / ἴσχεο, παῦε δὲ νεῖκος ὁμοιίου πολέμοιο, / μή πώς τοι Κρονίδης κεχολώσεται εὐρύοπα Ζεύς. Odysseus "obeyed"; the alternative would have led to a continuation in the working out of the anger of Zeus. How to end vengeful anger becomes a tragic problem as well: there are points in common between the endings of the *Oresteia* and the *Aeneid*.

[34] A point emphasized especially by the Stoics (e.g., Sen. *De ira* 1.7–8). Cf. the end of *Georgics*. 1 for a nightmare vision of the unstoppability of "epic" violence.

[35] Anxiety about limits marks the end of the other showcase of Roman power at 6.869–71 (of Marcellus), *ostendent terris hunc tantum fata neque ultra / esse sinent. nimium vobis Romana propago / visa potens, superi, propria haec si dona fuissent.*

[36] *Quis furor*: *Aen.* 5.670; Luc. 1.8. *Quis modus*: Luc. 1.334; Stat. *Theb.* 7.161, 12.573. Virgil had already posed the second question in a closing poem at *Ecl.* 10.28: *"ecquis erit modus?"* inquit, *"Amor non talia curat"*; with Gallus's submission to the omnipotence of *Amor*, the impossibility of limitation within the dramatic world of the poem is acknowledged (69), and in the next line the poet invokes a more formal kind of closure (70), *haec sat erit, divae, vestrum cecinisse poetam* (though to speak of an exit from the fictional to the real world of the poet would in this poem be problematic). Rather similar is the Statian strategy of closure at the end of the *Thebaid*, on which see below.

action: *stetit . . . Aeneas*. He stands stock still, and checks his right hand, the instrument of anger, only his eyes in motion. The juxtaposition of *armis / Aeneas* is a variant of the epic opening *arma virumque*; stasis is imparted to the epic itself. Within the structure of Book 12, the words *stetit acer in armis /* Aeneas also halt the impetus given to himself by Aeneas at 12.107–8, *nec minus interea maternis saevus in armis / Aeneas acuit Martem et se suscitat ira*, where *saevus* is a near-synonym for *acer*, and *acuit* contains the root of *acer*.[37] But things seen, rather than things heard, retain the power to provoke further action; *acer* may be taken closely both with *in armis*, "fierce," and with *volvens oculos*, "keen-sighted."[38] In 940, *cunctantem* is now used of Aeneas, not Turnus, and words, *sermo*, lead to the beginning of an ending (*coeperat*), from which we are once more diverted in the *cum-inversum* clause. The rest takes only ten lines to tell; the suddenness of the ending is partly an effect of the painful series of delays to that ending.

So far I have followed the plotting of the ending at the level of the human action. The death of Turnus is also the result of decisions taken by the gods. The human opponent of Aeneas is ultimately powerless beneath the weight of divine intentions, but the divine words and actions, as well as forming part of the chain of causality that leads inexorably to the ending of the human story, can also be read as a parallel story, so that again we have to do with alternative endings, one on earth and one in heaven. These are alternative ways of ending the wrath theme. If *mora* is the concern of actors on earth, the divine actors speak more directly of an end. Jupiter begins the final interview with Juno with the words *quae iam finis erit, coniunx? quid denique restat* (793)?[39] Ten lines later the question becomes a simple statement, *ventum ad supremum est* (803), and three lines later Jupiter concludes with a command, *ulterius temptare veto* (806). Turnus will conclude his appeal with *ulterius ne tende odiis* (938); Jupiter's words, however, are to be obeyed, and sibling diplomacy leads to reconciliation[40] as Juno's wrath (*irarum tantos volvis sub pectore fluctus*, 831) is converted into joy (*laetata*, 841), and Juno makes her exit from heaven (*excedit caelo nubemque relinquit*, 842 as she had already left earth, *terras invita reliqui*, 809).

The contrast between easy reconciliation in heaven and the irreversible effects of earthly anger is one that Virgil takes from the beginning of the *Iliad*, where at the end of the first book strife on Olympus is dissolved in

---

[37] Cf. 12.102, *oculis micat acribus ignis*, where *acribus* seems to be echoed in *acuit* six lines later.

[38] *Oxford Latin Dictionary* s.v. *acer* 3. There is perhaps a hint of the piercing power of the eyes (on the *acer/acies* pun, see Harrison 1991 on 10.308–9).

[39] One of the many features of ring composition connecting this interview with the interview between Jupiter and Venus in Book 1: *quem das finem, rex magne, laborum?* (241). On the use of *quis finis?* in Lucan, see Masters 1992, 251–53.

[40] But on the provisionality of even this reconciliation, see Feeney 1984.

the laughter roused by Hephaestus, while the wrath of Achilles still has many books and deaths to run. Malcolm Davies has shown how this contrast in the first book of the *Iliad* is inverted in the final book, where mortal reconciliation (Achilles and Priam) is at odds with the relentlessness of the animosity of the immortal gods;[41] but their animosity is directed in the first place against humans, rather than against each other. Virgil brings out the lines of his mortal/immortal contrast much more clearly through the stricter parallelism of his divine and human scenes (the scene in heaven is a rapprochement *between* gods, rather than a softening of Juno toward her mortal enemies, as the final exchange of the poem is one *between* mortals).

Virgil further stresses the contrasting parallelism of the final scenes of gods and humans by inserting between them a scene that shows a being intermediate between the divine and the human, Turnus's sister Juturna, compensated by Jupiter for his rape of her virginity with the gift of immortality. And where both the scenes that precede and follow *do* (with all due qualification) yield an ending, Juturna is condemned to a torture that is as unending as it is undeserved. Spatially the link between heaven and earth is made by the descent of the Dira to warn off Juturna (12.843–68); symbolically the Dira is an outpouring of divine wrath, but of Jupiter, not Juno, *dei ira* (worrying, if we thought that the theme of divine wrath was played out in this epic). Her effects are more akin to the piercing power of steel than to the persuasive balm of words: she is compared in a simile to a poisoned arrow (856–59). Fittingly for one located between the divine and the human, Juturna's last speech and departure partake, in an ironic mode, of *both* Juno's *and* Turnus's endings.[42] Her words are addressed to her brother (*germana*, 872; cf. *es germana Iovis*, 830). Juno hears and obeys the words of Jupiter; Aeneas hears and ultimately ignores the words of Turnus; it appears that the third possibility holds for Juturna: her words are not heard (and are therefore ignored) by her stunned brother. She both echoes Jupiter's opening question and uses the human language of *mora* (873–74): *aut quid iam durae superat mihi? qua tibi lucem / arte morer?* Like Juno she announces her departure, recognizing the futility of opposing Jupiter's commands: *iam iam linquo acies* (875). But for her the impossibility of an ending results from her status as an immortal with mortal attachments; hers is a futile wish for a limit to her passion (of grief, rather than anger): *possem tantos finire dolores* (880). Unable to accompany Turnus into his *umbrae* (881), she is condemned to a parodic imitation of the real death that limits

[41] Davies 1981, 59.

[42] Barchiesi's (1978) excellent discussion of this passage is vitiated by the insistence on the total isolation of Juturna and her point of view from the normative ideologies of the poem; he fails to see the extent to which the scene functions as a middle term between the divine and the human, despite his initial recognition (100) that, like the weeping Hercules of Book 10, she is a "figura intermedia fra il divino e l'umano."

her brother's existence (885–86),[43] shading her head in her robe, the gesture of the mourner but also of the suicide;[44] and descending into her river, where *her* groans will continue indefinitely (*multa gemens*, 886), as opposed to Turnus's single dying *gemitus*.

The death of Turnus is also caught in an intricate and extensive net of structural patterning that reaches over the whole poem. From the point of view of closure, the most important vectors take us to the beginnings of Books 12 and 1, to the night of the sack of Troy in Book 2, and to the finale of the Shield of Aeneas.

Inversion links beginning and end of book 12: fiery in his passion and proud at the start (*ardet / attollitque animos*, 3–4), at the end Turnus is first humbled and then chilled in death (*humilis*, 930 *solvuntur frigore membra*, 951). His failure to persuade Aeneas to spare his life through the appeal to the thought of his own father and the father of Aeneas is no more than poetic justice after Turnus's deafness to the appeals of Latinus (12.43–46):

> "miserere parentis
> longaevi, quem nunc maestum patria Ardea longe
> dividit." haudquaquam dictis violentia Turni
> flectitur; exsuperat magis aegrescitque medendo.

Compare 12.934 (*Dauni miserere senectae*) and 940–41 (*cunctantem flectere sermo / coeperat*). That the book should continue beyond the appeal of Latinus is the result of the unboundedness of Turnus's violent anger (*exsuperat*). This is of course one of the places where the advocate for Aeneas can take comfort: words themselves seem to exacerbate Turnus's passion.

The connections between the closing scenes of Book 12 and the opening scenes of Book 1 are extremely dense: the interview between Jupiter and Juno corresponds to the interview between Jupiter and Venus at 1.223–96; the storm imagery applied to Aeneas's final spear-throw picks up and inverts Juno's use of the storm force in Book 1;[45] the sense that the very last action is the ending is reinforced by the repetition in the penultimate line of the words that give us our first sight of Aeneas in the poem (*extemplo Aeneae solvuntur frigore membra*, 1.92): first and last things for Aeneas and Turnus respectively, with the strongest inversion. But if the *Aeneid* has more than one ending, it also has more than one beginning. If we look to the first (in absolute chronology) entrance of Aeneas onto the epic stage, we find not inverse but direct repetition: the emotions that impel the hero into action on the night of the sack of Troy, led by what he sees and hears

---

[43] The confusion of an immortal who wishes for death is mirrored in the paradox of a *threnos* uttered for one who is *not yet* dead (Barchiesi 1978, 110–13).

[44] Barchiesi 1978, 121 n. 31; Waltz 1939, esp. 296, for examples of self-veiling before suicide by drowning.

[45] See Hardie 1986, 177–80.

into ignoring the words of the ghost of Hector, are not to be distinguished[46] from the emotions that lead him to ignore Turnus's plea at the end:

> arma amens capio; nec sat rationis in armis,
> sed glomerare manum bello et concurrere in arcem
> cum sociis ardent animi; furor iraque mentem
> praecipitat pulchrumque mori succurrit in armis.

$$(2.314-17)$$

> ille, oculis postquam saevi monumenta doloris
> exuviasque hausit, furiis accensus et ira
> terribilis.

$$(12.945-47)$$

Comparison of the passages from Books 1 and 2 makes the ending of the poem even more problematical: the inversion of Aeneas's helplessness before the violence of the storm suggests a well-rounded and satisfyingly concluded plot, a long path successfully traveled, whereas the repetition of Aeneas's frenzy in the burning Troy leaves us with the feeling that he has been running hard to stay in the same place.

In the context of the endings of the other surviving completed Latin epics, the ending of the *Aeneid* remains unusual in its abruptness. Both the *Thebaid* and the *Punica* give us a version of the last scene of the *Aeneid* but then continue with closing scenes of ritual, triumph in the *Punica* and figurative triumph plus ritual lament in the *Thebaid*. In both cases the triumph alludes to the triumph of Octavian viewed as the ulterior ending of the *Aeneid*; the Statian funerals take us back to Homeric origins, the funeral of Hector at the end of the *Iliad*, but combined with allusion to the death of Turnus in a way emblematic of Statius's combinatorial imitation of both Homer and Virgil throughout the poem. In addition, the *Thebaid* receives a separable envoi in the form of an address by the poet to his completed poem, based largely on Horatian and Ovidian models, which drives a wedge between the degree of closure allowed by the subject matter and that imposed by the poet.

STATIUS *THEBAID*

The twelfth book of the *Thebaid* plays with its own status as a supplement, an ending after an ending. As a final book resolving the problem of burial outstanding after earlier killing it follows the model of *Iliad* 24, but the Statian resolution is brought about through a renewal of all-out war, when

---

[46] Attempts to make a distinction do not convince: Cairns 1989, 82–84, with Thomas 1991b.

an army from another city, Athens, repeats the earlier expedition from Argos (an example of "microcosmic recapitulation"). There is Homeric precedent in the reopening by the suitors' relatives at the end of *Odyssey* 24 of the violence of the killing of the suitors in Book 22; there is also the Virgilian parallel of the renewed outbreak of total war after the *foedus* intended to bring it to an end. The final encounter between Aeneas and Turnus is thus played out twice in the *Thebaid*, once in the mutual fratricide of Polynices and Eteocles in Book 11, and again in Theseus's killing of Creon near the end of Book 12. The last pages of Book 11 parade dismembered fragments of the ending of *Aeneid* 12 to increase our sense of a new beginning in the continuation of Book 12: a suppliant, Antigone, appeals to the "winner" Creon to take pity on an old father and pleads for "burial" (11.737–39):

> miserere senis, maestosque parentis
> hic, precor, hic manes indulge ponere: certe
> Thebanos sepelire licet.

Compare *Aeneid* 12.932–36:

> miseri te si qua parentis
> tangere cura potest, oro (fuit et tibi talis
> Anchises genitor) Dauni miserere senectae
> et me, seu corpus spoliatum lumine mavis,
> redde meis.

Creon is moved (*flectitur adfatu*, 748; cf. *Aen.* 12.940, *flectere sermo*), but grants only part of Antigone's prayer (as we may suppose that Aeneas will at least grant Turnus's prayer for the return of his body to his family),[47] assigning the borderlands of Thebes as the appropriate habitat for the "shadow" that is Oedipus (*umbris*, 753), a sort of halfway house to full flight into exile. The last five lines switch to an account of the ignominious, real flight of the Argive survivors, but into an unworthy life, not death, under cover of darkness and without a groan (*eunt taciti passim et pro funere pulchro / dedecorem amplexi vitam reditusque pudendos*, 759–60). The last line converges on the last word of the *Aeneid*:

> nox favet et grata profugos amplectitur umbra.
>
> (*Theb.* 11.761)

> vitaque cum gemitu fugit indignata sub umbras.
>
> (*Aen.* 12.952)

---

[47] Though for considerations to the contrary, see Lyne 1989, 113.

But if the Virgilian echoes had lulled us into thinking that we had finished, the first two words of the next book set us straight: *nondum cuncta*.[48]

The final scenes of Book 12 strike a fine balance between the narration of *cuncta* and the suggestion of incompletion. The single combat of Theseus and Creon is heavily marked by signs of closure: lexical items of completion (repetition of forms of *extremus* at 755, 759, 777, 781); foreshadowing (*frustraque extrema minantem*, 755; *audax morte futura*, 760; *frustra periturum missile*, 755); allusion to the final scene of the *Aeneid* (the image of the killing as sacrifice, 771; *oculis . . . solutis*, 777: cf. *solvuntur . . . membra*, *Aen.* 12.951). In two respects the finality of the death of Turnus is tightened up: the first throw of Theseus's massive spear brings certain death, and in the last words of his taunt to the dying man Theseus assures Creon of the burial that Aeneas *might*, conceivably, wish to deny to Turnus (if we press the Iliadic model of Achilles' response to Hector's request for burial).[49]

In the sequel, Statius at first rushes with almost unseemly haste to tie up the loose ends: in joyful disorder the two sides make peace, *medio iam foedera bello* (783, eliding the expected sequence of *foedera post bellum*, in a positive instance of the confusion of distinctions that is a central theme of the whole epic). The rest is a mixture of celebration and lamentation, triumph and funeral, even triumph as funeral (in Virgilian terms, the Marcellus coda to the Parade of Heroes combined with the triumph of Augustus on the Shield, two very different endings to two comprehensive reviews of Roman history).[50] Theseus's entry into Thebes and the joy of the Theban women (12.784–87) reworks topics from the triumph of Augustus at the end of the Virgilian Shield of Aeneas (*Aen.* 8.714–15 *at Caesar, triplici invectus Romana triumpho / moenia*; and *omnibus in templis matrum chorus*, 718: in Statius there are *only* women to celebrate the "triumph"; the men are dead).[51] The closing simile comparing the Theban women to the Ganges rejoicing in its new subjugation to the victorious Dionysus exploits the Theban connections of the god to suggest the tri-

[48] Henderson (1991, 66 n. 54) spots *nondum cuncta*. In other ways the ending of Book 11 of course demands continuation; Venini (1970) ad loc. notes the closural effect of nightfall, but correctly stresses that the book *lacks* the dramatic ending of the other books in the second half of the *Thebaid*.

[49] But for ways in which the victory of Theseus may not be so unambiguous, see Hardie 1993c, 46–48.

[50] The Parade of Heroes itself combines triumphal and funereal elements; for other epic confusions of triumph and funeral, see *Aen.* 11.53–54; Lucan 3.288–92 (catalogue-as-triumph-as-funeral); Stat. *Theb.* 12.88, 578–79. On the extraliterary links between triumph and funeral, see Versnel 1970, 115–29 (skeptical of Brelich's [1938] hypothesis of an original connection between the two, but allowing for the obvious triumphal elements of the *funus imperatorium*.

[51] Theseus has already appeared as the Roman triumphator at his entry to Athens after his Amazonian victory: note esp. 12.532–33, *niveis victorem . . . vectum / quadriiugis*.

umph of Dionysus as a mythical type for the later Roman institution,[52] and adds another to the catalogue of conquered rivers with which Virgil rounds off his triumphal procession:

> qualis thyrso bellante subactus
> mollia laudabat iam marcidus orgia Ganges.
>
> (*Theb.* 12.787–88)

Compare *Aeneid* 8.726, *Euphrates ibat iam mollior undis*.

But our sense of an ending is rudely disrupted at line 789 with the sudden (*ecce*) arrival of another group of females, the Argive women, following Theseus more slowly from Athens. In another Bacchic simile they are compared not to peaceful acolytes of the god, but to *Bacchea ad bella vocatae / Thyiades amentes, magnum quas poscere credas / aut fecisse nefas* (791–93). Commenting on *bella*, Ahl points out that the women's cries of lamentation are "the first stirrings of those emotions which will send the descendants of the Seven to try—and to succeed—where their fathers had failed."[53] Moreover, their movement from the mountain (Cithaeron) to the city reverses the normal escape of Maenadic women from the city to the wilds (archetypically in Latin epic at *Aen.* 7.385–405),[54] seriously infringing the integrationist thrust of triumph and funeral as closural rituals. This context lends fresh force to the conventional paradox of the pleasure of weeping at 793–94: *gaudent lamenta novaeque / exsultant lacrimae*.

In the next thirteen lines the poet begins to detach himself from his epic, prior to the envoi that personifies the poem as an object separate from its maker. The last line, *et mea iam longo meruit ratis aequore portum* (809), seems a curiously trite use of a poetic cliché as a closing formula; perhaps that is deliberate, an admission of the impossibility of any adequate epic conclusion to a boundless subject. Indeed, the closest model for this brusque and arbitrary management of an intractable topic would appear to be non-epic, Virgil's use of the image of poetry as sea journey in the *Georgics*: at 2.39–46 that image is combined with the "hundred tongues" topos as here, and at 4.116 ff. Virgil "sails past" the subject of gardens as Statius here decides that it is time for his ship to enter port.[55]

The "hundred tongues" topos is here unusually employed at the end of a poem.[56] When it is applied in the middle of an epic, before a catalogue or

---

[52] "Triumph" of Dionysus: Versnel 1970, 251–54; Cairns 1972, 96–97.

[53] Ahl 1986, 2898.

[54] Statius uses the Virgilian model near the beginning of the narrative of the Lemnian women at *Theb.* 5.92–94.

[55] *Theb.* 12.797 *non ego* = *G.* 2.42.

[56] See Skutsch 1985, 627–29; Austin (1977) on Verg. *Aen.* 6.625ff. Note in particular its use at Ovid *Met.* 8.533–35 to express the poet's inability to catalogue female utterances of grief over a death that results from intrafamilial strife.

wherever, the suggestion is of a local excessiveness that is bounded by the narrative that surrounds it; here the effect is to leave the poem as a whole open-ended. Statius exaggerates the hyperbole of grief[57] to suggest that what is left over is nothing less than a whole epic of mourning. This is the implication of line 808, *vix novus ista furor veniensque implesset Apollo*, the spirit and the god that are needed at the beginning of an epic;[58] it is also the implication of a comparison of this closing *praeteritio* with the proemial material at the beginning of the first book. What we find is ring composition—in itself a signal of closure—but ring composition that brings us to a close on another opening. The closing lines are also an exemplification of the problems of setting limits that is an explicit theme of the proem.[59]

The catalogue of laments by the womenfolk of Argos corresponds first to the catalogue of the men that they mourn at 1.41–45.[60] But as *praeteritio* the closing catalogue corresponds to the epic subjects that Statius in the proem either refuses to sing of or postpones. At 1.4–16 the previous history of the house of Cadmus *ab origine* is sketched and then passed over: material for a different kind of epic, a *perpetuum carmen* (and in fact the *gemitus et prospera Cadmi* form a substantial part of Ovid's epic, Books 3 and 4 of the *Metamorphoses*). Statius is adamant about setting a limit to *his* epic (*limes mihi carminis esto / Oedipodae confusa domus*, 16–17). And yet what kind of "limit" or "path" is to be found in the tale of a "house of confusion"?[61] The attempt at self-limitation with regard to the totality of the legendary subject-matter is then followed by the demarcation of the pretensions of *this* epic with regard to a subsequent epic magnification of the wars of Domitian (*quando Itala <u>nondum</u> / signa nec Arctoos <u>ausim</u> spirare triumphos*, 17–18). Statius's careful gradation of his epic flights is, however, fatally compromised by the very subject matter of the *Thebaid*:

> tempus erit cum Pierio tua fortior oestro
> facta canam: nunc tendo chelyn satis arma referre
> Aonia et geminis sceptrum exitiale tyrannis
> nec furiis post fata modum.

$$(1.32-35)$$

---

[57] The conventional hyperbole is parodied at Lucr. 3.907–8: *insatiabiliter deflevimus, aeternumque / nulla dies nobis maerorem ex pectore demet*.

[58] Cf. 1.3: *Pierius menti calor incidit*. In the *novus furor* it is impossible in a poet writing after Lucan not to hear a contamination of the poet's inspiration with the epic emotions of his characters. Note Theseus's reformulation of Lucan's question *quis furor, o cives*? (*Bellum civile* 1.8) at *Theb.* 12.593, *novus unde furor?*: it is Creon's "new madness" in refusing to allow burial that has occasioned this extra book after the end of the story of the two brothers.

[59] Ahl 1986, 2817–22.

[60] Despite the lack of a complete one-to-one correspondence, because of the exigencies of plot.

[61] See Henderson 1991, 34–39.

This is an epic without limit, *modus*, in which the most emphatic of endings, death, is no ending. The anger of Polynices and Eteocles survives them (and in the wider perspective is a part of the curse of the Labdacid house that will lead to further epic action by the Epigoni—the Seven against Thebes is the classic example of an epic tale to be continued); and even if death could bring to an end the furious violence of epic men, it provokes the boundless frenzy of female grief.[62]

Here one is reminded of the unending mourning that is Juturna's lot at the end of the *Aeneid*. The concluding catalogue of untellable female sorrow also uses the very last lines of the *Aeneid* both to comment on its own unendingness and to mark itself as some kind of closure. Virgil takes his leave with the dying groan of one man:

> vitaque cum gemitu fugit indignata sub umbras.
>
> (*Aen.* 12.952)

Statius proclaims himself unequal to express the innumerable groans of Argive lament:

> non ego . . .
> tot pariter *gemitus dignis* conatibus aequem.
>
> (*Theb.* 12.797–99)

But some attempt to convey the quality of that lament is made in the three-line expansion (12.805–7) on the last of the dead heroes to be mentioned, Parthenopaeus.[63] In the first place, the threefold repetition at the beginning of successive lines of *Arcada* is itself formally suggestive of closure;[64] second, the number three further hints at the ritual practice of calling for the last time on the dead thrice;[65] third and last, the repetition points to the repetition (twofold) of the name of another Arcadian youth in the last words of Aeneas in the *Aeneid*:

> Pallas te hoc vulnere, Pallas
> immolat.
>
> (*Aen.* 12.948–49)

THEBAID 12.810–19

The *praeteritio* that is no ending is capped by an epilogue to the whole epic that is very different in closural effect.[66] The separation between poet and

---

[62] The first hero listed in the catalogue at 1.41–45 is *immodicum irae / Tydea*.
[63] See Hardie 1993c, 48.
[64] For "closural repetition," see Smith 1968, index s.v. "repetition.".
[65] E.g., *Aen.* 6.506: *magna manis ter voce vocavi*.
[66] On *Theb.* 12.810–19, see Vessey 1986, 2974–76.

his work implied in the distinction between the author's "ship," which has reached port, and the pressure of the narrative itself to continue its journey indefinitely before the gale of the Argive women's laments becomes explicit in the ten-line coda or envoi, in which the poet addresses his own work and looks forward to its survival after his own demise. As a closural device this is contrary to Homeric and Virgilian practice, and presents the epic as a completed whole that is immune to continuation; the epic model is above all the nine-line epilogue at the end of Ovid's *Metamorphoses*, 15.871–79, which in turn has non-epic precedents, Ovid's own elegy (*Amores* 3.15.19–20; cf. *Tristia* 3.7.49–54) and, above all, Horace's lyric, especially *Odes* 3.30. This last work may return us to epic models, for its topics probably owe much to a passage on the durability of epic praise when compared to physical monuments at the beginning of the continuation in a sixteenth book of Ennius's *Annals*.[67] It is certain that the *Annals* was introduced with an elaborate reference to the poet himself and his task, in the dream of the phantom of Homer. The invocation of the Muses before the dream seems likely to have formed a ring with the account at the end of Book 15 of Nobilior's importation of the statues of the Muses to Rome after his Aetolian victory,[68] creating a coincidence of historical and poetic themes; this might have been the occasion for further self-reflection by Ennius concerning the nature of his achievement at the *end* of the poem. Some have suspected that Ennius's lines comparing himself to a retired race-horse (522–23 Skutsch) come from the end of *Annals* 15; if that were so, then we would have a closural device of the same kind as Statius's image of the ship that has earned its rest in port at *Thebaid* 12.809.

This is all speculation, but there remains a possibility that the Ovidian and Statian epilogues develop an Ennian technique of closure that is lacking in the sudden ending of the *Aeneid*.[69] What is unusual about the Statian envoi is its modesty, certainly when compared with Horace *Odes* 2.20 and 3.30 or the end of Ovid's *Metamorphoses*. The irony is Horatian, modeled on *Epistles* 1.20, in which the book of *Epistles* is personified as a slave-boy running away from his master.[70] By separating the work from its author, it is freed to undertake its own future career, in the image of an epic journey under the aegis of a guardian divinity, *praesens Fama*, an externalization of the power to immortalize through renown that is the epic's own prerogative. The temporal structure of the ten lines lends it its own completeness: it falls into five groups of two lines, the symmetry broken only by the

---

[67] See Suerbaum 1968, 165ff.

[68] Skutsch 1985, 144–46.

[69] Virgil may well displace some of this Ennian proemial/closural self-consciousness to a point in midstream: the famous reference to the power of his poetry at *Aen.* 9.446–49 is probably heavily indebted to the beginning of *Annals* 16.

[70] Perceptively on the irony, Henderson 1991, 38–39.

spilling over of the name *Thebai* into emphatic position in the first foot of the third line. The sequence of (recent) past (812–13), present (814–15), and future (818–19) is introduced by a concerned question about the future of the (more distant) past achievement (810–11), and punctuated by injunctions for the future (816–17) that draw confidence from the previous consideration of past and present. Just as the poet's own boat earned its rest in harbor (*meruit*, 809), so after the poet is no more the poem will receive its well-earned tribute of (perhaps divine)[71] honors, the final closing ritual. This little narrative of pious obeisance to a poetic monarch (Virgil) and orderly inheritance from a poetic master (Statius) is the complete opposite of the Theban tale that we have just read. One might read this as another reworking of the Virgilian double ending: but where the *Aeneid* contains both the end of the narrative (the death of Turnus) and the larger ends (the foundation of Rome and the triumph of Augustus) that somehow complete it, in the *Thebaid* the end of the narrative invokes a larger end (poetic fame) that completes it (if at all) from outside the poem.[72]

SILIUS *PUNICA*

The closural effects in the *Punica* are easier to define than in the *Thebaid*, but they are not without sophistication, and Silius, too, plays with the possibilities of reopening stories that seem to have reached a conclusion, largely through reworkings of Virgilian endings. Furthermore Silius indicates at various points through his epic that his, too, is a story to be continued. The final victory of Scipio Africanus is a decisive ending of a war, but it is only a stage in the much larger history of Rome.

At the end of *Punica* 17 Silius adopts the same basic pattern as Statius, that is, a version of the end of *Aeneid* 12 followed by the triumphal ending of *Aeneid* 8 (and perhaps drawing also directly on the ultimate model at the end of Ennius *Annals* 15). Unlike Statius, Silius sets a clear limit between the fighting and its celebration (*hic finis bello*, 17.618). A close immediately followed by the voluntary opening[73] to Scipio of the walls of Carthage, as Theseus is welcomed by the citizens of Thebes, is in Silius not a prelude to a "triumphal" entry but rather an example of *victorque volentis / per populos dat iura* (Virg. *G*. 4.561–62). The description of the triumph itself is introduced with a statement of the permanence of Scipio's glory, *mansuri compos decoris per saecula rector* (625 epic κλέος ἄφθιτον), and the final return to Rome (*referens*, 626; *repetit*, 627). An echo of *Aeneid* 8 introduces the tri-

---

[71] See Hardie 1993c, 111.

[72] For these closing formulations I am indebted to Francis Dunn.

[73] *Reserantur*, a word associated with poetic openings in Ennius *Ann*. 210 Skutsch and in Lucretius 1.11.

umph: *repetit per caerula Romam / et patria invehitur sublimi tecta triumpho* (627–28; cf. *Aen.* 8.714–15: *at Caesar triplici invectus Romana triumpho / moenia*); images of Gades, the end of the world, and of Gibraltar, the limit of Hercules' achievements, suggest as much of the Augustan claim to world empire as is appropriate for Scipio. We watch the procession unroll before us, until the last and most important figure appears, Scipio himself (*ipse*, 645). What we see is not actually the man himself, but a climactic series of comparisons to gods and great men. This closural synkrisis echoes the comparisons with Hercules and Bacchus that conclude the panegyric of Augustus at *Aeneid* 6.801–5; the expanded Silian list runs: Mars; Bacchus, Hercules; Romulus-Quirinus, Camillus. The last two pairs provide mythological and historical precedents for the Roman triumph of Scipio. A provisional resting-place is reached at 650 with the picture of Hercules "touching the stars" after the defeat of the Giants, a resumptive allusion to a hero and a myth central to the imagery of the whole poem; the last word of the sentence, *astra*, suggests the source of legitimacy for Roman power and also the destination of apotheosized heroes like Hercules, Bacchus, and Romulus—the destination, too, of Virgil's Aeneas and his descendants. Scipio, of course, is not one of that band of deified men, but the comparison with gods facilitates the final turn of the epilogue to the form of the hymn, using the closural *salve* convention of that genre.[74] The claim that Scipio yields nothing to Romulus or Camillus implies a superlative.[75] The last two words of the last line provide a crashing final chord: *Roma Tonantis*, the epic voice thundering to the last; but not without a twist, for this climax to a triumph looks to a Lucanian climax to a funeral address, the last lines of *Bellum civile* 8 (which have as much claim to be an ending as anything in that poem):

> atque erit Aegyptus populis fortasse nepotum
> tam mendax Magni tumulo quam Creta Tonantis.
>
> (Lucan 8.871–72)

> nec vero cum te memorat de stirpe deorum,
> prolem Tarpei mentitur Roma Tonantis.
>
> (*Punica* 17.653–54)

The inversion only makes the allusion more emphatic (a lie in Lucan, a truth in Silius); in both cases the claim points to the superhuman preten-

---

[74] Archaic Greek epic begins with a detachable hymn; the hymnic close is paralleled in the final address to the heroes at the end of Apollonius's *Argonautica*, beginning ἵλατ' ἀριστήων μακάρων γένος, where ἵλατε is "la formula propria della divinità" (Livrea [1970] ad loc.). Silius also has in mind the closing address of the hymn to Hercules sung after the Cacus narrative at *Aen.* 8.301: *salve, vera Iovis proles. Invictus*, the epithet applied to Scipio, is a cult title of Hercules at Rome.

[75] Smith 1968, 183–85.

sions of the hero, or, more correctly, to the power of fame, and of epic *fama* in particular, to elevate the great man to a more than human status.

In the earlier part of Book 17 Silius has to step rather nimbly in order to bring to this triumphal ending what is essentially unfinished business (the stumbling block is the historical fact that Hannibal met neither death nor capture). At 201ff., informed of Scipio's destructive progress through Africa, Hannibal makes the painful decision to return from Italy. It seems to the Romans that this is a final decision (*tandemque resolvat / Ausoniam*, 205–6). Hannibal departs with groans (*multumque gemens*, 202), but soon changes his mind, like the dying Turnus unable to endure the thought of his unworthy flight (*hoc nunc / indignus reditu. . .?* in an ironic question to himself, 221–22). No, he will return (232–33): *ibo et castrorum relegens monumenta meorum, / qua via nota vocat, remeabo Anienis ad undas.* There is, then, a threat of the same replay of a war apparently completed that we find in the last books of the *Aeneid* and the *Thebaid*; to avoid this return to a beginning Silius has recourse to another beginning, the storm of *Aeneid* 1.[76] Like Aeneas, Hannibal is blown to the coast of Carthage, but with the difference that now it is Neptune, working for the Roman cause, who raises the storm in his own domain. This will not, then, mark the beginning of a new odyssey or iliad of woes for the Romans; the danger is rather the opposite one, that this display of elemental violence will result in premature closure. Excess of the epic emotion of anger here endangers the possibility of a measured continuation:

> tum Venus, emoti facie conterrita ponti,
> talibus alloquitur regem maris: "hoc satis irae
> interea, genitor; satis ad maiora minarum.
> cetera parce, precor, pelago."[77]
>
> (*Pun.* 17.283–86)

Hannibal and Scipio draw up their forces at Zama, and we seem once more to be on course for a version of the final confrontation of Turnus and Aeneas. There is another interview between Jupiter and Juno (17.341–84) to discuss endings: *quis erit, quaeso, germana . . . / . . . modus?* (348–49); *tempus componere gentes. / ad finem ventum est; claudenda est ianua belli* (355–56). Juno again consents, on condition of minor adjustments to the finality of the ending: Hannibal will be allowed to escape, and the walls of Car-

---

[76] For the play with ends as beginnings in epic, see Hardie 1993c, 12–14; Zetzel 1983, 261. On the Virgilian elements in the Silian storm, see von Albrecht 1964, 176–77.

[77] The main Virgilian model is Apollo's restraint of the excessive spirit of Ascanius at *Aen.* 9.653–56. At the beginning of Statius's fragmentary *Achilleid*, Neptune turns down Venus's request for a storm to destroy Paris returning with Helen to Troy: here a replay of the opening Virgilian storm, by removing the cause of the Trojan War, would stop an epic about the great deeds of Achilles in its tracks.

thage will stand until the coming of Aemilianus. Silius catches something of the provisionality of the Virgilian reconciliation of Juno.[78]

Battle is joined; after mighty slaughter Silius introduces the Virgilian theme of delay at 509: Scipio is impatient of delay (*cunctari taedet*) and attempts to single out Hannibal. At this point Silius must find an alternative ending to that provided by *Aeneid* 12; the solution is to replace that model with the postponement (*mora*, *Aen.* 10.622) of the final meeting engineered in Book 10 by Juno through the delusive phantom that leads Turnus out of the battle (*Aen.* 10.606–88).[79] This trick is followed by Juno's striking dead Hannibal's war-horse under him, and finally by the direct intervention of Juno in the disguise of a shepherd to lead Hannibal astray again; there is a hint that Hannibal has strayed out of the epic world into a pastoral world, where Juno is determined to keep him for the time being,[80] diverting him from the path that would lead to a Virgilian epic ending.[81]

At last Juno brings Hannibal to a halt (*fessum . . . tandem . . . / sistit*, 597–98) on a hill from where he can see the irreversible finality of the Carthaginian defeat, as an inverted image of his past career of victories flashes before his eyes (600–603: a version of the "microcosmic recapitulation"). In his final words and departure (605–17) various models compete to guide our interpretation, balanced between flight and permanence. Line 605 alludes to *Aeneid* 9.371, *iamque propinquabant* castris murosque subibant, preparing us for the flight of Hannibal in the footsteps of Nisus and Euryalus. His following soliloquy asserting (correctly) the eternity of his own fame may be compared to the Virgilian apostrophe of the dead Nisus and Euryalus at *Aeneid* 9.446–49, but Hannibal diverges from this in the sequel, where he claims in addition that he will survive in person to pose a threat to Rome (*nec deinde relinquo / securam te, Roma, mei*, 610–11—an attempt to prevent closure). The use of *vivam* (612, 615) perhaps reminds us of the last word of Ovid's *Metamorphoses*. Yet Hannibal does accept a limit to his ambition in 613–15 (*mihi satque superque, / ut me Dardaniae matres atque Itala tellus, / dum vivam, exspectent nec pacem pectore norint*), and the reader, aware of the agreement between Jupiter and Juno, will understand that there is no real threat here. Hannibal may be *patriae superstes* (611), like Aeneas at the end of *Aeneid* 2, but he will found no new cities.

---

[78] As analyzed by Feeney 1984.

[79] Von Albrecht 1964, 168–71. Instead, a version of the final Virgilian duel was offered to us in the encounter of Hannibal and the Saguntine Murrus at *Pun.* 1.456–517 (an ending at the beginning).

[80] 17.570–71: *quaenam te silvis accedere causa subegit / armatum nostris? num dura ad proelia tendis. . .?* The Virgilian model is the appearance of Venus disguised as a huntress to Aeneas in the woods at *Aen.* 1.314–17.

[81] 579: *fallens regione viarum*, modeled on *Aen.* 9.385, *fallitque timor regione viarum*.

All through this book Hannibal's pretensions to be an Aeneas have been undermined by the superimposition of Lucan's Pompey, written as a negative Aeneas, on the Virgilian model. The several models are combined in the last two lines:

> sic rapitur, paucis fugientum mixtus, et altos
> inde petit retro montes tutasque latebras.

> (*Pun.* 17.616–17)

Hannibal makes for the mountains like Aeneas going into exile at the end of *Aeneid* 2 (*cessi et sublato montis genitore petivi*, 804). The flight into the wilds also repeats Pompey's attempt to hide himself after Pharsalia (*deserta sequentem / non patitur tutis fatum celare latebris*, Luc. 8.12—13; Hannibal will in fact be more successful). But it should not be overlooked that this flight into obscurity also repeats the final flight of Turnus (*fugit . . . sub umbras*, *Aen.* 12.952).

There is no doubt that the Silian ending is far more self-contained than the end of the *Thebaid*. But enough has been said throughout the *Punica* to leave us with the awareness that however emphatic this ending is in personal terms for the individual Scipio, and only slightly less so for Hannibal, it is not quite yet the end of the city Carthage. At 1.8–14 Silius tells us that his epic will tell only of the middle (if most critical) of a series of three wars between Carthage and Rome. But the continuation that really matters, of course, is the story not of Carthage but of Rome, and Silius frequently points forward to the coming decline of Roman moral and political life, finding even in the epoch of Rome's greatest solidarity in the face of the Punic threat the seeds of the civil wars to come.

CHAPTER 8

Final Exit: Propertius 4.11

W. R. JOHNSON

> Wind up, though, on a moral note
> That Glory may go bang.
> —*Auden*

CORNELIA AND HER INDETERMINACIES

It is an interesting paradox that the London that saw the young Housman replicate the modern, Romantic version of Propertius *amator* in person by projecting onto it his feelings for Moses Jackson would, a generation later, witness Pound celebrating the end of his youth (in the thirty-second, not the thirtieth, year of his age), by donning his supreme mask, that of Propertius *faber*.[1] Housman had became obsessed with what he took to be (he did not call it that) a paradigm of the glories of erotic humiliation, of a self devoured by ecstatic delusions that alone made life worth living and throwing away. Pound, needing another sort of model for another sort of passion (*wozu Dichter in dürftiger Zeit?*), brilliantly collapsed Propertius's second and third books; then, focusing at the beginning and at the end of his collage on his model's challenge to the social forces that had threatened the integrity of his art, Pound thereby both stumbled into his own masterpiece and invented later styles of reading Propertius, which, emphasizing his debts to the Alexandrians and his response to his social situation of discourse, have come to dilute various romantic versions of the poet and to restore what seems a reasonable balance here, one in which the poet's artistry is in countervailing tension with, if it is not actually in control of, his fictive (or real or both) amative neuroses.

But having sensed that the heart of this poetry (and this poet) was constructed of *aporia* and *recusatio*, Pound made the mistake of ignoring the poet's fourth book and of sailing off to paradise and Mussolini.[2] He wanted

---

[1] See Thomas (1983) for speculations both about what his Propertius meant for the development of Pound's grasp of poetic self-and-mission at this time (39, 43, 47–48) and about the nature of his deliberate distortions of his "model" (56–57).

[2] See Ruthven's archaic fulminations against Pound's sure touch with regard to logopoeia

to write epic (that is, he wanted to remake history and the great world, in his head and on the page). Book 4 might have told him (did he think that Propertius had there copped out?) that poetry (usually) remakes the world only very obliquely and very imperceptibly (if at all), that poets who have no interest in praising the system of signs they find themselves born into will gladly turn to demystifying that system and its signs (but can hardly expect the system and its signifiers to reward them richly for their labors). Unlike Pound, Propertius did not sail away, he stayed to demystify. He stayed to promise the system that he would praise it, then went on to have his "sing to say" about the troubles with praising the signs and their multiple signers (Augustus, inevitably, becomes the sign for all the signers—except for the sign/signer, Maecenas—and he is, in this configuration, more sign than signer).[3]

It is plausible, of course, that Propertius finally decided to yield gracefully to necessity, to throw in the towel: to craft metrical panegyrics that proffered and proffer still every guarantee of sincerity. That plausibility rests, however, on reading 4.1 as a sincere palinode (one in which the demystifying Umbrian and Alexandrian decadent has found himself transformed into a born-again Roman of the born-again Golden Age).[4] The sincerity of this palinode, however, must be inferred from the sincerity of the remaining poems in the volume (whose sincerity, it is felt, the palinode guarantees), and not least from the sincerity, the admiration, and, indeed, the awe that (in this version) conspire to conceive and execute that supreme icon of the aristocratic Roman matron, Cornelia. Suppose, however, that Cornelia gives no such warrant for so tumultuous a change of heart? Suppose she does not ratify the conversion of 4.1 but rather calls it into question? What is needed in this closing poem, what is needed in any closure that partakes of the repertory of realism and its illusionism (which this version of Cornelia relies on), is for the reader to find herself in a place that furnishes a uniquely privileged perspective, one from which everything in the volume that has gone before (each of the earlier poems in Book 4 *and* all the earlier poems in the earlier volumes that 4.1 claims to

---

(1990, 120–21); Pound may have fumbled with the terminology, but he saw well, in some important poets, of what this variety of lexical discord/ *Verschiebung* consists.

[3] My sketch of the communication system involved here, literature/propaganda/demystification, is based on Foulkes's configuration of Ellul, Charles Morris, and Barthes (1983, 10–14, 18–36, 105–7). Though Zanker's "Geflecht von Interaktionen" (1987, 105, 171) of signers (and their signs) represents a vast improvement over the notion of a ministry of propaganda, it is still much less flexible than what Foulkes is working toward, and (pace Wallace-Hadrill [1989, 159, 160]) Zanker's Augustus, along with his helpers, tends to remain very much at the center of his web.

[4] For a good sketch of these difficulties, see Paratore 1986, 92–93. For the stylistic *aporias* of the poem, if the poet was trying to write it "straight," see La Penna (1977, 93–95), who is usually sensitive to the gaps and excesses that mark Propertian disunities.

disavow) can be viewed as a whole "in a single, intelligible, and all-embracing vision."[5] If the reader can sympathize with Cornelia sufficiently to imagine her as being possessed of an impeccably Roman (and "Augustan") morality and of the transparent gaze that attends it, if she is the incarnation of the system of Roman signs at its purest, its least heterodox, its least indeterminate, if she defies any and all of the strategies of demystification, then she can, transforming the reader into herself and her text, position the reader as "the unified and unifying subject of [her] vision."[6] The rest is a piece of cake: with Cornelia as transcendent subject/reader sponsoring it (she reads herself and her life in the poem as the reader reads her and/in her poem), the sincerity of 4.1 is beyond question. So crucial this closure is. But does it deliver what an unironic (sincere) Propertius/Cornelia/reader want(s) it to?

THE POEM'S "STRUCTURE(S)"

Cornelia's speech can, with a view to its rhetorical strategy, be divided into seven parts: 1) lines 1–10, exordium (to her husband, Paullus); 2) lines 11–28, address to the underworld courtroom; 3) lines 29–48, her ancestry; 4) lines 49–60, her female ancestors in particular; 5) lines 61–72, her children and her brother; 6) lines 73–98, address to Paullus; 7) lines 99–102, peroratio. The poem can be divided, of course, in other ways, in which more or fewer parts would be distinguished (fusing 1 and 2, for example, as exordium, or parts 3 and 4, as a single topic), but this patterning offers the rhetorical significance I'm after.

The locale of the situation of discourse that is established in part 1 seems to be the room where the grief-stricken husband sleeps when he is visited by the ghost-dream of his recently dead wife. Using the full resources of tragic style and the iconography both of poetic hell and of the speaking tomb, Cornelia bids her husband to weep for her no more and reminds him that his sorrow cannot persuade Hell to relinquish her.[7] In part 2 she moves (or leaps) from talking to her husband to addressing a more complicated and less specific audience, but even here Paullus remains her *audiens* (as we, through him, become the poem's) for what we gradually realize is Cornelia's dress rehearsal for the oration to Public Opinion, which she plans to deliver when she comes face to face with the Judges of the After-

---

[5] From Belsey's refiguring (*à la Macherey*) of cinematic narrative problems (1980, 78); for a "classic" construction of Cornelia's role in supplying unity for Book 4, see Grimal 1952, 449–50.

[6] Belsey 1980, 78.

[7] See Tolman 1907, 61–65, for the conventions of Hades as these appear in Buecheler's *Carmina epigraphica latina*; for those of the speaking tomb, 2–3, 10, and passim.

life (*at si quis posita iudex sedet Aeacus urna*, 19ff.): it is a speech in self-defense, an *apologia pro vita sua*.

Part of her strategy for exculpating herself she bases on an accusation against fate, blaming it for her premature death.[8] She feels, not unreasonably, that she has been cut off while she is still rather young, and before her children have grown up (shimmering near the surface of this complaint, illogical perhaps but not wholly inconsistent with her class ideology, is the notion that her blue blood has somehow served her poorly by letting her die). In any case, whether she is more concerned with accusing her destiny or with defending her life to ensure from the court a condign verdict (that is, she doesn't want to end up where the bad women are), her speech as a whole, which subtly mingles recrimination and self-defense, is essentially a summation of who she is/was and what her life means/meant. *Ipsa loquor pro me—si fallo poena sororum / infelix umeros urgeat urna meos* ("I plead my own case—if I lie, may the sisters' atonement, the dread jar, weigh down my shoulders," 26–27). Whatever one finally makes of the whole poem, there is a certain magnificence here, a certain stern bravery. She speaks for herself, and her rhetoric is, though she has had, probably, little or no formal training in this masculine genre, shrewd and skillful (perhaps the ghost of Hortensia is prompting her?). Surely it is more than bravado, surely it is genuine innocence that leads her to challenge the court to make her serve her eternal sentence in the company of the notorious husband-killers, those worst of wives, if it determines that her claim to perfect virtue is untrue? Or does she protest so much in this dream of Paullus's because she feels that she died before her time as a punishment for a hidden crime? Is that why she is so fervent in her denial of charges that no one seems to have brought against her? (Or is it an unfaithful Paullus who in this section of his dream of her projects some guilt of his own on her? This situation of discourse emphatically recalls this poem's companion piece, 4.7, the celebrated Cynthia-ghost poem, where the poet is clearly guilty of the charges of infidelity that Cynthia levels against him—but then, neither is she innocent.)[9] Whatever her mood or her method at the outset of her speech, the

---

[8] For this and related talking-tomb clichés, see Tolman (1907, 32–44), who nevertheless finds her, on balance, extravagant in her topoi (44). Her (and Propertius's) crucial stategy of imagining the courtroom in the afterlife is certainly unusual: for this, see Galletier 1922, 51–52, 55, 200, 268 (of interest here are the borrowings in the epitaph for M. Lucceius Nepos [Buecheler, B1109] not only of Cornelia's vision of hellfire but also of her celestial transfiguration).

[9] For Wyke (1987), Cynthia is "no longer stage center" (153), having been replaced, along with "the earlier authorial narrator," by "a new and final female narrator" (171); for Sullivan, she is, as she is in 7 and 8, "the heart of the book" (147), which means that she is illumined by the closure she illumines: Cornelia exists for her sake, not she for Cornelia's. It is her power that fuels the ironies of the closure. Cotterill (1988, 235–36) would appear to be affirming a position similar to Wyke's.

end of part 2 shows Cornelia, in the darkness of her death, imagining herself standing there in the brackish waters of the Styx (*vada lenta, paludes, / et quaecumque meos implicat ulva pedes*, 15–16), waiting for Charon to ferry her over to the place where she will face the inquisitors whom she now begins to imagine, begins to orate to.

In part 3 Cornelia displays her ancestors to the courtroom of her mind, a frieze of notables that rhetorical decorum allows her to present, and even requires her to present. On her father's side she can boast the Scipios, on her mother's, the Libones. Nor did she disgrace that birthright in any way. Her epitaph (she undertakes to write it herself) can be constructed from 35–36: *iungor, Paulle, tuo sic discessura cubili, / ut lapide hoc uni nupta fuisse legar* ("Thus doomed to leave it so early was I joined to your marriage bed, Paullus, that people who read my tomb's inscription will see that I was wed to one man alone"). For her times, as the poem will, with oblique wit, soon remind us (when we get to her mother, Scribonia, to her mother-in-law, Livia, and to her half-sister, Julia), this is a rare claim, one that allows Cornelia to close this section of her defense superbly. Not only did she not damage the achievements of her glorious male ancestors, but she also added to their store of glory: *non fuit exuviis tantis Cornelia damnum: / quin et erat magnae pars imitanda domus* (43–44; Cornelia caused such splendid trophies no impairment; instead she herself became a wife whom the women of the house of the Scipios might take for their model). Her life (and her entire adult life *was* her marriage) was beyond reproach. Between marriage torch and funeral torch (*inter utramque facem*, 46) she lived a spotless life, not because she was afraid of public opinion (before which she now pleads), but because blood tells, because her nature legislated her behavior: *mi natura dedit leges a sanguine ductas, / nec possis melior iudicis esse metu* (47–48). In short, what has shaped this woman, what she now relies on to save her, is a natural law, one that is genuine in Roman eyes because it is unmetaphysical, because it is genetic, "all in the genes," where (along with the furrow, the larder, the boundary stone, the battle line and the counting-house) Roman reality is at its most real.

In part 4 Cornelia continues her argument from the previous section and enhances it with her assertion that whatever judgment is passed on her (the bravado of the lines on the Danaids is echoed here), she has lived up not only to the standards set by her male ancestors but also (more crucially) to those set by her female ancestors (49–50). As an earnest of this claim, she calls on that Claudia who, back toward the end of the Second Punic War, had succeeded in verifying her own chastity (which had been called into question) by dragging ashore the reluctant image of the Magna Mater; this great, newly important goddess would not have allowed herself to be touched by a woman guilty of sexual misconduct. Cornelia then appeals to an Aemilia who, accused of having let Vesta's fire go out, proved her religious diligence and her chastity (for it was held that had she remained a virgin the fire would have continued to burn) by rekindling the fire in a supernatural manner. These two venerable ladies set a very high standard of sexual purity, one that Cornelia, their later incarnation, has preserved untarnished and thus magnified.

Perhaps just to shape a conventional triad, Cornelia finally evokes a model nearer to her in time, cries out, in fact, to her own mother Scribonia: *nec te, dulce caput, mater Scribonia, laesi: / in me mutatum quid nisi fata velis* (55–56: "Nor, my dearest mother, have I brought shame to you; what would you have different in me—except my doom?").[10] Here we are just past the center of the poem (arithmetically speaking, and, I think, formally speaking, just at its center). Can Scribonia, the woman Octavian had divorced, really be an example of the Roman matron at her finest? Certainly her collocation here with Claudia and Aemilia, those paragons of the old good times, makes no sense if she is not a proper exemplum of heroic housewife; nor, unless she is a genuine emblem of such virtue, can she be the link between ancestral models of the matron and their living contemporary, her daughter, the newly dead Cornelia at whose funeral she now grieves.

That connection and transition, the clan's virtuous matrons and the persistence of its gene for feminine conjugal virtues to the present day, the grief that the loss of Cornelia occasioned for all concerned (image of the funeral, *maternis laudor lacrimis urbisque querelis*, 57), lead elegantly to the mention of an exceptionally important mourner at the funeral, who had devoted a good part of his reign, especially in recent years, to refurbishing the ideology of domesticity: *defensa et gemitu Caesaris ossa mea* (58). My bones, my death and my life, my reputation—these the groan of sorrow from the breast of Caesar saves from any malice, from any accusation: *ille sua nata dignam vixisse sororem / increpat et lacrimas vidimus ire deo* (59–60: "He [thundering like Jove] makes loud his lament that I, worthy to be his daughter's sister, have finished my life, and we saw that a god can weep"). I will return shortly to this interesting trio, Scribonia, Augustus, and Julia, but for the moment it suffices to say that the living god's grief for her death is the index of his approval for her life, and, in this concatenation of proofs of her worthiness, the eloquence of his grief is decisive: the defendant who can show at her funeral the lamentations of an emperor and the tears of a god needs no further witnesses for her case.

Yet in part 5 Cornelia does go on. Perhaps it is the emperor's entrance

---

[10] For Richardson (1976, 486), "her apostrophe of her mother seems unfortunately, if appropriately phrased"; the oxymoron of luckless decorum hits a mark that most commentators ignore.

into her discourse that reminds her that she nevertheless survived long enough in her marriage and in her life to receive the matron's robe of honor for having borne three children, thus setting an example for re-populating the nation, for challenging decadent sexuality with matronly procreation, for standing up, in short, for the domesticity of yore. Augustus's wife, Livia, of course, not Scribonia (did Livia go to the funeral?), had also received this honor (though neither of her sons, alas, had been fathered by Augustus), and the honor seems to have been part of the emperor's reinvention of familial tradition, of which the Lex Julia of 18 B.C.E. was a central strategy. In this configuration, then, the grieving presence of the emperor at the funeral and the honor for patriotic sexuality and public virtue are superbly juxtaposed. The mention of the robe of honor leads naturally to her thinking of her children, her boys, Lepidus and Paullus; of her brother, who achieved that best of the glittering prizes, the consulship, just about the time death came to get her; and of her little daughter. This daughter's birth authenticates the righteousness of her father's censorship,[11] and her mother explicitly enjoins her to follow in her mother's footsteps (thus preserving this clan's grand female tradition) and to marry only one man (*fac teneas unum nos imitata virum*, 68, which neatly echoes, like mother, like daughter, *ut lapide hoc uni nupta fuisse legar* at 35).[12] This brief section on her closest blood relatives, those who really belong to her, who really testify to who she is (and in whom, through her, the blood of the Libones is mingled with that of the Scipios), following as it does hard on the approval bestowed on her by Caesar, ends with a final summation of her many weighty pieces of evidence: *haec est feminei merces extrema triumphi, / laudat ubi emeritum libera fama torum* (here's the biggest thrill in a woman's victory parade—when public opinion acknowledges that her marriage was, from start to finish, a success).

In part 6 (73–98), the decorum of ring composition reminds Cornelia that it is essentially her husband to whom she is talking. Having proved her case (she assumes) to the imaginary courtroom (where in fact her superego

---

[11] Lilja (1978, 236), allowing that tastes (ancient/modern) differ, designates *specimen censurae paternae* as "particularly awkward"; it's a nice instance of the poet's brand of logopoeia.

[12] See Hallet 1984, 241, for a good discussion of the ideology of domesticity behind the code phrase *unum virum*. Whether Cornelia is a "sender" of the code (see Papangelis 1987, 61) or purely its dupe is a question that may not have been interesting to readers before Foucault, but it is now. See Schor's discussion of what's at issue in a poem like this one, 1987, 106–9. For a clear discussion of what the code meant, see Wyke 1989, 40–43; for what it meant to Propertius, see Anthony 1976, 21–22. See also Stahl 1985, 262: "A flesh and blood paradigm of the legislated Augustan womanhood." Wallace-Hadrill's fascination with Dionysius of Halicarnassus's housewife/whore antinomy (1989, 159, 161) illumines the code and maybe even Propertius's parodic strategy in seeming to let Cornelia drive Cynthia from the volume they share so violently.

presides), she now logically turns back to her husband, whom she had used as prelude to her trial.[13] She is now getting ready to go off to her just reward, to her heavenly destination, and, good wife and mother that she is, she has a few last words of advice to the husband she leaves behind her (the homage to Euripides' masterly imagination of this variety of smugness is subtle and effective). She particularly asks that he take good care of the children. He should not, she cautions him, weep in front of them, but instead should set them a cheerful example. He can grieve alone at night in the privacy of the bedroom they shared and in dreams of her (like this one) that come to him sleeping there (81–82). In offering the widower these suggestions (but they are more in the nature of commands—*mandata* is Cynthia's word, 4.7.71, at a similar place in this poem's negative image), she seems to think that his love for her is such that he will not remarry. Or rather, this is what she wants to think, but reality intrudes and with it thoughts of the ubiquitous *noverca*. She therefore turns to address her children and to give them some tips on handling this woman when and if she should turn up (Cornelia has, it seems, few illusions on this score, having felt her way through the problem). Her poor children should flatter this new woman in their lives and then she will like them. But they shouldn't always be talking about their real mother and how she did things, or Daddy's new wife will get annoyed with them (89–90). This gratifying turn in her train of thought (and subconscious feelings) cheers her up. Maybe their father won't take a wife after all, maybe he'll respect the urn that contains her ashes (91–92). She catches herself in this instant's lapse into self-pity, forgets herself (the *noverca* in any case has vanished from her considerations), and thinks only of them and of him. Her jealousy, her resentment, all the ugliness, are banished. She is once again the model matron. She prays that the life taken from her prematurely may be added to her children so that they will always be there to take care of her husband (that excellent husband who has shunned the temptation of dishonoring her urn) and to cheer his declining years.

Part 7 offers the briefest of perorations. In fact, she says, *causa perorata est* (99). Back at 71–72 she had guessed what the verdict must be (womanly triumph), but here the formal verdict is handed down, by herself to herself. The defendant, who was her own defense attorney, was, it turns out, her own judge as well. She dismisses all the loyal, wonderful witnesses her apostrophes have subpoenaed. She is content to die: the earth will now receive her, *grata humus* (grateful and pleasing both: grateful for her nurturing life, pleasing to her who, having won her vindication, is reconciled to sleep with her ancestors). But this thought (it should be the last thought, and in most other poets it would have been the last thought) triggers another one. Since 15ff. (see also 70), she has indeed been steeling herself for the encounter with the judges of Hell, rehearsing her defense before them. So, yes, she would cross the Styx; yes, she would submit herself to the examination that none could escape; she would, winning her acquittal, go off to where the virtuous women went. So said the conscious mind. But, deep beneath the rational ego of the normal Roman matron, the Lacanian imaginary mirror-child has a very different agenda for crafting its unified futurity. Where exactly do the good women go? Some *vates* say one thing, others say another. Ready at last for her final journey, her farewells said to her nearest and dearest, her eyes are downcast on the soil that will lie light upon her, but they happen to glance up to the radiant heavens: *moribus et caelum patuit: sim digna merendo, / cuius honoratis ossa vehantur avis.* Gone to glory! Heaven's her destination, not some lovely island somewhere off in Hell, crammed with nice women who lived their lives nicely. It's the stupid poets who pretend to a knowledge of moral geography in the afterlife. Cicero knew a lot more than they did. There was that wonderful story he told, about how virtuous Romans, her own ancestors among them, were transfigured into stars when they seemed to expire. Descended from a line of heroes, both male and female, stepdaughter of a living god who would eventually become a star like his father (that is, his great-uncle) before him, she could not but know herself summoned now to join that visionary company. *Sim digna merendo*—and up she goes, maybe in a sort of Euripidean machine, like Iphigenia, another heroic female, who had learned at Aulis that glory was as much her birthright as it was any male's. It is not a mere lock of her hair, but Cornelia herself, body and soul, womanly virtue incarnate, that is about to be translated, back with her ancestors, up into the stars.[14]

THE TALE BEHIND THE STORY BEHIND THE POEM

A noble Roman matron, recently dead, expresses her feelings and thoughts about her death and about the meaning of her life. Her appearance to her husband, moreover, presents the mirror-image of dead Cynthia's appearance to her poet in 4.7 (sane, virtuous, and dull matron, paragon of feminine *Romanitas* countervailing—or countervailed by—mad, wicked, and enthralling mistress, paragon of everything that Rome hates and rejects). Unlike Cynthia in all else, Cornelia echoes her, as the convention requires,

---

[14] For her timely (mis)quotation (no *l'esprit d'escalier* for her) of the Ennian *caelum patuit*, see Jocelyn 1986, 135–36.

by admonishing the living and by advising them. But, as I have emphasized, it is the image of judgment, visualized in the images of poetic afterlife, that her discourse turns on, and most of her discourse accordingly
takes the form of a defense of her life. That defense in turn finds its center
of gravity in her death, or rather, as Curran shrewdly observes, in her
funeral.[15] The story that the woman in the poem tells, obliquely, fragmen-
tarily, anxiously, is the story of a life that gathered its meaning from its
death and its funeral. What story is that, what kind of story is that?

It is, essentially, the story of manifold resentments, of a long and painful
civilized discontent. Cornelia had, of course, everything that a Roman
woman could have: wealth, position, a husband, children. In the end she
had, one could say, bad luck, but she herself doesn't seem to see it that way
(except at the outset of her speech, where her cry that she is the victim of
fate and a handful of dust, 13–14, is essentially formulaic). For her, death,
premature and therefore initially unwelcome, has come as something that
liberates her—from what? From the anxiety that she will somehow go
astray, that she will, like those naughty women whom the judges of Hell
condemn, actually do something dreadful, something that will bring dishonor on her family? That her children will die before she does? That she
will be one of those women whose husbands, for reasons that have nothing
to do with their wives' conduct, decide to divorce them? Worse, that she
will become one of those women whom their husbands want to divorce or
need to divorce because their conduct has become so notorious? When she
swears by all she holds sacred (the glory of her family) that she has committed no indecency (41–42), we may well believe her, refusing to let her
shrillness evoke our cynicism; nevertheless we may doubt that she has
never felt lust (or boredom) in the heart, or that Samuel Johnson's remark
to the Abbess might not be decorously directed to her: "Madam, you are
not here for the love of virtue, but for the fear of vice." By turns whining
and smug, what she hides beneath the mask of the perfect matron are the
terror and the anger that a few decades of being a gilded cipher, being a
baby factory, being on public display, being exploited by men who had
little interest in and less knowledge of her feelings and her needs have
reduced her to being.

As we saw, when Cornelia is about to unpack her conscious thoughts
for the judges' inspection (at the border, have you anything to declare?), it
is the Danaids and their crime that come (from her unconscious mind) as
the appropriate negative index to her innocence and honesty (I am not like
them). I doubt that it's coincidental that when Cynthia, having subtly and
copiously informed her lover that she is permanently lodged with the good
women in the underworld, magnanimously refuses to list his infidelities

---

[15] Curran 1968, 137.

(*celo ego perfidiae crimina multa tuae*, 7.70), she verifies her innocence and honesty, which she has claimed back in 53 (*me servasse fidem*), by associating herself with Hypermnestra, the single good Danaid (I am like her). They are both lying, Cornelia unconsciously, Cynthia (who is in fact off, contentedly, with the bad women and has never set eyes on Hypermnestra) consciously. Cornelia may well have wanted to kill her husband (and her brother and her father and assorted other male relatives) for making a wretched life excruciating. Her story, in short, whatever its unique pains and pleasures, was the common one of aristocratic Roman women who were, from cradle to pyre, through birth or through marriage, the pawns of the men who were "in" their lives. (This, naturally, is only half the truth perhaps, but since it is the half that the poem seems to leave out and that readings of the poem always leave out, it seems worthy, here, of such hyperbole and distortion.)

But that is not the whole story. The whole story, the one Cornelia tells along with what we infer from it, all but conceals the deeper tale that generates it—the tale of sexual misconduct out of which was (re)constructed the current (and timeless, universal, essential, natural) ideology of domesticity and its (incarnate) pattern of conjugal virtue and bliss (on which the ironic palinode and the ironic closure and their volume depend).[16] At its arithmetical and symbolic center is a frieze, the figures that Cornelia summons to represent her funeral procession: Claudia, Aemilia, and Scribonia (her female models); Scribonia, Julia, and Augustus (her human mourners); Cybele, Vesta, and Augustus (the divine ones who verify the chastity and the virtue of Cornelia and those whose blood flowed in her veins). So far, so good: a divine iconic moment that generates for ocular hermeneutics a patriotic myth in a patriotic poem in a collection of patriotic poems. But the tearful god and the somewhat awkward juxtaposition of Scribonia and Augustus at this solemn moment present the reader, that "unified and unifying" subject, with difficulties that must be met before all of Book 4's varied and not quite compatible "grandeurs" can be gathered up and knotted neatly.

Let me take these difficulties in reverse order, beginning with what must be a difficult moment at the funeral, the rare and perhaps tense encounter

---

[16] I'm concerned here not merely with distinguishing Cornelia's *discours* (where her resentments are apparently mostly unconscious) from its *histoire*, the whole story of mother and daughter and their lives and times (where her resentments and especially her mother's would be discernible), but also with speculating that Propertius, the connoisseur of erotics, knows and wants to demystify the ideology of Roman patriarchal imperialism. See Macherey 1978, 58–59, 80, 85–89, 132, and 195 (on this last page, it looks as though a writer can in fact detect the ideology's "absent sun" well enough to produce a partial image of it [the ideology], well enough to "put it into question"). For Propertius's "Tadel durch scheinbares Lob," see Anthony 1976, 63 n. 104.

between Cornelia's mother and the emperor. Scribonia and Augustus. Scribonia and Octavian? The bell rings, faintly for some, less faintly for others. Twenty-two years before the date of the funeral that unites them once again in the pompous frieze, they had been a pair, had been (briefly, as the commentaries chorus it) married: Scribonia, the first wife of the man who would be emperor, had borne him his only offspring, his daughter, Julia.[17] He had divorced Scribonia at the beginning of 38 B.C.E. in order to marry Livia, who was already the mother of one son, the one who would become, on his stepfather's death, the emperor Tiberius. When Octavian's divorce took place (just prior to his new marriage), Livia chanced to be still married, so she needed a quickie divorce. There was another, no less pressing complication: she was three months' pregnant (in some versions more) when she got divorced and came to live in Augustus's house and then married him as soon as the extra-legal divorce came through. Tongues would have been wagging that it was Octavian, not her recent husband, Tiberius Claudius Nero, father of the second Roman emperor, who had sired the child yet unborn, but history has determined that it was in fact the Claudian husband who begat Drusus, who would grow up to marry the younger daughter of Marc Antony and would beget on her both Germanicus and Claudius.[18]

Such are the bare bones of the old (buried but not really forgotten) gossip that haunts the center of Cornelia's funeral and her poem. What does the tale mean? And what is it doing here (for it is *in* the poem, having been summoned into it by this gauche, unnecessary juxtaposition)? Back in 39 B.C.E., maybe toward the middle of it, Octavian has come to want Livia, and in early 38 B.C.E. he gets her. He does this by divorcing his wife Scribonia (*pertaesus morum perversitatem eius*, says Suetonius in his life of him, 62), by forcing Nero to divorce Livia, pregnant though she is, and by flouting a law that requires the space of a year's time between divorce and a marriage. The details of these conjugal alterations are obscure and inconsistent, can be read in various ways, and perhaps it is wise not to try to make too much of them; but these rearrangements do seem to have created some

[17] The fable is told with verve (it's a little, *mutatis mutandis*, like something you might find at the checkout counter of your supermarket) by Carcopino (1958), and his guesses about some of its indeterminacies are more than entertaining; its shreds of evidence and hearsay are carefully assembled by Leon (1951) into a sober, useful pattern. Syme (1986) conducts us through his vast labyrinth of information, but "facts," for the dust and clutter, are hard to come by there. The presence of Julia at the funeral perhaps inspires us to *imagine* what her reception, as one of the poem's first (and maybe most eager) readers, might have been. She had been groomed to be everything that Cornelia claims to be—and she rejected the job: see Richlin's superb re-de-constructions of Julia's subject-positions, 1992, 74–79.

[18] Some of the scandal may have been nourished by his circle's efforts to represent Octavian as "an energetic, though selective, womanizer": see Hallett 1977, 159–60, where the time period in question is wittily probed.

scandal when they occurred, and reverberations of the scandal continued, certainly into the time when Propertius was writing and beyond it. Augustus's proponents, however, pay little attention to it, and in the grand mural of World Historical Destiny and of the Roman beginnings of Europe's Manifest Destiny the scandal matters very little—so why should it matter to readers of Propertius 4.11 now? When one looks at the standard commentaries or discussions that express the consensus, the identity of Scribonia is tersely noted and then ignored. Why then am I making so much of it?

I confess that a merely personal dislike of "Augustus" (it began in the McCarthy era, not with the Vietnam War) has something to do with my focus on the weeping god at the funeral. (The question remains whether those who admire the god's tears or all but erase him from the poem are innocent of subjectivity or of politicizing the text of this poem in other ways—ways that seem to them "transparently clear" or "natural.") Nevertheless, looking at the poem's center, I find Augustus's intrusion into Scribonia's grief peculiar. What reason is there for Augustus to be in the poem? What reason is there for his being not only in the poem but also at or very near its center? Would the poem be essentially what it is without him weeping in it? Would it be a worse poem without his tears? A better poem?

That Cornelia should adduce him, the father of her half-sister, as a member of the funeral party (which he may in fact have been) is perfectly unremarkable. Viewed in this way, this piece of familial verisimilitude would be not only defensible but also elegant and exact. That, however, she should, propelled by ruinously subconscious logic, connect him (in respect of divinity) with Cybele and Vesta, then (in a context of female rectitude, of sexual propriety and fidelity) with Aemilia, Claudia, and Scribonia, the wife he had been unfaithful to and had divorced, is a felicitously Freudian lapse. The clustering of images and nuances in this magnetic field are not activated by a need to give glory to the dead (that is, by the poet's having Cornelia say, "Augustus was, as it were, my stepfather") but by a gratuitous reactivation of the sniggering jokes of January, 38 B.C.E. Cornelia may want him in the poem, and, as these things go, she has a right to have him in the poem. But Augustus does not want to be in the poem, especially not in *this* configuration of divinity (Cybele yet!) and immaculate domesticity, and, since he is related to the deceased only by virtue of a dissolved marriage, he has a right not to be there.[19]

[19] Cybele as member of the wedding presents no problem for Wiseman (1984), who is apparently beguiled by the patriotic and sentimental reconfigurations of Cybele by Virgil and their composite incarnation on the *gemma Augustea* (Oikoumene); Becher (1988) shows that the other poets were not engaged in or persuaded by this pious and ludicrously impossible prestidigitation-transformation.

Though authors always tell us about how their characters "take over the story from them," there are some authors (not their characters) who have the blue pencil, the wastebasket, the finger on the deletion key. The truth of the matter is that Propertius didn't have to write this poem at all. Or, if he had wanted to write a patriotic poem about the largely unsung glories of an aristocratic matron's life-in-virtue (something that could close his palinodic volume with a bang, that also would, for good, shut the excluding door on Cynthia), if he had wanted to write a poem that evokes Roman women's sacrifices for their patriarchs in rich detail, in a dazzling tirade, why not use a fictive matron, or at least one not so problematic? Or, having chosen Cornelia and the risks she posed, why not at least—it was not so difficult to do—avoid the worst baggage she brought with her by not mentioning Julia or Augustus? Or, having mentioned Augustus, why not (carefully) refrain from mentioning Scribonia (at least by name; mention of Julia by herself might have worked) and, above all, from alluding, in a heavily clumsy fashion, to something the emperor did not like having mentioned unless it was produced with exquisite opacity: his divinity (which was, at the time the poem was written, a topic mostly for export to the Orient).[20] With this gauche reference to the emperor's celestial hankerings, the poem's movement veers off in a new direction, cannot any longer be seen from a single angle (that patriotic angle promised by the unironic *recusatio* of the book's opening).

The man who divorced Scribonia was no god, the god who weeps at the funeral and gestures piously to the kinship of his Julia with the dead woman is not the young whoremonger of yore, naughty hero of an aristocratic dirty joke. They are not the same person. Except that they are.[21] Which means that the god, for all his copious tears, is human-all-too-human, and his epiphany here in the volume's final poem echoes (solemnly, lugubriously) the hilarious epiphany in the volume's central poem, *sum deus*! (6.60), Julius's cartoon shock of divine self-recognition at Actium.[22] So far, then, from avoiding the pitfalls inherent in his plan, the poet placed them smack in the middle of his poem, then zestfully bellyflopped into them. He mentioned Scribonia, he mentioned Augustus, he mentioned that Augustus was a god. That deft economy, that sly, sudden rematching of the sundered parties, one of them a tedious, expended wife, one of them a god very much concerned with chastity and the sanctity of marriage, causes the poem (along with the book it closes) to collapse in upon itself.

[20] See Zanker 1987, 299–301, 313–14; Hallett 1985, 83 n. 28.

[21] For a succinct and accurate statement of the deconstructive meshings in process here (in the imperial sign-systems and the poet's demystification of them), see Patterson on identity/difference, 1993, 70–73.

[22] See Johnson 1973, 168; cf. Pasoli 1982, 74–75.

THE CLOSURE(S)

This is not to say that Propertius's main purpose in this poem was to fling yet another spitball at the system of signs of which Augustus was the chief sign. But two of his ancillary purposes happened not to be incompatible: to write an ambiguous (and maybe funny) poem about the splendors and miseries of being an upper-class Roman *materfamilias*, and to remind the system of signs and its various signers, one last time, why it was he would not (hadn't, never could = *aporia*) write poems about the Roman imperial reality in its most recent renewal. In their fusion, these purposes admirably serve the poet's master purpose in this volume: to sum up the nature of his art, what it was and wasn't, to celebrate the realities that were his to celebrate (eros, art, freedom).

In the opening poem of this volume, the poet had elaborately proclaimed a change of mind and art, had announced his conversion, had forsworn his earlier obsession with trivialities. If it is troubling that his speech is immediately followed (whether or not in the same poem hardly matters) by the rantings of a mad astrologer who forbids him to pursue the new goals he has set himself and orders him to return forthwith to erotics, to the themes and the moods that are proper to his genius, readers who were relieved (and convinced) by the poet's palinode are apparently heartened when they unroll the next poem and find it deals with Vertumnus (though rather oddly); this meditation on Roman antiquities appears to answer these readers' hopes that the poet will in fact mend his ways and, after what has seemed an eternity of flippant derelictions of duty, write some really Roman poems. Then comes a rather self-centered letter from a Roman wife (whose name, disconcertingly, is Greek) to her soldier husband. Then comes an abrasive, not wholly convincing, rather too sympathetic portrayal of Tarpeia (more antiquities, yes, so he's performing what he promised, but he's not doing it very well). Then comes a totally un-Roman poem about a disgusting madame, a vivid but hardly edifying picture of her and of her brothel (she, like the soldier's wife and Tarpeia, gets to do too much of the talking—why doesn't the poet, in his own mask, tell us about how they threaten Roman family values; better still, why doesn't he just burn these poems himself before others have to?). Finally, there is a poem about Actium whose content is impeccable, but the *Stimmung* is a trifle strained, a bit overripe: still, it's at least trying to be Roman, it has maturity of vision and some sweetness and light, it grapples (weirdly) with significant events. Then comes another poem about a woman who, once again, is allowed to talk too much—well, to be honest, it is a poem about Cynthia, who is not even supposed to be in this volume, which is supposed to be about Rome, not about depraved, psychotic harlots. The fact that she is dead saves nothing. If anything she is worse dead than she was alive. One rolls her up, having skimmed her, with a sigh of relief; holds one's breath for fear of what's coming next. Will it be a patriotic poem? It is, in fact, feigning from the start to be about Roman antiquities, *another* Cynthia poem. But this one is worse than the one where she was dead and shrieking. Here she is alive again, still shrieking, because she has discovered Propertius involved in a ludicrous and disgusting three-way. One is tempted to just roll the volume up and cast it aside. Dare one continue? Since we've got this far, we might as well. The next poem is about the Ara Maxima. Hercules is raping some maidens, but that's all right, at least it is about antiquities as it's supposed to be (but the tomentose chest not adequately concealed with a brassiere has to go).[23] The next (we must be getting toward the end by now) is again antiquarian, is about the *spolia opima*, and that is all to the good, except that the poem is rather clumsy and rather dull, and its closure, which is disastrously feeble, fiddles foolishly with folk etymologies. The last poem, very ennobling and possessed of genuine grandeur (would he had always written so, in this volume and in the others!), is about the tragic Cornelia and her early death and the virtues that she is emblem of. Finis.

One rerolls it (not glancing much at the columns of writing) with very mixed feelings. The last poem was superb, and the poet's intentions were, for the most part, commendable, but, on balance, it was a curiously uneven and curiously inept performance. The truth of the matter is that his instincts were right after all: he had no talent for serious verse whatever; he really was very limited—to a sort of soft porn on the edges of the perverse. A weak, demented mind; a gifted creature, but very oversexed and incurably spoiled. Hardly surprising that women enjoy him. Still, there's no real problem here. This fourth (and mercifully final) volume will very quickly and very mercifully be forgotten. The earlier volumes will never become part of the school curriculum. Which means, he'll last for a while as a not uninteresting specimen of a particular variety of light blue literature, and gradually he'll vanish. So a faintly tolerant, common reader of the early empire might have responded; so, *mutatis mutandis*, have later readers responded.

But, unless one can find pleasure in its frosty nobility, the last poem of the last volume is the last straw, deliberately and delicately positioned on a house of cards; it is the last domino that a hand that exuberant malice has carefully disciplined puts in its fatal place. His first astonishing volume had been about the painful and blissful realities of erotic illusion, about that and about a youthful and baffled political disenchantment. Then the dynamics of the system of signs (these poems and other poems contemporary with them call that system "Maecenas" or "Augustus") began to crowd him.

---

[23] See Sullivan 1976, 135.

His Umbrian (or Italian) feel for being one's own guy, joined with his devotion to Callimachus and his belief in the truth of erotic identity, set free in him an anarchic imagination. From then on, Propertius's response to the pressures of the sign system was as implacable as it was inventive. He continued re-inventing the game of *recusatio* and enjoying the resources of its spiraling ironies until, for some reason not yet got at and probably forever inaccessible, he decided to close down the fun house with a gala celebration of *recusatio* and what it was capable of. In Book 4 he constructed a definitive handbook on how not to flatter the will to power, and, to finish up (and off) his construction, he imagined the patriarchy's perfect "own petard," a paradigm of its perfect victim at her most vulnerable and most pathetic, and (simultaneously, deconstructively) of its smugly complicit slave at her most simpering and most monomaniacal, the sad, stupid woman who is everything, alas, that his wonderful, dreadful, delicious, incomparable Cynthia is not. As a spokesperson for the patriarch, Cornelia both has and is the last word.

Well, almost, but not quite, since her last word is in the poet's mouth ("And none so soon either shall the pharce for the nunc come to a setdown secular phoenish": so, the grand artificer of [un]closure in his closing opus). Quintilian thought that the whole life of Socrates was a figure, that of irony.[24] In a not dissimilar way, Propertius lived most of his adult life, from the time he finished the first book, from the instant he crossed the threshold of Maecenas's salon, *sub specie recusationis*. All the other Augustan poets needed *recusatio* also, and all of them ironized it in various ways, but for Propertius it became a career, a fate. Like a fox terrier fastened on a trouser leg, the poet grabbed hold of *recusatio* and wouldn't let go. This strategy, this compulsion, was, to be sure, a way of defending Cynthia, or what she stands for still, the truth of sexuality, the erotic core both of identity and of creativity; but beyond even that, it was a way of refusing to accept domination by the sign system, of insisting, instead, on producing demystifications of the system. (It was also a way of having fun.)

Once this sort of thing has begun, once one has chosen to do and be this sort of thing, a sort of living *Recusatio*, process and product become almost indistinguishable, the life becomes the art, which (the mode is one of limitless ricochet) in turn becomes the life. So, when one skims through the collected elegies of Propertius, one may become aware that he is singularly unsuited to the *florilegium*; separate poems of his may be put on display, under glass, in the museum, but that presentation somehow doesn't work for him. Not because there is some narrative sequence that must here be preserved, without which the individual poems would fail of their resonance and bite, but rather because without the constant context of the

---

[24] See Vlastos 1991, 33, on Quintilian *Inst.* 9.2.46.

recusatio we miss the heart of the collection, which is a sort of Empedoclean *ricorso*. When we have finally gotten to Cornelia, whose central message is that the game of *recusatio* has ended, overwhelmed by her chilly sublimities and conquered by the powers of her Roman Truths and Virtues—when the performance ends and the silence begins, we may be shocked to hear Cynthia laughing loudly at the lachrymose deity and the metonymic skid that has now enfolded him. And then turn back, almost inevitably, to her poems in Book 4, then to its first poem, to the wicked mendacity of its palinode in-and-of a palinode, then go (back) to trace the splendid zigzag of this poet's adventures in daredevil rhetoric back through Book 3 and through Book 2 to the first book where (before the *recusatio* begins) the figure of Cynthia, for which the *recusatio* exists, takes on her glittering polyvocities, her abundant life-as-text. Then back again, through all the poems, to Cornelia—then, turn, and back again.

Cornelia, the matron whom the patriarch reveres (and depends on), arrives with her spotless morality, her patriotic gore, and her whining bathos, to lock up the love nest (such perils circle in on the Signs), then throw away the key. But she remains there at the end of the fourth volume and the whole collection, not as grand finale, not as closure, but as subversive signal (Let's Go Round One More Time), as revolving door.

CHAPTER 9

Endgames: Ovid's *Metamorphoses* 15 and *Fasti* 6

ALESSANDRO BARCHIESI

MY THEME is the completeness of the *Metamorphoses* and the incompleteness of the *Fasti*. I start from the traditional idea that the former is a complete text and the latter is not. My discussion will bring tension and play to this traditional picture, for which, perhaps, a brief explanation is necessary.

My true starting point is the theatrical quality I find in Ovid's poetic strategy. The poet introduces his audience to a scene full of illusions, and holds open a perpetual alternative between naive participation and detachment, credulity and irony. The reader confronted with so many tricks one after another gets used to assuming an alias, becoming a "duped" reader who is seized by the narrative unawares. This credulous reader who loses his way seems endowed with a voice of his own, a voice that sometimes sounds demanding, and official—dare I say, imperial? The authoritative voice implies a privileged reader, set apart from the anonymous majority and able to make himself heard in the poetic text; he pays dearly for this privilege because he is—much more than the general reader—a decoy, a "duped" reader.

I shall explore this ironic triangulation (an authorial voice, a duped yet privileged reader, a detached and self-conscious reader) in the endings of the two most ambitious and official works that Ovid composed. Endings are by nature textual spaces laid out with great expectation. The usual way of reading them is to look for a solution, a settling of narrative tension or a realization of its designs. We shall see (and this is not just a truism) that the end of the *Metamorphoses* has something to say about transformations, and that the (provisional?) end of the *Fasti* demands a re-reading of the poem and a revision of its calendrical poetics. But with a poet such as Ovid, reading is a more interactive, agonistic process than following a musical score. Readers who look for a stable structure will be greatly misled. To begin, then, let us see what happens when we try to map the narrative structure of the *Metamorphoses*.

UNCLEAR BOUNDARIES

Agreement between readers is so scarce that one could replace it with a handful of quotations from Ovid. Ovid must have had a plan: how else could he control this huge list of characters and the complexities of mythological chronology? But he has deliberately confused his tracks: *ponit opus turbatque notas et lumina flexu / ducit in errorem variarum ambage viarum* (8.160–61). Like Daedalus in the labyrinth, the artist seems lost in his own work: *vixque ipse reverti / ad limen potuit: tanta est fallacia tecti* (8.167–68).[1] The chronological axis of the poem, which could favor a linear reading, is disrupted by advances and backtrackings, just as the Meander River runs through its own course, speeds up, and plays with the linearity of its fluvial nature:

> non secus ac liquidis Phrygius Maeandrus in undis
> ludit et ambiguo lapsu refluitque fluitque
> occurrensque sibi venturas adspicit undas
> et nunc ad fontes, nunc ad mare versus apertum
> incertas exercet aquas.
>
> (8.162–66)

The length of this reflexive work creates an illusory perspective that unifies in the distance what is disconnected and independent at close range: *spatium discrimina fallit* (8.578). Transitions from one theme to another are so fluid they go unnoticed, as if one tried to distinguish the colors in a rainbow: *transitus ipse tamen spectantia lumina fallit* (6.66). It is not surprising that the editorial pauses between one book and the next become places of deception and frustrated expectation.[2] There is a profound lack of agreement on the details of Ovid's plan, and on our chances (even on the legitimacy) of reconstructing it. Only a broad articulation unmarked by formal divisions seems acceptable to most scholars, one that divides the general project into three principal sections: Gods, Heroes, and History.[3] It happens that there are dividing lines—accepted by scholars, but not indicated by the narrator—between 6.420 and 421 and between 11.193 and 194. In

[1] Crabbe 1981 is perhaps the finest attempt to lay out the poem's structure. The idea of a "perfect labyrinth" is important in the poetics of Italo Calvino; I take the title of this section from that of a preface by Calvino to an (unsuccessful) Italian edition of the *Metamorphoses*. Quotations below follow the Latin editions of Haupt, Korn, Ehwald, and von Albrecht 1966 (*Metamorphoses*), and Alton, Wormell, and Courtney 1985 (*Fasti*).

[2] On the role of the divisions between books in the poem, see in particular Fowler 1989b, 95–97, who is also important generally in opening new questions on the subject of closure.

[3] There is at least partial agreement among, e.g., Crump 1931, 274; Ludwig 1965, 12–13, 60, 72–73 (with a less linear approach); Otis 1970, passim ("The Avenging Gods" ends at 6.400, and the following section ends with Book 11; and Kenney 1986, xxvi; see also Wilkinson 1955, 147–48 and n. 1. More noteworthy for our purposes are the reservations expressed by Schmidt (1991), who can see "keine Zäsur, keine Grenze" before 6.421 (125) and is reluctant to separate different parts "im Erzählfluss" (122)—this last metaphor seems written under the semiconscious effect of the Ovidian image of the Isthmus; compare Kenney 1986, 439: "The Trojan war tended to mark the *dividing line*" (my emphasis) between myth and history.

spite of the narrator (who is no help here), the change in topic is clear: 6.421 introduces the story of Tereus, who, after a section dominated by the gods and their loves, brings to the stage human characters, heroes and wars. At 11.194 we are shown for the first time the city of Troy, a city so important to the following books and the first peg for something like historical chronology (*ex Ilio capto*). Now, if we read without prejudice the two transitional zones, we find a narrator who in his customary manner uses temporal, spatial, and analogical means to stitch together different stories:

> quaeque urbes aliae bimari clauduntur ab Isthmo
> exteriusque sitae bimari spectantur ab Isthmo;
> credere quis posset? solae cessastis Athenae

> (6.419–21)

(after a long list of Greek cities, arising from the preceding story); and

> ultus abit Tmolo liquidumque per aera vectus
> angustum citra pontum Nepheleidos Helles
> Laomedonteis Latoius adstitit arvis

> (11.194–96)

(after the vendetta on Midas, when Apollo leaves the region of Tmolus and reaches Troy). If we read these same lines with prejudice, we find a coincidence: the jump from one story to another is mediated by two brief geographical descriptions. First, the Isthmus of Corinth joins two lands and divides two seas, a space that closes (*clauduntur*) and opens (*spectantur*) a view of separate realities. Two mirroring clauses (*-ntur ab Isthmo*) reinforce the pause. Second is the Hellespont,[4] a thin line of sea (*angustum*, 11.195) where two continents almost fuse.[5] The Isthmus and the Strait are both important yet elusive borders—thin separations that help to define pairs of lands and pairs of seas, yet offer easy transitions; tropes that invite the reader to gloss the paradox of imperceptible textual demarcations.

---

[4] Note also the closural force of departure (*abit*), the ideological importance of *ultus* (compare Galinsky 1967, 188 n. 18), and the solemn Virgilian tag *liquidumque per aera* (*Aen.* 6.202, from the Golden Bough episode); the whole line could be an echo of the *opening* of Catullus 101, introducing a very different arrival to the Troad. The idea of founding Troy with great effort (199: *novae primum moliri moenia Troiae*; 200–201: *susceptaque magna labore / crescere difficili nec opes exposcere parvas*) suits a new epic impulse after the competition between lyric and bucolic in the preceding story.

[5] This may have been a strategic narrative site long before Ovid: if Herodotus truly ended with the seizure of Sestus on the Hellespont, the ending is well suited to a long historical tale on the confrontation of East and West. See now Dewald, Chapter 4 in this volume.

METAMORPHOSES 15 AND THE EFFECT OF CONCLUSION

Our treacherous narrator could not finish simply. The example of Pallas—a traditionalist poet, authoritarian in content, clear and hierarchical in form—shows how one can close with irrevocable clarity: *operi Victoria finis / . . . (is modus est) operisque sua facit arbore finem* (6.82; 102). The best way to end is with an ending or, to be clearer, the word "END" twice used as the end of the verse.[6] The narrator of the *Metamorphoses*, for his part, has elaborated an interminable ending: the entire last book can be read as an extended coda.

This summarizing function is clear in the first part of Book 15, the revelation of Pythagoras, which recapitulates the principal theme of transformation (and which should not be taken as a confession or credo[7]). But there is more to say on the following episode, which moves from Pythagoras to Augustan farewell. In the forests of Ariccia is Virbius, the Double Hero, who can say in reply (15.497ff.): *Fando aliquem Hippolytum vestras, puto, contigit aures,* "I will amaze you. Surely you have heard of Hippolytus. (Yes, it is the title of Euripides' masterpiece—rather, of two works by Euripides; is this why you call yourself 'The Double Man'? By the way, the formula you have used to introduce yourself recalls the beginning of a famous story by Virgil, which *has* reached my ears: *Fando aliquod si forte tuas pervenit ad auris / Belidae nomen Palamedis*" [*Aen.* 2.81–82]. It is the story of another ill-starred tragic hero, Palamedes; I remember the confusing story, a mixture of truth and fiction, with some unease. But continue.) Surprise! I, Virbius, am that Hippolytus! I can tell you the end of the tragedy (of the twin tragedies): a messenger speech on my frightening dismemberment. But now I am the messenger. This is much more believable, since who could know more directly than I how I was killed by my horses? Ironically, when I was a Euripidean character (*Hipp.* 1078–79), I uttered this very wish: that I could look at myself from the outside, leave myself and become a spectator. There were some changes, I must admit, and a simple questioner might doubt my identity. But as Virbius I would have no other story to tell you.[8] Yes, there were some changes: I live in a land far from my origin, I am older (not by nature, with god's help!), my appear-

---

[6] A strategy dear to artists of the preceding generation, and therefore out-of-date for Ovid. The last word of the *Epodes* is *exitus*; *Satire* 1 finishes with *subscribe libello*; Propertius 3 (24.38) with *eventum formae tuae*. Compare Aristotle's *Rhetoric*, ending (3.1420b) with the quotation of a traditional formula for ending a speech (like, for instance, Lysias 12.99). Having arrived at Book 4 of the *Odes*, Horace concludes with a future, *canemus*, and sets a precedent that Ovid (*vivam*) will know how to appreciate.

[7] Barchiesi 1989, 73–83.

[8] "We have no legend that may be called simply the Virbius legend: the figure which we see is always the composite one, Virbius-Hippolytus," Gordon 1932, 182.

ance is changed, and I have been rebaptized: 'you who were Hippolytus will now be the same person, Virbius.'" Divine power, like poetry, changes the world into itself.[9]

The episode, as is typical of endings, reviews and puts in perspective some central themes of the poem. Virbius plays with credibility, and with the credulity of his audience—the nymph Egeria, widow of Numa—just as Ovid plays with the credibility of his own tale and with the involvement of his readers. Moreover, in the end the tale lacks any practical effect. Hippolytus the Second wants to convince the mourning nymph that her pain is not the worst condition possible. (In Euripides *Hippolytus* 1425–30 Hippolytus's sad story will try to relieve brides of their suffering.) To reassure Egeria, he narrates again his moral and physical trials and his horrible death—but in the end the story concerns a character that dies and lives again; not an example best suited to the comforting frame of *non tibi soli*.[10] This irony is representative of the entire poem, a fabric of tales that constantly undermine their own didactic or practical intentions.

Virbius is also a bilingual character. He has a double life split between Greece and Latium. His name is double, whether in Latin (*vir* + *bis*) or in Greek (*heros* + *bios*, "reborn as a hero"; compare *Met.* 15.492); and he is double, the copy of a Euripidean hero brought to Rome—just as the *Metamorphoses* are doublings and recreations of Greek myths transferred to Rome in a different language. It is not by chance that the last two books of the poem are imbued with a strong sense of movement, of translation to the West.[11]

This sense of movement from Greece to Italy predominates in the last narrative panel of the poem, Asclepius's voyage from Epidaurus to Rome. Even before this, we find a unique (and strange) piece of republican history. The praetor Cipus finds he has sprouted a pair of horns, a miraculous sign of royal power over the city. But he runs from the opportunity and chooses a solitary life outside Rome. This curious legend of missed opportunity is relevant to Augustan political discourse;[12] the story of Cip(p)us,

---

[9] "The danger of literature lies in its power to change the world into itself" (so Mary Beard, *New Statesman*, May 16, 1990, reviewing an Ovidian novel, *Die letzte Welt*, and citing, I presume, Mallarmé).

[10] Especially since Romulus, a king anything but superior to Numa, ascended into heaven thanks to his divine credentials and to the authoritative precedent of Ennius's *Annals*.

[11] This translation is tied to a rising momentum of the *Metamorphoses* typical of the "Roman" books of the poem; Porte (1985) has good comments on this momentum, but is less receptive to possible countereffects.

[12] For some political interpretations of the episode, see Galinsky 1967; Lundström 1980, 67; Schmitzer 1990, 260. I think we do not need to look for allegories to a particular event in Roman history, such as the crown presented to Julius Caesar. The political reference is effective precisely because it implies a concentrated political discourse; Ovid explores a way of representing power, not a specific situation. On Roman politics and *Metamorphoses* 15, see

apparently a "boundary stone," is that of a man who does not want to be king, and of a magistrate who limits his own power before crossing the *pomerium*. It would be possible to read the episode as a brief eulogy to Augustus, who refuses titles such as lord and king and who with his irrefutable word guarantees the continuity of ancient institutions. And all the while Ovid avoids or passes over the history of the republic in his universal chronicle.

Yet this history, while replacing and even erasing the republican tradition, might have more complex implications. It is impossible to ignore the horns, which are the central metamorphosis and striking event of the episode. Cipus undergoes a physical change, and then refuses a constitutional change. We have the right to ask what happens to the horns when the knot is untied and Rome is safe from being transformed into a monarchy. The horns are not destroyed but simply covered, masked by a crown of laurel. This crown is an eminent attribute of Augustus, full of triumphal and Apollonian associations (*Met.* 1.562); the gesture of hiding something underneath is highly suggestive. Will this honorific crown be a substitute for monarchy, or a veil for it? The story allows both conclusions: it is given as a substitute, but functions as a veil. The story rests on uncertainty between two possible interpretations of the Augustan principate;[13] one can imagine, for example, a synoptic reading according to both Mommsen and Syme. The archaic Cipus rejects the laurel crown, reveals the horns, and is rewarded by the people with a crown (again of laurel, or just a crown?) and, following contemporary custom, with a piece of land. His compensation for the kingdom was as much land as one could plow from sunrise to sunset: *quantum . . . conplecti posses ad finem lucis ab ortu* (15.618–19). The reward is suited to a nobleman of the past, but Ovid's language allows another reading: *ad finem lucis ab ortu* belongs to the coded language of imperial power, "from the distant East to the furthest West." A world empire instead of a monarchy? Ovid will use the same phrase to describe the worldwide power of the princeps:

> qua nihil in terris ad finem solis ab ortu
> clarius excepto Caesare mundus habet.
>
> (*Pont.* 3.1.127–28)

With horns under his crown, and as much land as he can take in from morning to night, Cipus is well paid for his refusal of empire. The narrative structure dramatizes the founding gesture of imperial power: not acceptance, but refusal. Because imperial power arises from the ritualized

---

the important paper by Philip Hardie (forthcoming). Another way to look at Cipus's horns would be (as Hardie and my editors independently point out) to investigate the twin projections on the head of Romulus in *Aeneid* 6.779–80.

[13] On ambivalent ideology associated with the principate, see Stevenson 1992.

refusal of honors and absolute power and is constructed as a surrogate, the princeps is a citizen who chose—as a republican magistrate could not—to decline the offer, and then accept it on new terms; this reduction is perhaps the true signifier of imperial power. The "boundary stone" of the *Metamorphoses*, Cipus suggests there is another metamorphosis to narrate, one on which the final panegyric will shed only indirect light.

THE SERPENT GOD

The sign of Cipus's horns is greeted with a strong sense of closure: *cornua . . . postibus insculpunt longum mansura per aevum* (15.620–21). To emphasize the permanence of a monument is a suitable move for a closing section; Ovid will soon speak of his own lasting fame and of the future of his works. (Here, again, is an implicit tension: the Romans of Ovid's age knew that these horns, *longum mansura per aevum* at the time of Cipus, have disappeared; no Augustan witness seems to have seen more than a trace of that monument.) We should also remember that the *cornua* of a papyrus roll mark the limit at which the reader stops following, and reading, a book: *explicitum . . . usque ad sua cornua librum et quasi perlectum* (Mart. 11.107.1; compare Ovid *Trist.* 1.1.8). Perhaps the poem begins to gloss its own closure.

The section on Asclepius's arrival at Rome opens with an impressive declaration:

> Pandite nunc, Musae, praesentia numina vatum
> (scitis enim, nec vos fallit spatiosa vetustas)
> unde Coroniden circumflua Thybridis alti
> insula Romuleae sacris adiecerit urbis.
>
> (15.622–25)

This manner of starting an episode is unique: nowhere else does the narrator invoke the Muses, not even in the prologue, where we clearly expect an invocation. Lafaye suggests that Ovid just got tired of thinking up clever transitions. More to the point, Kenney observes that as we read the final pages of the poem, a certain seriousness, the formal tone of *Musenanruf*, serves to prepare for the praise of Augustus.[14] But the appeal to the Muses has no direct relation to the Augustan section: Ovid has reserved this tradi-

---

[14] See respectively Lafaye 1904, 82, and Kenney 1986, 464 ("giving emphasis and weight"). There are those who acknowledge the difficulty; Holleman 1988, 384, n. 16: "Für diese Anrufung gibt es bis jetzt keine oder doch keine befriedigende Erklärung"; compare La Penna 1988, 287: "Una nuova invocazione alle Muse . . . maschera la difficoltà del legame con quanto precede," although to call it "new" conceals the difficulty that there are no other appeals to the Muses in the entire poem.

tional resource for the story of the serpent who travels from Epidaurus to Rome, bringing the new cult of Asclepius that will be located in the temple founded on the first of January, 293 B.C.E., on the island in the Tiber. This is, in fact, the last independent narrative in the *Metamorphoses*.

Such datability is a curious anomaly in this panchronic work. No other episode in the poem (no extended episode, that is; the founding of Rome is mentioned in two half-lines, 14.774–75, making room for the names of Actaeon's nearly forty dogs) is conceived as a true and precisely datable historical event before the poet arrives *ad sua tempora*. No other fact of republican history, except the coronation of Cipus, finds a place in the poem's chronology. The Muses are invoked as witnesses who preside over the *spatiosa vetustas* precisely when, for once in the poem, there is no need for them; that is, when the theme is recent history, well documented in written sources. The anniversary of the temple of Asclepius is a day marked on the first line of every surviving Roman calendar: the Kalends of January, AESCULAPIO IN INSULA. The first of January is an exciting date for Ovid, who is planning and writing an extensive poem that will complement the *Metamorphoses*: a work on time again, but not a universal history; a work on the calendar that will have as its starting point the first day and the first festival of the Roman year. So the *Metamorphoses* closes, in its last narrative, with the first of January, when the *Fasti* has its official beginning. Perhaps Ovid, while working on two poems so rich in cross-references and purposeful differences, wanted to give the proem of the *Metamorphoses* an ambiguous reference: here the poet will bring his poem *prima ab origine mundi . . . ad mea tempora*, while *tempora* is the first word of the *Fasti* and could serve as an alternative title for that poem on the Roman year.[15] The plot of the *Metamorphoses*, from the beginning of the world to the height of Rome, intersects, on the first day of the year, with the plot of the *Fasti*, the circle of Roman months.

But a long poem that mentions the Muses only in the last book is still surprising. A considerable precedent is that of Lucretius, an epic poet who works on a similar scale, and arranges his *Musenanruf* in a similar way. The only appeal to the Muses in *De rerum natura* appears unexpectedly in the last book (6.92–95). The similarity is greater if we remember that the final episode of Lucretius Book 6 is an important model for Ovid's story of Asclepius; the endings of Lucretius and Ovid are closely interwoven.

The similarities entail opposites. The arrival of Asclepius at Rome is framed by the crisis of a plague:

> Dira lues quondam Latias vitiaverat auras,
> pallidaque exsangui squalebant corpora morbo.

[15] For other suggestive examples of *tempora* used to imply the poem, *Fasti*, see below, and Hinds 1987b, 21; 1992, 87 n. 7.

> funeribus fessi postquam mortalia cernunt
> temptamenta nihil, nihil artes posse medentum,
> auxilium caeleste petunt.

(15.626–30)

Asclepius arrives as a savior: *finem . . . luctibus inposuit* (15.743–44). The description of the crisis is similar to that of the plague at Athens. Some allusions recall a crucial paragraph at the end of Lucretius, a text that should probably be taken (despite most editors of Lucretius) as the end of the Plague and the conclusion of *De rerum natura*:[16]

> lacrimis lassi luctuque redibant;
> inde bonam partem in lectum maerore dabantur,
> nec poterat quisquam reperiri, quem neque morbus
> nec mors nec luctus temptaret tempore tali.

(6.1248–51)

The Athenians yield to pain and sorrow. The return home after the burials is the final image, perhaps alluding to the last scene of the *Iliad*. The Romans in Ovid, *funeribus fessi* as their counterparts in Lucretius were *lacrimis lassi* (in parallel alliteration), do not yield, but seek a solution Lucretius had not conceived. The supernatural help given by Apollo and Asclepius is a narrative turn that antagonistically supplements Lucretius: *luctus*, a powerful force in the last verse of *De rerum natura*, finds an appropriate answer in the final episode in Ovid:

> et finem specie caeleste resumpta
> luctibus inposuit venitque salutifer Urbi.

(15.743–44)

Ovid looks to the highest models an epic poet can have. The last story of the *Metamorphoses*—the omnivorous epic that swallows up every model and uses up the resources of narrative—supplements and corrects the final episode of Lucretius; at the same time, the story of a plague and an appeal to Apollo brings the text back to where it all began, to the first book of the *Iliad*.

The healer is the son of Apollo, the god who re-created Virbius from the dead Hippolytus. Asclepius puts an end to the suffering, and his arrival is a kind of historical coronation. Moving from Greece to Italy, he fills a final void in the Roman pantheon and seals the ancient epoch in which

---

[16] In favor of regarding 1247–51 as the conclusion, see P. Fowler 1983, 564; compare D. Fowler 1989b, 85; an opposite view is Ferrarino 1986, 371–72. In the first verse of the Ovidian plague, the position of *quondam* and *morbus* corresponds with Lucr. 6.1138 (*haec ratio quondam morborum*) and with his literary successor, the beginning of the plague of the animals in Virgil *Georgics* 3.478 (*hic quondam morbo caeli*). On closure in Lucretius, see Peta. Fowler, Chapter 6 in this volume.

nulli cura fuit externos quaerere divos (Prop. 4.1.17). The next step, as will be clear a few verses later, is the birth of the divinity *in situ*. Asclepius is the last importation from Greece, and his arrival on the island is like a sign of completion for Roman culture:

> unde Coroniden circumflua Thybridis alti
> insula Romuleae sacris adiecerit urbis.
>
> (*Met.* 15.624–25)

The epithet for Asclepius, "Son of Coronis," is well suited to the situation. The god arrives at Rome in the form of a serpent, and the long journey is marked by his winding coils: *incurva . . . carina* (15.644); *flectitque sinus . . . tendit ad incurvo munitos aggere portus* (689–90); *torta coronatae solvunt retinacula navis* (696); *inposita premens puppim cervice recurvam* (698); *deus explicat orbes / perque sinus crebros et magna volumina labens* (720–21; the god *explicat* himself and, like Ovid's work, is made of long, winding *volumina* to unwind and wind again); *innixus moderamine navis in alta / puppe caput posuit* (726–27); *erigitur serpens summoque adclinia malo / colla movet* (737–38). The god's ship is crowned, as befits the end of a prosperous journey—and the envoi of the book (as in Prop. 3.24.15; Ovid *Rem.* 812; compare Rutherford, chapter 3 in this volume). The serpent is an icon taken from the cult of Asclepius, but it can also represent the end, the conclusion of a text. For ancient readers, whose books were rolls, the sign of the conclusion is a line curved at each end: Ƨ.

Meleager personifies this sign of the end when he concludes his *Crown* (Στέφανος—but Κορωνίς may also mean "crown") by giving voice to the "coronis," the symbol that is added to a complete text to show that the roll must be rewound:[17]

> I, who announce the final lap's finish, the coronis,
>   trustiest keeper of the bounds of written columns,
> I declare that Meleager has finished, he who enrolled
>   in this book the labor of all poets gathered
> into one, and that it was for Diocles he wove with flowers
>   a wreath, whose memory is evergreen.
> But I, curled in coils like the back of a snake, I am fixed here
>   enthroned beside the limits of this learned work.
>
> (*Anth. Pal.* 12.257; trans. Peter Bing)

[17] On the coronis, see esp. Stephen 1959; also Griffiths 1970, 37–38; Bing 1988, 33–35; Fowler 1989b, 105–7. Compare 615, *festam imposuere coronam* (with 624–25, *Coroniden . . . adiecerit*); both κορωνίς and κορωνός can mean "with curved horns," and κορωνίς is attested as "crown, wreath" (Stesichorus 187.4 PMG); with the other Latin examples I cite, compare κορωνιάω, "to arch the neck," and κορωνίς, "stern" (Aratus 345) or "curve," a Homeric epithet for ships; etymological dissemination, figurative repetitions, and bilingual word-plays interweave and reinforce one another.

In a parallel example, Philodemus crowns a collection of love epigrams with a simpler invitation: "Muses, write a coronis for my love" (*Anth. Pal.* 11.41). The serpentine nature of the coronis, conceived as the coils of a snake, blends with the serpentine incarnation of Coronis's son, whose appearance puts an end to the long textual journey of the *volumina* that land at Rome.[18]

THE PRESENCE OF AUGUSTUS

Another closing strategy is involved in the epiphany of Asclepius in Book 15. The god that revives Virbius had been himself revived; his skill at restoring life was punished by the bolt of Jove, and his own existence as a serpent-god is a return from death. The myth is anticipated at length in Book 2. The nymph Ocyroe, before being struck silent by a mysterious divine intervention, predicts the strange fate of Coronis's young son:

> eque deo corpus fies exsangue deusque,
> qui modo corpus eras, et bis tua fata novabis.

> (2.647–48)

As is typical of prophecies, the language reveals but also conceals further mysteries. The splitting of Asclepius's destiny is more complicated than it appears; not only "from a god, a dead mortal, and then a god once again," but also "from a serpent, a god," that is, "you will be reborn as a snake in order to become again a god," a message that perhaps is hidden in *ex(s)angue*. The child's mission of salvation is already explained in the first words that the prophetess tells to him: *"toto"* que *"salutifer orbi / cresce, puer!" dixit* (2.642–43), and this language is mirrored, across no fewer than thirteen books of poetry, when the narrator has his last word on Asclepius's presence at Rome: *venitque salutifer urbi* (15.744). A solemn, hymnlike harmony closes and sets in unison the destinies of the world and of the mother city. Making himself *praesens* at Rome (15.646), the god is also guarantor of a cultural transference and of a *translatio imperii*.

There is much to recommend a political reading of this concluding tale. Apollo, the father and healer of Asclepius, has a central role in the assimilation of religious symbols that was so important to Augustan political discourse. *Salutifer* is an appropriate epithet for the image of savior that the emperor projected on the world stage of his empire. The omen *cresce puer!* makes one think of a politicized, Augustan interpretation of Virgil's fourth eclogue. Some maintained that the birth of Augustus resulted from a visit by Apollo: Atia was supposedly visited by the strange figure of a serpent

---

[18] *Coronis nota tantum in fine adponitur*, Isid. *Orig.* 1.21. The *Metamorphoses* is identified as *volumina* in *Trist.* 1.7.35; 1.1.117 (= 3.14.19).

(Suet. *Aug.* 94.4). There is a recurring temptation to close the circle, from Asclepius to Augustus and vice versa, but this has curious results. Some identify Augustus with the serpent through Asclepius; the result is a warning to the Romans that Augustus is in fact "eine verräterische Schlange, ein amphibisches Ungeheuer."[19] La Penna accepts the connection, but sees it as indirect praise, and recognizes the difficulty. Asclepius is one of the few cases of mythological apotheosis not usually associated with the imperial cult, although La Penna argues that Augustus, even if Ovid makes no explicit reference, will likewise free Rome and the empire from the ruin of civil war. True, Asclepius is seen as "already" a god, but to some extent he anticipates the divinizations of Caesar and Augustus, a connection made by no Augustan poet, but which Ovid perhaps implied. "Perhaps," La Penna concludes, because we must acknowledge that Ovid did not make clear the connection between Asclepius and Augustus.[20]

Both Holleman and La Penna, with opposite intentions, try somehow to mediate between imperial discourse and the cult of Asclepius, and La Penna's argument is very suggestive. In fact, Asclepius's healing serpent is no favorite of, nor a common analogy for, the saving role of Augustus. Augustan discourse privileges other religious icons. Of course, we cannot forget that the serpent is connected with the idea of apotheosis: by shedding its skin each year, the snake embodies victory over age and sickness (Macrob. 1.20.2). In Ovid there is a clear example of a serpent representing the change between human being and immortal:

> utque novus serpens posita cum pelle senecta
> luxuriare solet squamaque nitere recenti,
> sic, ubi mortales Tirynthius exuit artus,
> parte sui meliore viget maiorque videri
> coepit et augusta fieri gravitate verendus.
>
> (9.266–70)

The rare, emphatic adjective *augustus* is seldom without purpose. Hercules, no lightweight as a mortal, is transformed by a process of growth: *augustus* works as a superlative of *maior*, and ties the apotheosis of Hercules to the "growing" idea of "Aug-ustus," the man who increases without limit (unlike Asclepius, Hercules is already a traditional signifier in political discourse, understood as referring to Augustus). After his human life, Hercules is reborn like a serpent changing its skin. This curious image is the same one Lucretius used to oppose belief in the immortality of the soul:

[19] Holleman 1988, 381.

[20] La Penna 1988, 286–87, concluding: "Dico forse, perché Ovidio, bisogna riconoscerlo, non ha fatto niente per rendere esplicite queste connessioni."

> quod si immortalis nostra foret mens,
> non tam se moriens dissolvi conquereretur,
> sed magis ire foras vestemque relinquere, <u>ut anguis</u>.

> (3.612–14)

The surprise ending *ut anguis* is the term of similarity in Ovid. Ovid affirms the existence of what Lucretius thought absurd (*vestemque relinquere* recalls *exuit*, *Met*. 9.268). We are asked to accept new rules, in a world constructed as a fantastic transgression, but these rules also apply to official discourse, which asked Romans to accept the divinization of the emperor following the precedents of Hercules and Romulus Quirinus.[21] If we remember the Lucretian "countertext," this connection is discredited, but if we accept the image of the reptile, it is difficult to separate it from its literary heritage. This imagery of apotheosis is thus seen from a dangerous perspective. The changing serpent has a double model in Virgil: *Georgics* 3.437–38 and *Aeneid* 2.473–75. In the *Georgics*, we see a threatening creature spewing poison, and the poet prays he will never meet it. In the *Aeneid*, the reptile has a chilling similarity to the cruelest figure in the entire epic, Neoptolemus, a serpent who brings new war and death. It follows that he is a less reassuring model of immortality than the benevolent and redeeming serpent who lives on the island of Tiber. The serpent is a figure of disjunction rather than connection; it does not integrate, but separates. The two saviors can be read as competing with one another. Two *Heilbringer* seem too much for an ending; it is true that these figures have an obvious closing potential, but we are used to meeting them one at a time. In separate places, Virgil adopts Octavian (*Georgics* 1) and Aristaeus (*Georgics* 4); Lucretius has Epicurus completely alone. The strange and untraditional juxtaposition of Asclepius and the emperor is not the way to show they are the same (whether the serpentine monster and tyrant of anti-Augustan readings or the savior-prince of pro-Augustan readings); but the juxtaposition produces a bifurcation, a redoubling of the conclusion that requires a choice. Asclepius is not a straightforward mirror for Augustus, and his episode, with its clear formal autonomy and intense generation of concluding signals, suggests a plausible ending for the *Metamorphoses* as a whole. This saturation has a curious result: it makes the Augustan section a kind of supplement, leaving Augustus out.

---

[21] It has already been observed (Due 1974, 32–33) that another simile for apotheosis, *ceu lata plumbea funda / missa solet medio glans intabescere caelo* (*Met*. 14. 825–26), has models close to the scientific language of Lucretius, but the item compared is entirely different (Lucr. 6.177–79, 306–8). The choice of *intabesco* (absent in the Lucretian model) has a curious suggestion of ruin and corruption, an antagonistic effect, while the narrative should exalt and make believable the change from human to divine. The problematic nature of this kind of apotheosis is stressed by Plutarch *Rom*. 28.7.

In fact, the apotheosis of Augustus is the central idea for what follows the epiphany of Asclepius.[22] The catasterism of Caesar is not an independent story; as the poet forcefully explains (15.760–61), this transformation is only a "foreshadowing" of the future deification of Caesar Augustus. The greatness of Caesar, which is a backward projection of his son, a future god,[23] transforms the master of war into a new star: *in sidus vertere novum stellamque comantem* (15.749), a lasting star or a comet—a star that falls? The tradition admits some uncertainty, and casts doubt on the stability of Caesar's promotion. It has been noted that a new star is the theme of another famous poetic epilogue, the constellation Coma Berenices, inserted as the last chapter of the *Aitia* by Callimachus (and perhaps transformed by Ovid into his *stellamque comantem.*[24] Thus Ovid, in the wake of Callimachus, aligns his own ending with the tradition of court poetry: the *Metamorphoses* replaces the *Aitia* and turns toward the Julian dynasty as Callimachus did to the Ptolemaic. But there is at least one more point. After having prayed for Augustus and having foretold his ascent to heaven, Ovid claims a destiny that is not just celestial: *super alta perennis / astra ferar* (15.875–76). This is more than catasterism; above the stars, the poet has a kind of ultra-Caesarean immortality: *iamque opus exegi, quod nec Iovis ira nec ignis / nec poterit ferrum nec edax abolere vetustas* (15.871–72). His work cannot be destroyed by *Iovis ira*, the most obvious sign of Augustan power. The thunderbolt, *ignis*, has received much attention, but the danger of *ferrum* is no less relevant. From his Horatian model (*Odes* 3.30), Ovid has taken only one of the destructive factors (*edax . . . vetustas*, 872, from 3.30.4–5, *innumerabilis / annorum series et fuga temporum*, with the attribute given to *imber* at 3.30.3), and it is significant that the heavenly agents of Horace are replaced by images with political overtones. Woodman suggests that mention of the sword, after the drastic images of fire and thunderbolts, is anticlimactic: "It is hardly a compliment to himself if Ovid says that a mere sword (*ferrum*) will not destroy his opus";[25] but I prefer to ask who alone could legitimately bear a sword in the pacified world of the late Augustan age. The slow decline foreseen by Horace gives way to weapons of immediate destruction that only one person can control. That same

[22] The narrative style and structure demonstrate that this part is a dedication *in exergo*, not a typical narrative section; see Little 1972, 399.

[23] On the importance of this father-son tie, see Barchiesi 1989, 94–95; the position of Caesar in Augustan ideology is explored by P. White 1988. Received into heaven, the father becomes witness (*videns*, 850) to the superiority of his son (*et vinci gaudet ab illo*, 851): *venit, vidit, victus est.*

[24] *Sidus . . . novum*, Catull, 66.64; ἄστρον . . . νέον, Callim, *Aet.* 110.64 Pf.; and *novum . . . sidus* (referring to Octavian), Virg. G. 1.32. On Ovid's transformation of Callimachus, see P. Knox 1986, 75–76; compare Herter 1973, 205: "So schlossen die Aitia mit einem Katasterismos wie Ovids Metamorphosen."

[25] Woodman 1974, 127–28.

person also has the right to wipe out names (876: *nomenque erit indelebile nostrum*).[26] Without doubt, Augustus is parallel to Jove (15.860), but the same bolt that had in vain destroyed the career of Asclepius will be a useless weapon against the *Metamorphoses*. The last word, *vivam*, connects with the distant proem *in nova*, closing the poem in a circularity of glorious rebirth, a continual transformation of the poet in his own book (15.879 + 1.1, and perhaps a coronis after *vivam*? Lines 871–75 have the amusing acrostic INCIP . . .).

The cumulative effect of this process is not easy to define; in fact, it is precisely this indeterminate closure that is the object of my analysis. An excess of concluding gestures can generate the structure of an open ending. The title of the work, *Transformations*, sharpens the reader's sensibility to all that is provisional, changing, and liable to revision. The signs and effects of closure tend to control this flux, but they are in turn exposed to continual rearrangement, and are displaced.

This dynamism is so strong that not even the miraculous rise of Augustus is untouched. It is time to examine the poet's parting words to the ruler, keeping in mind the coronation in the story of Asclepius (*venitque salutifer Urbi*, 744) and the ending spoken by the narrative voice ("I will live").[27] It is helpful to remember that the emperor lives beyond the reach of change; his image, always the same, inviolable and spread everywhere in thousands of copies, guarantees stability: "For the last thirty-five years of his rule the portraits do not age: we have no representations of the seventy-five-year-old emperor."[28]

> tarda sit illa dies et nostro serior aevo,
> qua caput Augustum, quem temperat, orbe relicto
> accedat caelo faveatque precantibus <u>absens</u>.
> iamque opus exegi.

(15.868–71)

The work is finished before the human life of Augustus comes to an end. A vow is expected: *voto finiendum volumen est*, says Velleius (2.131). If we think the words have an important position in the verse and a privileged position in the clause, the effect is hard to overestimate. Ovid prays for the long life of Augustus, as every citizen must in the ritualized *vota pro salute*

---

[26] But since Ovid will live on the tongues of the people (15.878), his name will be less erasable than that of Caesar, which is written on monuments and temples (listed, apparently, in a prayer a few verses before, 861–66, on which see Feeney 1991, 214–22).

[27] "It is a dangerous thing to propose a grand climax and then to top it with another, for it inevitably raises the possibility that it too will be ante-climactic, and so on *ad infinitum*"; thus Winkler 1985, 219, discussing Apuleius's novel, another text with an overdetermined conclusion.

[28] Price 1984, 172.

principis,[29] and only the last word refers to the distant future when the emperor, now seventy years old, will leave Rome and reveal his divine nature: *vocabitur hic quoque votis*. But the last word is, in fact, *absens*.[30]

One can, of course, analyze the epithet from different points of view. Augustus, as everyone knows, is an analogue of Jove; Ovid has just equated the two (15.860: *pater est et rector uterque*), and Horace began *Odes* 3.5 by describing the move from god to emperor: *Caelo tonantem credidimus Iovem / regnare: praesens divus habebitur / Augustus*. But will the emperor's destiny be a true progress if, after having been *praesens*, a θεὸς ἐπιφανής, he becomes an *absens* god? Asclepius, as we have seen, must be *praesens* in order to employ his virtue: "Als Überwinder des Pesttodes in Rom ist er abschliessend präsent: *venitque salutifer urbi* . . . Prototyp für Augustus ist nicht nur der Jupitersohn und Held Hercules, sondern auch der Apollosohn und Heiland Aesculapius."[31] To turn to an absent divinity, however, is proverbial for wasting words (*deos absentis testis memoras*, Plaut. *Merc.* 627). To the poets, the Muses are *praesentia numina* (15.622), and certain charismatic individuals in human society are *praesentes divi* (compare Virg. *Ecl.* 1.41). Even worse, not all gods are good, and some are invoked to secure their absence from mortal affairs. In *Fasti* 4.931–32 we meet a negative, malign goddess, Robigo. She must be honored, but the poet hopes that she will accept gifts and prayers in absentia:

> at tu ne viola Cererem! semperque colonus
> absenti possit solvere vota tibi.

MULTIPLE ENDINGS

Ovid writes in an age that does not like easy conclusions; Livy will bear witness. The expectation of apotheosis, supported by propaganda, is becoming too concrete. Ovid's next work, the *Fasti*, will have to be rewritten in part to confront the great theme of succession. By writing the word "end" to the *Metamorphoses*, the poet shows that Augustus can be inserted; but for his readers, readers of a distant (15.878) and not so distant future, there is a way to come to terms with new transformations, and even to prepare, if they wish, for a future without Augustus. So many strategies of closure are exhausted one after another: recapitulation (Virbius), anticipations of modernity (Cipus), thematic inversion (the Lucretian ending sub-

---

[29] On the chronology of relations between "actual" and stylized literary prayers, see Gomez Santamaria 1991.

[30] The emphasis of *absens* placed at the end of verse, sentence, book, and work is well observed by Moulton 1973, 7; also Schmitzer 1990, 296–97. Feeney 1991, as far as I can see, is now the best study of the "Augustan" ending of the poem.

[31] Schmidt 1991, 137.

verted and "cured"), deification and panegyric (the *Aitia*), a prayer for the ruler, a prophecy of literary fame (*exegi*: Horace's ending to Books 1–3 of the *Odes*)[32]—all these rival strategies invite the reader to negotiate a new idea of closure that controls the form of the text. The apotheosis can be a climax, but also a kind of expulsive contraction: the work is almost without its *caput Augustum*. Ovid presents the emperor with his text "completed" as a *maius opus, quod adhuc sine fine tenetur* (*Tr.* 2.63); a text without ending, indeed.

THE YEAR OF SIX MONTHS

Looking over his work from exile, Ovid finds that his *Metamorphoses* and *Fasti* have something in common:

> carmina mutatas hominum dicentia formas
> infelix domini quod fuga rupit opus.
>
> (*Tr.* 1.7.13–14)

> sex ego Fastorum scripsi totidemque libellos
>
> . . . .
>
> idque tuo nuper scriptum sub nomine, Caesar,
> et tibi sacratum sors mea rupit opus.
>
> (*Tr.* 2.549–52)

rupit opus conveys a sense of violence more than simple interruption; the destiny of the two poems (as we see in *Tr.* 1.7.14 and 2.552, respectively) matches the destruction of the work of Arachne, a work beyond envy but not beyond the hysterical anger of Athena: *rupit pictas, caelestia crimina, vestes* (*Met.* 6.131). With exile, Augustus has damaged beyond repair (so it seems) two poetic masterpieces still "in progress." Ovid uses indirection because, as we know from elsewhere, the *Metamorphoses* was more finished, and the *Fasti* less finished, than the poet lets us believe (although it is important to remember that his words are directed, especially in *Tristia* 2, to a very important reader). Two possible intentions can be discovered, "in the former case literary and in the latter political."[33] The ostensible incompleteness of the epic casts upon Ovid's exile the sublime literary myth of Virgil's will: exile as Death of the Artist, obsession for perfection, the decision to burn a masterpiece. The analogy is literary, but not without political significance. After having personally intervened to save the *Aeneid* from destruction, the emperor now provokes cremation of the *Metamorphoses*. I shall have something similar to say about the political background of the *Fasti*.

[32] On the imitations of Horace, Rosati is convincing (1979, 119–21).
[33] Hinds 1987a 137 n. 23.

Ovid makes it clear that he has already written all twelve books of the Roman Year. His banishment from Rome affects a work that should be dear to Augustus, and now the poem is cut short.

It is strange that the *Fasti* was broken into two exact halves, just as the unmetrical *duodecim* is cut into *sex . . . totidemque*. Chance and compromise can impart various forms to a literary text, but this is one of the most curious: more than incomplete, the poem is literally half-complete. Books 1–6 are as complete as the *Metamorphoses*, while Books 7–12 have disappeared without a trace. It does not matter what Ovid wished to say or suggest with *scripsi*, because, whatever we want to see in the verb, *sex . . . totidemque* can only mean twelve. Six books published, twelve "written." Stopping halfway can be seen as a particular act of incompleteness: the missing part is highlighted, and the poet does not entirely renounce his capacity for the project and for unitary form. Of course, the plan of the *Fasti* presupposes a break in the middle: each book is a well-formed unity, and we expect a gravitational point after the first six. With remarkable insight, an obscure later writer produced an introductory distich for *Fasti* 7:[34]

> tu quoque mutati causas et nomina mensis
> a te qui canitur, maxime Caesar, habes.

The result is a parallel between the second, missing part and two famous Second Parts: the second pair of the *Georgics* (*tu quoque, magna Pales*) and, above all, the second half of another poem organized in twelve books (*Aen.* 7.1: *tu quoque litoribus nostris*, also with a character, Caieta, who gives her name to something); a common beginning unites them.

Ovid behaves, if one may put it this way, as if the entire second part of the diptych has been a victim of the poet's exile, while the first part remains unharmed. Yet we know very well that *Fasti* 1–6 have been rearranged more than once, and not superficially. Why the complete silence about *Fasti* 7–12? One possible answer is that the exiled poet lacked his primary tools: sources and books. It should be clear, however, that this situation did not prevent Ovid from drafting a thesis on mythology such as the *Ibis*, and that the language used by Ovid to lament his lack of books (*Tr.* 3.14.37) is intended as literary allusion: Ovid recalls a poetic book, Catullus 68.33–36, in which a poet lamented, "I have no books."

A better clue emerges when we examine the possible themes for *Fasti* 7–12. The twin proems to Books 5 and 6 analyze the names "May" and "June," and discuss competing aetiologies. A similar investigation was not possible for the next two months, whose names leave no room for discussion. A dramatic intervention in the history of the calendar renamed the

---

[34] Alton, Wormell and Courtney 1985, v–vi.

months for two members of the Julian family. Each reader of the poem should feel the effect of surprise that arises when the text fails to reach its promised political climax: the celebration that could have been an effective center of the poem is deferred *sine die*. A quick look at the official agenda would present the bard of the civil year with the following: July 1, Augustus Renounces Consulship; July 4, Ara Pacis Augustae; July 12, Birthday of Divine Julius; July 20 (and ten following days), Games for Venus Genetrix (of the Julian line); August 1, Octavian Takes Alexandria; August 9, Pharsalus; August 13–15, Augustus's Triple Triumph; September 2, Actium. This list does not include lesser occasions and, most important, growing expectation for September 23—the cosmic date on which whole districts of Asia had chosen to reform their own calendars, beginning the year with the emperor's birthday. Looking at these dates, one can see that Ovid was reluctant to take up the task or, rather, that he wanted to arrange a postponement: time and leisure to complete the Roman year, with its nettling Augustan dates, in Italy instead of in Tomis. But this remains hypothetical (and if others want to use this argument to support a traditional reading of the *Fasti* as conformist, I do not). It is interesting in this regard to look at the final part of *Fasti* 6, a text crucial to all these questions. My starting point is the fact that this text had a regular circulation, as Ovid acknowledges. It appeals to a public, and although it is just half of the project, it is not a stolen manuscript: this half has the right to be considered as a text.

We need to take the question of an audience very seriously. All Ovid's work suggests that the author is aware of being in contact with a vast, anonymous public that determines literary success. The Romans who were Ovid's regular readers for some twenty years expected clever manipulations and surprising turns. The poet accustomed his audience to interventions that changed even the physical text with which they had made a "literary agreement." Reading Ovid is a contract that can be renegotiated at any moment. The *Amores* was reduced from five books to three, a reduction that embodies a lighter, more "slender" poetics. Tragedy interferes (3.1) with the *Amores*, which has already resisted (and taken advantage of) incursions by epic (1.1) and *gigantomachia* (2.1). The *Ars* begins as a work dedicated to manly love, and without warning brings in a third book on the Amazons. The *Remedia* declares war on the *Ars*. The *Ibis* claims to be the precursor of an impending iambic work. The *Metamorphoses* has a brief, mysterious proem, but the *Tristia* is concerned with publishing a new preface adapted to the author's changed fortunes.[35] *Tristia* 2 offers a complete catalogue of Ovidian poetry, framed by a tendentious manual of literary history, with a timely "authentic" reading of the *Ars amatoria* that decon-

[35] Hinds 1985, 24–25.

structs the alternative reading proposed by the emperor. Finally, the *Metamorphoses*, as I have tried to show, has a redundant tendency toward completion and closure, but ends up introducing a "metamorphic" reading that opens the way to less conclusive and authoritative readings of texts.

If there is a common factor in all these manipulations, I would say that the form of Ovid's texts, their stable scheme and structure, is open to constant negotiation with the reader. Are we so sure that the *Fasti* is just an interrupted utterance and that the interruption cannot be a communicative "gesture"? The personal situation of the author invests the damaged year with at least a potential metaphorical meaning: the time of Ovid's life is severed like the structure of the poem.

LET US COUNT THE DAYS

Some comment is necessary on the last ten days of *Fasti* 6. In general, there is a recurrent sense that time is escaping:

> Iam sex et totidem luces de mense supersunt . . .
> Tempora labuntur, tacitisque senescimus annis,
>   et fugiunt freno non remorante dies . . .
> Tot restant de mense dies quot nomina Parcis . . .
> Tempus Iuleis cras est natale Kalendis.
>
> (6.725; 771–72; 795; 797)

Tacitisque senescimus annis: it would be difficult to find a more appropriate, and particular, context for this trite cliché: we are reading it (as we, too, grow old) in the context of a poem that represents the year. In a poem so concretely identified with the measurement of time (each month a book, the numbering of the days always intertwined with the progress of writing and reading), the increased use of temporal signs suggests the presence of an approaching deadline. Is the book about to "expire"? The *Parcae* (795) are not only a figurative presence, motivated by an elegant reference to the number three, but also a reminder of transience and interruption. The years (771) are "quiet" as soon as the yearly poem is about to become silent. The days run away (772) as if the poet were losing his grasp on the flux of time. Besides the normal thematic formula of pressing time (Virg. G. 3.284, on the work, its themes and composition: *sed fugit interea, fugit inreparabile tempus*), *tempora labuntur* reminds us that *tempora* is not only the didactic theme of the *Fasti*, but also the initial word of the poem,[36] appropriate as a title. The work also flees. While time and the poem on Times are both passing, there are only seven days before the month of June ends:

---

[36] Above, note 16. On the theory that the first proem is a successor to an original proem that still surfaces in the proem to *Fasti* 2, I agree with Miller 1991, 143–44.

post septem luces Iunius actus erit (6.774). Thirteen days remain, seven, three, and one: no other book in the *Fasti* has a similar countdown. The themes of the last days before the Julian Kalends offer other suggestive developments.

June 21

The last narrative section of the poem (6.733–62) has a familiar ring for readers who are acquainted with *Metamorphoses* 15 and its multiple endings. The actor Asclepius and the supporting actor Hippolytus/Virbius are central figures in the conclusion of the epic. Again, the story of Asclepius is significant. Jove destroyed him with his thunderbolt, but then repented and allowed his rebirth (759–62); Asclepius is a kind of victorious Prometheus, achieving the very height of his art in spite of Jove's divine anger and opposition. There are many other meaningful connections between the *Metamorphoses* and the *Fasti*. The legitimate prologue of the elegiac poem, Janus, divine caretaker and god of beginnings, has explained (1.103) that he is identifiable with Chaos: a connection with the beginning of the epic is implied, where Chaos is the original state before the creation of the world and of narrativity (*Met.* 1.5–9). Thus the two poems have a slender thread of common plan, from chaos to the regenerated (and regenerating) Asclepius (who is also, like Janus, a god of the first of January).

The suggestion of closure contained in the name of the god Coronides (6.746, see above) is picked up by the description of the crowned ship (6.779: *coronatae . . . lintres*) and the crown for the Lares (792: *ubi fit docta multa corona manu*). Crown, coronis, and coronation achieve a ceremonial poetic of closure.

June 24, 25, 26

The last celebration of June, addressed to *Fortuna Fortis*, has the air of a plebeian festival. The wine runs (780: *multaque per medias vina bibantur aquas*; 778: *nec pudeat potos inde redire domum*), and the effects of alcohol mark the following days (785–89: *rediens male sobrius . . . aliquis . . . at si non esset potus*). As drinking prepares for the solstice, this protracted carnival bypasses a date that has a very different meaning for Roman society.[37] On

---

[37] The conspicuous omission is noted by Syme (1978, 33–34). This omission is crucial for Syme's theory that Ovid cut off his work on the *Fasti* some years before his exile. The poem nevertheless had a circulation even earlier (*Tr.* 2.549), was worked on for some time, updated in several places, and changed to keep in line with new turns in the succession and with the accession of Germanicus (Fantham 1986). If one accepts that the text is meant to be read as a poem in six books, the absence of Tiberius is strange and cannot simply be explained as a

June 26, 4 c.e., Augustus solemnly adopted his successor. The national calendar celebrates the event, but as the people descend to the river, and as the wine causes them to forget the day (6.789–90), Ovid fails to record the epiphany of a new emperor.

Such an omission requires interpretation. If we assume, as a reasonable starting point, that the poet had something to do with the circulation of his text in the years following Tiberius's proclamation, then he was presumably not indifferent to public reaction. The absence of Tiberius might have been either a great mistake or a conscious omission. There is another aspect to the problem: the importance of the omitted anniversary places in relief what the poet decided not to omit, namely, the traditional celebration of Fortuna Fortis. This cult has deep roots in the lives of the Roman masses, whereas the Claudii, the family of the new emperor, are a pinnacle of aristocracy, with a well-known reputation for intolerance and arrogance. (In 6.770, the battle of Metaurus is described without mention of its victor, Claudius Nero.) Syme observes that Tiberius was undoubtedly reacting against this antiplebeian tradition and trying to win back popular support, and he cites news of Tiberius's efforts (about 16 c.e.) to strengthen the cult of the plebeian Fortune.[38] But this is not enough when the text we have not only hides Tiberius's accession to the throne, but also gives evidence for another, very different coronation:

> plebs colit hanc, quia qui posuit de plebe fuisse
> fertur, et ex humili sceptra tulisse loco.

(6.781–82)

In this aetiology, the new king is Servius Tullius, son of a slave, champion of a very different kind of monarchy. To speak of his accession to the throne is not at all diplomatic if the day should be dedicated to a more recent successor; the king celebrated for his humble origins is not an appropriate substitute for Tiberius.

26 June

To speak of the solstice has some meaning in a text that follows the development of the seasons. The equinox that balances day and night (3.878: *tempora nocturnis aequa diurna*) was placed at the end of the third book, and

---

result of composing in layers. The new prologue to Germanicus was a clear sign of adjustment to an era in which a lack of interest in the new successor would be dangerous. Only a reader like Syme, careful, rigorous, and with a strong sense of history, could be satisfied with the conclusion that the main body of the poem continues to reflect an earlier political context. It is interesting to compare the observations of Nicolet (1991, 44–45) on the effect of the "Parthian triumph" that Ovid "anticipates" in *Ars Am.* 1.213ff.

[38] Syme 1978, 34.

divides the six surviving books into two corresponding halves.[39] The autumnal equinox and the winter solstice will never be mentioned. The former is Augustus's birthday, and the latter the day of his zodiac sign, Capricorn.

June 30

No other book of the *Fasti* has a final day so well marked by the narrative voice:

> Tempus Iuleis cras est natale Kalendis:
> Pierides, coeptis addite summa meis.

(6.797–98)

Tomorrow the Kalends will arrive, honored by the name of the Julii; the poet and his readers know the strength of this name. For a moment one would be tempted (with Holleman) to explain *summa* as a reference to the Augustan culmination that should inaugurate the next month: "Diese Worte implizieren, dass der Dichter sich unmittelbar vor der Klimax (*summa*) des Werkes befand."[40] But this cannot be the literal meaning: *addite summa* indicates that the poet is asking for a full and proper conclusion, as if this could be the final touch to the *summus liber*[41] of the calendrical project. The promise of a continuation under the sign of the ruling family is threatened by a sense of closure, and resulting exclusion.

Seen in this light, the aetiological theme of the last day is not without resonance. The temple of Hercules and the Muses vowed in 33 B.C.E. by L. Marcius Philippus suggests in its dedication a celebration of poetry, well suited to the epilogue of a work in verse. The genealogy of the founder is a

---

[39] The proem of Book 4 has a certain similarity to the tradition of "proems in the middle" studied by Conte (1992): it contains a dense discussion of poetics and even a "doubling" of the proem of Book 1 with a literal citation (4.11; *tempora cum causis*). "Proems in the middle" are a classical way of placing in relief the closure of a text, marking its architectonic completion. Once more, the condition of the *Fasti* as a "half" poem is paradoxical.

This work was complete before the publication of Feeney 1992, a fascinating essay that I think complements my own. Feeney discovers in the poem a growing consciousness of a premature end, while I read (paradoxical) signs of closure in the end of Book 6. These two ways of reading can easily be combined, because there is a common factor, the growing tension between the poetics of the work and its reference to Augustan discourse. On this topic, Hinds 1992 is now indispensable.

[40] Holleman 1988, 390.

[41] An expression used by Quintilian (*Inst.* 3.8.42) to identify the last book of his work. *Coepta* is for Ovid the project and the development of a work; compare *Met.* 1.2; 8.200–201, *postquam manus ultima coepto / inposita est*; *Ars Am.* 1.30; *Ars Am.* 1.771, *pars superat coepti* (the second book; the third book comes as a surprise); *Tr.* 2.555–56, *quamvis manus ultima coeptis / defuit* (on the *Metamorphoses*). References to *coepta* often occur at beginnings, and the use of beginnings in allusive endings is an Alexandrian strategy noted by Zetzel (1983, 261).

knot of stories and compliments. Philippus's father was the stepfather of Augustus. His wife, Atia, brings an important name to the family of the two Caesars. The family, the Marci Reges, goes back via Ancus Martius to Numa, tracing another connection between the family of Julius Caesar and the prestigious background of its origins.[42] The temple, as Ovid surely knew, replaced an *aedicula* created by Numa, the figure from ancient Rome who receives the most favorable treatment in the *Fasti*.[43] From the marriage of Philippus is descended the chaste Marcia, whom Ovid praises for her beauty, her morality, and her family ties to the Caesars: a conspicuous choice in a poem that has little space for private individuals, and even less for women, however distinguished. It may be worth noting that the last elegy in the "Roman" book of Propertius (the poetic project that the *Fasti* takes as its model) is dedicated to the praise of another matron, a noblewoman related to the family of Augustus. The language used by Ovid in 6.800, *cui dedit invitas victa noverca manus*, sounds like an allusion to the same elegy, 4.11.86–88 (*noverca . . . dabit . . . illa manus*). Both Cornelia and Marcia have a connection with the emperor emphasized by the poet.[44] By a curious coincidence there appears in both texts a political figure with a great name and an unclear future. A promising son of Cornelia, Lucius Emilius Paullus, will be swept away by the events of 8 C.E. Marcia's husband, Paullus Fabius Maximus, will have a similar destiny some years later. He is certainly the political protagonist with the most space in the *Fasti* (except, of course, for members of the imperial family). He is the center of attention when Ovid praises the *gens Fabia* and its powerful cognomen Maximus. This man will be swallowed up (in 14 C.E.) by a mysterious intrigue, often interpreted as the last attempt to stop the accession of Tiberius: fragmentary testimonia from the last years of Augustus's reign suggest that Paullus was not only independent of Tiberius but "the foremost among his enemies."[45]

Syme imagines that the poem was already essentially complete by 4 C.E., and is therefore not concerned that it combines (in the "neutral" succession of the calendar) a censored imperial anniversary with a tribute to the Fabian gens, the omission of Tiberius with interest in relations between Augustus and the Fabii. From this perspective, he can see the celebration of

---

[42] The connection is important for the self-fashioning of the Julii because Numa is a figure of peace and wisdom that complements the militarism of Romulus, and also because Romulus is less present in the genealogical tree than would be desirable. He is related to Aeneas (and Venus) and Mars, but the current view is that he died without sons; besides, he is seen more as a common ancestor of the race than as a specific progenitor of the Caesars.

[43] On the importance of Numa in the *Fasti*, see Hinds 1992.

[44] Compare Propertius 4.11.55–60, and the discussion of this poem by Johnson in Chapter 8 of this volume.

[45] Syme 1978, 146.

the temple of Philippus as "an innocuous point of termination."[46] Yet it is difficult to see Fabius, who is no longer Horace's *centum puer artium* (*Odes* 4.1.15), as an innocuous figure, cut off from the current of political tensions that accompanies the entire period of succession—a period in which the *Fasti* has every right to be placed, interrupted in 8 c.e. and reworked for several years afterwards. Whatever the details of its composition, it is crucial to observe that the poem *says* it was revised and brought up to date; recent political developments such as the death of Augustus and the rise of Germanicus are mentioned with so much emphasis that the poet assumes a heavy responsibility for the rest, including what has been excluded from the rearrangement and can be seen as a deliberate omission.

The reader cannot be sure that the ending of the *Fasti* is isolated from the tensions of political discourse. This peaceful family album includes shadows and dangers. Paullus Fabius Maximus, the talented young man who began the last book written by Horace, now marches (with his wife, the chaste Marcia) across an arena of dynastic intrigue. After asking the Muses about the history of the temple, and after listening to the Muse of history, Ovid ends on a note of quiet approval:[47]

> sic cecinit Clio, doctae adsensere sorores,
> adnuit Alcides increpuitque lyram.
>
> (6.811–12)

The consent and approval of Hercules and the Muses are the last published words of the *Fasti*. The Muses are reunited after the discord of 5.9 (*dissensere deae*). Clio (perhaps by chance) has the last word after having been the first informant to speak in the *Aitia* of Callimachus (p. 19, 30 Pf.). The approval of Hercules repeats the approval of Germanicus, who had been invoked in the proem (1.15: *adnue conanti*), and the parallelism is a further tribute to the new prince. *Increpuit* recalls a message that ended Ovid's elegiac production at the close of the *Amores*: *corniger increpuit . . . Lyaeus* (3.15.17). The harmony of the lyre, a final gesture (in half a text!) toward peace and coronation, reflects the last poem published by Horace:

> Phoebus volentem proelia me loqui
> victas et urbis increpuit lyra.
>
> (4.15.1–2)

---

[46] Ibid., 35.

[47] Once again, the effect of unanimity is in contrast to its background. The poet finishes with praise of Hercules and asks the Muses who placed them next to the hero, *cui dedit invitas victa noverca manus* (6.800), an interesting way to end a book marked with the name of Juno and aggressively claimed by her in the proem (6.26, 77) against the cautious claims of Hercules's wife. Propertius's fourth book is again a relevant model (4.9.71–72).

Ovid has just praised what had been the theme of *Ode* 4.1, the marriage of Paullus Fabius Maximus, so there was an additional reason for invoking the last book of Horace's lyrics. The sound of the lyre was a call for Horace: Phoebus was demanding respect for lyric verse in a book of poetry dangerously fond of sublimity and solemn celebration. But now, in Ovid, the lyre plays a harmony of approval: the meaning of Apollo's warning is inverted. The approval of Hercules and the Muses is the deserved reward for a poet who has discovered how to write a poem that is Roman and official, but also protected against war and epic catastrophe;[48] Hercules of the Muses replaces Phoebus—a god who is surprisingly missing from the pantheon of the *Fasti* (a celebration postponed to the second semester?). It is possible that the vignette of Hercules also suggests the hopes that the poet places on Paullus: the Fabii are descendants of Hercules (when he visited ancient Latium), and Ovid elsewhere observes in the politician Paulus Fabius Maximus the gifts of a *Herculea simplicitas* (*Pont.* 3.3.100).[49]

This might be the end, but, as in other Ovidian endings, there is still room for doubt. The history of the temple of Hercules Musarum includes a glaring omission, almost a historical inaccuracy, a serious defect of memory for a poet inspired by Clio and authorized to sing the aetiology and antiquity of Rome. The new temple is not as new as it seems: more precisely, it is a second edition, a restoration, of one of the most famous monuments of the republic. The ancient temple of Hercules Musarum was designed and dedicated by Fulvius Nobilior, the patron of Ennius. The symbolic apparatus of the temple was an impressive homage to the official status of poetry and art, and to the growing integration of Greek and Roman traditions. More important, the temple was the first official repository of the Fasti of Rome, edited and commented on by the same Nobilior. One can think of few sites better suited to closing a poem called the *Fasti*. Ovid's annals, an original version of the traditional record, glance back to a remote predecessor, and to a place that was a repository for the ancient material used in this poem. The Muses who are questioned about the origins of the temple are, after all, the Muses who long survived in that same site, transferred there from Ambracia by Nobilior (compare Pliny *HN* 35.66). The lack of a direct indication of continuity shows that antiquarian interest (an important theme in the *Fasti*) can not only reinterpret the past, but also make it unreadable by erasing its tracks.

---

[48] The intervention of Apollo turns the epilogue of the lyric book into a celebration of Augustan peace. There is a clear tie with the return of Augustus in 13 B.C.E. and with the senatorial decree that dedicates to the emperor the project of the Ara Pacis Augustae. The decree has a date to insert in the imperial Fasti, July 4. Without moving from the Campus Martius, and at a short distance on the calendar, Ovid would have confronted this anniversary. It is clear that his Hercules of the Muses is less bound to official celebrations than was Horace's Apollo.

[49] See, in general, Syme 1986, 403–20.

This might be the end, but a subtle suspicion remains. Nobilior's dedication was a direct consequence of the capture of Ambracia; it was designed to commemorate a war using Greek religious symbols, and to refigure victory and triumph with the transfer of new gods. Bringing the Muses to Rome was no minor distinction for a victorious general, himself Musagetes. The fall of Ambracia was told in Book 15 of Ennius's *Annales*; the author was a client of Nobilior, a devotee of the Greek Muses, and an expert on Pythagorean imagery. It has already occurred to students of Ennius[50] that the end of *Annales* 15 (for some time, before a later addition, the absolute end of that narrative, and preserved as such in some editions) would have been the right place for some allusion to the figurative and cultural program of the new temple: military victory sung by Ennius, and the promise of a *Musenweihe* of Roman culture directed by Ennius. The Muses, already invoked by Ennius at the beginning of the first proem, were thus able to give a clear sign of their presence at Rome. If these speculations have any basis, I think Ovid would have been interested in the coincidence. The restored divinities seal with their consent a work of poetic archaeology that claims to bring to light the most ancient of annals: *sacra recognosces, annalibus eruta priscis* (*Fast.* 17; compare 4.11, *tempora cum causis, annalibus eruta priscis*).

QUAE IAM FINIS ERIT? (*AENEID* 12.793)

To bring something to an end is a clear sign of power. This is a recurring complication in my study of Ovidian endings; I cannot separate poetic closure from the politics of closure.

We cannot define closure simply in terms of poetic form, because more than the responsibility of form or the control of poetic architecture is at stake. In two great projects, the *Fasti* and the *Metamorphoses*, the act of ending offers the reader a political analogy. Both texts involve, for different reasons, the dimension of Augustan time, time as appropriated by Augustan discourse:[51] the progress of universal chronology from the beginning

---

[50] The idea was put forth by Skutsch in 1944 (= Skutsch 1968, 18–20) and since then has remained speculative, even if several scholars find it attractive. For archaeological and historical data, see Richardson 1977 and the very complete Martina 1981. Conjectures on the end of *Annales* 15 have a special importance because the series of Books 1–15 was conceived as a closed entity and given independent circulation (compare Skutsch 1968, 20; Hofmann [1986, 225] even thinks that the number of books in Ovid's *Metamorphoses* was influenced by the three pentads of Ennius). Feeney (1992, 24 n. 64) now proposes a connection between Ennius and Ovid with respect to the temple of Hercules of the Muses, and I think the analogy is stronger if we consider that the temple was the first location for the Fasti. This "closural allusion" to the *Annales* is likely enough in a passage that, as I have tried to show, cites the final poems of the final books of Ovid (*Amores*), Propertius, and Horace (*Odes*).

[51] See the illuminating work of Wallace-Hadrill (1987).

to the empire, and the rotation of the Roman year in which the emperor is continually present. Augustan discourse gives a common slant to these methods of taming time: the flux of history has a culmination and conclusion in universal peace; the Roman year absorbs the transformation of Rome into its *telos*, the Restoration of the New Order that puts an end to change and disturbing memories. Augustan discourse is naturally directed toward a unifying and totalizing end. If we see closure as the degree to which a work can resolve in a satisfying way the expectations and tensions developed by its growth, then the discourse that motivates the Augustan constitution seems an extreme example of closure. Augustus completes and stabilizes all that was in flux, incomplete, open. To write an ending to the annals of triumphs, a supplement to the *carmen arvale*, to close Janus, to reclaim the Golden Age, to gather the *Annales maximi*, to describe an accurate geography of the known world: Augustus defines himself not only as the First, but also as the Last and Definitive Man of Rome.

THE FIRST SPECTATOR

Readers who take the closure of the *Metamorphoses* as an Augustan synthesis "from chaos to imperial cosmos"[52] are prisoners of that *Zeitgeist* to which they themselves contribute, with their tendentious imaginations about ancient Rome. But who protects from similar dangers those who go in search of dissonance and deviant voices? "Anti-Augustanism"[53] is a weak position, with a very weak name; who really knows what it meant to be "against"? But it is precisely the poetic text, with its erratic irony, that creates and makes necessary these contrasting roles of the Augustan and anti-Augustan. The "opponents" pay a high price; they are forced to read the text with the eyes of an informer or "mole," and are therefore profoundly vulnerable to the totalizing ideology that they say they want to reshape. The "Augustans," for their part, are welcomed with a smile and escorted to the empty seat of the privileged spectator, who is seized unawares by the narrative and by its theatrical games.[54]

---

[52] I use Pfeiffer's language only by way of example: "Vom ersten Wandel des chaos in den Kosmos bis zum letzten Wandel des politischen chaos in den neuen Kosmos der augustischen Ära" (1934, 48).

[53] On this the analysis of Kennedy 1992 is critical.

[54] I would not know how to place myself outside this contradiction.

I wish to thank some friends (Philip Hardie, Stephen Hinds, and Denis Feeney) for useful comments on a first draft (dated 1990); more recent material has been included only occasionally in the bibliography. Thanks also to my editors for helping me with (yes!) closural strategies.

CHAPTER 10

How Novels End:
Some Patterns of Closure in Ancient Narrative

MASSIMO FUSILLO

SINCE ITS BEGINNING, literary theory has been concerned with the concept of closure. In the *Poetics,* Aristotle frequently stresses organic unity as a necessary quality of the artistic work: its beginning, central section, and ending must be coherently unified (7.50b). It is significant that the same polysemic word τέλος indicates both spatial ending and finality.[1] Without any prescriptive rule, however, modern criticism has employed similar concepts. In particular, Neoaristotelianism and New Criticism in the United States, and semiotics and structuralism in Europe, have insisted on the artistic text as an autonomous system: that is, as a closed model apart from the open flow of existential time. Jurij Lotman synthesizes this theoretical approach in an incisive way: a work of art is "a finite model of an infinite universe."[2]

This general statement seems to have special validity in the case of fictional texts, which construct a possible world. In this regard we might compare Ricoeur's work on time and narrative, which stresses the philosophical value of fictional "configuration," on the levels both of semiotic theory and of creative literature (especially in Woolf, Proust, and Mann).[3]

The last decade has been marked by the poststructuralist trend: the concept of the closed text itself, and therefore that of closure, are passing through a crisis. Two theoretical movements in particular have criticized the fetishism of the text typical of semiotic analysis: pragmatics and deconstructionism. Although there is a great deal of discussion we cannot treat here, especially concerning the reader's creativity, the process of pragmatic reception must be addressed in discussing problems of closure. Semantic and structural paths, whether consciously intended by the author or not,

---

[1] For spatial meaning, cf. 18.55b29, 32; 20.57a7; 23.59a20, 32; 24.59b20; for finality, 6.50a18, 22, 23; 25.60b24, 25, 27; 26.62a18, b15.

[2] Lotman 1977, 210, and, in general on the modeling function of the end, 215–17; see the canonical work by Kermode (1967), and Friedman (1966, ch. 2 and 7).

[3] Ricoeur, especially vol. 1 (1983) and vol. 2 (1984).

allow the reader to transform the abstract text into a concrete work.[4] Anyway, it is only the definitive kind of closure that was strongly criticized, for example by gender theorists; closed meanings and male power are in fact considered equivalent, opposed to the open fluidity of women's discourse. On the other hand, New Historicism seems to create new perspectives for this issue, linked with problems of politics and power (see the essays by Don Fowler and Francis Dunn, chapters 1 and 5 in this volume).

The subject of this essay is the ancient novel—at least those that are completely preserved. The roots of the fluid literary phenomenon we now call the novel are chiefly in Hellenistic culture (and even earlier in the *Odyssey*). In that period, literature became a metaliterary laboratory, created by poets who were at the same time philologists and librarians; for this and other reasons we find in the Alexandrian texts a stronger closural strategy linked, at the sociological level, with the evolution of the book industry and of a larger reading public.

This observation leads us to the problem of the relationship between written literature and closure. It has been stated that oral poetry should be more open than written, and generally, this seems a valid observation.[5] But the problem is more complicated: the openness or closure of a text depends upon numerous factors, including its cultural context, its genre, and its own thematic and formal structure. Moreover, the use of written texts began very early in Greek literature, while aural reception lasted until the Hellenistic period and later. To state a direct relationship between strong novelistic closure (opposed to the epic openness) and Hellenistic culture may be suggestive, but is inevitably schematic.

It is necessary at this point to make some further preliminary remarks. Though there are many different usages of the term in recent criticism, closure generally indicates a sense of completeness, integrity, and coherence, both formal and thematic, that the reader experiences at the end of the work. This critical perspective, especially widespread in English-speaking countries, was introduced by Barbara Herrnstein Smith's book (1968) on sonnets and other short poems. Although this study offers many analytical tools and some theoretical categories (revised according to French semiotics by Philippe Hamon in 1975), the problems of fictional texts are basically different from those of poetry.

A typology of the forms of closure in the novel was sketched by Mari-

---

[4] The basic contribution to these theoretical problems is Iser 1978; for the difference between text and work, cf. Brioschi 1983, Introduction. The deconstructionist view is maintained by Miller (1978).

[5] Hamon 1975, 500; Zumthor 1984; on the peculiar case of the tragic work (a written text for an oral performance), cf. Segal 1986. Other generic polar oppositions (Western/Eastern; classic/romantic; postmodernist/modernist) are mentioned by Fowler (1989b, 79–80).

anna Torgovnick in the introduction to a book dealing with various modern novels from George Eliot to Virginia Woolf (1981). Some of her terms, especially those that concern the relation between the narrative and its ending, I shall make use of below: *circularity*, when the ending recalls the beginning "in language, in situation, in the grouping of characters, or in several of these ways";[6] *parallelism*, when it repeats important points of the narrative; the *tangential ending*, when the ending introduces a new topic; and the various ways in which the ending may or may not coincide with the reader's horizon of expectations (*complementary, incongruent, congruent, confrontational*). These interesting suggestions must be integrated, in my opinion, with the new rhetoric of "narrative discourse" (the narratology of the *discours*) described in Genette's *Figures III*.[7] For the analysis of closure, the following categories seem to me particularly useful: (1) *succession*, a proleptic reference to the future of the story beyond the limits of the novel (an ending with analepsis—comparable to beginning *in medias res*—is extremely rare; I can mention only one contemporary example, *Equal Affections* by David Leavitt); (2) *duration* (of a closing scene or summary); (3) *perspective*, i.e., whether or not we conclude with a character's point of view; (4) *voice*, that is, whether a narrator or character is speaking. This typology, together with thematic structure, also describes "infratextual closure," the articulation of narrative into units such as chapters and books.[8]

Before dealing with the narrative endings of ancient novels, we should begin with paratextual endings. The paratext was defined by Gérard Genette, who devoted a book to this subject (1987), as the borderland of titles, subtitles, intertitles, epigraphs, prefaces, dedications, commentaries, and interviews. In ancient literature the paratext was almost always incorporated into the text and not separated from the narration.[9] Its use becomes more and more important in the Hellenistic period thanks to its strong metaliterary character. For example, in Alexandrian poetry we find the paratextual *explicit* in the *Aitia*, which has a metaliterary ending based on the hierarchy of genres: Callimachus declares that he will proceed to the lower genre of the *Iambi* (Μουσέων πεζὸν . . . νόμον: 113.3 Pf.; probably imitated by Ennius in his *Saturae*);[10] the paratext here not only plays a

---

[6] Torgovnick 1981, 13.

[7] Genette 1980.

[8] Cf. Stevick 1967; Fowler 1989b, 82; Hamon 1975, 496 and 509 ("clausule interne / clausule externe").

[9] Genette 1987, 152–54, on the prefaces: "préfation integré."

[10] According to Knox (1985), this epilogue was originally placed at the end of a first edition in two books, looking forward to a new work that was later included in the definitive edition; Pfeiffer (1953, xxxvi–xxvii) thinks that it first marked the transition to the *Iambi* in a complete edition made by Callimachus at the end of his life; see also the important revision due to Parsons (1977, 49–50): first edition, two books framed by the Muses; second edition, four, the second two framed by *Victoria* and *Coma Berenices*: "The result was a

closing role, but also connects one work with another (supratextual closure, as Don Fowler calls it;[11] this second function will be picked up by Propertius at the end of Book 3, by Virgil at the end of the *Georgics*, and by the author of the false proem of the *Aeneid*; cf. La Penna 1985 on the "raccordo editoriale"). More integrated in epic objectivity and in fictional illusion, but equally paratextual, is the epilogue to the *Argonautica*. With an affective apostrophe, Apollonius of Rhodes takes leave of his heroes, saying that they have come to the end of their toils, and wishing himself success (the salutation to one's own work is a widespread topos in ancient and modern literature[12]).

Ancient novels use many paratextual devices, usually to give a sense of (historiographic) authenticity to the fiction (the embedded preface of Chariton and Longus Sophistes, the programmatic declaration addressed to the reader by Apuleius,[13] the introductory epistles of Antonius Diogenes anticipating many modern devices used by Potocky, Poe, Manzoni, Eco, and others, and finally the peculiar parodical preface of Lucian's *True Histories*). Among erotic novelists, only Chariton begins with a preface and ends with another paratextual device, the *explicit*:[14] τοσάδε περὶ Καλλιρόης συνέγραψα, "That is my story about Callirhoe" (trans. Reardon[15]), or, as Georges Molinié freely translates in the Budé edition: "Tel est le roman de Callirhoe." From a formal point of view, the brief sentence preserves the historiographic style of the *incipit*, with the author presenting himself as a secretary (συγγραφεύς) who transcribes a true love story; it ennobles a newborn genre and motivates a private plot in which the historic dimension plays a secondary role.[16] The *explicit* also gives thematic precedence to the female character, an interesting Charitonian feature we shall deal with later.

It is significant that Heliodorus's novel has no preface, but a more ex-

---

bipartite *Aetia*, to which a new prologue (fr. 1) and a new epilogue (fr. 112) gave external unity"; the connection with the *Iambi* is stressed by Van Sickle (1980); for other suggestions, see Hollis 1986, 467–71; on Catullus 116.7–8 as a similar transition to a book of mimes, see Wiseman 1985, 185–87.

[11] Fowler 1989b, 82–88. For some examples inside a lyrical collection, see Santirocco 1984.

[12] See Citroni 1986.

[13] See the convincing new interpretation by Harrison (1990): the "I" in the prologue is the book itself (neither Apuleius nor Lucius nor a prologue speaker), according to a widespread ancient and modern topos.

[14] See Smith 1968, 172: "explicit self-closural references," very rare in lyrical poetry.

[15] Translations of the Greek novels are from *Collected Ancient Greek Novels*, edited by Brian Reardon (1989).

[16] On the subordinate position of the historiographic material in comparison with the central role of eros, cf. Müller 1976, 126; Hägg 1987, 184–204; Fusillo 1989, 57–68 (= 1991, 56–66).

panded *explicit* than that of Chariton: "So concludes the *Aithiopika*, the story of Theagenes and Charikleia, the work of a Phoenician from the city of Emesa, one of the clan of Descendants of the Sun, Theodosios's son, Heliodoros" (trans. Morgan). From the fascinating and mysterious beginning *in medias res*, the *Aethiopica* is characterized by a gradual disclosure of the narrator's voice. In the first part of this complex novel, his presence is almost imperceptible because of the long story-within-a-story (the "meta-diegetic" narration of the priest Kalasiris); at the end, the author's control is made clear by invoking theatrical metaphors and the power of the god, "that had staged this whole drama" (ἐσκηνογράφησεν, 10.38.3). The culmination of this gradual climax is the *explicit*, where the narrator-author reveals his birthplace, his family, and, with the very last word, his name. In a novel unified by religion and the cult of Helios, we should consider the possibility of a pseudonym (another paratextual device[17]), but the wide distribution of this proper name in that area leaves the question uncertain.

Finally, this pattern is parodied by Lucian in the ending of the *True Histories:* "What happened to me in the other world I'll tell you in the following books." As the preface has already declared, every word of this text is a lie, and the ending is no exception; there will be no more books, and Lucian negates his ending by parodying this historiographic gesture.[18]

Western fiction begins with two poems that literary critics regard as opposing literary archetypes (epic vs. novel, tragic vs. romantic, and so on). This contrast also includes techniques of closure. Although the *Iliad* employs strong closural strategy (Helen's lamentation for Hector and the Trojan funeral rites supply the typical "closural allusions" described by Smith[19]), the basic tension of the poem remains unaltered. The poet alludes to continuation of the war (*Il.* 24.801–3), and the public knew that the war would continue.[20] This is the end of the limited subject chosen by the poet (Achilles' second anger is definitely over), but not the end of the mythic *fabula*: we could actually define it as an open ending (see the discussion of "incomplete closure" by Murnaghan, chapter 2 in this volume). The ending of the *Odyssey*, on the other hand, has a stronger closural character, although it preserves the basic openness typical of both Greek and Latin epic poems (in chapter 7 above, Hardie discusses significant examples). Everything that concerns the story of return is brought to a definitive end: the reunion with wife and father, and the revenge against the suitors. Nevertheless, the final battle is interrupted by Athena with some

---

[17] Genette 1987, 46–53; on the important function of the proper name in the paratextual technique from Hesiod onward, see 38–40.

[18] Stengel 1911, 94.

[19] Smith 1968, 101 on lyrical allusions, and 117–21 on the closural use of natural, extra-literary moments (death, marriage, etc.) in fiction.

[20] See Rutherford 1982, 158–60; Fowler 1989b, 81–82.

abruptness, and Teiresias's prophecy about Odysseus's new journey looks toward the future.[21]

Unlike Virgil's poem, the Alexandrian epic by Apollonius of Rhodes is more informed by the model of the *Odyssey* than by that of the *Iliad*. The fourth book in particular rewrites the *nostos* pattern, with many allusions to the second Homeric poem. The ending, however, is open in the manner of the *Iliad*. The reader of the *Argonautica* would certainly feel a sense of completeness at the end because the chief subject, the journey of the Argonauts, has been fully realized (although its last phase, rapidly repeating the hymnal beginning, has often been criticized—incorrectly—as anticlimactic[22]). But the tensions between Jason and Medea, strongly presented in the second part of the poem, are not definitively solved at the end; the Euripidean future of the story, to which the poet often alludes, especially by ekphrasis and simile, hangs over this apparently peaceful ending like the war over the ending of the *Iliad*.[23] (I cannot agree that the last line of the *Argonautica* is an intentional allusion to the presumed Alexandrian ending of the *Odyssey*;[24] apart from the problem of Homeric philology involved, the allusion would be purely formal, while on the thematic level Apollonius concludes not with conjugal reunion, but with foreshadowing of a tragic conflict.)

On the other hand, the Greek novel clearly follows the Odyssean pattern, stressing its closed and harmonious ending. Conjugal reunion with Penelope is the archetype, a pattern relived and rewritten on the private level. Together with this sense of finality, the most typical feature of novelistic closure is circularity—which does not come from the *Odyssey*. With the exception of Heliodorus, all the erotic novels end by reestablishing the initial situation. At the beginning the protagonists fall in love; in the center we have a series of adventures and trials; and at the end the couple is

[21] See the critical discussion of A. Heubeck on 23.297 and on 24.1–204; and Griffin 1987, 76–77: "odd," but authentic; for the interpretation as a spurious addition, see West 1989; on Teiresias's prophecy, see Peradotto 1990, 59–93.

[22] Incorrectly, because the part summarized does not contain any important events. So it is called "the most abrupt stop in literature" by Hadas (1932, 53); cf. Mooney 1912, 47: "anticlimax"; Wilamowitz 1924, 2:223–24; Carspecken 1952, 173; H. Herter 1944/55, 400; abruptness is considered by Fränkel (1968, 622–26) a consequence of the archaic norm, reflected in Orpheus's song (cf. especially 624: "ein offenes Ende"); a positive valuation by Wyss (1931, 40); the effect of performance due to the hymnic element is stressed by Goldhill (1991, 296). On the concept of completeness coexisting with the open form, cf. Richter 1974, ch. 1.

[23] Allusions to the development outside the poem are, for example, 3.1203–6; 4.423–34, 1062–67; see Fusillo 1985, 307–11 and 338; on the Iliadic openness, see Paduano 1972, 109–12.

[24] Cf. Adam 1889, 92; Meyer 1894, 478–79; Rossi 1968, 151–63; E. Livrea (1973) on 4.1781, and *SH* 947, with Haslam and Griffiths referred to ad loc.; contra Bethe 1918, 444–46; Campbell 1983, 154–55.

reunited and (if they were not in the first part) they are married. Bakhtin described this scheme as "an extratemporal hiatus between two moments of biographical time":[25] after infinite adventures the protagonists are still young and beautiful. It is a structure that celebrates and eternalizes reciprocal eros, and concretizes an unconscious trend toward symmetry, corresponding to the desires of a presumably large public. The obsessive parallelism of this genre seems to make concrete the trend toward symmetry that Ignacio Matte Blanco described as a fundamental feature of unconscious logic. It is especially evident in the symmetrical unity of the leading couple, which corresponds to an erotic desire for fusion beyond space and time (poetically expressed by Aristophanes' myth in Plato's *Symposium*), and thus to the expectations of the sentimental reader.[26] However, this pattern has many variants, making each novel different and reflected in many particular kinds of closure.

The first period of the Greek novel, including the works of Chariton and Xenophon of Ephesus, has a strong consolatory character: that means, on the thematic level, an absence of tragic conflicts, of problematic ambiguities and ideological depths, and a concentration on private values and erotic passions, destined to an optimistic triumph; whereas the expressive level shows a linear structure and an absolute predominance of narrative elements. Those features are typical of entertaining literature (or "paraliterature"),[27] and suggest a popular reader who enjoyed the progression toward a happy end. This can be seen in an interesting passage in Chariton, directly addressed to the reading public:

> And I think that this last chapter will prove very agreeable to its readers: it cleanses away the grim events of the earlier ones. There will be no more pirates or slavery or lawsuits or fighting or suicide or wars or conquests; now there will be lawful love and sanctioned marriage. So I shall tell you how the goddess brought the truth to light and revealed the unrecognized pair to each other. (8.1.4–5)

The happy end is described with the Aristotelian term *katharsion*. It is a pleasant purification of the melodrama that satisfies the readers with a long series of topoi, concluding with reunion and legitimate marriage. The happy ending is for the author a necessary limit to the unending narratable,

[25] Bakhtin 1981, 90.

[26] See Matte Blanco 1978, passim; for an application to the Greek novel, cf. Fusillo 1985, 3.2, a perspective developed by Konstan (1994). On parallelism as a narrative figure, see Todorov 1967, 70–73; as a peculiarity of the Greek novel, Marcovaldi 1969, 57–58 and 69–74 (a somewhat Jungian interpretation); Ruiz Montero 1988, 83 n. 2, 154, 202 (a functionalist interpretation); and Molinié 1982, pt 1.

[27] See the introductory essay by Couégnas (1992).

to the unlimited repetition of the adventures of Fortune; and for the reader, it is a pleasant antidote to saturation.[28]

It is perhaps not by chance that these two novels of the first period have proleptic endings ("aftermaths," in Deborah Roberts's terminology) that allude to a wonderful future for the leading couple outside the story. This gives further narrative force to the sentimental utopia of eternal unity. But there are important differences between these works.

From a macrostructural point of view, Chariton's pseudohistoriographic novel is framed with perfect circularity by two popular assemblies.[29] At the beginning, after a rapid introduction telling how the protagonists fell in love and describing the political rivalry of their families, the first assembly induces the famous general Hermocrates to accept the power of Eros and consent to the marriage. In the last book, another assembly, described at greater length, plays a closural role with a clear sense of *mise en abyme*.[30] The people of Syracuse ask Chaireas for a detailed narrative of all his adventures, and with this theatrical solution we hear at the end of the work a summary of the entire plot, told by a character using the same narrative techniques as the author. Beyond this metaliterary role, the scene gives a public endorsement to the private love story, thus conforming to the values of Greek novels in general.[31] It has another closural function: summarizing the plot at its end intensifies the reader's sense of completeness and organic structure. And as the character's voice recalls that of the author, the passionate curiosity and sentimental involvement of the Syracusan people evoke the effects Chariton wants to produce in his public. Chariton often uses recapitulation, both on the authorial level and at the level of characters' discourse (the theatrical monologues),[32] and it may be that these recapitulations were addressed to a less cultivated part of the public, which wanted to hear the end described. (There were similar summaries in the *feuilletons*, and there are many in soap operas today.)

But this last recapitulation is not the last word of the text; Chariton differs from the other Greek novelists chiefly in his psychological interest, as Ben Edwin Perry emphasizes.[33] The romantic triangle, for example, is represented more ambiguously by a favorable characterization of the rival

[28] On the dialectic between infinite narration and closure, see D. A. Miller 1981, passim, especially the preface and the afterword; for the concept of "saturation," already dealt with by the Russian formalists, see Smith 1968, 42, inspired by Gestalt psychology.

[29] Cf. Gerschmann 1975, 128–31.

[30] For this critical concept, developed by André Gide, see Dällenbach 1989.

[31] I restricted my analysis to these functions in my previous work on the novel (Fusillo 1989, 137).

[32] Cf. Hägg 1971, 246–67 and, on the last item, 286: "to call forth the emotive reaction of the audiences, fictitious as well as real."

[33] Perry 1930, 115–23 (especially the minor characters); see also Rackcinska 1971, 600–601; García Gual 1970, 203 and 218–20.

Dionysius. This psychological interest is facilitated by a large proportion of direct speech and by the timely use of focalization restricted to a character.[34] We find both of these in the final scene, just before the *explicit*, in Callirhoe's prayer to Aphrodite:

> "Thank you, Aphrodite!" she said. "You have shown Chaereas to me once more in Syracuse, where I saw him as a maiden at your desire. I do not blame you, my lady, for what I have suffered; it was my fate (ταῦτα εἵμαρτό μοι). Do not separate me from Chaereas again, I beg of you; grant us a happy life together, and let us die together! (καὶ βίον μακάριον καὶ θάνατον κοινὸν." (8.8.15–16)

To end with Callirhoe's thoughts, emotions, and personal history provides a subjective solution completely in accord with her prominence throughout the novel (a prominence illustrated by her pathetic monologues in the second book in which she decides to marry Dionysius in order to save Chaereas's son). The projection of erotic triumph into the future is thus not stated by the author but is represented in the main character's vow, and in her utopian desire for a common death. This ending is less proleptic than scenic, and focalized upon the main character; the resulting subjectivity lessens its optimistic character.

In the novel of Xenophon of Ephesus, the consolatory character of the Greek novel finds its purest form. Parallelism and circularity are realized in an extreme way, with no difference between the two main characters— they are really two sides of the same coin—and without the subjective subtlety of Chariton. Furthermore, his popularizing attitude is evident in the narrative style, which is absolutely impersonal and pragmatic, as in the fable.

Xenophon's ending is also fablelike. The last part of the action is devoted to the gradual recognition of the leading couple in Rhodes, where they made the first stop of their travels together, before the long series of adventures apart. Narrative circularity is thus particularly marked, and the triumph of eros dissipates the labyrinthine peripeteia caused by Fortune. After the reunion, solemnly celebrated by the people of Rhodes (5.12), the narrator summarizes the future of the story. For Habrocomes and Anthia, "the rest of their life together was one long festival" (trans. Anderson: ἑορτὴν ἄγοντες, 5.15.3); the two slaves, Leucon and Rhode, will live with them in Ephesus, and their friend Hippothous will live with his lover Cleisthenes, whom he adopted after erecting a monument to his former lover, Hyperanthes. Thus Hyperanthes, having earlier been both Abrocomes' friend and Anthia's opponent, finally abandons this contradictory

---

[34] Cf. Hägg 1971, 91–92 and 114–19; Ruiz Montero 1988, 318–19; Stark 1984, 260; Fusillo 1989, 120–22 (= 1991, 126–28).

role. The exaltation of the couple is stronger because it includes both the lower social level of the slaves and homosexual love (which is less common in the Greek novel than in the Roman[35]). Xenophon's ending is therefore the most impersonal and consolatory, offering a proleptic summary spoken by the narrator, an explicit aftermath stated as reality, without direct speech and without focalizing upon the characters' emotions.

Another ancient novel of a popular character, the *Historia Apollonii regis Tyrii*, concludes with a prolepsis that spells out the happy future awaiting King Apollonius: seventy-four years of peaceful rule. The last word, however, is metaliterary authentication (like the more complicated frame of Antonius Diogenes' novel implied in Photius): the narrator says that Apollonius wrote his story in two books, one for his own personal library and one for Diana's temple in Ephesus, with both available to the public.[36] This seems the embryo of an interesting modern pattern in which the end coincides with the beginning of composition, as in the fascinating example of Proust's *Le Temps retrouvé.*[37]

Longus's novel also ends with a proleptic summary, but this has a very different tonality. And like the *Ephesiaca, Daphnis and Chloe* has the narrative style of folktale, but is far more complex. On closer analysis, these features turn out to reflect the author's irony rather than an attempt to satisfy the public's expectations. Having renounced the topos of separate adventures followed by return to the native land, Longus will find another kind of circularity. The work ends with a marriage (as in novels of the second period, whereas those of the first begin with marriage); like death, marriage is a biographical event with strong closural force,[38] beloved by the modern novel and by all forms of consolatory art (such as Hollywood movies). The penultimate paragraph (4.39) is a proleptic summary that is fuller than that of Xenophon. We are told that Daphnis and Chloe will lead a pastoral life, worshiping the gods who played a part in their story (Eros, Pan, and the Nymphs); they will have two children, and they will let them be suckled, the boy by a goat and the girl by a sheep, as they had been themselves (and as the narrator reported at the beginning of the novel, 1.2 and 5). Longus's circularity thus involves the biological cycle, as a new generation repeats the story of the protagonists. And it involves a typically bucolic idealization of nature. Although the main characters are the children of rich urban families, they prefer to live in the country and artificially recreate their past experiences for their children. Daphnis and

[35] Cf. Effe 1987, 95–108: Chariton and Heliodorus, as opposed to Xenophon and Achilles Tatius, follow the epic norm, which imposes reticence and allusion on this subject.

[36] See the edition with commentary by Kortekaas (1984).

[37] Cf. Mortimer 1985, 23: "La «fin-commencement»."

[38] Smith 1968, 117–21.

Chloe create their own myth, reflecting the artistic process of transforming life into narrative.

But this text has further semantic density. The last paragraph returns to the time of the narration, that is, to the rough *hymenaion* sung by the shepherds and to the couple's first night. And the last sentence is an ironic commentary by the author on sexual intercourse:

> Daphnis did some of the things Lycaenion taught him; and then, for the first time, Chloe found out that what they had done in the woods had been nothing but shepherds' games (ποιμένων παίγνια). (4.40, trans. Gill)

To conclude a work with a pun is a common closural device, which Armine Mortimer calls a "tag line" or "clôture épigrammatique";[39] here the joke reveals a global tension peculiar to Longus's novel, a Freudian *Kompromissvorstellung*. On the one hand, he contaminates the erotic novel with bucolic poetry, thus celebrating sentimental innocence and love of country life. On the other hand, the text discloses a repressed voyeurism, a latent urban perspective pointed out by Bernd Effe.[40] The woman who initiates Daphnis into sex, and thus violates the important novelistic norm of fidelity, comes from the city; the mention of her name, Lycaenion,[41] is not by chance. The ending of *Daphnis and Chloe* condenses both factors of this basic dialectic: repressive bucolic idealization and repressed urban voyeurism. The proleptic summary is characteristic of the first and represents the natural cycle and pastoral life, while the narrative details of the first night belong to the second, revealing an ironic author with ambivalent feelings for his characters.[42]

The second period of the erotic novel (which includes Longus) is much more refined, showing complex narrative strategies, semantic games with the reader, nuances and ambiguities in the topical celebration of reciprocal eros and of the heterosexual couple. Achilles Tatius's *Leucippe and Clitophon* presents an interesting variation on the pattern of circularity. At the beginning of the novel we read a long first-person ekphrasis by the narrator-author, who meets a young boy looking at the same picture. This gives

[39] Mortimer 1985, 21–22.

[40] Effe 1982. On the complex dialectic of this ending and of Longus's vision of sexuality, see Winkler 1990, 124–26; and Zeitlin 1990, 457–60.

[41] On this figure, see Levin 1978.

[42] The novel of "Lucius" involves a different kind of epigrammatic closure. After being turned back into a man, Lucius, the protagonist and narrator, visits the woman who loved him as an ass. After dinner she throws him out, disappointed by his human member. Lucius spends the night on the beach, completely nude, and leaves town the morning after, happy he is no longer the ass curiosity made him (§56). The obscene pun, conforming to the stylistic level of this comic novel, shows that the ass was in fact a formal and thematic vehicle for the exploration of a grotesque world. Cf. van Thiel 1971, 190–94.

occasion for the long autodiegetic narration by Clitophon, the protagonist of the love story. At the end of the novel the frame is not resumed. This has been criticized as a fault, or considered a sign of incompleteness or textual irregularity,[43] but such criticisms raise the wrong questions. It is common for a frame not to be repeated (e.g., Plato's *Symposium* and Theocritus 13): the introduction in this case has an authenticating function that gives the "effet de réel,"[44] but does not require the author to repeat at the end that he heard the story from Clitophon.

Yet the ending has a strange and unsatisfactory rapidity. The last paragraph is a dense summary of events to follow: resolution of the legal action against the rival Tersander; the journey to Byzantium, where the long-desired marriage is celebrated (with a single line); the journey to Tyre, with celebration of the supporting couple's marriage; and finally, the decision to spend the winter there before going back to Byzantium (8.19). This closural weakness can be adequately explained only with reference to the thematic and structural peculiarities of the entire novel. The novel of Achilles Tatius differs from others chiefly in its morally elastic attitude toward fidelity and chastity; hence its polyphonic presentation of eros, its interest in "realism" and everyday life, its lack of ennoblement and idealization, its freer, all-encompassing structure, and its ironic multiplication of novelistic topoi. For all these reasons, I consider his work an ironic and ambivalent pastiche of the Greek novel.[45] Giving such limited space to the crowning marriage does little to celebrate the chaste and faithful couple, while breaking off the narration frees it of organic structure. Furthermore, the introduction sets the action in a contemporary setting (unlike the ennobling historical setting in Chariton and in Heliodorus), an everyday world in which the speaker meets Clitophon by chance, and which ends abruptly, without explanation. The sentimental reader of the typical love novel might find this ending unsatisfactory; but the implied reader of this strange work—who must follow its sophisticated, metaliterary play—might find it more acceptable. The aesthetic response Achilles Tatius aims to provoke in his public is as ambivalent as his authorial attitude toward the erotic novel: something like the "ironical identification" defined by Hans Robert Jauss.[46]

[43] See E. Vilborg (1955) on 6.19.3, reporting Jacobs's theory of textual incompletion.

[44] Cf. Hägg 1971, 125; Plepits 1980, 28; Hunter 1983, 38–40; and especially Bartsch 1989, 168–70: "An intentional omission . . . a deliberate artistic creation" to stress the artificiality of his own work; on the contrary, a sharp criticism by Romberg 1962, 33–38; see also Most 1989.

[45] For similar interpretations of Achilles Tatius's peculiarity, cf. Calderini 1912, 61–81; Durham 1938 (still very useful, although the main thesis—Heliodorus's parody—is no longer tenable); Reardon 1971, 363–65; García Gual 1970, 245 and 258–59; Cresci 1978; Napolitano 1983–84; my definition as "pastiche" is in Fusillo 1989, 98–109.

[46] Jauss 1982, 2:10.5.

Smith concludes her study of poetic closure with mention of the anti-closural tendency in modern poetry.[47] In the novel this tendency goes back much earlier, to the so-called self-conscious novel of the comic tradition. Sterne's entire work, for example, is dominated by a systematic negation of (conventional) closure and finality, and *Jacques le fataliste* by Diderot follows the same path.[48] Unfortunately, we have few traces of a similar trend in antiquity. The fragments we still possess of Petronius's *Satyricon* shows its remarkable multiple parody and structural openness, but we can only guess about its closure.[49] Achilles Tatius is the only Greek erotic novelist to have some points of contact with the comic novel: ironic use of the first person, parody of the magic scene (3.15–22), and sexual themes (2.34–38, 5.27). But there is nothing in his novel that compares with the parodic negation of unity we can find in Sterne and can suppose in Petronius. To sum up: *Leucippe and Clitophon*'s ending can be explained as anticlosural from the cultural and thematic point of view, even if not in the strict and programmatic sense we find in Menippean literature (for the concept of anticlosure, see Francis Dunn's discussion of Euripides' *Heracles*, chapter 5 in this volume); the novel ends in fact with a deliberate and expressive weakness, a solution that reminds me of Stendhal's problems in bringing the flow of narrative to a final point (and we can remember that for Henry James, novelistic closure is always an oxymoron).[50]

The novel of Heliodorus, by contrast, has a marked closural strategy, perhaps the strongest in ancient narrative. In comparison with other Greek novels, the *Aethiopica* has a more complex architecture without circularity; or to be more precise, the plot is circular insofar as it begins *in medias res* and goes back to the antecedent, while the story is linear, because it is directed to a future goal, and does not go back to the starting point (in the other Greek novels is just the opposite: linear plot and circular story). In Torgovnick's terms we have an ending based on parallelism, one that recalls not the beginning, but some other point in the text.[51]

Heliodorus's denouement is a long one, filling the entire tenth book. In the penultimate paragraph King Idaspes, at the instigation of the Ethiopian

[47] Smith 1968, 233–43: Eliot, Keats, Cummings, and, in fiction, Robbe Grillet; see also Lotman 1977, 216–17, on the end as "anti-beginning," as "a struggle between the text and cliché" as "continual de-automatization of the codes employed."

[48] See Alter (1975), who analyzes this trend from Cervantes to Nabokov; and, on the parody of the chapter division, see Stevick 1967, 182–83: "Life, for Sterne, is not lived in chapters. . . . What this internal, associationist, apparently capricious organization effects is precisely that radical reorientation of the gestalt-making mechanism."

[49] See Schmeling 1991: starting from the technique of the episodes and from the way that they defeat expectations, he argues for an open, maybe unfinished, "picaresque" ending; see also Slater 1990, Introduction, 1–23.

[50] Cf., on Stendhal's closure, Miller 1981, ch. 3.

[51] Torgovnick 1981, 13.

priest Sisimithres, proclaims the marriage of Theagenes and Chariclea and their consecration to Helios and Selene. The proclamation must then be confirmed by the proper rites, which are celebrated by Sisimithres in the last paragraph. Charicles, Chariclea's putative father, as he watches the boys in white mitres, suddenly remembers the oracle they heard at Delphi, and the narrator quotes three lines of this text (which closes the second book):

ἴξοντ' ἠελίου πρὸς χθόνα κυανέην,
τῇ περ ἀριστοβίων μέγ' ἀέθλιον ἐξάψονται
λευκὸν ἐπὶ κροτάφων στέμμα μελαινομένων.

To the black land of the Sun will they travel
Where they will reap the reward of those whose lives are passed in virtue:
A crown of white on brows of black.

The novel ends before the *explicit*, with a scenographic procession to the Ethiopian capital Meroe, where the protagonists will celebrate their marriage. As in Achilles Tatius's novel and in contrast to those of Xenophon and Longus, there is no reassuring prolepsis of a happy future outside the story; yet unlike Achilles Tatius, Heliodorus ends not with synthetic summary but with a "baroque" scene. The structural difference mirrors an ideological one: Achilles Tatius is materialistic (see, e.g., the scientific excursus on emotions, 2.29) and ironic, while Heliodorus is mystical, Neoplatonic, and Neopythagorean, with a religious exaltation of the couple. That is why the narrative represents the consecration to Helios and Selene but not the marriage at Meroe; and that is why, in a form of parallelism, quotation of the oracle repeats the end of the second book (2.35) and other moments at which characters recall or try to decipher the prophecy. John Winkler has shown that an important *Leitmotiv* in Heliodorus is the process of gradual deciphering: he treats events as texts to be interpreted both by the characters inside the narrative and by the reader outside.[52] Hence the plot is dense and complex from the beginning, and its mystery depends upon a restricted focalization that leaves the happy ending uncertain throughout the action[53] (even though the basic outline of the plot is foreshadowed by the Delphic oracle, and is reinforced at the end by quoting it again).

This brings us to Heliodorus's relationship with his public. Although we have little information about the readers of the ancient novel,[54] those we have dealt with so far seem to be striving for a complementary relation that will satisfy their readers' expectations. The metaliterary passage in Chariton

[52] Winkler 1982, pt. 2.
[53] On this feature, see Morgan 1989a.
[54] Perhaps just because of this thorny problem, the subject has been treated extensively in recent years: see, among others, Levin 1977; Wesseling 1988; Treu 1989; Bowie 1992.

quoted above implies for the first period of the Greek novel a sentimental addressee who enjoyed a happy ending and legitimate marriage. We have seen that the question becomes more complicated when we turn to Achilles Tatius and his play with conventions, which presupposes a more refined reception. Heliodorus's implied reader must also apprehend his mystical and philosophical rewriting of the popular genre, while following a more stratified plot. In Torgovnick's terms, this relationship is "confrontational,"[55] disappointing the expectations of the common reader (who is mirrored in the action by the narratee Cnemon and by the Ethiopian people) by describing the consecration but not the marriage, while provoking the cooperation of an ideal reader.[56] A sentimental reading is not out of place: the Ethiopians, even though they have difficulty understanding Greek, are moved by the final recognitions, just as Cnemon is moved by Theagenes and Chariclea falling in love (4.4.2), and this emotive reaction surely has the aesthetic effect Heliodorus desired; but it is only one level of a manifold and polysemic work.

The same confrontational relationship with the reader can be traced in the closure of Apuleius's novel, which, for all its differences, shares with Heliodorus a mystical perspective. What makes his work distinctive is the postponement of this perspective, which is clearly expressed only in the last book (this, together with the tale of Cupid and Psyche, is the only part that is certainly by Apuleius). After the symmetrical metamorphosis from ass back to man, the eleventh book is completely devoted to the initiation into the mysteries of Osiris. The Greek Lucius suddenly disappears, the African rhetor from Madaura appears, and the novel is partially transformed into autobiography. In terms of narrative structure, the ending is not circular or parallel but tangential, introducing a new topic, unconnected to the rest of the work.[57]

This new topic imposes on the reader a "retrospective patterning" (in Barbara Herrnstein Smith's phrase)[58] or reassessment of the entire story as an allegorical series of picaresque adventures. The priest of Isis spells out such a reading: *sed utcumque Fortunae caecitas, dum te pessimis periculis discruciat, ad religiosam istam beatitudinem inprovida produxit malitia* (11.15). The metamorphosis into a lowly animal, described by Isis in person as *pessima mihique detestabilis iam dudum belua* (11.6), was a journey into the lowest world, a journey necessary for purification from the condition of an ass

---

[55] Torgovnick 1981, 18 and ch. 5: "Discomforting the Reader: The Confrontational Endings of *Vanity Fair* and *L'Education Sentimentale*."

[56] On Cnemon as the narrative personification of the *lector non scrupolosus*, see Winkler 1982, 139–47; contra Morgan 1989c; on the metaliterary relationship narrator/narratee, see Fusillo 1989, 2.5; on the concept of Ideal Reader ("Lettore Modello"), see Eco 1979, ch. 3.

[57] Cf. Torgovnick 1981, 13–14, quoting as example Gide's *Les Faux Monnayeurs*.

[58] On this closural device in fiction, see Smith 1968, 117–21.

(metaphorically equivalent to that of a slave[59]) to that of the high priest and member of the *collegium pastophorum.*

But an allegorical reading does not do justice to the vitality and complexity of this text. Using the highly restricted focalization of the experiencing "I," Apuleius does not make any proleptic allusion to the mystical ending: we never hear Lucius saying, for example, "I had to suffer this terrible degradation for the sake of a higher vision," as we might expect in a first-person narration. Throughout the novel until the last book, the reader enjoys a work that is stylistically and thematically polyphonic, ranging from the most grotesque and obscene novellas to fable and to a comic rewriting of the tragedy of Phaedra. We underestimate Apuleius's artistry if we regard the ending as an addition to the Greek novel about the ass; we would do better to consider it a conscious tribute to *delectare* and to narrative suspense for the sake of *docere*, or religious perspective. But I am inclined to see in this polysemic contradiction a deeper conflict, not fully expressed, in which mystical closure fails to repress comic subversion and cannot give shape to an uncertain reality.[60]

These observations also apply, in general terms, to infratextual closure. Closure at this level was already an interest of the Alexandrians: the definitive edition of Callimachus's *Aitia* was divided into four books, the first two framed by the dialogue with the Muses and the second two by symmetrical homages to Berenice;[61] and another work in four books, the *Argonautica* by Apollonius of Rhodes, was thematically and formally divided into a first half on the outward journey and a second on the return, with an invocation to Erato in the center—a "proem in the middle" as Gian Biagio Conte has called it.[62] In Chariton, infratextual closure has a marked psychological interest, as we might expect (notably at the end of the seventh book), whereas there is none at all in Xenophon. His factual narration has the frantic rhythm of a silent movie: it is a succession of small units that together produce an impersonal objectivity.[63] In Longus some infratextual strategy is perceptible, but is concealed by a simple and fluid narration that strives for naiveté.

---

[59] For this sociological implication, see Giannotti 1969, ch. 1.

[60] See Heine 1978, 25–42: the allegorical ending might have been conceived during the composition of picaresque chaos; on *delectare/docere*, see Giannotti 1969, ch. 4; Apuleian ambiguity is brilliantly described by Winkler 1985.

[61] See Parsons 1977, 49–50.

[62] Conte 1992 (originally published in 1980). See in general Campbell 1983.

[63] A vague intentional symmetry can be recognized between the endings of the third and fourth books, both consisting of a dangerous situation for the main characters; but this narrative parallelism is obsessively repeated in the entire novel. Of course, the absence of clear book articulation might depend on the hypothetical epitome of the original text, but I agree with Tomas Hägg (1966) in rejecting Bürger's (1892) critical thesis of an epitome and in considering original the text we possess.

As for Achilles Tatius, we can expand upon our discussion of the tension between openness and closure by looking at his use of digression or excursus (and I must disagree with Tomas Hägg's rejection of every intentional book division in *Leucippe and Clitophon*[64]). The theoretical and paradoxographical excursus is a novelty of the second period of the Greek novel, a feature of its greater rhetorical elaboration and its connection with the Second Sophistic. Achilles Tatius makes greater use of this device than Heliodorus;[65] but the digressive nature of his excursus is often limited by its location at the end of a book, where it produces the narrative equivalent of a caesura. The first book ends with a long paradoxographical dialogue between Clitophon and his slave Satyros on the power of Eros in all areas of nature; in this case the digression has a narrative purpose as part of Leucippe's courtship (1.16–19). The second book ends with a long and autonomous exchange, an anomalous philosophical dialogue within the novel, in which pederasty and heterosexual love confront one another. At the end of the third and fourth books we find an exotic paradoxography with two digressions about strange animals, the phoenix (3.25) and the crocodile (4.19). We might compare D. Sedelmeier-Stöck's observations on ekphrasis at the beginning of the first, third, and fifth books:[66] each description metaphorically condenses the basic themes of the two following books, organizing this part of the plot into three blocks dealing with courtship, rape, and erotic intrigue respectively. Both types of digression show Achilles Tatius using book articulation to shape a polyphonic work that is richer in digressive material than others of the same genre.

Infratextual closure is used for thematic purpose in the second half of the novel, when the rhythm changes: no more adventurous journey and ethnographic experiences, but a static erotic intrigue in Ephesus. The endings of the fifth and sixth books represent the different reactions of the couple to this intrigue. At the end of the fifth book, Clitophon tells of his sexual intercourse with Melite; although he stresses that he did it just to heal a sick soul and to obtain her help in finding Leucippe, it represents a marked deviation from the norm of fidelity peculiar to the Greek novel, and will later be concealed by total reticence (this episode and that of Lycaenion in Longus are the only examples in the Greek novel of betrayal by a protagonist, as well as the only descriptions of sexual intercourse). By contrast, the end of the sixth book depicts Leucippe's heroic resistance against Thersander; her direct speech, closing the book at 6.22, resembles the literature of martyrs, with a sublime tone extremely rare in this ironic

---

[64] Hägg 1971, 77 n. 2 and 314 n. 4; on the Charitonian division, surely authorial, see 252.
[65] See Rommel 1923; and, for the different technique and the different semantic value between the two authors, Fusillo 1989, 68–77 (= 1991, 67–76).
[66] Sedelmeier-Stöckl 1958, 77–90; see also Friedländer 1912, 47–51; and, on the visual aspect, Garson 1978.

novel. I think the contrast between these two internal endings is intentional: Achilles Tatius uses book divisions to stress the dissonance in the relations of his leading couple, who are not the perfect pair favored by the popular and consolatory Xenophon and, to a degree, by other novelists. This dissonance coincides with his ambivalence toward the genre, and with his hesitation in celebrating marriage, as his almost anticlosural ending demonstrates. Nevertheless, as is the rule in this polymorphic author, deviation from the norm is corrected; the last section involves the reunion of the couple—although in an anomalous way, since the presence of Leucippe's father inhibits their embrace and requires them to communicate by glance alone (7.16).

Heliodorus has a more complex rhythm in which internal endings play an important if not central role, often accompanied by metaliterary passages or by theatrical metaphors typical of this author.[67] In the long metadiegetic narration by Calasiris, the endings of the second and fourth books (on Delphi and the Delphic oracle) are especially full of suspense; in the second part told by the narrator, the ends of the sixth and eighth books are rare instances of prolepsis of the happy solution.

As in the picaresque novel, Apuleius's narrative is a linear succession of pressing adventures; the infratextual pauses are therefore not so strongly emphasized as in most Greek novels, but are still used as a rhythmic device. His peculiar type is the reference to sleep as a moment of expectation (at the end of the first, second, fourth, and tenth books). Another type of internal ending in Apuleius involves the epigrammatic pun, which we have already seen in the novel of the ass. The proverbial ending of the ninth book may be considered epigrammatic, and even more the Menippean ending of the seventh. To free himself from the violent attack of a woman who believes the ass is responsible for her son's death, the ass uses his excrement, and concludes the narration with a mythological pun: *ceterum titione* [the woman has thrown a firebrand to the ass] *delirantis Althaeae Meleager asinus interisset* (7.28). But generally speaking, the adventures of Lucius the ass in a grotesque world do not allow sharp division or articulation (and we can assume the same was true of Petronius).

With its low birth and unofficial status, the ancient novel does not know the many-faceted resolutions of the modern novel; but it would be a serious mistake to classify all these works under a broad category of consolatory endings, typical of entertaining literature. One must be always very cautious in applying this concept to ancient texts, because it depends on different cultural systems and different aesthetic responses. Chariton's sub-

---

[67] Cf. Walden 1894; on the closural metaphor in 10.39.2, see Fowler 1989b, 107. An intentional book division in Heliodorus is maintained by Feuillatre (1966, 14) and Morgan (1989a, 310); rejected by Hefti 1958, 121–22.

jective solution, Xenophon's fablelike aftermath, Achilles Tatius's provocative openness, Longus's ambiguous play on sexuality, Heliodorus's mystical ennoblement, are all reinterpretations of the same pattern, the triumph of eros, though with different creativity, while Apuleius's mixture of grotesque and sublime shows the vitality of the comical and picaresque novel. This poliedric range of solution proves that "happy ending" is a very nonspecific category, which does not exclude deep tensions and contradictions—as countless examples from Greek tragedy (*Eumenides, Oedipus at Colonus, Philoctetes*) to the modern novel and cinema would confirm.[68]

[68] This text was first presented at the meeting of the Classical Association at Oxford in 1992, and subsequently given as a paper at Harvard, Brown, and Princeton universities; I would like to thank David Konstan, Gregory Nagy, Alessandro Schiesaro, Charles Segal, and Froma Zeitlin.

CHAPTER 11

Is Death the End? Closure in Plutarch's *Lives*

CHRISTOPHER PELLING

CLOSURE in biography may seem straightforward. This form of historical writing might even evade the constant worry of those who stress the textuality of history, the role of the writer in imposing beginning and end points that are essentially factitious, simplifying a messy continuum.[1] Human life does have a clear beginning and it does come to a full stop, and that would seem to be that:[2] death is surely the place to end. But in Plutarch it really is more complicated. For one thing, his artistic unit is not the individual *Life*, it is the pair: the end of a single *Life* is a temporary resting point, no more. And even the second *Life* of a pair does not conclude it, for it is usually[3] followed by a comparative epilogue, or synkrisis, picking up a selection of themes and comparing the two characters. Just as all the lines of a *Life* may seem to be brought together, the whole pair moves into a new register in these synkriseis, and the way the themes are revisited will emerge as interesting and bold.

OTHER PEOPLE'S DEATHS

Is death the end? Often it is; but it is striking how often a *Life* ends with someone else's death, not the principal's. Thus *Caesar* ends with the death of Brutus,[4] and *Crassus* with that of King Orodes. More than a quarter of Plutarch's forty-six *Parallel Lives* fit this pattern: the other examples are *Numa, Lucullus, Marcellus, Pelopidas, Agesilaus, Demosthenes, Brutus, Camillus, Marius,* and *Cato minor.* There are five further cases where deaths are hinted

---

[1] Bibliography on this point could be equally endless; perhaps most influential has been White, especially 1973, 1978, and 1987. Mink (1987, esp. 47–48, 68–72, and 136–37) emphasizes the linkage of ending and explanation, as a story's configuration becomes clear retrospectively: cf. also Fusillo, Chapter 10, p. 223 in this volume. On particular endings in classical historiography, cf. recently D. Fowler 1989b, 116–17; Henderson 1989; Kennedy 1991, 177; and Dewald, Chapter 4 in this volume.

[2] Cf. Nuttall 1992, 201.

[3] There are four exceptions, which are considered below.

[4] The last word is in fact ἀπέθανεν, "died": so also in *Caesar, Cato minor, Marius, Camillus,* and *Flamininus* (if we treat the transitional sentence as part of the synkrisis; cf. note 5).

at rather than described, or where another person's death provides the last significant incident, though not the ending itself: *Eumenes, Coriolanus, Pompey, Sertorius,* and *Flamininus.*[5]

These make an interesting set of cases. Several of them deal with a sort of posthumous vengeance, tracing the way in which a man's killers met their end: *Crassus, Eumenes, Demosthenes, Pelopidas, Pompey,* and most elaborately *Caesar,* a case to which I shall return.[6] Or the point may rather be a telling contrast with the principal: Tullus Hostilius caught religion in his old age, but it was a poor equivalent of Numa's genuine religious feeling, and Tullus was duly blasted by a thunderbolt. Then there are cases of what we might call the completion of the principal's own death, instances where a second individual found his or her own destiny so entwined that the two deaths were almost inseparable: Porcia, wife of Brutus, swallowing the coals to share his death; or Cato's son and his follower, who both found an appropriate death at Philippi, where Cato's cause finally died too; the death of Sertorius's associates, or of the son of Marius at Sulla's hands. In *Flamininus* it is the completion of the life rather than of the death: Flamininus hounded down the aged Hannibal in a way that rounded off Flamininus's own career, marking an unsettling culmination of his aggressive "love of honor," *philotimia.*[7] All this needs to be put in a wider setting, and we will find that many of the other *Lives* fit into the same categories. Such "completion of the death" is especially interesting: another person's death is not the only way in which that can be marked, as we shall see. But this listing already suggests two preliminary points.

First and obviously, Plutarch's readiness to carry on the story some way beyond his principal's death. *Antony* is the most spectacular example among the other *Lives,* with ten chapters devoted to Cleopatra's last days when Antony is already dead. There are good reasons for such an expansion:[8] this is another case where two deaths have become entwined, and the two lovers' stories have become one (so much so that Antony's death is not even directly stated, but only implied in a participial phrase at 78.1). Plutarch has no rules for ending a *Life,* and he can carry on the story until it reaches several different sorts of rest. Statistics are here suggestive. The *Parallel Lives* average forty-five Teubner lines devoted to posthumous mate-

---

[5] Thus *Flamininus* gives its closing chapters to the death of Hannibal, then notices Flamininus's own demise in a brief sentence of transition (*Flam.* 21.15): "We have not discovered any further political or military achievement of Flamininus, but he met with a peaceful death: so it is time to consider the comparison." This is conventionally printed as part of the *Life*; it might equally be regarded as the first sentence of the synkrisis. As, e.g., with *Demetr.* 53.10 and *Gracch.* 1.1, such questions and divisions are artificial.

[6] See below, pp. 246–49, where the closing chapter is quoted.

[7] I have said more about this in Pelling 1986 and 1989.

[8] Cf. Pelling 1988, esp. 16–17; D. Fowler 1989b, 116.

rial, between one-and-a-half and two pages. That is something like 4 per-cent of the *Lives'* total bulk. And that is quite a lot: a representative sifting of modern biographies would show a much smaller figure. In Plutarch, the average conceals quite a large spread. *Camillus* has nothing at all; five *Lives* have more than one hundred lines, *Antony*, *Romulus* (boosted by an apo-theosis), *Pelopidas*, *Caesar*, and *Lycurgus*. There seems to be an attempt to keep a balance between paired *Lives*, and also between ends and begin-nings. Thus *Camillus* has nothing before the hero's birth as well as nothing after his death; and *Solon–Poplicola* makes an interesting example, a pair that could easily have had some expansion at both beginnings (on historical background) and both ends (on aftermath or family), but in fact has very little in any of the four places. Then there is *Agis–Cleomenes–Gracchi*, the elaborate double pair, which has similar amounts of posthumous material in all four *Lives* (44, 61, 62, and 62 lines) and develops similar themes across the four cases—their countrymen coming to miss them, their noble womenfolk, some shared deaths, the continuing struggle, the emergence of adversaries in their true colors. In this chapter I shall take several *pairs*, rather than *Lives*, as test cases: if one *Life* is posthumously interesting, its pair tends to be posthumously interesting as well.[9]

The second preliminary point is rather different. It will already be clear that the *Lives* exploit closural devices familiar from other genres: Barbara Herrnstein Smith's work on English lyric poetry has here already acquired the status of a classic.[10] Death is a prime example of a motif that conveys a closural feel, but other "natural" ends are also frequent, especially in poetry and the novel: dusks, departures, journey's ends, winters, old age, and so on. Thus the ending of *Sertorius*, which dwells not only on the deaths of the man's old associates but also on one person who "grew old in penury," may look doubly appropriate. Other devices explored by Smith include some self-referential authorial intrusion; then also, less predictably, a closing generalization (an "unqualified assertion," and one not always the most obvious or natural to draw from the preceding work) or an arresting vi-gnette of one sort or another. I now pass to considering some ways in which the other closural devices recur in Plutarch's work.[11]

---

[9] The pervasive importance of the comparative technique is increasingly realized: cf. espe-cially Erbse 1956b; Stadter 1975 and 1983–84; Pelling 1986; Larmour 1988 and 1992; Swain 1989 and 1990; Walsh 1992.

[10] Smith 1968; for fuller bibliography, cf. esp. D. Fowler 1989b.

[11] As we shall see, they recur throughout the *Parallel Lives*, and also in the self-standing works *Aratus* and *Artaxerxes*; but not, interestingly, in *Otho*, though *Galba* has a strong enough closure. That is further confirmation that the *Lives of the Caesars* was conceived as a continuous series: the reader is not expected to stop at the end of *Otho*, and it looks as if *Otho* 18.3–4 could equally have been considered as the opening of *Vitellius*.

TERMINAL DEVICES AND TERMINAL RESTFULNESS

First, the authorial intrusion. It may be a straightforward self-referential transition, particularly when Plutarch moves over to the concluding synkrisis: "These, then, are the things that seemed to us worth recording among the traditions concerning Marcellus and Pelopidas" (*Marc.* 31 [1].1); "So, Sosius, you have the life of Demosthenes on the basis of what we have read or heard" (*Dem.* 31.7).[12] Or, though surprisingly rarely, it can be a cross-reference to another work, something that is a feature of many a cycle of modern novels (and indeed of scholarly articles): "The details are given in my *Life of Scipio*" (*Gracch.* 21.9) or "in my *Life of Timoleon*" (*Dion* 58.10).[13] It can be a reference to a tradition, an honor, or just a family that extends down "to our own day," as in *Themistocles, Antony, Aristides,* or (outside the *Parallel Lives*) *Aratus.* I shall return to these in a moment.

There is also a subtler form of authorial intrusion. One pervasive characterization within Plutarch's *Lives* is easy to miss, and that is his characterization *of himself.*[14] Self-characterization as well as self-reference is relevant here, that projection of the generous, perpetually interested and curious, ethically concerned but sympathetic, learned and knowledgeable, sometimes bumbling scholar with a taste for a good story and a warm feeling for humanity.[15] Many of these endings leave a particularly strong impression of Plutarch the man. We often see authorial generosity toward a hero in defeat, or the desire to find some sort of compensation for his death: such features evidently fit the self-projection as a figure of sympathetic humanity. We may also notice how often Plutarch ends a *Life* with a parade of

---

[12] Cf. *Cic.* 50(1).1, with a very similar formulation leading into the pair's synkrisis. That has the effect of ringing and marking off the whole of *Cicero,* and also of drawing attention to his own role as researcher: cf. below. For further self-referential transitions, cf. *Flam.* 21.15 (see above, note 5); *Lys.* 30.8; *Demetr.* 53.10; *Alc.* 40(1).1; *Popl.* 24(1).1; *Quaest. Rom.* 30(1).1. For the modern tendency to terminal self-reference, D. Fowler 1989b, 109–13; for ancient instances, notice Xenophon's conclusions to *Hellenica, Cyropaedia,* and *Lacedaemonion politeia;* also Fusillo, Chapter 10 in this volume, pp. 212–13.

[13] Also *Cat. min.* 73.6; *Cor.* 39.11. For modern novel-series, cf. Torgovnick 1981, 13–14, 23. The end of *Crime and Punishment* is a striking example. An interesting variation is the terminal suggestion that another story is beginning, which *could* be the subject of a second work (ibid.).

[14] Stadter (1988, 292 and 1989), xlii) has written perceptively on this.

[15] Or, in Stadter's formulation (1.c): "The feeling of being in contact with an understanding and intellectually curious person, someone who is serious yet not stuffy, aware of life in all its manifestations, yet deliberately avoiding the unseemly and trying to present the best side of his subjects" (1988, loc. cit.). Stadter was writing in particular about the proems; they are mirrored in this respect by the conclusions.

scholarship, presenting himself as a figure of learned detachment.[16] In *Aristides*, for instance, he accumulates the evidence for Aristides' poverty by quoting Demetrius of Phalerum three times, Callisthenes, Hieronymus of Rhodes, Aristoxenus, Aristotle (with a cautious note on authenticity), and Panaetius; other, less spectacular examples are found in *Theseus*, *Romulus*, *Solon*, *Themistocles*, *Brutus*, *Lysander*, and *Sulla*. In several of these *Lives*, especially *Aristides* and *Solon*, the closing scholarship matches and mirrors a similar parade in the opening chapters;[17] and we again notice a tendency to find similar phenomena in paired *Lives* (*Theseus* and *Romulus*, *Lysander* and *Sulla*).

Some of these parades figure in the more pedantic and scholarly *Lives*, such as *Theseus*, *Romulus*, and even *Solon*. Plutarch works particularly hard to make these figures on the borders of myth look like the stuff of authentic, rationalized history (*Thes.* 1.5, "to purge them of the mythical and make them look like history"), and a list of scholarly authorities here makes the whole enterprise look more sober and respectable. But it is also notable how often such parades conclude very different sorts of *Lives*, works that have reveled in the dramatic, the vivid, and the immediate: *Themistocles*, *Brutus*, *Lysander*, *Sulla*. In such cases it is rather a stepping back from an exciting story, one that has sometimes been told in admiring tones (*Aristides*) but more often with moral disquiet (*Lysander*, *Sulla*), to move into a register of judicious and knowledgeable detachment. Such a tone is then appropriate for a new start and a new level of engagement, perhaps for the second *Life*, perhaps for the moral summing-up of the synkrisis.

The "summarizing vignette" is another category where Plutarch aligns with the patterns familiar from other genres: Peden, for instance has brought out how frequently Catullus closes poems in that way,[18] and the last chapter of Herodotus would be another example (though not a straightforward one).[19] In Plutarch such anecdotal vignettes often capture something important. Take *Philopoemen*, for example. When Corinth fell,

---

[16] Cf. note 12 above. Livy, too, sometimes ends books in this way (Books 4, 7, 8, 30, 37, 39). I here put this point in terms of the relation of the author (or implied author) to the material, or more precisely in the projection of this relation to the implied audience, a matter in Genette's terms of "voice" (Genette 1980, 31–32, 211–62). It could equally be phrased in terms of the emotional engagement encouraged in the readers. Such an assumed harmony between authorial and audience engagement is not unusual, though it is not universal either; but in Plutarch the harmony is unusually close and complete. That reflects the persuasive and rhetorical charm whereby he assumes the same moral standpoint in his audience as in himself, something that in its turn helps to make his further moral inferences more acceptable. Stadter (1988, 293) again has some perceptive remarks.

[17] On the proems of *Aristides* and *Solon*, see Stadter 1988, 287–88; on *Aristides*, Pelling 1990, 22–23.

[18] Peden 1987; cf. Schrijvers 1973, 154, on Horace.

[19] On which see Herington 1991, and Dewald, Chapter 4 in this volume.

an unnamed Roman wanted to destroy all Philopoemen's statues and other memorials, but Mummius and the Roman envoys refused to allow him: their respect for Philopoemen's virtue was too great, even in an enemy. In *Lysander* we find several such vignettes. After his stormy final years, Plutarch now stresses the respect felt by the Spartans when they discovered his poverty. Then an anecdote reprises several of the *Life*'s themes: Agesilaus wanted to reveal a document showing Lysander's revolutionary plans, but the wise Lacratidas said that it was better to let his plans die with him. The final note is one of more respect, with the Spartans fining the men who wished to marry Lysander's daughters but gave up their suits when they discovered their poverty. *Cicero* also has two anecdotal vignettes:

> I gather that many years later Augustus was visiting one of his grandsons. The boy had a book of Cicero in his hands and, terrified of his grandfather, tried to hide it under his cloak. Augustus noticed this and, taking the book from him, stood there and read a great part of it. Then he handed it back to the young man with the words: "A learned man, my child, a learned man and a lover of his country."
>
> Directly after Antony's final defeat, when Octavian was consul himself, he chose Cicero's son to be his colleague. It was thus in his consulship that the senate took down all the statues of Antony, canceled all the other honors that had been given to him, and decreed that in the future no member of the family should bear the name of Marcus. In this way Heaven entrusted to the family of Cicero the final acts in the punishment of Antony.[20] (*Cic.* 49.5–6)

These three instances have different styles, but they also have something in common. I have called them *summarizing* vignettes, but that is not quite right: in each case they recall the tumult and passions of the man's life—Philopoemen's honorable battles with Rome, Lysander's revolutionary ideas and his rift with his countrymen, Cicero as victim of both Octavian and Antony; but in each case the point is now the sense of rest, the passion spent, the respect of the old antagonists, the end of the struggles rather than the continuation.[21] So it is rather a *modifying* vignette, just as in other authors and genres we often find a modifying generalization.[22] That also recalls some of the instances in our preliminary listing of *Lives*, those which

---

[20] Notice the summarizing "in this way . . . ": some dozen of the other *Lives* end similarly. Cf. Peta Fowler on Lucretian *epiphonemata*, Chapter 6 in this volume, pp. 116, 120. For further points about the *Cicero* anecdotes, especially their elaboration of earlier themes in the *Life* and the pair, cf. Moles 1988, 200–201.

[21] This does not exclude the possibility that the issues might reappear in later generations, including Plutarch's own: in particular, the tensions between Greek contentiousness and Roman oppressiveness (*Philopoemen*) and between philosophical culture and autocratic domination (*Cicero*) would both have contemporary resonance.

[22] Cf. Smith 1968, index s.v. "terminal modification." This category seems to prove particularly illuminating for ancient texts: cf. Nagle 1983 and Reeve 1984.

ended with someone else's death. Here we find some of the same categories. It may be the posthumous revenge, as in *Cicero*, with his son's revenge on Antony. But in all three of these new cases there is also something of the "completion of the death," with the stress on the magnanimous respect of old antagonists (Mummius, the Spartans, Augustus), and the feeling that with the death of the principal the issues died too.[23] These are not endings that pose questions, that cast in doubt the man's greatness, that point to struggles that outlive the principals: these are endings that are calm, that close themes down, that point respite after conflict. It is all restful: quite skillful, not difficult, not—so far—very challenging.

We can add some other restful, reassuring elements. Let us take another typical category of posthumous material, the tracing down of the fortunes of the family. Sometimes it is mainly for interest's sake: in *Themistocles*, for instance, whose descendant and namesake was one of Plutarch's schoolfriends (*Them.* 32.6); and perhaps *Marcellus*, suitably lugubrious and morbid as the name of the younger Marcellus might be (*Marc.* 30.10–11). But even in these cases, the respect enjoyed by a man's descendants also underlines the generous appreciation paid by posterity to the man, however qualified the impression we may just have received of his final years. Such notices can be more suggestive, even if they are not specially elaborate. Take *Cato maior*. So much of that *Life* has centered on the way in which Cato managed his own household. There have been reservations, especially on his attitude to his slaves; but at least he has been enlightened about his own children, always trying to get home for bath time, and giving great care to their proper education. He even wrote the *Origines* for their benefit (ch. 20). It is a pleasing continuation of that idea to have the younger Cato coming out so satisfactorily a few generations later, at least as he is briefly presented here (27.7).[24]

Antony is the most interesting case. The *Life* had started with an interest in heredity, with an anecdote about Antony's prodigal father. Now, after the finest death scene of all, we have something of a false closure.

> So died Cleopatra. She had lived for 39 years; of those 22 had been as queen, and more than 14 as joint ruler with Antony. As for Antony, some say that he was 56, some 53. Antony's statues were taken down; Cleopatra's remained standing, for Archibius, one of her friends, had given 2,000 talents to Octavian to save them from sharing the fate of those of Antony. (*Ant.* 86.8–9)

[23] There is an eloquent contrast here with *Lycurgus*, one of the *Lives* with the greatest bulk of posthumous material: his achievement did not die with his death, which indeed he engineers to safeguard his achievement; the final story therefore needs to be taken down to Agis and Lysander. This, too, is a "completion of the death," but in the case of Lycurgus it takes centuries. Cf. also *Tim.* 39.7.

[24] This interest in Cato's descendants mirrors that in his ancestors at *Cat. mai.* 1.1–3: cf., *Antony*, discussed below.

But the *Life* does not in fact end there. We still have a chapter to come, and it is a very enterprising one, tracing Antony's own descendants through five generations and subtly suggesting how many of the same themes come back with them: heredity once again, just as in that first chapter. Finally we reach Nero, "who reigned in our own day and killed his mother and almost destroyed the Roman empire with his frenzy and lunacy:[25] he was descended from Antony in the fifth generation." The links between Antony and Nero are evidently more than casual. Like father, like son, and like great-great-great-grandson, too: the parallel with the two *Cato*s is an interesting one. But there are also parallels with those other *Lives* which feature posthumous vengeance. Antony's family won in the end, and Octavian was eventually succeeded by Antony's descendants. Contrast the end of *Cicero*, with that different emphasis—Cicero's son as consul at the time when the senate decreed the destruction of Antony's statues and the prohibition on the name Marcus in Antony's family. If Plutarch had so chosen, *Antony* too could have finished on that item, which would have marked a completion of the death in a different way. But that would be too ungenerous, too annihilating for Antony's own *Life*. This wider perspective of the five generations is more thought-provoking, and even for Antony it allows the reflection that defeat was not total.

One feature may not seem to fit. This may be a more generous ending toward Antony himself, but it is scarcely generous to Nero: "He reigned in our own day and killed his mother and almost destroyed the Roman empire with his frenzy and lunacy." The moralism is particularly crude and blunt, and it grates after the closing chapters, where Plutarch has become so dramatically involved in the death scenes. There has earlier been moralism of this dismissive stamp, but largely in the first third of the *Life*, and the moralism has recently been more subtle and muted. True, this cruder moralism here focuses on Nero rather than Antony; but Nero, too, is afforded rather more sympathy elsewhere in Plutarch's work—after all, he did liberate Greece.[26] But again the change in moral register is pointed, and it prepares for the similarly blunt moralism of the following synkrisis. I have already suggested that the typical parades of scholarship, apart from presenting Plutarch as a learned researcher, are also helpful in shifting the tone in preparation for the more detached estimates of the synkrisis. This is something of the same technique, except that in *Demetrius–Antony* the moral tone of the synkrisis is not at all detached. It ends, for instance, with

[25] This assumes the reading ἐπιμανῶς (Solanus, Jones) rather than ἐπιφανῶς at 87.8. For more detailed commentary on the closure, cf. Pelling 1988, 322–327.

[26] *De sera numinis vindicta*, 567a; cf. Jones 1971, 16–19, 120; Russell 1973, 2–3; for a different view, Brenk 1987 and 1992, 4356–75.

shrill disapproval of the manner of Antony's death, something we should not have inferred from the narrative itself.[27] This final chapter of *Antony*, with its shift toward moral disapproval, marks a stepping back of a different sort from the dramatic involvement and sympathy of the death scenes; it is once again a transitional device.

NEW PERSPECTIVES?

Some of these features—the posthumous revenge, the respect of the antagonist, the notion that defeat is not total—are reminiscent of a technique familiar from tragedy: for tragedy, too, typically offers some "restitution" or "compensation" in a closing scene—a posthumous honor, perhaps, or a festival, something to satisfy our feeling for humanity.[28] Of course, we have to be careful how we put this. In Plutarch and in tragedy, it evidently does not make everything all right, it is not as bland as all that. It is cold comfort for Hippolytus, for instance, to think of the virgins of Troezen offering hair-offerings *before their marriage*,[29] just as it is not that reassuring a thought that Antony's final compensation will almost lead to the destruction of the Roman world.

When we think of the ends of tragedies, it is more the differences than the similarities that strike us. For instance, it is familiar to find discordant tensions at the end of a play: at the end of *Medea*, audience members may find it unsettling to reflect on what they have been brought to sympathize with earlier in the play, and certainly feel uncomfortable that Athens, of all places, will now play host to the child-killing murderess. That is a different degree of discomfort from anything we might feel at the end of *Antony*. We might compare Sophocles, too—all those plays that end with discordant strands:[30] *Oedipus at Colonus*, with the loyal daughters trudging back to Thebes to discover what they will find there; *Trachiniae*, with Hyllus forced to marry Iole, and "all this is nothing but Zeus"; *Philoctetes*, and the ethically sensitive young Neoptolemus warned to "respect the gods" as he sets off back to Troy, where Priam and the altar await him—and perhaps Heracles' epiphany only adds to the disquiet. Here again we have to be careful how we put it. These new strands evidently do not deconstruct the whole earlier texture of the play; but we are still presented with thought-provoking new perspectives, with a feeling of open questions and of the

[27] *Ant.* 93(6); cf. Pelling 1988, 19–26, 325.
[28] Stinton 1990, 143–85 (= Stinton 1975); cf. Moles 1988, 24, 200; Pelling 1988, 323. I am not implying that such emotional "restitution" is the only, or even the main, reason for including such *aitia*.
[29] Eur. *Hipp.* 1422–30.
[30] Cf. esp. Roberts 1987 and 1988.

provisionality of any response. Tragedies, or at least many tragedies, do not have the same taste for the comfortable resting-point as we have been tracing in Plutarch.

In historiography, too, we sometimes find the radically new perspective, though this is seldom so uncomfortable as in tragedy. The end of Dio 56 is one example, with its redirection of our attitude to Augustus;[31] the various emotional strands at the end of Livy 22 are also interestingly disconcerting. There is even a case for considering *Annals* 6.51 in this context, given how strangely that final summary sits with Tacitus's own earlier narrative.[32] Elsewhere in this volume Dewald brings out the multiple strands of thought suggested by Herodotus's final chapter: several of those strands problematize any straightforward polarity of Greek and barbarian, East and West. Particularly illuminating here is a different case, the end of Sallust's *Bellum Iugurthinum*; with it we shall take the first of our extended examples, *Cimon and Lucullus*.

TERMINAL GENEROSITY: CIMON AND LUCULLUS

First, the closure of the *Bellum Iugurthinum*.

> At the same time our generals Q. Caepio and Cn. Mallius fought badly[33] against the Gauls. All Italy had been quivering in terror. At the time, and to our own day, the Romans have felt that all else is prey to their valor, but that they fight with the Gauls not for glory but for survival. Still, after news arrived that the African war was finished and that Jugurtha was being brought to Rome in chains, Marius was elected consul *in absentia*, and Gaul was assigned as his province. As consul he celebrated a triumph, very gloriously, on January 1. And at that time all the city's hopes and resources rested with him. (*Iug.* 114)

That is a marvelous end, especially as Marius and Sulla have been brought so close together in the closing narrative, and especially as the corresponding initial frame (5) has made the suggestion of the coming civil war explicit.[34]

---

[31] Cf. the exhaustive discussion of Manuwald 1979, 131–67, and more cogently Rich 1989, 104–8.

[32] See recently Woodman 1989, though I am unconvinced by his attempt to minimize the discordance between obituary and narrative. A version of the view of Koestermann (1963, 1:38), rejected by Woodman, is more attractive: different parts of Tacitus's narrative suggest to the reader different, and not straightforwardly reconcilable, explanatory strands.

[33] *male pugnatum*: the important combination of a moral register ("badly") with one of success and failure is hard to capture in English, but is important to the passage's suggestions.

[34] On the end of the *Jugurtha* and its function within the work, see esp. Levene 1992; on

It is also very different from Plutarch's technique. Plutarch can certainly use a final chapter to set his story in a wider historical perspective, but he tends not to use that perspective to cast new or ironic or qualifying shadows in the manner of *Jugurtha*. Contrast the end of *Cimon*.

> After his death no Greek general was to win another brilliant success against the barbarians. Instead, a succession of demagogues and warmongers arose, who proceeded to turn the Greek states against one another, and nobody could be found to separate or reconcile them before they met in the headlong collision of war. In this way the Persians gained a breathing space, but the power of Greece was incalculably weakened. It was not until several generations afterwards that Agesilaus carried the Greek arms into Asia and fought a brief campaign against the king's generals along the Ionian coast. Yet even he achieved nothing of great consequence before he was overwhelmed in his turn by a flood of dissensions and disturbances within Greece and a second empire was swept from his grasp. In the end he had to return, leaving the tax-gatherers of the Persian Empire still collecting tribute among the allied and friendly cities, whereas not one of these functionaries, nor even so much as a Persian horse, was to be seen within fifty miles of the sea, so long as Cimon was general. (*Cim.* 19.3–4)

And then the posthumous honors for Cimon.

The similarity and the contrast with *Jugurtha* are both clear. The *Jugurtha* passage has the effect of putting the African war in its place, of rather diminishing it; the real struggle is only just beginning. We are reminded of the great storms ahead for Rome, especially civil storms, and the transience of this present collaboration of Marius and Sulla. The *Cimon* passage, too, introduces reflections that could easily have diminished Cimon's achievement: it could have become an "all in vain" passage—Cimon's work did not come to much, his successes were soon wiped out by a flood of a different sort of history, those internal Grecian wrangles that not even Cimon had been able to prevent. Yet, clearly, that is not the tone at all. The failures of his successors do not diminish his achievement, they heighten it: they project the gloom against which Cimon's brilliance stands out. The closing sentences of our two passages bring the point out. Plutarch's transition to the honors is natural after such enthusiasm for Cimon. In the last sentence of the *Jugurtha*, the "hopes" founded on Marius sound a quizzical and ironic note.

So subsequent failures in Plutarch highlight success, and do nothing to undermine it. It is the same effect as at the end of *Philopoemen*, mentioned

---

spes in Sallust, so often illusory or frustrated, see Scanlon 1987, esp. 1, 40, 61, on the final sentence. The end of *Catiline* is also forward-looking and thought-provoking, though in slightly different ways: cf. Peta Fowler, Chapter 6 above, p. 134.

earlier:[35] there we have the flash forward to subsequent Roman respect, but its context—Mummius, the destruction of Corinth, the Roman take-over—could again have served to underline the "all in vain" suggestion; within a generation Rome could afford to pay that sort of bland respect, because the cause he had fought for had died. But once again that is not the effect. The hint of subsequent reversals does not diminish Philopoemen; instead, it underlines how great was his achievement, when so much of the tide was running against him.[36] There are cases where Plutarch goes even further to avoid the "all in vain" suggestions: the ends of *Nicias* or *Demosthenes*, for instance, where "all in vain" would not be too far to seek, but again we find the generous mode instead. Nicias had always known it would end in tears, Demosthenes had always known the dangers of the venal sycophant: less "all in vain" than "I told you so."[37] The main exception is *Aratus*,[38] where we do have a foresnap of how his unsatisfactory son wrecked everything and his cause was lost. The tone there is genuinely much more negative than in the otherwise closely similar *Philopoemen*. *Aratus* is a self-standing *Life*, outside the series of parallels, and therefore does not have a synkrisis to follow.[39] That may be significant: I shall return to this.

If comparison is important, we ought to consider *Lucullus*, the pair of *Cimon*. Lucullus was very much Plutarch's sort of person: a public man, who accepted the responsibility of the talented to serve the states; but also a man of intellect and culture, who would feel the pull of a quieter, more civilized style of life. He belongs with Epaminondas, Scipio Aemilianus, Pelopidas, Marcellus, and Cicero. It was men like these to whom Plutarch turned first when be came to write the *Parallel Lives*, and all of these figured in the first five pairs of the series.

In Lucullus's case, the pull eventually became too great, and his final years were spent in torpor, luxury, and excess: too old, he thought, for statesmanship, he lived the life of the glutton and the roué instead. Or so, at least, people claimed. This drift into retirement was naturally essential to

[35] Above, p. 233.

[36] The end of *Pericles* is similar. We are given a hint of the way the war will go, the abandonment of his advice, the rise of the demagogues. But there is nothing of the "all in vain" here; this is simply a pointer to how much Athens would come to miss him. This is terminal laudation once again, not terminal redirection.

[37] *Nic.* 30.3, *Dem.* 31.6.

[38] And to an extent *Marius* and *Alcibiades*: cf. below. *Demetr.* 53.8–9 might also belong here, with its survey of the generations until Macedon fell to Rome; but the principal point here is to aid the transition to the "Roman drama" of Antony, 53.10, and the tone is not specially charged.

[39] Here and elsewhere, its moralism is also cruder than that of the *Parallel Lives*. The *Life* is written for the impressionable sons of his friend Polycrates, and filial imitation is a suggestive theme.

any moral evaluation, and Plutarch was in a difficult position. His own view was clear: even in old age, an able man has no right to turn his back on public life; a drift into torpor and luxury is the most undignified retirement of all. That is set out clearly in *Should an Old Man Engage in Politics?* In that moral essay Lucullus himself serves as a powerful example—and a wholly negative one (785f–786a, 792b–c).

Yet too strident a disapproval would sit uncomfortably in this *Life*. That was partly for reasons particular to the pair. Plutarch begins by mentioning a specific debt of his hometown Chaeronea to Lucullus (*Cimon* 1–2). There had been a scandal when the commander of the local Roman garrison was sexually harassing a local boy, and it had ended with the murder of the commander and his entourage. Lucullus had stepped in to exonerate the town: now this *Life* should be a grateful tribute in recompense. But there are more general reasons, too. Plutarch favors ethical generosity in treating human weakness, for reasons he sets out in the introduction to this very pair: one should not suppress human frailties, but like a portrait-painter one should not overemphasize them either (*Cimon* 2.3–4). We have also seen that he does not like to end a *Life* on an uncomfortable note. Quiet, respectful repose is rather the appropriate terminal register.

The way he handled the problem is interesting. The pairing with *Cimon* itself helps: Cimon, too, had a shady private life, and the scandal in his case was a good deal less respectable than in the case of Lucullus—incest with his loose-living sister, a series of affairs, not to mention lack of education. All that in the first chapter of the narrative of *Cimon* (4): it is an astonishing way to begin a basically sympathetic portrait, but one that immediately establishes private lapses as a typical concomitant of public achievement. Then the treatment of Lucullus's retirement itself is a good deal less strident than the tones of *Should an Old Man Engage in Politics?* might lead us to expect. Plutarch does not conceal it: indeed, some six chapters are devoted to it (38–43). As he had said at *Cimon* 2, one should not suppress such things. Nor does he play down the moral issue. His disapproval of the banqueting is especially clear (ch. 40), and the section is introduced by a long debate where the case for and against such retirement is aired (38.2–5). Yet the balance of that chapter is still generous. Much more space is given to excuse than to denunciation, and the criticisms are devalued by giving them to biased rivals. "Here he was, abandoning himself to this life of pleasure and extravagance: did he not realize that he was too old for dissipation, not for politics or command?" But that is what "the supporters of Pompey and Crassus" said (38.5). It is what Plutarch had said, too, in the moral essay: but he does not say it here.

Hellenism also helps. Plutarch is always generous to lovers of Greece and Greeks: here he has prepared the theme earlier, with specific acts of generosity to Greeks, as well as with a general emphasis on Lucullus's civilized justice in dealing with subject states and individuals.[40] Now it is Greek visitors he is regaling at his mansion in 41.2 (the story does not depend on it, and Plutarch did not need to say so); the scholars who visit his library at 42.1–2 are again, naturally, Greeks: his house is a "genuine home away from home for the visitors to Rome, a pavilion of Greek culture." Then Plutarch stresses his interest in Greek philosophy (42.3–4). This passage, like that on the libraries, has no particular connection with his retirement, and it uses material relating to a much earlier period of his life. But Plutarch prefers to delay the points to here, and the effect is to distract attention from the torpor and the gluttony and to redirect it toward the culture and the scholarship. This is a civilized retreat, not a self-indulgent wallow. That indeed is how the opening chapter had proleptically introduced the motif: "When he grew older this [his culture and education] became a type of retirement after a life full of rivalry and contests; he allowed his intellect to find rest and leisure in philosophy, and cultivated the contemplative side of his mind, curtailing his ambition and granting it a timely demise after his struggle with Pompey" (1.6). We now revisit the theme in much the same terms, and the ring composition is of a simple kind.

The final illness, too, tells a story, but here the ring is subtler, and is part of a wider pattern of thematic recall.

> Cornelius Nepos claims that it was not age or disease that took away his mind, but it was caused by drugs, administered by one of his freedmen called Callisthenes. The drugs (says Nepos) were given him to win his affections for Callisthenes, for this was supposed to be their effect; but in fact they weakened and destroyed his intellect, so that even before his death his brother Marcus had to take over his property to administer. (*Luc.* 43.2)

A sad end, though one that is partly and typically retrieved by the popular affection shown at the funeral (43.3). But it is also an end that recalls many of the man's best qualities. The brotherly closeness is one thing; that is the note on which Plutarch ends the *Life* at 43.4, just as he had included it in the first chapter (1.8–9). The tale also recalls some of that story of Chaeronea that had begun the pair, an erotic liaison of superior and inferior that goes murderously wrong.[41] In several ways we have come full circle, and the closing chapters recall the opening, not merely of *Lucullus* itself (the brother), but also of *Cimon* and of the pair (the sexual liaison).[42]

---

[40] Generosity to Greeks: 18, 29.3–5, 33.4; Murena, Plutarch emphasizes, was hamfisted in comparison, 19.8–9. General justice: 4.1, 7.1–3, 20, 23.1–3, 24.6–7. Contrast Tigranes, whose friction with Greeks is stressed only here (21.3–5, 22), not for instance in *Pompey*.

[41] *Cim.* 1–2.

[42] On similar rings in the novel, cf. Fusillo, Chapter 10 in this volume; but biography is naturally more wistful, with the earlier themes re-emerging in death rather than in a restitution of initial order.

But that is only part of the recollective pattern, for "Callisthenes," the misguided freedman, is surely a Greek. The philhellenism, so stressed throughout, has gone awry.[43] Any form of repetition, particularly if it has some variation suggestive of finality, can be a force for closure: that is emphasized by Smith.[44] This sort of flashback mirroring is therefore particularly suitable for the end of a *Life*, and it is an unsurprising trait of Plutarch's writing to recall a hero's glorious moments as he declines and dies.[45] This is not the clearest case, but there is something of that here.

In *Lucullus*, then, we have a more extended example of terminal generosity, even after a *Life* that has opened up most serious moral problems. It is striking that a large proportion of such delicate moral issues tends to be opened up toward the end of *Lives*—Flamininus hounding down Hannibal, Pompey forsaking the duties of a commander by giving in to pressure to fight at Pharsalus, Lysander turning into a revolutionary, Fabius resenting Scipio, Philopoemen destroying the Spartan educational system, Brutus maltreating an ally, Theseus raping Helen, and so on. The questions are opened, but Plutarch feels the need to close them down before the *Life* finishes. We have seen how final chapters tend to be unproblematic, and *Lucullus* is now a clearer case of how Plutarch may work for several chapters to end his *Life* with a friendly, sympathetic envoi.

Perhaps we do not find that very surprising: we, too, do not like to be rude about the recently departed. But the modern analogy may be misleading. Perhaps we would be wise to appeal to the influence of funeral rhetoric in explaining the ancient phenomenon,[46] not to a shared cross-cultural human sensibility and feeling of propriety.

TERMINAL SYNKRISIS: THE QUESTIONS REOPENED

If we move on to the synkrisis chapters themselves, we find one reason why we should not appeal to that simple feeling of propriety, for Plutarch is very ready to introduce perspectives that swiftly qualify that terminal generosity. In *Life* after *Life*, the synkritic chapters do raise the awkward moral questions; the ends may have closed the issues down, but the synkriseis open them straight up again. In the case of *Cimon and Lucullus*, the first question of the synkrisis broaches the contrast with Cimon, the man who died at the peak of energetic activity, not drifting into excess. That is

[43] Compare the way in which "Philologus" plays a crucial role in the demise of the philhellene Cicero: *Cic.* 48.2, with Moles 1988, 200.

[44] Smith 1968, esp. 31, 42–44, 48–49, 155–66.

[45] For clearer cases, cf. the closures of *Pelopidas* and *Marcellus*, briefly discussed in Pelling 1989.

[46] Cf. especially Dihle 1987.

not atypical: take *Dion and Brutus*. I have argued elsewhere that *Brutus* in particular tends to avoid moral problematic.[47] That is true of the *Life*, but it is certainly not true of the synkrisis. Should Brutus have turned against Caesar, when Caesar had done so much for him? That was conventionally *the* great moral issue about Brutus,[48] and in the *Life* Plutarch sidesteps it— but he confronts it squarely in the synkrisis. The comparison with Dion poses the question, whose tyrannicide was the purer? However alien we find that mode of comparison, it gives the question immediacy and bite. And did Caesar deserve to be killed at all? There was a view that Caesar was the least harmful remedy for the ailing state, and Plutarch airs it here[49] —but again in the synkrisis, not in the *Life* itself, where the tyrannicide had been cloaked in unquestioned respectability.

Other epilogues, too, raise awkward moral questions that the *Lives* themselves had elided. *Aristides*, for instance, had painted its hero's famed poverty in admiring tones, whereas *Cato maior* had been appreciative of Cato's old-fashioned diligence in caring for his home; it is the synkrisis that brings the two themes together, and makes each of them seem more morally ambivalent. The same is true of Crassus's extravagant military aspirations, which the synkrisis discusses more thoughtfully than the *Life* does; elsewhere new doubts are expressed, on Cleomenes' revolutionary tactics, for instance, or on the circumstances of several deaths—Antony, Eumenes, Nicias, and Philopoemen.[50] Elsewhere the moral questions are not new ones, but nonetheless counter the restfulness of the end of the narrative. Thus *Demosthenes–Cicero* reopens the awkward questions of earlier parts of *Cicero*—the badly timed witticisms, the self-praise, the undignified and unconstructive behavior in exile, the unprincipled fostering of Octavian;[51] *Theseus–Romulus* reminds us of Theseus's rapes, the forgetfulness that killed Aegeus, and the deaths of Hippolytus and Remus. There are times, too, when particular actions are recolored in the synkriseis, and usually the principal's motives come out worse than in the corresponding narrative. In *Coriolanus* itself, Plutarch rejects a story that Coriolanus sent a disastrously deceptive message to the Roman magistrates (26.2); in the synkrisis, he accepts it, and puts it down to the man's extreme anger (*Alc.* 41 [2].4).[52] In *Demetrius*, the Macedonian regent Alexander seemed to be plotting to kill Demetrius, and Demetrius struck him down in self-defense (*Demetr.* 36,

---

[47] Cf. Pelling 1989, 222–28.

[48] Cf. esp. Rawson 1986.

[49] *Brut.* 55(2).2; similar praise at *Ant.* 6.7.

[50] Aristides' poverty: *Cat. mai.* 30(3)-31(4). Crassus's aspirations: *Crass.* 37(4). Cleomenes' tactics: *Gracch.* 44(4).2–3, 45(5).2; deaths: *Ant.* 93(6).6 (discussed above), *Eum.* 21(2).7–8, *Crass.* 38(5).4, *Flam.* 22(1).7. Cf. Pelling 1988, 20.

[51] Cf. Moles 1988, 200, on *Cic.* 49.3–6 and the following synkrisis.

[52] Russell 1963, 21.

esp. 36.12); in the synkrisis, the charge of Alexander's plotting appears to be "false," a disingenuous fabrication of Demetrius himself (*Ant.* 92 [5]).[53] Such inconcinnities do not show Plutarch at his best, but they do reflect the wider sense in which the synkriseis are less morally generous than the narrative.

Today's response to the synkriseis tends to be one of impatience. We do not find the nursery moralism attractive, and the whole principle of comparison seems artificial. Carelessness and superficiality are not far to seek.[54] But another way of looking at it would be to see these chapters as reopening these issues which the closing chapters have closed. The modern, or postmodern, taste is for aperture rather than closure; if we could only stomach the questions that Plutarch finds it so natural to ask, we might join all those generations who have found the synkritic chapters admirable. They do raise thought-provoking moral issues, and they usually leave the fundamental comparative questions—who is the better man, whose was the greater achievement—open in the fullest sense, or at least declare a draw.[55]

TERMINAL IRREGULARITY: PAIRS WITHOUT EPILOGUES

There are four pairs that lack a concluding formal synkrisis—*Phocion–Cato minor*, *Themistocles–Camillus*, *Pyrrhus–Marius*, and *Alexander–Caesar*. It used to be assumed that they had been lost, but Erbse (1956b) argued that Plutarch deliberately omitted synkriseis for those pairs;[56] he suggested that the similarities were either so great (*Phocion–Cato minor*) or so slight (e.g., *Pyrrhus–Marius*) that there was nothing very illuminating to say. That particular explanation is not cogent: similar problems did not stop Plutarch writing synkriseis elsewhere. But Erbse may still have been on the right lines, and our present angle, relating this to the closures of the respective *Lives*, might be more productive.

---

[53] Pelling 1988, 20.

[54] Cf. the criticisms formulated in Pelling 1986, 88–90, and 1988, 19, where I perhaps put the point too strongly; contra Larmour 1992, 4156, 4159–62.

[55] The verdict is left open explicitly at *Luc.* 46(3).6, and implicitly in most of the other cases. Even in pairs where the rhythm of the argument seems to tilt the scales toward one man or the other, this is not made explicit, and the issues are usually made to seem finely balanced: *Theseus–Romulus, Aristides–Cato maior, Pericles–Fabius, Dion–Brutus, Aemilius Paulus–Timoleon*. A draw seems suggested by those summaries which give each man the advantage in a particular area; *Sulla* 42(5).6, *Flam.* 24(3).5, and *Gracch.* 45(5).7. Some equality between the subjects of comparison was in fact an expectation of ancient rhetorical theory: cf. Swain 1990, adducing Theon *Prog.* 2.112.20ff. Sp., and Hermogenes *Prog.* 19.14–19 Rabe.

[56] Contra, Swain 1990, 111.

Certainly, in each of these pairs the second *Life* has a striking end. *Phocion* and *Cato minor* are linked by the Socratic elements in each man's death, though the comparison is not straightforward. Cato cannot finally manage the calm and dignity of Socrates or Phocion: he cannot even deliver the death blow very well because he has just injured his hand striking a slave, and the final agonized struggles are not pleasant or serene. But it is clear that this final scene of the *Cato* is peculiarly dramatic, even given Plutarch's general capacity to surpass himself at the end; one can understand if he was reluctant to compromise so fine an ending with a formal synkrisis, and preferred to leave it as it is, especially as the implicit comparison with the dying Phocion is so loud. Some of the material he might have used is transposed into the introduction to *Phocion*, where he has an unusual amount to say about the Roman as well as the Greek.

Then there is *Pyrrhus–Marius*. We earlier noticed Plutarch's taste for the favorable ending, avoiding terminal disquiet in the *Life* even if he goes on to raise it in the synkrisis, and there are few exceptions to this "friendly farewell." One disquieting end was that of *Aratus*, mentioned earlier: no synkrisis there, for that is outside the series of *Parallel Lives*. There are perhaps two other exceptions, and one of them is indeed *Marius*.[57] That ends without sympathy for Marius, so undignified in his final ambition, and then with the even worse younger Marius, who himself fell in battle against Sulla a few years later. Thus what is exceptional in one way again turns out to be exceptional in another: Plutarch's usual terminal rhythm could not have worked here.

Themistocles–Camillus is exceptional in a different way. *Camillus* is the one *Life* that is the nil case at either end,[58] and both its terminus and its beginning are the most perfunctory of them all. Admittedly, it is not clear to a modern audience why that should have excluded a synkrisis; we might rather have expected it to make a different sort of rounding off more desirable. But our own tastes may be an unreliable guide. We should simply notice that the absence of a synkrisis is again found in combination with an ending that is irregular in a quite different way.[59]

What about *Alexander–Caesar*, our last example? No one can doubt that

---

[57] The other is *Alcibiades*, a genuine exception.

[58] See above. Notice also that there is no transitional sentence between the *Lives*.

[59] A skeptic might retort that the terminal abruptness of *Camillus* could equally suggest that a more leisurely ending has dropped out of the manuscript tradition. But the precise phrasing of the final words—"Camillus's death grieved the Romans more than those of all the others who at that time, and in that plague, met their deaths"—fits a regular closural pattern: cf. above. Further, in view of the regular symmetry between the beginning and the end of *Lives*, the irregularly abrupt beginning of *Camillus* lends support to an equal irregularity at the end.

Caesar ends marvelously—perhaps the finest ending of them all. It bears extended quotation.

> Caesar died at the age of fifty-six, outliving Pompey by a little more than four years. He had sought dominion and power all his days, and after facing so many dangers he had finally achieved them. And the only benefit he reaped was their empty name, and the perils of fame amid his envious fellow citizens.
>
> His great guardian spirit, which had watched over him in life, continued to avenge his murder, pursuing and tracking his killers over every land and sea, until not one remained, but everyone had been punished who had had any contact with the killing in thought or in execution. The most remarkable human event concerned Cassius, who after his defeat at Philippi killed himself with the very dagger he had used against Caesar. As for the supernatural, there was the great comet that shone brilliantly for seven nights after Caesar's death, then disappeared; and also the dimming of the sun's rays. For that entire year the sun rose pale, with no radiation, and its heat came to earth only faintly and ineffectually, so that the air hung dark and thick on the earth because of the lack of radiance to penetrate it. The crops consequently never matured, but shriveled and withered away when they were only half-ripe because of the coldness of the air.
>
> More than anything else, it was the phantom that appeared to Brutus which gave a particularly clear sign that Caesar's killing had been unwelcome to the gods. It happened like this. Brutus was about to transport the army from Abydus to the other continent: it was nighttime, and he was resting as usual in his tent. He was not asleep, but deep in thought about the future. They say that this man needed less sleep than any other general in history, and spent many hours awake and alone. He thought he heard a noise by the door, and looked toward the lamp, which was already burning low. He saw a terrifying apparition of a man, a giant in size and menacing to look at. At first he was frightened, but then he saw that the apparition was doing nothing and saying nothing, but just standing silently by the bed. Brutus asked him who he was. The phantom replied: "Your evil genius, Brutus. You will meet me at Philippi." For the moment Brutus calmly replied "I will meet you there," and the phantom immediately went away.
>
> In the following months Brutus faced Antony and the young Caesar in battle at Philippi. In the first battle he defeated and forced back the detachment stationed opposite himself, and drove on to destroy Caesar's camp. When he was about to fight the second battle the phantom visited him again at night. It said nothing, but Brutus recognized his fate, and plunged into danger in the battle.
>
> Yet he did not die fighting. After the rout he took refuge on a rocky prominence, and forced his breast against his naked sword, with a friend, they say, adding weight to the blow. So he met his death. (*Caes.* 69)

And perhaps I should leave it there, just commenting on the fineness of the ending: no wonder Plutarch was content to leave it there too. Still, we can also adopt the same approach as with *Phocion–Cato minor*, and wonder if there is some *implicit* comparison with Alexander here, which is as thought-provoking as any formal synkrisis—to us, indeed, with our distaste for the formal comparisons, distinctly more interesting. The point could be summarized as the relation in the two *Lives* between the religious and the secular, or (better) the supernatural and the down-to-earth and human. This apparition does not come wholly from the blue; the pair has done something to prepare the way.

First, *Alexander*. That *Life* also has a finely wrought ending; death has been in the air for some time. The replies of the Gymnosophistae were decidedly morbid (*Alex.* 64); just before that point his horse Bucephalus[60] and his dog had both died, and he had extravagantly founded cities to commemorate both (61). He himself was wounded all but fatally (63.12), just before (expressively) coming to the bounds of his conquest and turning back. Then we have other deaths—memorably Hephaestion, with Alexander playing Achilles to his Patroclus;[61] that Homeric reminiscence has its own suggestions, and we know that Alexander's own death, like Achilles', cannot be far away. First we meet Calanus, the suicidal Indian sage (69), who builds his own pyre and bids the Macedonians farewell. His parting words are powerful ones. "He will see Alexander soon, at Babylon" (69.6): the closeness to *Caesar's* "You will meet me at Philippi" is clear. The most moving aspect is the taut, emotional response to all this. The atmosphere is bizarre, with Alexander himself dismayed and gloomy at the omens and the deaths, but responding with strained, extreme passion—his grief, his drinking bouts, his terror, his rage. It seems an unreal world, except that we know that death is near, a death that is very real; so are the dangers to people like Cassander (74.2–6). Alexander had begun as a pupil of Aristotle, in particular learning medicine (8): the difference between the clean and healthy Greek atmosphere of the beginning and the fevered hypochondria of the end, deep in an alien world, is beautifully conceived and executed.

One thing is continuous from beginning to end; Alexander's divine aspiration. The end of *Alexander* has been lost, but I have argued that we have a fragment from it:[62]

It is said that, as Alexander realized his life was departing, he wanted to drown himself secretly in the Euphrates: his object was to disappear and leave behind

---

[60] Given the prominence of Bucephalus and the Achillean suggestions that are beginning to crowd into the *Life*, it may not be fanciful here to think of Achilles' horse Pedasus, the mortal animal who keeps pace with his divine companions (*Il.* 16.152–54), but whose death comes to prefigure Patroclus's at *Il.* 16.467–69.

[61] Cf. Mossman 1988.

[62] In Zonaras 4.14 (p. 304): cf. Pelling 1973.

the story that he had now returned to the gods, just as he had come from them. But Roxane realized what was in his mind, so they say, and stopped the plan; Alexander said to her with a groan, "So you envied me, wife, the fame of apotheosis and immortality."

The passage expressly recalls the beginning of the *Life*—"He had now returned to the gods, *just as he had come from them.*" That is the "story" that Alexander now wants to "leave behind him"—but Plutarch's early narrative had left a different impression. Chapters 2–3 raised the possibility of divine birth, but the end of each section was there rationalistic and deflating. Plutarch discussed whether Olympias had been visited by a snake: he aired several possibilities, but gave most emphasis to the most rationalistic, the version that Olympias simply practiced cultic snake-handling. He also included the story that Olympias confided a divine secret to Alexander, but again ended with an alternative and less supernatural version, with Olympias bursting out, "Won't Alexander stop slandering me before Hera?" The *Life* includes other Hammon material as well, but Plutarch remains largely detached and noncommittal. Our new fragment fits perfectly. Alexander is pathetically foiled, and the divine aspirations are deflated yet again, here by his wife as initially by his mother.

In *Caesar*, death is again in the air, but it is all dealt with in a much more political and pragmatic way.[63] Caesar is politically forced, by the pressure of rule, to use unsatisfactory friends (esp. *Caes.* 51); they make him unpopular; the forces of opposition are gathering. There are omens (esp. 63), more omens than in *Alexander*, and Shakespeare was to find them useful for *Julius Caesar*, even Plutarch's Caesar is a little disturbed, but he is still inclined to minimize them. What he finds unsettling is Calpurnia's reaction rather than the omens themselves (63.11), and it is a point about people rather than about the firmament. Here it is not Plutarch who is doing the deflating, but Caesar himself; Alexander unduly deflated the religious register, Caesar is dangerously playing it down. True, Calpurnia finally persuades him to change his mind; but Decimus Brutus readily persuades him back, partly with, once again, the *political* argument, 64.5: What will the senate think? How will his friends be able to deny that this is a matter of tyrant and slaves? The political atmosphere is already too fraught for him to frustrate them like this. Caesar goes, and he dies.

The death itself is in the main realistic and human; then its first sequel, the lynching of Cinna the poet, again points to the force and violence of the human passions. That takes us to 69.1, which is phrased so as to sound strongly closural:

---

[63] Cf. Mossman 1988, 92; Pelling 1996.

Caesar died at the age of fifty-six, outliving Pompey by a little more than four years. He had sought dominion and power all his days, and after facing so many dangers he had finally achieved them. And the only benefit he reaped was their empty name, and the perils of fame amid his envious fellow citizens.

Yet that closure is a false one. Rather as we saw with the similar false closure in *Antony*, there are still themes unfinished; and here the themes touch on something more than human. The omens have already suggested that there is something more in the air; that is also stated by the element in the death scene that was not strictly human and rationalistic, the place where it all happened:[64]

All that [the story of Artemidorus, and his failure to force his way through to Caesar with news of the conspiracy] might simply be the result of coincidence, but it is harder to explain the place where the senate had gathered on that day, the scene of the murder and the violence. For it had a statue of Pompey lying on the floor, and the whole building had been dedicated by Pompey as one of the additional decorations to his theater. That gave an indication that there was some heavenly power directing events and guiding the plot into action at this very spot. Indeed, there is a story that Cassius looked at the statue of Pompey before they attacked, and called him silently to his aid, even though Cassius was sympathetic to the teachings of Epicurus; but it would seem that, in this critical and terrifying moment, a type of frenzied emotional transport drove out those earlier rational calculations. . . .

He fell by the pedestal on which Pompey's statue had stood, perhaps by chance, perhaps dragged there by the assassins. It was drenched in streams of blood, so that it appeared that Pompey himself had presided over the vengeance inflicted on his enemy, lying there beneath his feet, still writhing convulsively from his many wounds. (*Caes.* 66.1–3, 12–13)

Here, too, Plutarch is careful to keep the focus heavily on the human side: the effect on Cassius is phrased in naturalistic and psychological terms; and it only "appeared" that Pompey presided over the death, when in fact this was a matter either of chance or of the conspirators' engineering. But the language remains clear: "That gave an indication that there was some heavenly power directing events"; and that supernatural register eventually asserts itself in that final chapter, after the false closure, with the demonic apparition. Alexander may have aspired to play a divine game, but it is Caesar who ultimately plays it.

I do not suggest that there is a crude or straightforward conclusion to draw from this. It is surely not that "the divine ultimately took more thought for Caesar, so Caesar must have been greater than Alexander," even though Plutarch is more inclined than we are to phrase questions in

[64] Cf. Mossman 1991, 117–18.

this "Who is the greater?" mode. It may even be that the final intrusion of the supernatural is a sort of commentary on the whole pair. However much anyone—Olympias, Roxane, Plutarch himself, Caesar—tries to evade a divine involvement, there will still be some supernatural accompaniment and concern with events as momentous as these, and men so great. But there is no need to pin down the suggestions in that way either. We can surely be content to leave the end as it is, open and thought-provoking. This is certainly a case where we find a new perspective and a new set of reflections, an exception to Plutarch's usual preference for avoiding such terminal redirection. There is a sense of rest as well, with the posthumous vengeance and the concluding death, but it is still rare to have so arresting a new perspective so close to the end. Again, this is not the usual closing rhythm; again, a closing formal synkrisis could not have fulfilled its usual role; again, the implicit comparison with *Alexander* could have struck Plutarch as enough, and not to be compromised by a lamer, formal equivalent.

ENVOI

Aristotle knew that the events of a single life were not enough to give a work unity (*Poet.* 8.1451a16–19); he also asked whether the end of a life might be too soon to allow an adequate judgment on its happiness (*Eth. Nic.* 1.10–11, 1100a10–1101b9). Cradle to grave may not be enough. That is doubly true of Plutarch, where a pair has two cradles and two graves, and the themes need much finer modulation. That modulation does not always follow the same pattern, for Plutarch does not write to formulas. But the synkritic framework is used thoughtfully and pervasively; and the variations in his style of closure are intimately related to those of his comparative technique.[65]

---

[65] My thanks to David Levene, John Moles, Philip Stadter, Judith Mossman, Simon Swain, and the editors for helpful criticism.

Afterword: Ending and Aftermath, Ancient and Modern

DEBORAH H. ROBERTS

ABOUT HALFWAY through the Marx Brothers' film *Animal Crackers*, Chico is playing the piano with his usual uncanny aplomb, and finds himself repeating the same sequence of notes over and over again, unable to extricate himself. This exchange follows:

> CHICO   (looking at Groucho, who is seated in the audience):
>   I can't think of the ending.
> GROUCHO: I can't think of anything else.
> CHICO   (after playing a few more bars):
>   I think I went past it.

As several of the essays in this volume have suggested, it is not unusual for a text that tells a story to go past its ending, that is, to acknowledge in some way an aftermath not part of the narrative (or drama) proper.[1] Such an aftermath may be narrated proleptically (by a narrator or a prophetic character), alluded to, or simply implied by the trajectory of the narrative in light of the reader's prior knowledge; Dewald suggests that a narrative may even by its mode of ending point to the existence (though not the nature) of an aftermath the author cannot know but knows the reader will.[2] In those instances in which the aftermath is only alluded to or implied, the role of the reader in the construction of closure seems to become especially prominent and problematic. In this afterword (not, please note, a conclusion), I consider the reader's desire for aftermaths, that is, for endings

[1] See in this volume Dewald, Chapter 4; Dunn, Chapter 5; Fusillo, Chapter 10; Hardie, Chapter 7; Murnaghan, Chapter 2; Rutherford, Chapter 3.

[2] Dewald, Chapter 4 in this volume; cf. Hardie (Chapter 7) on the gradual obsolescence of the annalistic ending. In his analysis of order and of what he terms anachronies in the novel, Genette (1980, 68–70) calls narrative anticipation of events beyond a novel's last scene "external prolepses" (as opposed to internal prolepses, which look ahead to events before the novel's end). Genette's very useful analysis does not take into account the possibility we will largely be concerned with here, that is, of external prolepsis that can only be understood and sometimes only recognized as such by someone with prior knowledge of later events. Cf. also below on Torgovnick 1981.

beyond the ending, some circumstances under which readers are provided with aftermaths or the wherewithal to construct them, and some effects of such construction on closure. After a brief sketch of the interpretive problems and possibilities raised by aftermaths known to the reader in ancient narrative, with a closer analysis of one instance, Bacchylides' fifth ode, I turn to the aftermath of our period and explore some analogues in modern narrative, again with a closer look at one text, Shirley Hazzard's *Transit of Venus*.

At the end of Homer's *Odyssey*, after defeating the suitors and being reunited with his family, the hero makes peace with the suitors' families at Athena's command. But although the poem ends here, we have been told that there is something more to come. According to the prophecy given to Odysseus by Tiresias in the underworld (11.121–37) and repeated by Odysseus to Penelope (23.267–84), he will set out on his travels once more, wandering far inland to sacrifice to Poseidon, and will eventually meet with a gentle death from the sea, in his old age, surrounded by a prosperous people.[3]

Some have seen in this passage a reopening of the closure produced by return, reunion, and reconciliation, a new beginning that undoes Odysseus's homecoming and thus foreshadows the later tradition of Odysseus's continued wandering in such writers as Dante and Tennyson.[4] But this passage may also be said not to counter but to defer closure, since it confirms in several respects our sense of an ending (to use Frank Kermode's phrase). It tells of another reconciliation, this time between Odysseus and Poseidon, and it brings Odysseus in prosperity to a peaceful death, to what we might call the real end of his story—happily ever after, with just one more journey first.[5]

The prophecy thus provides an ending beyond the ending, an aftermath.

---

[3] On the meaning of *ex halos* (irrelevant here) and on Tiresias's prophecy, see most recently Falkner 1989; Hansen 1977; Heubeck, Hainsworth, and West 1989–92, vol. 2, ad loc.; Nagler 1980; and Peradotto 1986, 1990.

[4] See, for example, Steiner 1959, 113–15; Falkner 1989; and especially Peradotto 1986, 1990. Peradotto's particularly subtle reading sees the prophecy as creating a kind of openness both because its fulfillment is never actually narrated (unusual, he suggests, for the impossible-task type of prediction) and because it is, like the earlier part of Tiresias's prophecy, in some sense conditional; Odysseus must perform certain tasks in order to achieve his peaceful end. For Peradotto, this openness involves a tension between mythic narrative and Märchen and makes the readers complete the poem (Peradotto 1990, 89–90); cf. Falkner 1989, 51.

[5] Peradotto (1990, 60) calls this the "*ultimate end*" of the story; Falkner (1989, 51) comments that "closure here is both secured and postponed." We have no solid evidence that this prophecy alluded to a story known from existing tradition; it is not incompatible with what we know of the events of the lost *Telegony* (ascribed to the sixth century B.C.E. Eugammon of Cyrene) with its somewhat bizarre permutations (Odysseus is killed by his son by Circe; Penelope marries the son, and Telemachus marries Circe, who makes them all immortal (Photius, epitome of Proclus's *Chrestomathia* in Allen 1912, 109).

We might also say that the way in which the prophecy is introduced in Book 23 comments on our desire as readers or as audience for such aftermaths. The *Odyssey* is an epic of storytelling, and Odysseus is the master storyteller, but here, for once, he is reluctant to tell his story. Immediately after his reunion with Penelope, he tells her that their sufferings are not over, since Tiresias has foretold further troubles, but then breaks off and suggests they go to bed. Penelope reassures him—he can go to bed whenever he wants to, since the gods have brought him home—but urges him to tell her the story, since she will in any case find out eventually and it is no worse to learn it now.

Odysseus reluctantly complies, evidently puzzled (he addresses her as δαιμονίη, 264) by Penelope's wish to learn what will give her no joy. But Penelope's desire is not only a familiar human desire to know the worst at once; it is also emblematic of an audience's or reader's desire to know how the story comes out, how it really ends—whatever that end may be.[6]

In modern literature, that desire is most often explicitly addressed in the epilogues once common at the ends of novels;[7] in these final passages the narrator sums up from some not necessarily specified later vantage point the course of events in her or his own voice, often with some self-conscious comment on the fact of doing so, and often with some reference to the reader's *insistence* on being given such information, that is, to the reader's desire to know how it all comes out. Dickens ends *The Pickwick Papers* with a reference to the author's misfortune not only in losing his imaginary friends but in being "required to furnish an account of them besides"; nonetheless, he goes on to say that "in compliance with this custom—unquestionably a bad one—we subjoin a few biographical words." Louisa May Alcott speaks (in the epilogue to *Jo's Boys*) of "forestalling the usual question, 'how did they end?' "[8] Such endings suggest not only the familiar desire of readers for endings but also a kind of contractual disagreement over what really constitutes an ending. The story ends, but the epilogue indicates that more is somehow being demanded. I do not mean to imply that these epilogues are all responses to factual demands by actual readers, although there is some evidence for such demands, just as there is evidence for the related demand for sequels, a demand that asks for more,

---

[6] Penelope's reaction to Odysseus's account is read quite differently by different readers; Peradotto finds it hard not to see some bitterness here (1990, 86), while Falkner sees Penelope as emphasizing the happiness that awaits them in the end (1989, 50).

[7] For a useful discussion of the epilogue and of particular epilogues, see Torgovnick 1981. A contemporary example may be found in Isabel Colegate's novel *The Shooting Party* (and the film made from the novel).

[8] Dickens 1986, 875; Alcott 1886, 365. Scott's novels contain a number of variants on the theme of the reader's insistence; see, among others, *Quentin Durward* and *Redgauntlet*, and see, on Scott's endings, Hart 1978.

too, but seeks continuation (if possible in perpetuity) rather than closure.[9] What is important here is rather that the reader's desire for an ending beyond the ending is inscribed in the text itself, so that the implied reader is somehow made responsible for the inclusion of the aftermath in the narrative.

But why should the reader, actual or implied, desire this ending beyond the ending? Presumably because the first ending in some way falls short of satisfactory closure. Part of what readers want from an ending seems to be the opportunity to look back over what has come before and interpret it, to engage in what Barbara Herrnstein Smith calls "retrospective patterning."[10] Only when the work has come to an end can we be confident that the patterns are as we see them and will not change. Our ability to read a work of literature is then end-dependent in a manner analogous to our ability to judge a human life; we can call no human being happy until death—that is, until the change inherent in the mortal condition has yielded to stasis. Indeed, it has been suggested that this is more than a mere analogy, and that our craving for endings in literature is rooted in our inability ever to experience our own death and thus understand our own life.[11]

In "The Story-teller," Walter Benjamin takes us one step further:

> The reader of a novel actually does look for human beings from whom he derives the "meaning of life." Therefore he must, no matter what, know in advance that he will share their experience of death: if need be their figurative death—the end of the novel—but preferably their actual one. . . . This stranger's fate by virtue of the flame which consumes it yields us the warmth which we never draw from our own fate. What draws the reader to the novel is the hope of warming his shivering life with a death he reads about.[12]

In other words, the figurative death a story's end provides may do, but the death of the character is really what we crave.[13] With a passion rooted in our inability to grasp our own end, we want to know how it ends for the characters. We may be satisfied with the implication that nothing *changes*

---

[9] The fact that even where we find epilogues now we tend not to find such references to reader's desires may have partly to do with the virtual end of serialization (and thus to the communication of readers' views while the work is in progress). It is interesting that it is films that now more often have epilogues, and that it is also films that are sometimes shown in preview with different endings and altered in response to audience reaction.

[10] Smith 1968, esp. 212–13.

[11] See, for example, Torgovnick 1981, esp. 3–5; and Brooks 1984, esp. 22–23, 28, 95–96.

[12] Benjamin 1968, 101; cf., on our responses to narratives of actual murders as well as to fictions of murder, Lesser 1993.

[13] On the other hand, the desire for sequels—perhaps a wish for a kind of immortality?—can lead to the resuscitation of characters the author has killed (Sherlock Holmes, perhaps Falstaff).

until their deaths—that is, with a "happily ever after" or the equivalent (note that from this perspective it is the "ever after" that matters more than the "happily"). We may be satisfied, in a more sophisticated way, with an ending that figures death by providing some other kind of closure. We may even enjoy the postponed or open ending. But there is always a chance that any ending short of death will be felt as merely provisional. In a short piece entitled "Happy Endings," after sketching a variety of plots about John and Mary, John and Madge, Madge and Fred, etc., Margaret Atwood continues:

> You'll have to face it, the endings are the same however you slice it. Don't be deluded by any other endings, they're all fake, either deliberately fake, with malicious intent to deceive, or just motivated by excessive optimism if not downright sentimentality. The only authentic ending is the one provided here:
> John and Mary die. John and Mary die. John and Mary die.[14]

One of the most frequently quoted formulations of the problem of creating an ending is Henry James's, in the Preface to *Roderick Hudson*: "Really, universally, relations stop nowhere, and the exquisite problem of the artist is eternally but to draw, by a geometry of his own, the circle within which they shall happily *appear* to do so."[15] Our involvement in the circle of mortality makes us struggle with the circle of the work of art and always raises the possibility that we will insist on knowing more. Such insistence may in fact emerge more strongly in certain readers and in response to certain narratives,[16] but it is in part the ascription of this insistence at some level to all readers that lies behind the epilogue or the prophecy that tells how things turn out.

But what if the reader or audience already knows how things turn out, at least in outline (which is all epilogues and prophecies ever give us)? We might imagine that in ancient literature, where plots are more often than not selected from a body of stories continuous and to some extent familiar, the author can present whatever part of the story he or she chooses, and the reader will be satisfied, knowing the rest even if not in detail, and knowing how it ultimately turns out. But of course things are much more complicated; in spite of the reader's presumed knowledge, texts often spec-

---

[14] Atwood 1983, 40; but on even death as no ending; see Hardie, Chapter 7, and Pelling, Chapter 11 in this volume.

[15] James 1934, 5.

[16] I once knew a boy who was so disturbed by the open ending of E. B. White's *Stuart Little*—in which Stuart sets off on his travels once more, in search of the bird he loves—that he not only wrote another and more satisfactory ending (complete with reunion and return) but insisted that his mother paste it into the book.

ify an aftermath, and where they do not explicitly do so it is often far from clear how (and whether) the reader's knowledge comes into play.[17]

Some ancient narratives based on traditional myth nonetheless provide the equivalent of an epilogue in the form of prophecy, both telling us that we are to bear the aftermath in mind and letting us know what that aftermath will entail. The *Odyssey*, the *Iliad*, and the *Aeneid* all provide examples of this treatment, but Euripides' concluding prophecies by deus ex machina most strikingly structure the audience's awareness and knowledge of the story's aftermath;[18] he uses such epilogue prophecies not only to inform or remind his audience of less-well-known variants, but also to reassert well-known futures when his story has departed from tradition.[19] It is also in Euripides that we come the closest to a reference to the audience's desire for knowledge of the future, if we read the almost excessive thoroughness of some of his concluding prophecies as parodic of that desire.

Even such relatively clear statements of the aftermath may complicate closure when the predicted ending stands in contrast with the narrated or enacted end. Odysseus's homecoming and Odysseus's renewed travels; Aeneas's slaughter of Turnus and the future of Rome; Orestes' mad plans in Euripides' *Orestes* and Apollo's reconciliatory conclusion—in all these instances, critics have noted what amounts to a kind of doubling of ends.[20] The interpretive authority of the second may seem greater in that it comes later and is in that sense more truly the *end*; but the first derives an authority of its own from enactment, from fuller narration, and sometimes (as in the epics cited) from the fact that it comes last in the narrative if not in the chronology of the story.

---

[17] Of course, not all ancient narratives are based on familiar stories; comedy and the novel are fiction in something like the modern sense. Ancient testimony on how familiar ancient audiences actually were with traditional myth is contradictory. In Antiphanes fr. 189 *PCG*, the comic playwright compares the easy life of tragedians, who need only mention a character for the audience to know all about him, with the more difficult lot of writers of comedies, who have to invent their characters and plots. Aristotle says on the one hand that "what is familiar is familiar only to a few" (*Poetics* 9.51b25–26), and on the other that the poet must not change the central elements of the received stories (*Poetics* 14.53b22–24). Modern critics tend to assume at least a basic knowledge on the part of audiences and readers and to ask instead when and how a text calls on that knowledge, that is, what constitutes an allusion or grants it significance. Among recent treatments of some aspects of the question of allusion, see Conte 1986; Garner 1990; Slatkin 1991; Stinton 1990.

[18] See Hardie, Chapter 7 in this volume, on Latin epic; Dunn 1996 on Euripidean endings generally.

[19] The *Electra* provides an example of the first strategy, the *Orestes* an example of the second; see Dunn 1996, 64–83.

[20] See Hardie, Chapter 7 in this volume; Peradotto 1990; cf. also esp. Sophocles' *Philoctetes*, on which most recently Hoppin 1990. Any uncertainty about the predicted aftermath of course adds further complications; see again Peradotto 1990 on the *Odyssey*; Dunn, Chapter 5 in this volume.

This sort of prophetic prolepsis, however, cannot be said to rely on the reader's prior knowledge, though it may in some way call upon it (say, to suggest contrasting versions of the story as predicted). Other narratives give the reader less assistance (or exert less control?). We may find explicit refusal to speak of later events, complete silence about later events, and what may or may not be hints of later events; it is often difficult to know whether the aftermath is being suppressed or evoked, or which of several different versions the text implies. Let me give a familiar example of each strategy.

1. *Refusal to speak of the aftermath.* Where explicit prophecies that look beyond the bounds of the narrative tell us to think of the aftermath, another sort of intervention (authorial, not divine), tells us not to consider the aftermath at all. Pindar's thirteenth Olympian ode includes the story of Bellerophon's taming of Pegasus; after recounting the hero's subsequent victories on the winged horse, the narration ends with the words: "I will be silent about his fate; but the ancient stables of Zeus on Olympus received Pegasus."[21] What is the effect of this refusal? On the one hand, the narrator tells us explicitly that the aftermath is not a part of his praise song;[22] on the other hand, his self-declared silence (clearly a kind of *praeteritio*, as critics have noted) is itself a reference to and thus a reminder of Bellerophon's ultimate fate, which as early as the *Iliad* (6.200–205) is a paradigm of wretchedness. Pindar's refusal to speak of Bellerophon's end, while ending his narration with the horse's happier future, seems to entail a doubled ending as much as any explicit prediction could do, with this difference, that the second ending is both deferred and indefinite. And it is hard to see how any declaration that the future must remain unspoken could work otherwise. Even something as simple as "I'll say no more" suggests that there is more to be said, and though such a statement might imply an aftermath to be kept from the reader, this is not possible when the reader knows the story.

2. *Hints of an aftermath.* A text may omit outright prophecy while still alluding to an aftermath in terms that can be understood by a reader who knows of that aftermath (and only by that reader). Heracles' warning at the end of Sophocles' *Philoctetes* about respect for the gods when sacking Troy (1440–41) seems clearly to hint at the tradition of Neoptolemus's future impiety during that sack at Troy. There are similar hints of Antigone's unhappy future at the end of *Oedipus at Colonus*; her brother has already requested

---

[21] *Olympian* 13.130–32; of Pindar's characteristic evasions, this is the one that most simply says that the aftermath will be no part of his story.

[22] In Hubbard's (1986) analysis of the use of the Bellerophon myth in the poem he comments on the declaration of silence, "It is significant that the poet alludes to Bellerophon's final hybris and downfall only by preterition. . . . In a sense, the poet's own verbal restraint balances Bellerophon's lack of restraint" (40).

(ominously for the knowledgeable) that his sisters see to his burial (1409–10), and now in the closing lines Antigone requests that Theseus send her back to Thebes to try to prevent the war between her brothers (1769–72). Here the audience's or reader's awareness of its events lead, as in the case of Pindar's *praeteritio*, to a kind of partial and indefinite deferral of interpretation: there is an ending beyond the ending in light of which we may have to revise our reading, but this ending is itself never stated (and thus never realized in the text), only alluded to in terms we could not understand if we did not have prior knowledge.[23]

3. *Complete silence on the aftermath.* A text may make no reference at all to later events. Sappho 44 tells the story of the arrival of Andromache in Troy for her wedding with Hector; the poem may have been an epithalamium.[24] If the poem as a whole ended where our fragment does, as seems probable, there is no reference to the sorrows in store for this couple: his death, her enslavement. Does the aftermath impinge on the joyful narrative we find here? If so, Sappho seems to have chosen an oddly ill-omened exemplum, and some scholars have argued that this poem cannot therefore be an epithalamium. We might instead suppose that the genre somehow controls the readers' frame of reference, so that in an epithalamium they think no further than marriage.[25] Or we might suppose that genre is a factor in another sense, that is, that lyric exempla may be limited in scope to what their immediate context requires.[26] But this is to argue in a circle: how can we be sure in advance what the context requires?[27] There is a further difficulty: can we ever be sure of a text's silence? Several critics have seen in this poem a pattern of verbal echoes that call to mind passages from the *Iliad* and thus by indirection summon up the characters' future fates.[28]

[23] I have discussed the role of such allusions in Sophocles at length elsewhere (Roberts 1988); see also Stinton 1990 and bibliography for both articles. On hints of the aftermath in Apollonius's *Argonautica*, see Fusillo, Chapter 10 in this volume, and Fusillo 1985, 307–11 and 338.

[24] Some scholars have in fact doubted Sappho's authorship of this poem primarily on linguistic grounds (her use of certain dialect forms); for brief accounts of the problem, see Burnett 1983; Kakridis 1966.

[25] Vases made especially for weddings could show scenes of Helen's wedding—an even more ill-omened occasion, one might think; see, for example, Boardman 1974, 190. (My thanks to Alan Shapiro for this observation.)

[26] So Burnett (1983), who argues that to consider the scene ominous "is to misunderstand the proper use of such magic and exemplary scenes . . . Surely we are not to suppose that when Sappho . . . likened a bridegroom to Achilles . . . she meant to introduce an ominous idea of death" (220 n. 26); cf. Rissman 1983, 138; and Rösler 1975, 277–78.

[27] Rissman (1983, 139–40) suggests that the ill-omened might even have a place in a wedding poem as a kind of apotropaic gesture, on the analogy of traditions of mockery at Greek and Roman weddings; the argument doesn't seem to me convincing, but I cite it as an example of the problem with assumptions about context.

[28] See Rissman 1983, 126–28, 135–39; Kakridis 1966, 25–26.

In fact, this category of complete silence on the aftermath is a problematic one, given the difficulty of determining what constitutes an allusion, and always threatens to collapse into the previous category. Sophocles' *Electra* is perhaps the most notorious example of this problem. Some find in this play no hint of the aftermath familiar from Aeschylus's *Oresteia*; Orestes completes his revenge successfully, is hailed by the chorus, and leaves the stage with no sign of pursuing Erinyes. Others see hints of difficulties yet to come in the final exchange between Aegisthus and Orestes, especially in the reference (in general terms) to the future misfortunes of the Pelopid family (1497–98). If we agree that direct indications of the aftermath are lacking, we still have to sort out how to read the ending in light of the reader's knowledge of the aftermath. Are we to assume an aftermath in which the Furies arrive, with all that follows? Are we to assume a version of the story in which they remain absent, and to what effect? Or are we to assume that since the focus of Sophocles' play is Electra's experience, not her brother's, we simply should not think about the aftermath? And is such evasion a possibility? If, on the other hand, we do see allusions, this play resembles the *Philoctetes* and the *Oedipus at Colonus* in its use of hints of a familiar aftermath.[29]

Hints in the text, then, may evoke a known aftermath; but it is the known aftermath that leads us to notice hints we would otherwise not see. The very audience knowledge that creates problems thus also creates possibilities: a narrative can incorporate allusions that take on meaning only in the context of a future not actually narrated and can establish patterns that make themselves known as patterns only in the context of that deferred and untold future. Ending and interpretation are thus both multiplied and rendered unstable; the reader's knowledge is crucial to both effects.

Bacchylides' fifth ode could be described as using all three of the strategies noted here, or rather as demonstrating how my categories tend to collapse into one another.[30] The first section, praising Hieron and the horse that won an Olympic victory for him, ends with the familar sentiment, "No mortal is fortunate in all things" (53–55), and is followed by an account of Heracles' trip to the underworld, his encounter there with the hero Meleager, and Meleager's telling of his own story. Heracles enters the realm of the dead to bring back the dog Cerberus; while there, he sees the innumerable dead, most striking among them the shade of Meleager. Alarmed, he prepares to draw his bow, but Meleager's spirit tells him it would be useless and unnecessary. Heracles asks Meleager the traditional

---

[29] See for examples and discussion of these divergent views esp. Winnington-Ingram 1980, ch. 10; Stinton 1990; Roberts 1988.

[30] See esp. Burnett 1985; Goldhill 1983; Lefkowitz 1969; Scodel 1984; Stern 1967. (I do not here offer a reading of the poem as a whole and so do not take into detailed account the epinician context of the narrative.)

questions asked of the living—who were his parents, where is he from; he also asks who killed him. But this second question is no mere politeness (as if one should conventionally ask the living where they were born, the dead how they died); Heracles asks because he fears that anyone great enough to kill Meleager might be sent by his enemy Hera to kill him as well. Meleager answers both questions by telling his story: the goddess Artemis, angry at his father Oeneus, sent first a wild boar and then a war. Because Meleager killed his uncles in this war, he was himself killed by his mother Althaea, who put on the fire a log the fates had destined to the same lifespan as Meleager's. Heracles responds to this story, for the only time in his life, with tears, and with another familiar saying, that it is better for mortals never to have been born. He adds, however, that nothing comes of complaining, and that one should declare one's intent, and then asks whether Meleager has a sister at home who resembles him and whom Heracles might marry. Meleager replies that he did indeed leave at home his young sister Deianeira, still inexperienced in love's enchantments. The narrator tells his muse to stop her chariot here (176–78) and returns to the topic of praise.

What should we make of the ending of this narrative? If we knew nothing about the rest of Heracles' story, we might simply read this way: the opening aphorism about the inconsistency of human happiness is exemplified both by Heracles' dangerous descent to the underworld (he, a son of Zeus, undergoes labors) and by Meleager's misfortunes. But the narrative ends on a movement of hope, as Meleager's death is balanced by the prospect of marriage between Heracles and the sister who is like him; this marriage seems indeed to be a kind of compensation for Meleager's loss, somewhat as the glory of Achilles' son Neoptolemus is a recompense for his father in the underworld in *Odyssey* 11.[31]

But the reader who knows the rest of Heracles' story knows that this marriage will lead to disaster. Heracles will marry Deianeira, and she will be the cause of his death.[32] From the perspective of this aftermath, a different pattern emerges. The narrative's opening aphorism, that no mortal is consistently happy, is reconfirmed: even what seemed a happy outcome is reversed. Heracles' closing aphorism (it is better not to have been born) speaks of his own fate as well as Meleager's; his unprecedented tears, Burnett notes, are for himself as well as for the hero he pities. Heracles' ignorance (he thought Meleager had been killed by a great warrior that might have killed him) reveals the deeper truth of what Burnett calls the congru-

---

[31] Among the numerous Homeric echoes in this poem, Lefkowitz (1969) notes several that recall Odysseus's journey to the underworld (65, 67, 69); cf. Burnett 1985, 145 n. 22, 23.

[32] See, on the history and versions of the story of Heracles and Deianeira, March 1987, 49–77.

ency of their tales:[33] Meleager and he are both killed by women and family members, and the poem presents us with what now proves to be a pattern of destruction by women: Artemis, Althaea, Deianeira. What we thought was the ending is not really the final ending, and the true ending or second ending of the poem provides no compensation, but instead redoubles loss. Heracles, like Odysseus, has journeyed to the underworld and returned to a marriage, but like Odysseus, too (though he does not know it), he has brought back from the underworld the prospect of an aftermath that replaces marriage with death.

Is it possible that Bacchylides' narrative evades this aftermath? When Bacchylides tells his muse to halt the chariot there, we might take this command as equivalent to Pindar's declaration that he will be silent on the fate of Bellerophon, and as a similar signal that we are not to think of the rest—perhaps even a more effective signal, given the absence of *praeteritio*. We might also consider taking this story as quite silent on the aftermath, given the absence of explicit indications of what follows. Deianeira's name is the only direct allusion to what will happen to Heracles, and as we noted in connection with Sappho 44, some have argued that names in lyric exempla may suggest only the part of the story the context calls for. On my first reading here, an allusion to a happy wedding might be just what we want.

In fact, however, most critics agree that Deianeira's name alone is ominous enough to summon up the untold future, perhaps because she has little story of her own in the tradition apart from the destruction she brings Heracles, perhaps also because of the meaning of that name.[34] Some have suggested other possible allusions as well; references to Deianeira's inexperience, to the goddess of love and her powers of enchantment, call to mind the later unknowing and fatal use of a supposed love charm.[35] But to understand these allusions as such, to understand the aphorisms as more widely applicable than we thought, and to perceive the patterns common to both heroes' lives and deaths requires a retrospective patterning that is possibly only for those who already know what lies beyond the boundaries of the narrative itself and can construct the ending beyond the ending[36]—

[33] Burnett 1985, 145.

[34] Cf. Stern 1967, 36; Goldhill 1983, 78 n. 31; and Burnett 1985, 145 (in interesting partial contrast with her remarks on Sappho cited above): "The spectator who hears the name of Daianeira, after such a narrative, understands perfectly. That name means death."

[35] Lefkowitz 1969, 86; for her, the words used here "describe the exact circumstances of Heracles' death."

[36] Goldhill (1983) argues that the emphasis on the story of Deianeira as a signifying unit "compels the reader to complete the narrative from, in this case, I am proposing the metatext of what we may term received myth" (78); cf. Scodel 1984 on Bacchyl. 17: "The effect is produced by the hearer's finishing the story for himself and his comparison of his own response to that of the characters" (142). Cf. also Peradotto 1990, 89–90.

and perhaps even an ending beyond that, if Heracles' death further implies his apotheosis.[37]

Then does the ending outside the story cancel the ending actually narrated? Not entirely; the reader is compelled at least momentarily to respond to the thought of the marriage as good news.[38] The double ending thus has the effect not only of making us read the poem in two different ways, but of making the reader experience, however briefly, the happiness-turned-sadness of the characters, that very uncertainty of human happiness the story sets out to illustrate.

In her study of closure in the novel, Maria Torgovnick includes among her types of closural strategy both the *tangential* ending, in which an ending introduces a new topic, and the strategy of *linkage*, in which the ending of one book looks ahead to later books in a series.[39] She discusses no such endings at length, however, since for her they "do not lend themselves to detailed analysis."[40] The ancient endings we have been considering here could be seen as examples of Torgovnick's categories, but the fact that the reader knows what comes next and the interpretive implications of that knowledge seem to allow for the detailed analysis she excludes. Can we find in modern literature as well analogues of the transformative yet tentative effects of "tangential" awareness of the aftermath, of the ways in which that awareness defers and complicates the experience of closure? There are of course still works that make use of ancient myth and exploit the reader's knowledge of such myth; Giraudoux's *La Guerre de Troie n'aura pas lieu* (for example) is all about a deferred but familiar ending. But reliance on shared knowledge of any story tradition (the Bible, the Arthurian cycle) is surely diminishing. When might a modern reader know what would come next without being told, and do modern writers exploit such knowledge? Several possibilities come to mind.

The most obvious source for a reader's knowledge of what comes next is history. When a work has a historical basis, the reader may of course know more than the narrative tells, and this is true whether the characters are themselves historical or are fictional but take part in or are affected by specific historical events (such as a war). Modern fiction shows approx-

---

[37] See Goldhill 1983, 78 and n. 31; Burnett 1985, 145; and see March 1987 on the place of the apotheosis in the tradition.

[38] That is, the reader responds as Heracles does; Lefkowitz (1969, 87) comments that "Heracles can now depart satisfied with the happier possibilities of Meleager's answer." She sees the poem as including two outcomes, either of which gives a sense of completion, and this seems right; but the fact of the second prevents the first from maintaining that sense of completion.

[39] Torgovnick 1981, 13–14.

[40] Ibid., 14.

imately the same range in dealing with historical aftermaths as ancient fiction does in dealing with mythical aftermaths. Just as epilogue prophecies may be found in ancient literature even where the aftermath is known, epilogues may be used in modern historical fiction.[41] But these are often (though not always) concerned not so much with well-known events as with the fates either of fictional characters or of less-well-known historical characters in the face of those events. They thus presume the reader's desire to know rather than the reader's knowledge, and are not our concern here. I have found no example of a historically based text that explicitly disclaims interest in later events, but as (perhaps) with Sappho 44, the aftermath may be suppressed or ignored; Chaim Grade's *Rabbis and Wives*, for example, is set in Eastern Europe in the 1930s but seems to give no thought to what awaits the characters beyond the narrative and outside their self-contained world. As with myth, however, it isn't clear that an aftermath well known to the reader can be successfully suppressed;[42] Dewald even suggests that a text may evoke a historical aftermath known to the reader but unknown to the author.[43] Finally, as with Sophoclean tragedy and Bacchylides 5, a narrative can allude to a historical aftermath known to the reader in terms only fully accessible to that knowledgeable reader; Tanizaki's *The Makioka Sisters*, preoccupied with daily life, includes passing references to events leading up to the Second World War.[44]

Sometimes, as with Bacchylides 5, knowledge of a historical aftermath allows new patterns to emerge, allusions to be understood, and events to

---

[41] See again Colegate's *The Shooting Party*. The beginnings of the historical novel show plenty of examples; see, for example, Scott's *Ivanhoe*. (His *The Talisman* concludes with the statement that "our story closes here, as the terms on which Richard relinquished his conquests are to be found in every history of the period" [Scott 1926, (356)]—an allusion not so much to the reader's knowledge as to the availability of that knowledge and perhaps the reader's responsibility for acquiring it.)

[42] As a child I once read a book about a family of orphaned children who successfully make their way together across North America in the nineteenth century and finally find a new home with a kindly couple who have settled in a valley in Oregon. I read the ending with great pleasure, and then learned (as I seem to recall, from an afterword or introduction) that the book was based on a historical episode, and that some five years after the children's arrival the original inhabitants of the area killed them all. I could never feel the same about the story and indeed could never reread it. (The book was probably A. R. Van Der Loeff's *Children on the Oregon Trail*, but the only edition I have been able to find includes no information about later events in the author's introduction, perhaps because such information so drastically undercuts the book's happy ending.)

[43] Dewald, Chapter 4 in this volume.

[44] Tanizaki 1957 (my thanks to Allen Bergson for this example). Among earlier novels it is often noted that the references to Pierre's activities and associations in the final chapters of *War and Peace* call to mind the Decembrists. On the impact of such elements, see Torgovnick 1981, 66–71.

become emblematic. Aharon Appelfeld's *Badenheim 1939* is set in Austria, in a Jewish summer resort.[45] As the story progresses, the residents are subject to increasing constriction and regimentation; the conditions of life decay, and new arrivals tell stories of mistreatment in the world outside. But the story ends with the characters getting on a train for Poland, where most of them still expect to continue with their lives and professions. In the absence of historical knowledge, what happens might seem surreal; with that knowledge, it is horribly realistic. The final arrival not of an ordinary train but of a freight train seals the characters' fate for the knowledgeable reader. The continued optimism of one of the characters is ironically juxtaposed at the last with an image of winnowing and with the demonic image of the train's seeming to rise from the ground. In light of what we know, earlier moments in the story also emerge as symbolic, in particular a strikingly anthropomorphic account of the behavior of fish in the hotel aquarium—the "massacre" carried out by certain blue fish, the sudden disappearance of the peaceful little green fish.[46]

The reader may also derive knowledge of the aftermath from intertextuality. If a book is based closely on another book, or uses characters from another book, we may know from that other book what lies beyond the ending.[47] A number of contemporary works are written not as sequels but in the interstices, as it were, of prior fictions, retelling the story from a different perspective: Tom Stoppard's *Rosencrantz and Guildenstern Are Dead*; Valerie Martin's *Mary Reilly*, which retells the story of *Dr. Jekyll and Mr. Hyde* from the viewpoint of a servant in the household; John Gardner's *Grendel* (*Beowulf* from the monster's viewpoint); Jean Rhys's *Wide Sargasso Sea* (the story of Mr. Rochester's first wife); Lin Haire-Sargeant's *Heathcliff: The Return to Wuthering Heights* (which proves to fill in certain gaps not only in *Wuthering Heights* but, as the knowledgeable reader soon sees, in *Jane Eyre* as well). None of these texts seems to me fully to exploit the reader's knowledge of the original ending in the ways we are concerned with, but Rhys's book comes close.[48] The narrator dreams the end of *Jane Eyre* (the fire, her own leap from the rooftop) and wakes intending to enact

[45] Appelfeld 1980. Cf. also his *The Retreat* and *To the Land of the Reeds.* Appelfeld's omission of historical events and his assumption that readers will know the facts comes up in the conversation between Appelfeld and Philip Roth in Roth's *Operation Shylock* (1993, 83–84).

[46] Appelfeld 1980, 51, 57.

[47] On the use of other fictions to create a "story world," see Laird 1993.

[48] Haire-Sargeant provides an alternative ending that partially changes the original. This interstitial genre continues popular; to the texts cited here, we may now add Bigsby 1994 (*Hester: A Novel About the Early Hester Prynne*) and Austen-Leigh 1993 (*A Visit to Highbury: Another View of Emma*).

the same events; it is our knowledge of the prior novel that confirms the coming reality of dreamed death and fire.[49]

A reader may know the aftermath if a work is part of a series of works that appear in other than the story's chronological order; in Faulkner's Yoknapatawpha novels, Quentin Compson is a suicide in *The Sound and the Fury*, but we meet him again as listener and narrator in the later *Absalom, Absalom*.[50] The availability of such knowledge is only partially dependent on the order in which the reader encounters the novel; the original readers, constrained by the order of publication, will read later works in the series with an awareness that later readers may miss if they read according to the chronology of the story, but this difference in experience applies only to a first reading.[51]

Just as we entertained the possibility (in discussing Sappho 44) that generic constraints on a work of ancient literature could tend to suppress the reader's attention to a known outcome, the generic constraints on a modern work could theoretically at least be so strong that even in the absence of any further indications the reader would know there was only one possible ending. This is what Shaw claims to fear for *Pygmalion* when he says that he is writing his account of what happened afterwards only because "our imaginations are so infeebled by their lazy dependence on the ready-mades and reach-me-downs of the ragshop in which Romance keeps its stock of happy endings to misfit all stories. . . . People in all directions have assumed, for no other reason than that [Eliza] became the heroine of a romance, that she must have married the hero of it."[52]

---

[49] Nicholas Meyer's detective story, *The Seven Per Cent Solution*, is an example of the use of a fictional character (Sherlock Holmes) in a new story whose ending alludes to the ending of the prior fiction. In fact, Meyer mingles historical characters (Sigmund and Anna Freud), another writer's fictions (Holmes, Watson, Moriarty—though a very different Moriarty), and his own creations. He uses Freud and Holmes much as earlier authors use mythical characters (characters on the borderline of history and fiction) such as Odysseus, or King Arthur, or Robin Hood. Meyer's ending makes a particularly witty use of prior fiction; Holmes refuses to return to England with Watson, and when the latter asks what he should tell Holmes's reader, Holmes replies, "Tell them anything you like—tell them I was murdered by my mathematics tutor—they won't believe you in any case" (169). Meyer has already established that Holmes's belief that his former tutor Moriarty is a master criminal is a delusion, and Freud has elicited the basis of this delusion and cured it. But Meyer's ending also alludes to the story in which Conan Doyle, attempting to end the Holmes series, had Moriarty kill Holmes—a death his readers refused to accept, ultimately compelling Doyle to bring Holmes back.

[50] Cf. Cooper's *Leatherstocking Tales*, and Balzac's *Comédie Humaine*.

[51] Cooper's original readers will have read some of the "later" stories first, and therefore will have known the aftermath of *The Deerslayer*, last written but first in the chronology of Natty Bumppo's life. See on Cooper's endings Martin 1978.

[52] Shaw 1965, 751. Note however that Shaw is not objecting to audience assumptions

It is tempting to include one further possibility. A reader acquainted with the author may have access to an aftermath the author had in mind but never wrote. Jane Austen shared with her family subsequent events in the lives of her fictional characters; we learn from the memoir written by her nephew James Austen-Leigh that

> she would, if asked, tell us many little particulars about the subsequent career of some of her people. In this traditionary way we learned that Miss Steele never succeeded in catching the Doctor; that Kitty Bennet was satisfactorily married to a clergyman near Pemberley, while Mary obtained nothing higher than one of her uncle Philip's [sic] clerks . . . that Mr. Woodhouse survived his daughter's marriage, and kept her and Mr. Knightley from settling at Donwell, about two years.

A further family tradition records Jane Fairfax's early death.[53] We might dismiss the idea of the effect of such aftermaths as frivolous either pragmatically (too few readers to count) or more theoretically (the text cannot be said to allow for such knowledge on the reader's part), but word can spread, and actual readers escape their implied duties. I wonder how many readers of *Emma* remain entirely unaffected by the last piece of news?

By any of these means, the ending may be revealed as not final, allusions may be revealed as significant, and patterns may shift; that is, the narrative may be read differently, conditioned by an aftermath that is not actually narrated. The aftermaths known may vary in specificity and in degree of authorial control—detailed knowledge of another text is different from general knowledge of a coming historical event—but the aftermath in all cases belongs to a different realm from that of the narrative at hand.[54]

Let me now discuss at somewhat greater length the text whose closural strategy I think comes closest to what we find in Bacchylides and in Sophocles, and to the consequent ironic deferral and doubling. Paradoxically, the technique used in this text is not one that relies in the strict sense on the reader's prior knowledge. It bears some resemblance to the use of em-

---

about the aftermath per se, since he adds (before proceeding to recount it in some detail) that "the true sequel is patent to anyone with a sense of human nature in general and of feminine instinct in particular."

[53] Austen-Leigh 1926, 157–58; on Jane Fairfax, see Austen-Leigh and Austen-Leigh 1913, 307. Genette (1987) would call this part of "l'epitexte privé."

[54] For this reason circular texts (see Mortimer 1985, 206–17 on Simon's *La Bataille de Pharsale*) and texts that move backwards in time (Pinter's *Betrayal*), although they do allow the reader to know the future when she comes to the end, present a different picture; the text contains the future, and it is fully narrated. (Cf. also Fusillo's comment [p. 211] on David Leavitt's *Equal Affections*, whose narrative ends with a scene earlier than the preceding scenes in story time, a scene thus read with prior knowledge of what follows.)

bedded external prolepsis as a form of epilogue Genette finds in Proust.[55] It is also reminiscent of a mode of prolepsis in fiction that can be found at any point in the story but that has little to do with the plot, or indeed with any line of action. George Eliot refers in *Middlemarch* to memories of Rome that were to recur for Dorothea in later life, and Tolstoy refers in *Anna Karenina* to Levin's and Kitty's later recollections of the early days of their marriage; in both these cases, the suggested aftermath involves only a kind of reliving of events in the story. We find a more detailed projection in the middle of Charlotte Brontë's *Shirley*, but here the futures the narrator sketches are those not of the central characters but of the children of a secondary character.[56]

Such embedded prolepses may, however, be much more pointed and much more transformative of closure, though I have found only one novel that fully exploits them, Shirley Hazzard's *The Transit of Venus*. The following sketch does no kind of justice to the complexity and interest of either the lives of the characters or Hazzard's narrative technique.

At the beginning of this novel, a young man, Ted Tice, and a young woman, Caro (Caroline) Bell, meet in an environment in which neither quite belongs. He is a young scientist from a working-class background, come to work with an eminent older scientist. She and her sister are Australians, and her sister is engaged to the son of the older scientist. Ted falls in love with Caro; she has only friendly feelings for him. We continue to follow their lives and the lives of other characters. Caro falls in love with a man she and Ted both know, but eventually marries (happily) someone else; Ted continues to love only her, but marries when she does. She remains his friend, he is still in love with her. Finally, in middle age, they come together again after the death of her husband. A revelation by her first lover about a past event (before the time of the novel, and new both to her and to the reader) has somehow changed what she can feel for Ted. They meet in Oslo, admit their love, and arrange to be together. Ted writes his wife to end his marriage, and sees Caro off on a plane to Rome, where he will join her.

This ending feels satisfying (and not, one hopes, simply because of a weakness for happy endings). Through the novel's many losses and dissatisfactions the idea of this coming together has persisted; the intelligences and concerns of these two people seem especially to matter and to match. But the author has concealed clues, allusions to an aftermath, that give us quite a different ending. Here are the clues:

---

[55] Genette 1980, 68.
[56] Tolstoy 1950, 566; Eliot 1988, 188; Brontë 1905, 215–16.

1. Early in the novel we read: "In fact, Edmund Tice would take his own life before attaining the peak of his achievement. But that would occur in a northern city and not for many years" (12).[57]

2. Nearer the end, Caro (now Caro Vail, her married name) visits a doctor; of him, we hear that "three months later he was to die in a plane crash on his way to an ophthalmologists' congress at Rome" (296).

3. A little later, we meet the concierge of Ted Tice's hotel in Oslo; "later that week he was to tell his family: 'He was in the hotel on Tuesday. Large as life.'" In the next sentence we read: "Edmund Tice was approaching the peak of his career" (329).

4. After their encounter, the day before she leaves for Rome, we read: "For the last time, Caroline Vail lay in a bed alone" (334).

5. As Caro waits in line in the airport, she catches sight of a familiar face among those in line with her: it is the ophthalmologist she consulted (336).

With this last clue, the aftermath is clear. Caro Vail will die in a plane crash, and Ted Tice—because he has lost her again, perhaps because it was he who put her on the plane—will kill himself.[58] And once we grasp the aftermath, the narrative changes; the ending now confirms the book's patterns of loss rather than providing a final fulfillment. Allusions that were ambiguous are now clear: the concierge told his family about Tice not because Tice was a well-known scientist but because of the news of Tice's suicide. Caro lay in her bed alone for the last time not because she would be with Ted from then on but because she would die and lie in no bed; indeed, the closing moments of the book, reconsidered, are full of such double language.[59]

In light of the aftermath we can now also understand the imagery of the last paragraph:

> Within the cabin, nothing could be heard. Only, as the plane rose from the ground, a long hiss of air—like the intake of humanity's breath when a work of ages shrivels in an instant; or the great gasp of hull and ocean as a ship goes down. (337)

Without our knowledge of Caro's death and of Ted's, these similes might have seemed excessive; why do we need such great disasters to de-

---

[57] On the context in which this sentence occurs and on its syntax, see the very interesting comments of Baym (1983).

[58] No critic seems to have missed the foreshadowing of the aftermath, though a few critics curiously refer to the work as *ending* with Caro's death and Ted's suicide (Rainwater and Scheick 1983a; Taylor 1984); on the openness of the ending, see esp. Bird 1985; on the complexity of Hazzard's narrative in general see Baym 1983; Bird 1985; Olubas 1992; Taylor 1984.

[59] There are a number of allusions to death that we might, before we are made conscious of the aftermath, take simply as closural motifs, unaware of their more literal appropriateness.

scribe a mere mechanical sound? And we might have read this excess merely as a generalized memento mori shadowing the lovers' reunion as death always shadows love. In light of the known aftermath, however, similes of disaster are specific, revelatory, and apt.

In Hazzard's text, then, although the reader has no prior knowledge of the aftermath in the sense in which an ancient reader might, such knowledge is suggested (almost hypnotically?) prior to the text's ending, though not to its beginning, and the reader thus arrives at the work's conclusion with an awareness of the future surprisingly like that of the reader of Bacchylides 5. And just as the reader of Bacchylides 5 must more fully construct the future from what she knows, with no detailed narrative provided, so the reader of Hazzard's text must in a somewhat different sense construct the future, given no detailed narrative of these later events.[60] (I exemplified such construction above when I assigned causes to Ted's suicide and explained the concierge's comments.)

I have stressed the reader's role in constructing the ending beyond the ending, both here and in the ancient texts discussed above. But critical writing on Hazzard characteristically describes her narrative technique as a way of asserting the narrator's control.[61] We might suppose that this contrast has to do with the fact that in the case of the ancient texts, the reader really does have access to knowledge beyond the narrator's control, whereas here the reader has only what the narrator gives her. If, however, we take ourselves to be concerned with the implied reader, the reader presumed by the text, then in both cases the narrative may be said to presume or construct this reader, who in turn must partly construct the unnarrated aftermath.[62] In neither case is the reader entirely in charge, since she cannot evade the text's hints of a future. But in neither case is the author's or narrator's control complete, since the hints do not constitute or even epitomize a narrative but leave it to the reader to construct that narrative. Where texts with a known mythical or historical aftermath seem to me to differ dramatically from texts such as Hazzard's is in the possible responses of actual readers, who, whatever the text's efforts to evade or elide the aftermath, may still insist on reading the text in its light.[63]

If the narrative strategy with which Hazzard complicates her ending is like that of Bacchylides 5, so are some of its effects. I commented above

[60] See Olubas 1992, 163.

[61] Cf. phrases such as "the supremacy of the narrator" (Sellick 1990, 88) and "the Deity of the plot" (Baym 1985, 225); others stress the elusiveness of the narrator (Olubas 1992) and the "writerly" qualities of the text (Bird 1985).

[62] Sellick 1990, 92; cf. Conte 1986, 30, on the presupposition or construction of the reader, and D. Fowler, Chapter 1 in this volume, on authorial control vs. the power of the reader.

[63] On this issue, see Lamont 1991.

that the aftermath revealed to us confirms the novel's patterns of loss. The losses in the novel are many: Caro loses a lover, a pregnancy, a husband, and Ted; her husband has lost a first wife, and fails to save a group of political prisoners he is struggling to defend. Caro's first lover is losing a son to illness. Her sister loses a man she loves but whose lover she cannot be. Ted loses Caro, and his wife loses him. By her way of ending the novel, Hazzard not only confirms this pattern for us but also makes us share the characters' sense of loss even more strongly than we would otherwise have done, since the happy ending is offered to us, then snatched away.

Indeed, Hazzard's ending seems to put her in the company of those who resist their readers' very desire for happy endings. I have already mentioned Shaw's epilogue to *Pygmalion*; we might also compare Fowles's *The French Lieutenant's Woman*, whose ending offers us, self-consciously, first reunion and then loss, and refuses to choose between the two. Hazzard similarly evades the happy ending, both as happy and as ending. But this evasion is hardly simply a critical comment on an outworn mode of reading or writing; it rather entails an insistence on change and chance that may at any time turn gain to loss, and thus recalls both a theme of ancient narrative in general and Bacchylides' particular evocation of that theme. Critical writing on Hazzard's work often focuses (guided in part by her comments in interviews) on her narrative technique as a means of creating a sense of fate, of what is preordained.[64] What seems to me more striking is the way her narrative, like that of Bacchylides, evokes the conflict between our desire to know our ends and the need to remain ignorant of them if we are to bear our existence. In Aeschylus's *Prometheus Bound* (concerned throughout with the question of the value of foresight) Prometheus tells the chorus that as one of his gifts to mortals he took away their ability to see the day of their death (548–51). In our brief sharing of the characters' ignorant enjoyment of the present and our subsequent construction of the future that awaits them, we feel in effect the value of Prometheus's gift even as we refuse to receive it.

In Hazzard's novel as in Bacchylides 5, and indeed as in the *Odyssey*, the ending beyond the ending gives us death instead of marriage, with change and chance thus figured once again by the traditional polarities of ending. There is even, here too, a journey to the underworld (traditional middle, traditional source of knowledge about the end) in the form of an allusion to ancient myth that itself constitutes a hint of the novel's aftermath—a hint that makes use of the reader's knowledge of ancient myth. After Ted and Caro's penultimate meeting, in London, still just as friends, he sees her off on the underground:

[64] See Rainwater and Scheick 1983b, 118.

He watched her red coat pass the barrier, move with the Down escalator, gliding, diminishing, descending: a rush-hour Eurydice. At the last moment she looked back, knowing he would be there. (295)

This should be an ominous allusion for the reader who knows the myth, but its ominousness is muted by the fact that in the immediate context the allusion involves several reversals of the tradition. In most versions of the story, neither Orpheus nor the reader sees Eurydice descending; her loss is sudden each time, and what is gradual is either Orpheus's journey down or their return together.[65] It is Orpheus, not Eurydice, who traditionally and fatally looks back, and his backward glance is a guarantee not of the beloved's presence, but of her absence. Hazzard's revisions and the progression of the narrative might seem to suggest a Caro-Eurydice in the role of a successful Orpheus; Caro will lose her husband to death but gain in Ted another love, and do so partly by looking back at his past and hers.[66] In light of the novel's aftermath, however, the allusion regains all its traditional force. Orpheus regains Eurydice only to lose her again (through his own action) and eventually to follow her in death; so it will be with Ted and Caro. The fiction that seemed to offer an escape from the familiar ending of this myth finally only confirms it.

I conclude with one recent fiction whose mythic title evokes a past to which, as to Eden, all presents seem mere aftermath. Tom Stoppard's play *Arcadia* moves in alternating scenes between early nineteenth and late twentieth century in Lord and Lady Croom's country house; most of the present-day characters are in one way or another trying to reconstruct the past.[67] As the play ends, the two times, always overlapping through shared space and physical objects, coexist more fully on stage; characters from both periods are present, although (with one possible exception) unaware of each other.[68] The nineteenth-century daughter of the house, Thomasina Coverly, is waltzing with her tutor Septimus Hodge on the night before her seventeenth birthday. They kiss; he returns an essay, warns her to be careful with the candle flame, and refuses her invitation to come to her room. After a brief exchange between two present-day characters, both pairs continue to dance as the curtain falls.

The kiss and the continued dance suggest erotic union in spite of Septimus's firmly resisting words. But we know, because we have earlier heard

[65] Cf. Ovid *Metamorphoses* 10.1–85; Virgil *Georgics* 4.453–527.

[66] And in a sense by confronting death, since the story her former lover tells her involves a death for which he was responsible and about which Ted knew.

[67] Stoppard 1993. My reading of this play is indebted to Amanda Irwin's fine interpretive study in her Haverford College senior essay (1995).

[68] The possible exception is the mysterious Gus Coverly, the unspeaking "genius brother" (Stoppard 1993, 32, I.2), who is played by the same actor as his nineteenth-century counterpart Augustus.

the present-day characters say so, that Thomasina will die that very evening in a fire; we know, or have good reason to believe, that Septimus will become the hermit of Sidley Park (the object of one of the present-day characters' historical research). As in Hazzard's novel and as in Bacchylides' poem, we are given only a glimpse of the aftermath—not narration, not enactment, not even epitome—and we must therefore to some extent construct it.[69] We may tell ourselves a story in which Thomasina will fail to pay attention to Septimus's warning, will read the essay too close to the candle, and will catch fire; in which Septimus's remorse at not accepting an assignation that would have saved her will lead him to become a hermit; but it is we who tell this story.[70] In Bacchylides' poem, as in other ancient works, our participation in reading the aftermath is forced by our knowledge of the untold myth; Hazzard reproduces a version of this effect without her readers' prior knowledge by means of the hints and withholdings of her narrator. Stoppard provides another modern variation; in a sense he, too, hints and withholds, but here the aftermath is figured not as a narrator's privileged possession of future fate but as a past that partially evades the present-day characters. Our participation in constructing the aftermath for the earlier characters is thus elicited by the combined eagerness and inability of the present-day characters fully to reconstruct that past.

There is in any case no evading the awareness of the aftermath and the responsibility for constructing it. And in the aftermath of Stoppard's play, once again, as with many of our other texts, marriage or its counterpart gives way to death. Stoppard may be said to anticipate this aftermath by the typically allusive and elusive memento mori in the play's title. If we have not already picked up the allusion to death, Stoppard reminds us through Lady Croom's grandiloquent mistranslation: "In short, [Sidley Park] is nature as God intended, and I can say with the painter, 'Et in Arcadia ego!' 'Here I am in Arcadia,'"[71] In case we still miss the point, Septimus declares a few lines later, as he listens to the guns of those shooting grouse, "What a calendar of slaughter. Even in Arcady there am I!" and Thomasina replies: "Oh, phooey to Death."

The Arcadia of Stoppard's play is clearly not only Sidley Park, but the lost and longed-for past. It is also, inevitably, because of its long literary history, a type for fiction itself, or at least for happy fictions, unchanging pasts to which we can return in imagination. The aftermaths of the *Odyssey*, of Bacchylides 5, of Sappho 44, of Hazzard's novel, and of Stoppard's

[69] Stoppard's play is thus different from texts (like those mentioned in note 54 above) that in reversing chronology fully play out the aftermath.

[70] Cf. A. Barton's (1995, 32) comments on Stoppard's "reticences" in her review of Stoppard's play and its New York production in the *New York Review of Books*.

[71] Stoppard 1993, 12, I.1. On the history of the Latin phrase, especially as used in works of art, and its readings and misreadings, see Panofksy 1955.

play, then, suggest that together with the delightful prospect of love, death is inevitably a part of the landscape of our fictive Arcadias, lurking in the untold future. The repeated substitution of death for marriage seems to confirm Atwood's declaration that all other endings are fake. But Stoppard's ending, in which Thomasina and Septimus dance on, still as present to us as the present-day dancers beside them, points to a reading in which the relegation of death to the aftermath also constitutes a gesture of defiance, reminding us that life, although transient, is necessarily more vivid than death. Death is always the aftermath, but death is only the aftermath. Memento mori; phooey to Death.[72]

---

[72] This essay is based on a talk given at a symposium at Swarthmore College in honor of Helen North (to whom it is gratefully dedicated) and at New York University. My thanks to those present on both occasions, to my co-editors, and to Aryeh Kosman for helpful questions and suggestions.

Bibliography

Introductory Note

The works that inaugurated the modern study of closure are Kermode 1967 and B. H. Smith 1968: they embody the two poles around which research has oriented itself, with Kermode demonstrating the wide implications of closure for the patterning of human life, especially in fiction, and Smith discussing in detail motifs and techniques, especially in lyric poetry. The review of the latter by Hamon (1975) is particularly important for relating Smith's work to the concerns of French narratology. W. Martin 1986, 85–89, offers a brief survey of work down to the mid-1980s: collections of essays include the 1978 issue of *Nineteenth Century Fiction* (with an important introduction by J. H. Miller), the 1984 issue of *Yale French Studies*, Montandon 1984, and Söring 1990. The focus in studies of modern literature has been especially on prose narrative and drama. Important general works (mainly) on the former include Richter 1974, Torgovnick 1981, D. A. Miller 1981, Mortimer 1985, and Krieger 1989: see also Adams 1958, Friedman 1966, Kuzniar 1987, Szegedy-Maszak 1987, Thickstun 1988, Rowe 1988, Stern 1991, and Morson 1994. On drama, see especially Klotz 1969, with Jagendorf 1969, Liouve 1984, R. S. White 1985, Willson 1990, Bache 1991, Hodgdon 1991, and H. J. Schmidt 1992. Bruckner 1993 focuses on twelfth-century French romance, but has many general observations, particularly in relation to closure and gender: on this aspect, see also P. A. Parker 1979, DuPlessis 1985, MacArthur 1990 (on epistolary fiction), Winnett 1990, Grudin 1992, and Booth 1993. Doherty 1995 offers some classical perspectives on this. Work on closure in music is often relevant to literature: cf. Agawu 1987, 1991, with Clément 1988, Robinson 1988, Hopkins 1990, and Abbate 1991. On closure in relation to history and historiography, see especially the work of H. White (1973, 1978, 1987), and cf. Mink 1987 and Bernstein 1994. On film, note the collection of material in Chesher 1992. For the issues raised by developments in hypertext, see Lanham 1989, Delany and Landow 1991, and especially Landow 1992. Finally, there are obvious parallels between inauguration and closure; see, for example, Saïd 1975, Nuttall 1992 with Martindale 1993, and the 1992 issue of *Yale Classical Studies*.

For a survey of the issues in relation to classical literature, with a partial bibliography of earlier work, see D. P. Fowler 1989b, which also includes (88–97) details of work on "infratextual" closure (book divisions, etc.) that are not generally cited here: D. P. Fowler 1994 expands on some of the wider issues involved. General and comparative studies of closure in classical literature are not common, but on Greek poetry, see Kranz 1961 and Van Sickle 1984, and on Latin, Schrijvers 1973 and Gómez Pallarés 1995. Other works with significant general reflections on ancient closure as well as specific discussion include Curtius 1953, 89–91, Van Groningen 1960, D. Parker 1969, Esser 1976, Goldhill 1984a, Peden 1987, Roberts 1987 and 1988, Morgan 1989a, Henderson 1989, and Dunn 1996. A complete bibliography of works dealing with ancient endings would be immense: in some cases (such as Virgil's *Aeneid*) almost all critical treatments involve discussion of closure. The following survey arranges by genre some other recent works in which discussion of specific texts may also be of more general interest.

On **epic** (cf. Murnaghan, Fusillo, Hardie, and Barchiesi in this volume), Van Sickle 1984 discusses closing motifs from Homer to Virgil, whereas the problems of the end(s) of the *Odyssey* have been explored in various ways by Bertman 1968, Stössel 1975, Hansen 1977, Wender 1978, Peradotto 1986, Falkner 1989, West 1989, Oswald 1993, and Doherty 1995. The interplay of resolution and continuance in the *Iliad* has been explored, for example, by Davies 1981 and R. B. Rutherford 1982, whereas the ending of Apollonius's *Argonautica*, and especially its relation to the supposed *telos* or *peras* of the *Odyssey* in Book 23, has been discussed by Rossi 1968, M. Campbell 1983, and Hunter 1993, 119–29. The politics of closure have been particularly explored in relation to Latin epic: see, for example, Feeney 1991, esp. 137–49, Quint 1989 and 1993, and Hardie 1993a and 1993b. The end of the *Aeneid* is a well-worn theme—see, for example, Farron 1982, Nagle (1982–83), Feeney 1984, Salat 1984, Renger 1985, Mitchell-Boyask 1996—but politics are also central to the closure of Ovid's *Metamorphoses* (cf., e.g., Segal 1969, Little 1972, Fowler 1995b), and to much recent "New Latin" work on Lucan, especially Masters 1992, and Flavian epic, especially Henderson 1991 and 1993 on Statius's *Thebaid*. In relation to **didactic** (cf. P. G. Fowler in this volume), the critical debate generated by the end of the *Aeneid* has been recapitulated in relation to the end of the *Georgics*; see especially Habinek 1990 and Thomas 1991a. For Lucretius, note Bright 1971 and P. G. Fowler 1983; for Manilius, D. P. Fowler 1995b. On Ovid's *Fasti*, note, in addition to his piece in this volume, Barchiesi 1994.

The subject of closure has also been central to the study of **tragedy** (cf. Dunn and Roberts in this volume). Kremer 1971 offers a general survey; Goldhill 1984a (cf. 1984b) deconstructs the language of the *Oresteia* and the imagery of end or goal that pervades it; the uncertainties of Sophoclean endings are explored by Hoppin 1990 and Roberts 1988, and the especially problematic endings of Euripides by Roberts 1987, Nicolai 1990, and Dunn 1996, whereas Roberts 1992 examines the issues in relation to Aristotle's theories of the tragic plot. There are many discussions of individual plays: see, for example, on Sophocles' *Oedipus Tyrannus*, Davies 1982; on *Trachiniae*, Kraus 1991; and on Euripides' *Trojan Women*, Dunn 1993.

Work on closure in ancient **prose narrative**, the central focus of much modern theory, has been surprisingly less in evidence, in part reflecting the lack of interest until the last decades in the ancient novel and the tendency for historiography to be the preserve of historians rather than literary scholars. Interest in the **novel**, however (cf. Fusillo in this volume) is now intense, especially in relation to the self-consciously complex and metaliterary *Ethiopica* of Heliodorus, for example, Winkler 1982, Bartsch 1989, and Morgan 1989a, and the challenges of the fragmentary *Satyricon*, for example, Zeitlin 1971 with the reply by Schmeling (1991). The end of Apuleius's *Metamorphoses* is another paradigm instance of the centrality of issues of closure to interpretation: Winkler 1985 suitably problematizes the ways in which Lucius's conversion retrospectively rewrites the earlier narrative. In **historiography**, the problems of ending a historical account are mirrored by the textual problems of many extant ends, either because the author is presumed to have left the work unfinished or because we have lost it: Henderson (1989) explores the ironies here in relation to Livy (and refrains from concluding his own account even with a full stop). On Herodotus (cf. Dewald in this volume), see especially Boedeker 1988 and Herington 1991; on the self-consciously "fragmentary" ending of Sallust's *Jugurtha*, see Levene 1992; and on the endings of Plutarch's *Lives* (and especially the synkriseis) in relation to our expectations of both history and biography (cf. Pelling in this volume), see Erbse 1956b, Stadter 1975, Pelling 1986, Swain 1990, and Larmour 1992.

Discussion of closure in **lyric**, **epigram**, and **elegy** (cf. Rutherford and Johnson in this volume) often involves both the endings of individual poems and the much-vexed question of their arrangement in poetic collections. In relation to the former issue in Latin poetry, both Schrijvers 1973 on Horace and Peden 1987 on Catullus make good use of the extensive discussion of lyric in B. H. Smith 1968: see also Zetzel 1983 on Catullus, Esser 1976 and Santirocco 1984 on Horace, Grondona 1977 and Reeve 1984 on Tibullus, Lefèvre 1966 (especially 131–56) and Curran 1968 on Propertius, and D. Parker 1969 on Ovid's *Amores*. On closure in poetic collections, cf., for example, Macleod 1973, Wiseman 1985, 183–89, and Dettmer 1989 on Catullus; Woodman 1974 on Horace; and Van Sickle 1981 on Gallus: a full discussion is promised in Krevans forthcoming. The complexities of the questions are well illustrated by the many discussions of Catullus 51, for example, most recently, O'Higgins 1990, Vine 1992, and Fowler 1994: Is the last stanza transmitted in the manuscript part of the preceding poem? If so, what is its effect? Was there an equivalent stanza or stanzas in the Sapphic model? How does the poem relate to poem 50? What of the intertextuality with the opening of Horace *Odes* 2.16? There has been much less discussion of closure in Greek small-scale genres: note, however, Race 1979, 1989, and 1990 on Pindar; Cerri 1991 on Theognis; and Parsons 1977 and P. Knox 1985 on Callimachus's *Aitia*, the latter again discussed in Krevans forthcoming.

References

Abbate, A. 1991. *Unsung Voices, Opera and Musical Narrative in the Nineteenth Century*. Princeton.

Adam, L. 1889. *Die aristotelische Theorie vom Epos nach ihrer Entwicklung bei Griechen und Römern*. Wiesbaden.

Adams, R. M. 1958. *Strains of Discord: Studies in Literary Openness*. Ithaca, N.Y.

Adkins, A.W.H. 1960. *Merit and Responsibility: A Study in Greek Values*. Oxford.

Agawu, V. K. 1987. "Concepts of Closure and Chopin's Opus 28." *Music Theory Spectrum* 9:275–301.

———. 1991. *Playing with Signs: A Semiotic Interpretation of Classic Music*. Princeton.

Ahl, F. 1986. "Statius' *Thebaid*: A Reconsideration." *ANRW* 2.32.5:2803–2912.

Alcott, L. M. 1886. *Jo's Boys and How They Turned Out: A Sequel to "Little Women."* Boston.

Allen, T. W., ed. 1912. *Homeri opera V*. Oxford.

Alter, R. 1975. *Partial Magic: The Novel as Self-Conscious Genre*. Berkeley.

Alton, E. H., D.E.W. Wormell, and E. Courtney, eds. 1985. Ovid, *Fastorum libri sex*. Leipzig.

Aly, W. 1921. *Volksmärchen, Sage und Novelle bei Herodot und seinen Zeitgenossen: Eine Untersuchung über die volkstümlichen Elemente der Altgriechischen Prosaerzählung*. Göttingen. Rpr. 1969 with corrections and afterword by L. Huber.

Andronikos, M. 1968. *Totenkult*. Archeologia Homerica 3. Göttingen.

Annas, J. 1982. "Plato's Myths of Judgment." *Phronesis* 27:119–43.

Anthony, H. 1976. *Humor in der augusteischen Dichtung: Lachen und Lächeln bei Horaz, Properz, Tibull und Vergil*. Hildesheim.

Appelfeld, A. 1980a. *Badenheim 1939*. Trans. Dalya Bilu. Boston.

———. 1980b. *To the Land of the Reeds*. Trans. Jeffrey M. Green. Boston.

———. 1984. *The Retreat*. Trans. Dalya Bilu. Boston.

Appleby, J., L. Hunt, and M. Jacob. 1994. *Telling the Truth About History*. New York.

Aristotle. 1965. *Poetics*. Ed. R. Kassell. Oxford.

Arrowsmith, W. 1956. "Introduction to *Heracles*." In D. Grene and R. Lattimore, eds., *Euripides II*, 44–59. Chicago.

Assmann, J. 1975. *Ägyptische Hymnen und Gebete*. Zurich.

Atwood, M. 1983. *Murder in the Dark*. Toronto.

Ausfeld, C. 1903. *De Graecis precationibus quaestiones*. Leipzig.

Austen-Leigh, J. 1926. *Memoir of Jane Austen*. Reprint of 1871 edition, intro. and notes by R. W. Chapman. Oxford.

Austen-Leigh, J. 1993. *A Visit to Highbury: Another View of Emma*. New York.

Austen-Leigh, W., and R. A. Austen-Leigh. 1913. *Jane Austen: Her Life and Letters, A Family Record*. New York.

Austin, R. G., ed. 1977. *P. Vergili Maronis, Aeneidos liber sextus*. Oxford.

Bache, W. B. 1991. *Design and Closure in Shakespeare's Major Plays: The Nature of Recapitulation*. New York.

Bakhtin, M. M. 1981. *The Dialogic Imagination: Four Essays*. Ed. M. Holquist, trans. C. Emerson and M. Holquist. Austin.

Bandera, A. 1981. "Sacrificial Levels in Virgil's *Aeneid*." *Arethusa* 14:217–40.

Barchiesi, A. 1978. "Il lamento di Giuturna." *MD* 1:99–121.

———. 1979. "Palinuro e Caieta: Due 'epigrammi' Virgiliani (*Aen.* 5.870ff.; 7.1–4)." *Maia* 31:3–11.

———. 1989. "Voci e istanze narrative nelle *Metamorfosi* di Ovidio." *MD* 23:55–97.

———. 1994. *Il poeta e il principe*. Bari.

Barlow, S. A. 1981. "Sophocles' Ajax and Euripides' Heracles." *Ramus* 10:112–28.

Barton, A. 1995. "*Arcadia*, A Play by Tom Stoppard, Directed by Trevor Nunn; *Arcadia* by Tom Stoppard." *New York Review of Books* 42:28–32.

Bartsch, S. 1989. *Decoding the Ancient Novel: The Reader and the Role of Description in Heliodorus and Achilles Tatius*. Princeton.

Baym, N. 1983. "Artifice and Romance in Shirley Hazzard's Fiction." *TSLL* 25:222–47.

Becher, I. 1988. "Augustus und seine Religionspolitik gegenüber orientalischen Kulten." In G. Binder, ed., *Saeculum Augustum*, vol. 2: *Religion und Literatur*, 143–70. Wege der Forschung 512. Darmstadt.

Belsey, C. 1980. *Critical Practice*. London.

Benjamin, W. 1968. "The Storyteller." In *Illuminations*, trans. H. Zohn, 83–107. New York.

Bernadini, P. A. 1983. *Mito e attualità nelle odi di Pindaro*. Filologia e Critica 47. Rome.

Bernstein, M. A. 1994. *Foregone Conclusions: Against Apocalyptic History*. Berkeley.

Bertman, S. 1968. "Structural Symmetry at the End of the *Odyssey*." *GRBS* 9: 115–23.

Bethe, E. 1918. "Der Schluss der Odyssee und Apollonios von Rhodos." *Hermes* 53:444–46.

Bignone, E. 1945. *Storia della letteratura latina*. Vol. 2. Florence.

Bigsby, C. 1994. *Hester: A Novel About the Early Hester Prynne*. New York.

Bing, P. 1988. *The Well-Read Muse: Present and Past in Callimachus and the Hellenistic Poets*. Hypomnemata 90. Göttingen.

Bird, D. 1985. "Text Production and Reception—Shirley Hazzard's *The Transit of Venus*." *Westerly* 1:39–51.

Bischoff, H. 1932. "Der Warner bei Herodot." Diss., Marburg. Pages 78–83 reprinted in Marg 1982a, 681–87.

Boardman, J. 1974. *Athenian Black Figure Vases*. New York.

———. 1975. "Herakles, Peisistratos and Eleusis." *JHS* 95:1–12.

Bockemueller, F., ed. 1873. Lucretius, *De rerum natura*. Stade.

Boedeker, D., ed. 1987. *Herodotus and the Invention of History*. Arethusa 20.

———. 1988. "Protesilaos and the End of Herodotus' *Histories*." *ClAnt* 7:30–48.

Bond, G. W., ed. 1981. Euripides, *Heracles*. Oxford.

Bonner, S. F. 1966. "Lucan and the Declamation Schools." *AJPh* 87:257–89.

Booth, A. 1993. *Famous Last Words: Changes in Gender and Narrative Closure*. Charlottesville.

Bornitz, F. 1968. *Herodot-Studien: Beiträge zum Verständnis der Einheit des Geschichtswerkes*. Berlin.

Bowie, A. 1993. *Aristophanes, Myth, Ritual, and Comedy*. Cambridge.

Bowie, E. L. 1992. "Les Lecteurs du roman grec." In *Le Monde du roman grec, Actes du colloque international*, 55–62. Paris.

Bowie, M. 1987. *Freud, Proust, and Lacan*. Cambridge.

Bowra, C. M. 1944. *Sophoclean Tragedy*. Oxford.

———. 1964. *Pindar*. Oxford.

Boyle, A. J., ed. 1993. *Roman Epic*. London.

Brelich, A. 1938. "Trionfo e morte." *SMSR* 14:189–93.

Brenk, F. E. 1987. "From Rex to Rana: Plutarch's Treatment of Nero." In A. Ceresa-Gastaldo, ed., *Il protagonismo nella storiografia classica*, Pubblicazioni del Dipartimento di Archeologia, Filologia Classica e Loro Tradizioni 108, 121–42. Genoa.

———. 1992. "Plutarch's Life 'Markos Antonios': A Literary and Cultural Study." *ANRW* 2.33.6:4347–4469.

Bright, D. F. 1971. "The Plague and the Structure of the *De Rerum Natura*." *Latomus* 30:607–32.

Brioschi, F. 1983. *La mappa dell'impero: Problemi di teoria della letteratura*. Milan.

Brontë, C. 1905. *Shirley*. Edinburgh.

Brooks, P. 1984. *Reading for the Plot: Design and Intention in Narrative*. New York.

Bruckner, M. T. 1993. *Shaping Romance: Interpretation, Truth, and Closure in Twelfth-Century French Fictions*. Philadelphia.

Bundy, E. L. 1972. "The 'Quarrel Between Kallimakhos and Apollonios.' Part I: The Epilogue of Kallimachos's *Hymn to Apollo*." *CSCA* 5:39–94.

Bürger, K. 1892. "Zu Xenophon von Ephesos." *Hermes* 27:36–67.

Burkert, W. 1983. *Homo Necans: The Anthropology of Ancient Greek Sacrificial Ritual and Myth*. Trans. P. Bing. Berkeley.

Burn, A. 1984. *Persia and the Greeks*. Stanford.

Burnett, A. P. 1971. *Catastrophe Survived: Euripides' Plays of Mixed Reversal*. Oxford.

———. 1983. *Three Archaic Poets: Archilochus, Alcaeus, Sappho*. Cambridge, Mass.

———. 1985. *The Art of Bacchylides*. Cambridge, Mass.

Cairns, F. 1972. *Generic Composition in Greek and Roman Poetry*. Edinburgh.

———. 1989. *Virgil's Augustan Epic*. Cambridge.

———. 1984. "Propertius and the Battle of Actium." In A. J. Woodman and D. A. West, eds., *Poetry and Politics in the Age of Augustus*, 129–68. Cambridge.

Calasso, R. 1993. *The Marriage of Cadmus and Harmony*. Trans. T. Parks. London.

Calderini, A. 1912. *Prolegomeni a Le avventure di Cherea e Calliroe*. Turin.

Cameron, A., ed. 1989. *History as Text: The Writing of Ancient History*. London.

Campbell, D. A. 1967. *Greek Lyric Poetry*. London.

Campbell, M. 1983. "Apollonian and Homeric Book Division." *Mnemosyne* 36: 154–55.

Carcopino, J. 1958. *Passion et politique chez les Césars*. Paris.

Carey, C. 1989. "Two Transitions in Pindar." *CQ* 39:287–95.

Carspecken, J. F. 1952. "Apollonius Rhodius and the Homeric Epic." *YClS* 13:33–143.

Cave, T. 1988. *Recognitions: A Study in Poetics*. Oxford.

Ceccarelli, P. Forthcoming. "La Fable des poissons de Cyrus (Hdt. 1,141): Son origine et sa fonction dans l'économie des *Histoires* d'Hérodote." *Metis*.

Cerri, G. 1991. "Il significato di <sphregis> in Theognide e la salvaguardia dell' autenticità nel mondo antico." *QS* 33:21–40.

Chalk, H.H.O. 1962. "ἀρετή and βία in Euripides' *Herakles*." *JHS* 82:7–18.

Chesher, R. D. 1992. *"The End": Closing Lines of over 3,000 Theatrically Released American Films*. London.

Citroni, M. 1986. "Le raccomandazioni al lettore: Apostrofe al libro e contatti con il destinatario." *Maia* 38:111–46.

Cixous, H. 1986. "Sorties." In H. Cixous and C. Clément, *The Newly Born Woman*, trans. B. Wing, 63–132. Manchester.

———. 1991. *Coming to Writing and Other Essays*. Cambridge, Mass. and London.

Clark, M., and E. Csapo. 1991. "Deconstruction, Ideology, and Goldhill's *Oresteia*." *Phoenix* 45:95–125.

Clay, D. 1969. "De rerum natura: Greek Physis and Epicurean Physiologia." *TAPhA* 100:31–47.

———. 1983. *Lucretius and Epicurus*. London.

Clay, J. 1986. "Archilochus and Gyges: An Interpretation of fr. 23 West." *QUCC* 53:7–17.

Clément, C. 1988. *Opera, or the Undoing of Women*. Minneapolis.

Cobet, J. 1971. *Herodots Exkurse und die Frage der Einheit seines Werkes.* Wiesbaden.

———. 1988. "Herodot und mündliche Überlieferung." In J. von Ungern-Sternberg and H. Reinau, eds., *Vergangenheit in mündlicher Überlieferung,* Colloquium Rauricum 1, 226–33. Stuttgart.

Cole, T. 1990. *Democritus and the Sources of Greek Anthropology.* 2d ed. Atlanta.

Colegate, I. 1980. *The Shooting Party.* London.

Commager, H. S. 1957. "Lucretius' Interpretation of the Plague." *HSCPh* 62: 105–18.

Conacher, D. J. 1967. *Euripidean Drama: Myth, Theme and Structure.* Toronto.

Conte, G. B. 1986. *The Rhetoric of Imitation: Genre and Poetic Memory, Virgil and Other Latin Poets.* Ithaca, N.Y.

———. 1992. "Proems in the Middle." In F. Dunn and T. Cole, eds., *Beginnings in Classical Literature,* 147–59. *YClS* 29. Cambridge.

———. 1994. "Instructions for a Sublime Reader: Form of the Text and Form of the Addressee in Lucretius' *De rerum natura.*" In G. B. Conte, *Genres and Readers,* trans. G. W. Most, 1–34. Baltimore.

Cotterill, R. 1988. "Sunt aliquid manes: Personalities, Personae and Ghosts in Augustan Poetry." In A. Benjamin, ed., *Post-Structuralist Classics,* 227–44. London.

Couégnas, D. 1992. *Introduction à la paralittérature.* Paris.

Crabbe, A. 1981. "Structure and Content in Ovid's *Metamorphoses.*" *ANRW* 2.31.4:2274–2327.

Cresci, L. 1978. "La figura di Melite in Achille Tazio." *A&R* 23:74–82.

Crump, M. M. 1931. *The Epyllion from Theocritus to Ovid.* Oxford.

Cupitt, D. 1991. *What Is a Story?* London.

Curran, L. 1968. "Propertius 4.11: Greek Heroines and Death." *CPh* 63:134–39.

Currie, H. M. 1993. "Closure/Transition and the nox erat Topos: Some Notes." *LCM* 18, 6:92–95.

Curtius, E. 1953. *European Literature and the Latin Middle Ages.* Trans. W. R. Trask. New York.

Dällenbach, L. 1989. *The Mirror in the Text.* Trans. J. Whiteley and E. Hughes. Cambridge.

Darbo-Peschanski, C. 1985. "Les 'Logoi' des autres dans les 'Histoires' d'Hérodote." *QS* 22:105–28.

———. 1987. *Le Discours du particulier: Essai sur l'enquête hérodotéenne.* Paris.

Davies, J. K. 1978. *Democracy and Classical Greece.* Stanford.

Davies, M. 1981. "The Judgement of Paris and *Iliad* 24." *JHS* 101:56–62.

———. 1982. "The End of Sophocles O.T." *Hermes* 110:268–77.

———, ed. 1988. *Epicorum graecorum fragmenta.* Göttingen.

———. 1990. "Popular Justice and the End of Aristophanes' Clouds." *Hermes* 118:237–42.

Day Lewis, C., trans. 1966. *The Eclogues, Georgics, and Aeneid of Vergil.* Oxford.

Delany, P., and G. P. Landow, eds. 1991. *Hypermedia and Literary Studies.* Cambridge, Mass.

Dettmer, H. R. 1989. "Closure in the Lesbia Polymetra 1–13." *CW* 82:375–77.

Dewald, C. 1981. "Women and Culture in Herodotus' Histories." In H. P. Foley, ed., *Reflections of Women in Antiquity,* 91–125. New York.

———. 1993. "Reading the World: The Interpretation of Objects in Herodotus'

Histories." In R. Rosen and J. Farrell, eds., *Nomodeiktes: Festschrift for Martin Ostwald*, 55–70. Ann Arbor.

Dickens, C. 1986. *The Pickwick Papers.* Ed. J. Kinsley. Oxford.

Diggle, J., ed. 1981. Euripides, *Fabulae.* Vol. 2. Oxford.

Dihle, A. 1987. *Die Entstehung der historischen Biographie.* SHAW 1986.3. Heidelberg.

Dingel, J. 1967. "Das Requisit in der griechischen Tragödie." Diss., Tübingen.

Doherty, L. E. 1995. *Siren Songs: Gender, Audiences, and Narrators in the Odyssey.* Ann Arbor.

Due, O. S. 1974. *Changing Forms: Studies in the Metamorphoses of Ovid.* Copenhagen.

Dunn, F. M. 1993. "Beginning at the End in Euripides' *Trojan Women.*" *RhM* 136:22–36.

———. 1996. *Tragedy's End: Closure and Innovation in Euripidean Drama.* Oxford.

DuPlessis, R. Blau. 1985. *Writing Beyond the Ending: Narrative Strategies in Twentieth-Century Women Writers.* Bloomington, Ind.

Durham, B. 1938. "Parody in Achilles Tatius." *CPh* 33:1–19.

Easterling, P. 1981. "The End of the *Trachiniae.*" *ICS* 6:56–74.

———, ed. 1982. Sophocles, *Trachiniae,* Cambridge.

———. 1987. "Putting Together the Pieces: A Passage in the *Bacchae.*" *Omnibus* 14:14–16.

Eco, U. 1979. *Lector in fabula: La cooperazione interpretativa nei testi narrativi.* Milan.

Effe, B. 1975. "Entstehung und Funktion 'personaler' Erzählweisen in der Erzählliteratur der Antike." *Poetica* 7:135–57.

———. 1982. "Longos: Zur Funktiongeschichte der Bukolik in der römischen Kaiserzeit." *Hermes* 110:65–84.

———. 1987. "Der griechische Liebesroman und die Homoerotik: Ursprung und Entwicklung einer epischen Konvention." *Philologus* 131:95–108.

Eisenstein, E. L. 1979. *The Printing Press as an Agent of Change.* Cambridge.

———. 1983. *The Printing Revolution in Early Modern Europe.* Cambridge.

Eliot, G. 1986. *Middlemarch.* Ed. D. Carroll. Oxford.

Elsner, J. 1991. "Cult and Sculpture: Sacrifice in the Ara Pacis." *JRS* 81:50–61.

Erbse, H. 1956a. "Der erste Satz im Werke Herodots." In H. Erbse, ed., *Festschrift Bruno Snell,* 209–22. Munich.

———. 1956b. "Die Bedeutung der Synkrisis in den Parallelbiographien Plutarchs." *Hermes* 84:378–424.

———, ed. 1969. *Scholia graeca in Homeri Iliadem.* Vol. 1. Berlin.

Esser, D. 1976. *Untersuchungen zu den Odenschlüssen bei Horaz.* Beiträge zur klassischen Philologie 77. Meisenheim am Glan.

Evans, J.A.S. 1965. "Despotes Nomos." *Athenaeum,* ser. 2, 43:142–53.

———. 1980. "Oral Tradition in Herodotus." *Canadian Journal of Oral History* 4/2:8.

———. 1991. *Herodotus, Explorer of the Past: Three Essays.* Princeton.

Fagles, R., trans. 1990. Homer, *The Iliad.* New York.

Falkner, T. 1989. "Ἐπὶ γήραος οὐδῷ: Homeric Heroism, Old Age and the End of the *Odyssey.*" In T. M. Falkner and J. de Luce, eds., *Old Age in Greek and Latin Literature,* 21–67. Albany.

Fantham, R. E. 1986. "Ovid, Germanicus and the Composition of the *Fasti.*" *PLLS* 5:243–81.

Farron, S. 1982. "The Abruptness of the End of the *Aeneid*." *AC* 25:136–41.

Faulkner, W. 1929. *The Sound and the Fury*. New York.

———. 1936. *Absalom, Absalom!* New York.

Feeney, D. C. 1984. "The Reconciliations of Juno." *CQ* 34:179–94.

———. 1991. *The Gods in Epic: Poets and Critics of the Classical Tradition*. Oxford.

———. 1992. "*Si licet et fas est*: Ovid's *Fasti* and the Problem of Free Speech Under the Principate." In A. Powell, ed., *Roman Poetry and Propaganda in the Age of Augustus*, 1–25. London.

Ferrarino, P. 1986. "La Peste nell' Attica." In *Scritti Scelti*, Opuscoli Accademici 15, 362–81. Florence.

Feuillatre, E. 1966. *Études sur les Éthiopiques d'Héliodore*. Paris.

Finley, M. I. 1985. *Ancient History: Evidence and Models*. Harmondsworth.

Flower, M. A. and Toher, M., eds. 1991. *Georgica: Greek Studies in Honour of George Cawkwell*. *BICS* suppl. 58. London.

Focke, F. 1927. *Herodot als Historiker*. Tübinger Beiträge zur Altertumswissenschaft 1. Stuttgart.

Foley, H. P. 1985. *Ritual Irony: Poetry and Sacrifice in Euripides*. Ithaca, N.Y.

Fornara, C. 1971. *Herodotus: An Interpretive Essay*. Oxford.

———. 1983. *The Nature of History in Ancient Greece and Rome*. Berkeley.

Foulkes, A. P. 1983. *Literature and Propaganda*. London.

Fowler, D. P. 1989a. "Lucretius and Politics." In Griffin and Barnes 1989, 120–50.

———. 1989b. "First Thoughts on Closure: Problems and Prospects." *MD* 22: 75–122.

———. 1990. "Brief Reviews: Roman Literature." *G&R* 37:235–42.

———. 1991. "Narrate and Describe: The Problem of Ekphrasis." *JHS* 81:25–35.

———. 1993. "Response" to Hardie 1993b. In Molyneux 1993, 73–76.

———. 1994. "Postmodernism, Romantic Irony, and Classical Closure." In I.J.F. de Jong and J. P. Sullivan, *Modern Critical Theory and Classical Literature*, 231–56. Leiden.

———. 1995a. "Horace and the Aesthetics of Politics." In S. J. Harrison, ed., *Homage to Horace: A Bimillenary Celebration*, 248–66. Oxford.

———. 1995b. "From Epos to Cosmos: Lucretius, Ovid, and the Poetics of Segmentation." In D. C. Innes, H. Hine, and C. Pelling, eds., *Ethics and Rhetoric, Essays for Donald Russell on His 75th Birthday*. Oxford.

———. 1996. "Even Better Than the Real Thing: A Tale of Two Cities." In J. Elsner, ed., *Art and Text in Roman Culture* 57–74. Cambridge.

———. Forthcoming a. "Laocoon's Point of View." In T. Habinek and A. Schiesaro, eds., *The Roman Cultural Revolution*. Cambridge.

———. Forthcoming b. "The Feminine Principal: Gender in the *De rerum natura*." In *Proceedings of the 1993 Conference "Epicureismo greco e latino*." Naples.

Fowler, P. G. 1983. "A Commentary on Part of Book Six of Lucretius *De rerum natura*." Diss., Oxford.

Fowles, J. 1969. *The French Lieutenant's Woman*. Boston.

Fränkel, H. 1968. *Noten zu den Argonautika des Apollonios*. Munich.

———. 1982. "Verknüpfung." In Marg 1982a, 737–47 (= H. Fränkel, *Wege und Formen frühgriechischen Denkens*, 65–67, 83–88 [Munich, 1960; originally published 1924]).

Friedländer, P. 1912. *Johannes von Gaza und Paulus Silentiarius: Kunstbeschreibung justinianischer Zeit.* Leipzig.

———. 1969. "Pattern of Sound and Atomic Theory in Lucretius." In *Studien zur antiken Literatur und Kunst,* 337–53. Berlin.

Friedman, A. 1966. *The Turn of the Novel.* New York.

Friedman, N. 1955. "Point of View in Fiction: The Development of a Critical Concept." *PMLA* 70. Reprinted in P. Stevick, ed., *The Theory of the Novel,* 108–37. New York.

Führer, R. 1967. *Formproblem Untersuchungen zu den Reden in der Frühgriechischen Lyrik* (Zetema 44). Munich.

Fusillo, M. 1985. *Il tempo delle Argonautiche: Un'analisi del racconto in Apollonio Rodio.* Rome.

———. 1989. *Il romanzo greco: Polifonia ed eros.* Venice.

———. 1991. *Naissance du roman.* Paris.

Gale, M. R. 1991. "Man and Beast in Lucretius and the *Georgics.*" *CQ* 41:414–26.

Galinsky, G. K. 1967. "The Cipus Episode in Ovid's *Metamorphoses* (15.565–621)." *TAPhA* 98:181–91.

———. 1968. "*Aeneid* V and the *Aeneid.*" *AJPh* 89:157–85.

———. 1975. *Ovid's Metamorphoses: An Introduction to the Basic Aspects.* Berkeley.

———. 1992. "Venus, Polysemy, and the Ara Pacis Augustae." *AJA* 96:457–75.

Galletier, Edouard. 1922. *Étude sur la poésie funéraire romaine d'après les inscriptions.* Paris.

Gallop, J. 1982. *Feminism and Psychoanalysis: The Daughter's Seduction.* London.

Gantz, T. 1993. *Early Greek Myth.* Baltimore.

García Gual, C. 1970. *Los origines de la novela.* Madrid.

Gardner, J. 1971. *Grendel.* New York.

Garner, R. 1990. *From Homer to Tragedy: The Art of Allusion in Greek Poetry.* London.

Garson, R. W. 1978. "Works of Art in Achilles Tatius' *Leucippe and Clitophon.*" *AClass* 21:83–86.

Genette, G. 1980. *Narrative Discourse.* Ithaca, N.Y. (Trans. J. E. Lewin from "Discours du récit," *Figures III,* Paris, 1972.)

———. 1983. *Nouveau discours du récit.* Paris.

———. 1987. *Seuils.* Paris.

Gerschmann, K. H. 1975. "Charitoninterpretationen." Diss., Münster.

Giannotti, G. F. 1969. *"Romanzo" e ideologia: Studi sulle Metamorfosi di Apuleio.* Naples.

Girard, R. 1977. *Violence and the Sacred.* Trans. P. Gregory. Baltimore.

Giraudoux, J. 1935. *La Guerre de Troie n'aura pas lieu.* Paris.

Glaser, K. 1935. "Das Schlusswort des Herodot." *Commentationes Vindobonenses* 1:12–20.

Goldhill, S. 1983. "Narrative Structure in Bacchylides 5." *Eranos* 81:65–81.

———. 1984a. *Language, Sexuality, Narrative: The Oresteia.* Cambridge.

———. 1984b. "Two Notes on τέλος and Related Words in the *Oresteia.*" *JHS* 104:169–76.

———. 1986. *Reading Greek Tragedy.* Cambridge.

———. 1987. "The Great Dionysia and Civic Ideology." *JHS* 107:58–76.

———. 1989. "Reading Performance Criticism." *G&R* 36:172–82.

———. 1991. *The Poet's Voice: Essays in Poetics and Greek Literature.* Cambridge.

Gómez Pallarés, J. 1995. *Per una poètica de l'oxímoron: Inicis i finals o el concepte d'unitat en poesia latina.* Barcelona.

Gomez Santamaria, I. 1991. "Sobre el deseo de larga vida al princeps." In A. Ramos Guerreira, ed., *Mnemosynum C. Codoner a discipulis oblatum,* 99–115. Salamanca.

Goold, G. P., trans. 1977. Manilius, *Astronomica.* Cambridge, Mass.

Gordon, A. E. 1932. "On the Origin of Diana." *TAPhA* 63:177–91.

Gossman, L. 1990. *Between History and Literature.* Cambridge, Mass.

Gould, J. 1973. "Hiketeia." *JHS* 93:74–103.

———. 1989. *Herodotus.* London.

Grade, C. 1982. *Rabbis and Wives.* Trans. H. Rabinowitz and I. H. Grade. New York.

Gregory, J. 1977. "Euripides' *Heracles.*" *YClS* 25:259–75.

———. 1991. *Euripides and the Instruction of the Athenians.* Ann Arbor.

Griffin, J. 1980. *Homer on Life and Death.* Oxford.

———. 1987. *The Odyssey.* Cambridge.

Griffin, M., and J. Barnes, eds. 1989. *Philosophia Togata: Essays on Philosophy and Roman Society.* Oxford.

Griffiths, A. H. 1970. "Six Passages in Callimachus and the Anthology." *BICS* 17:32–43.

Grimal, P. 1952. "Les Intentions de Properce et la composition du livre IVe des 'Élégies.'" *Latomus* 11:437–50.

Grondona, M. 1977. "Gli epigrammi di Tibullo e il congedo delle elegie (su Properzio e Tibullo)." *Latomus* 36:3–29.

Grudin, M. 1992. "Discourse and the Problem of Closure in the Canterbury Tales." *PMLA* 107:1157–67.

Habinek, T. 1990. "Sacrifice, Society, and Virgil's Ox-Born Bees." In M. Griffith and D. J. Mastronarde, eds., *Cabinet of the Muses,* 209–23. Atlanta.

Hadas, M. 1932. "Apollonius Called the Rhodian." *CW* 26:41–46 and 49–54.

Hägg, T. 1966. "Die Ephesiaka des Xenophon von Ephesos: Original oder Epitome?" *C&M* 27:118–61.

———. 1971. *Narrative Technique in Ancient Greek Romances: Studies of Chariton, Xenophon of Ephesus, Achilles Tatius.* Stockholm.

———. 1987. "Callirhoe and Parthenope: The Beginnings of the Historical Novel." *ClAnt* 6:184–204.

Haight, E. 1943. *Essays on the Greek Romances.* New York.

Haire-Sargeant, L. 1992. *Heathcliff: The Return to Wuthering Heights.* New York.

Halleran, M. R. 1986. "Rhetoric, Irony, and the Ending of Euripides' *Herakles.*" *ClAnt* 5:171–81.

Hallett, J. P. 1977. "Perusinae Glandes and the Changing Image of Augustus." *AJAH* 2:151–92.

———. 1984. *Fathers and Daughters in Roman Society: Women and the Elite Family.* Princeton.

———. 1985. "Propertius' Cornelia-Elegy and the *Res Gestae* of Augustus." In R. Winkes, ed., *The Age of Augustus,* Archaeologia Transatlantica 5, 74–88. Providence, R.I.

Hamilton, R. 1974. *Epinikion: General Form in the Odes of Pindar*. The Hague.

———. 1985. "Slings and Arrows: The Debate with Lycus in the *Heracles*." *TAPhA* 115:19–25.

Hamon, P. 1975. "Clausules." *Poétique* 6:495–526.

Hansen, W. F. 1977. "Odysseus' Last Journey." *QUCC* 24:27–48.

Hardie, P. R. 1986. *Virgil's "Aeneid": Cosmos and Imperium*. Oxford.

———. 1990. "Ovid's Theban History: The First 'Anti-*Aeneid*'?" *CQ* 40:224–35.

———. 1991. "The *Aeneid* and the *Oresteia*." *PVS* 20:29–45.

———. 1992. "Augustan Poets and the Mutability of Rome." In Powell 1992, 59–82.

———. 1993a. "After Rome II: Renaissance Epic." In Boyle 1993, 294–313.

———. 1993b. "*Ut pictura poesis?* Horace and the Visual Arts." In Rudd 1993, 120–39.

———. 1993c. *The Epic Successors of Virgil*. Cambridge.

———. 1993d. "Tales of Unity and Division in Imperial Latin Epic." In Molyneux 1993, 57–71.

———. Forthcoming. "Questions of Authority: The Invention of Tradition in Ovid *Metamorphoses* 15." In T. Habinek and A. Schiesaro, eds., *The Roman Cultural Revolution*. Cambridge.

Harrison, S. J. 1990. "The Speaking Book: The Prologue to Apuleius' *Metamorphoses*." *CQ* 40:507–13.

———, ed. 1991. Vergil, *Aeneid 10*. Oxford.

Hart, F. R. 1978. "Scott's Endings and the Fictions of Authority." *Nineteenth Century Fiction* 33:48–68.

Hartog, F. 1988. *The Mirror of Herodotus*. Trans. J. Lloyd. Berkley.

Haupt, M., O. Korn, R. Ehwald, and M. von Albrecht, eds. 1966. Ovid, *Metamorphoses*. 2 vols. Zurich.

Hazzard, S. 1980. *The Transit of Venus*. New York.

Heath, M. 1988. "Receiving the κῶμος." *AJPh* 109:180–95.

Hefti, V. 1958. *Studien zur Erzählungstechnik des Heliodorus*. Vienna.

Heine, R. 1978. "Picaresque Novel Versus Allegory." In B. L. Hijmans Jr. and R. Th. van der Pardt, eds., *Aspects of Apuleius' Golden Ass*, 25–42. Groningen.

Henderson, J. 1989. "Livy and the Invention of History." In Cameron 1989, 64–85.

———. 1991. "Statius' *Thebaid* / Form Premade." *PCPhS*, n.s. 37:30–79.

———. 1993. "Form remade / Statius' *Thebaid*." In Boyle 1993, 162–91.

Herington, J. 1991. "The Closure of Herodotus' *Histories*." *ICS* 16:149–60.

Hershkowitz, D. 1991. "The *Aeneid* in *Aeneid* 3." *Vergilius* 37:69–76.

———. 1994. "Sexuality and Madness in Statius' *Thebaid*." *MD* 33:123–47.

Herter, H. 1944/55. "Bericht über die Literatur zur hellenistischen Dichtung seit dem Jahre 1921. II Teil: Apollonios von Rhodos." *Bursians Jahresber.* 285:213–410.

———. 1973. "Kallimachos." *RE* suppl. 13:184–266.

Heubeck, A., S. West, and J. B. Hainsworth. 1988–92. *A Commentary on Homer's Odyssey*. Vols. 1–3. Oxford.

Heuzé, P. 1985. *L'Image du corps dans l'oeuvre de Virgile*. Paris.

Hinds, S. 1985. "Booking the Return Trip: Ovid and *Tristia* I." *PCPhS*, n.s. 31:13–32.

———. 1987a. *The Metamorphosis of Persephone: Ovid and the Self-Conscious Muse.* Cambridge.

———. 1987b. "Generalising about Ovid." *Ramus* 16:4–31.

———. 1992. "*Arma* in Ovid's *Fasti.*" *Arethusa* 25:81–153.

Hine, H. M. 1981. *An Edition with Commentary of Seneca "Natural Questions" Book Two.* New York.

Hodgdon, B. 1991. *The End Crowns All: Closure and Contradiction in Shakespeare's History.* Princeton.

Hofmann, H. 1986. "Ovid's *Metamorphoses*: *Carmen perpetuum, carmen deductum.*" *PLLS* 5:223–41.

Hollander, J. 1981. *The Figure of Echo: A Model of Allusion in Milton and After.* Berkeley.

Holleman, A.W.J. 1988. "Zum Konflikt zwischen Ovid und Augustus." In G. Binder, ed., *Saeculum Augustum II*, 378–93. Darmstadt.

Hollis, A. S. 1986. "The Composition of Callimachus' *Aetia* in the Light of P.Oxy. 2258." *CQ*, n.s. 36:467–71.

Hopkins, R. G. 1990. *Closure and Mahler's Music: The Role of Secondary Parameters.* Philadelphia.

Hopkinson, N., ed. 1988. *A Hellenistic Anthology.* Cambridge.

Hoppin, M. C. 1990. "Metrical Effects, Dramatic Illusion, and the Two Endings of Sophocles' *Philoctetes.*" *Arethusa* 23:141–82.

Hornblower, S. 1987. *Thucydides.* London.

———. 1991. *A Commentary on Thucydides.* Vol. 1. Oxford.

How, W. W., and J. Wells. 1928. *A Commentary on Herodotus.* Vol. 2. Oxford.

Hubbard, M. 1975. *Propertius.* New York.

Hubbard, T. K. 1986. "Pegasus' Bridle and the Poetics of Pindar's *Thirteenth Olympian.*" *HSCPh* 90:27–48.

Hult, D. F., ed. 1984. *Concepts of Closure.* YFS 67. New Haven, Conn.

Humphreys, S. 1987. "Law, Custom and Culture in Herodotus." In Boedeker 1987, 211–20.

Hunter, R. L. 1983. *A Study of Daphnis and Chloe.* Cambridge.

———. 1988. "'Short on Heroics': Jason in the *Argonautica.*" *CQ* 38:436–53.

———. 1993. *The Argonautica of Apollonius: Literary Studies.* Cambridge.

Hurst, A. 1967. *Apollon de Rhodes, manière et cohérence: Contribution à l'étude de l'esthétique alexandrine.* Rome.

Immerwahr, H. R. 1954. "Historical Action in Herodotus." *TAPhA* 85:14–45.

———. 1966. *Form and Thought in Herodotus.* Cleveland.

Iser, W. 1978. *The Act of Reading: A Theory of Aesthetic Response.* Baltimore.

———. 1989. *Prospecting: From Reader Response to Literary Anthropology.* Baltimore.

Jacoby, F. 1913. "Herodotos." *RE* suppl., 2:205–520. Stuttgart. Reprinted in *Griechische Historiker* (Stuttgart, 1956).

Jagendorf, Z. 1969. *The Happy End of Comedy.* Newark, N.J.

James, H. 1934. "Preface to *Roderick Hudson.*" In R. P. Blackmur, ed., *The Art of the Novel: Critical Prefaces by Henry James*, 3–19. New York.

———. 1948. "The Art of Fiction." In M. Roberts, ed., *The Art of Fiction and Other Essays by Henry James*, 3–23. New York.

Jauss, H. R. 1982. *Ästhetische Erfahrung und literarische Hermeneutik.* Frankfurt.

Jebb, R. C., ed. 1907. *Sophocles, The Plays and Fragments, Part VII. Ajax.* Cambridge.

Jocelyn, H. D. 1986. "Propertius and Archaic Latin Poetry." In G. Cantanzaro and F. Santucci, eds., *Bimillenario della morte di Properzio, Atti del convegno internazionale di studi properziani*, 105–36. Assisi.

Johnson, W. R. 1973. "Propertius and the Emotions of Patriotism." *CSCA* 24: 151–80.

Jones, C. P. 1971. *Plutarch and Rome.* Oxford.

Junghanns, P. 1932. *Die Erzählungstechnik von Apuleius' Metamorphosen und ihrer Vorlage.* Leipzig.

Kakridis, J. T. 1961. *Der Thukydideische Epitaphios: Ein stilistischer Kommentar.* Munich.

———. 1966. "Zu Sappho 44 LP." *WS* 79:21–26.

Kallendorf, C. 1989. *In Praise of Aeneas: Virgil and Epideictic Rhetoric in the Early Italian Renaissance.* Hanover, N.H.

Kamerbeek, J. C. 1966. "Unity and Meaning of Euripides' *Heracles*." *Mnemosyne* 19:1–16.

Kauffman, L. S. 1986. *Discourses of Desire: Gender, Genre and Epistolary Fictions.* Ithaca, N.Y. and London.

Kennedy, D. F. 1991. Review of Cameron 1989. *JRS* 81:176–77.

———. 1992. "'Augustan' and 'Anti-Augustan': Reflections on Terms of Reference." In A. Powell, ed., *Roman Poetry and Propaganda in the Age of Augustus*, 26–58. London.

Kenney, E. J., ed. 1971. Lucretius, *De rerum natura, Book III.* Cambridge.

———. 1977. *Lucretius. Greece & Rome* New Surveys in the Classics 11. Oxford.

———. 1986. "Introduction" and "Notes." In A. D. Melville, trans., *Ovid, Metamorphoses*, xiii–xxix and 381–466. Oxford.

Kermode, F. 1967. *The Sense of an Ending: Studies in the Theory of Fiction.* Oxford.

Kinney, C. R. 1992. *Strategies of Poetic Narrative.* Cambridge.

Kirk, G. S. 1972. "Greek Mythology: Some New Perspectives." *JHS* 92:74–85.

Kleingünther, A. 1933. *Protos Heuretes: Untersuchungen zur Geschichte einer Fragestellung.* Leipzig. Reprinted 1976.

Klingner, F. 1964. "Philosophie und Dichtkunst am Ende des zweitens Buches des Lukrez." In *Studien zur griechischen und römischen Literatur*, 126–55. Zurich.

Klotz, V. 1969. *Geschlossene und offene Form im Drama.* Munich.

Knox, B.M.W. 1964. *The Heroic Temper: Studies in Sophoclean Tragedy.* Berkeley.

———. 1979. *Word and Action: Essays on the Ancient Theater.* Baltimore.

Knox, P. 1985. "The Epilogue to the *Aetia*." *GRBS* 26:59–65.

———. 1986. *Ovid's* Metamorphoses *and the Tradition of Augustan Poetry. PCPhS*, suppl. 11. Cambridge.

Kock, T. 1884. *Comicorum Atticorum fragmenta.* Vol. 2. Leipzig.

Koestermann, E. 1963. *Cornelius Tacitus: Annalen.* Heidelberg.

Köhnken, A. 1971. *Die Funktion des Mythos bei Pindar: Interpretationen zu 6 Pindargedichten.* Berlin.

Konstan, D. 1987. "Persians, Greeks and Empire." In Boedeker 1987, 59–73.

———. 1994. *Sexual Symmetry: Love in the Ancient Novel and Related Genres.* Princeton.

Kortekaas, G.A.A. 1984. *Historia Apollonii regis Tyrii: Prolegomena, Text, Edition of the Two Principal Latin Recensions, Bibliography, Indices and Appendices.* Groningen.

Kranz, W. 1961. "Sphragis. Ichform und Namensiegel als Eingangs- und Schlussmotiv antiker Dichtung." *RhM* 104:3–46, 97–124.

Kraus, C. 1991. "λόγος μέν ἐστ' ἀρχαῖος: Stories and Story-Telling in Sophocles' *Trachiniae.*" *TAPhA* 121:75–98.

Kremer, G. 1971. "Die Struktur des Tragödienschlusses." In W. Jens, ed., *Die Bauformen der griechischen Tragödie,* 117–41. Munich.

Krevans, N. Forthcoming. *The Poetic Book in Antiquity.*

Krieger, M. 1989. *A Reopening of Closure, Organicism Against Itself.* New York.

Krischer, T. 1965. "Pindars Rhapsodengedicht (zu Nem. 2)." *WS* 78:32–39.

———. 1974. "Herodotus' Schlusskapitel, seine Topik und seine Quellen." *Eranos* 72:93–100.

Krummen, E. 1990. *Pyrsos Hymnon: Festische Gegenwart und mythisch-rituelle Tradition als Voraussetzung einer Pindarinterpretation (Isthmie 4, Pythie 5, Olympie 1 und 3).* Berlin.

Kullmann, W. 1955. "Ein vorhomerisches Motiv im Iliasproömium." *Philologus* 99:167–92.

———. 1956. "Zur Διὸς βουλή des Iliasproömiums." *Philologus* 100:132–33.

Kurke, L. 1991. *The Traffic of Praise: Pindar and the Poetry of Social Economy.* Ithaca, N.Y.

Kurtz, D. C., and J. Boardman. 1971. *Greek Burial Customs.* London.

Kuzniar, A. 1987. *Delayed Endings, Nonclosure in Novalis and Hölderlin.* Athens, Ga.

Lafaye, G. 1904. *Les métamorphoses d'Ovide et leurs modèles grecs.* Paris.

Laird, A. 1993. "Fiction, Bewitchment and Story Worlds: The Implications of Claims to Truth in Apuleius." In C. Gill and T. P. Wiseman, eds., *Lies and Fiction in the Ancient World,* 147–74. Austin, Tex.

Lamont, C. 1991. "*Waverley* and the Battle of Culloden." In A. Easson, ed., *History and the Novel, Essays and Studies,* The English Association, 14–26. Cambridge.

Landow, G. P. 1992. *Hypertext, The Convergence of Contemporary Critical Theory and Technology.* Baltimore and London.

Lang, M. 1984. *Herodotean Narrative and Discourse.* Cambridge, Mass. and London.

Lanham, R. 1989. "The Electronic Word: Literary Study and the Digital Revolution." *New Literary History* 20:275–90.

La Penna, A. 1977. *L'integrazione difficile: Un profilo di Properzio.* Turin.

———. 1985. "*Ille ego qui quondam* e i raccordi editoriali nell'antichità." *SIFC* 78:76–91.

———. 1988. "Brevi considerazioni sulla divinizzazione degli eroi e sul canone degli eroi divinizzati." In D. Porte and J.-P. Neraudeau, eds., *Hommages à Henri Le Bonniec: Res Sacrae,* Collection *Latomus* 201, 275–87. Brussels.

Larmour, D.H.J. 1988. "Plutarch's Compositional Methods in the *Theseus and Romulus.*" *TAPhA* 118:361–75.

———. 1992. "Making Parallels: *Synkrisis* and Plutarch's 'Theseus' and 'Romulus'." *ANRW* 2.33.6:4154–4200.

Lateiner, D. 1989. *The Historical Method of Herodotus.* Toronto.

Latte, K. 1956. "Die Anfänge der griechischen Geschichtsschreibung." In *Histoire et historiens dans l'Antiquité,* Entretiens Hardt sur l'antiquité classique 4, 3–37. Geneva.

Lausberg, H. 1960. *Handbuch der literarischen Rhetorik.* 2 vols. Munich.

Lawall, G. 1966. "Apollonius' *Argonautica*: Jason as Anti-Hero." *YClS* 19:119–69.

Leavitt, D. 1989. *Equal Affections.* New York.

Lefèvre, E. 1966. *Propertius Ludibundus.* Heidelberg.

Lefkowitz, M. 1969. "Bacchylides' Ode 5: Imitation and Originality." *HSCPh* 73:45–96.

Legrand, Ph.-E. 1968. *Hérodote, Histoires: Livre IX, Calliope.* Paris.

Leon, E. F. 1951. "Scribonia and Her Daughters." *TAPhA* 82:168–75.

Lesser, W. 1993. *Pictures at an Execution: An Inquiry into the Subject of Murder.* Cambridge, Mass.

Levene, D. S. 1992. "Sallust's *Jugurtha*: An Historical Fragment." *JRS* 82:53–70.

Levin, D. N. 1977. "To Whom Did the Ancient Novelists Address Themselves." *RSC* 25:18–29.

————. 1978. "The Pivotal Rôle of Lycaenion in Longus' Pastorals." *RSC* 25:5–17.

Levitan, W. 1993. "Give Up the Beginning? Juno's Mindful Wrath (*Aeneid* 1.37)." *LCM* 18:14.

Lidov, J. B. 1974. "The Poems and Performance of Isthmians 3 and 4." *CSCA* 7:174–85.

Lieberg, G. 1982. *Poeta Creator: Studien zu einer Figur der antiken Dichtung.* Amsterdam.

Lilja, S. 1978. *The Roman Elegists' Attitude to Women.* New York.

Liouve, M. 1984. "Fin de partie, ou le point final au théâtre." In Montandon 1984, 183–91.

Lipsius, J. H. 1902. "Der Schluss des Herodotischen Werks." *Leipziger Studien zur Classischen Philologie* 20:195–202.

Little, D. A. 1972. "The Non-Augustanism of Ovid's *Metamorphoses.*" *Mnemosyne* 25:389–401.

Livrea, E., ed. 1973. *Apollonii Rhodi, Argonauticon, liber quartus.* Florence.

Lloyd-Jones, H., and N. G. Wilson. 1990. *Sophoclea: Studies in the Text of Sophocles.* Oxford.

Lobel, E., and D. Page. eds. 1955. *Poetarum Lesbiorum fragmenta.* Oxford.

Loraux, N. 1990. "Herakles: The Super-Male and the Feminine." In D. M. Halperin, J. J. Winkler, and F. I. Zeitlin, eds., *Before Sexuality: The Construction of Erotic Experience in the Ancient Greek World*, 21–52. Princeton.

Lotman, J. 1977. *The Structure of the Artistic Text.* Trans. R. Vroon. Ann Arbor.

Ludwig, W. 1965. *Struktur und Einheit der Metamorphosen Ovids.* Berlin.

Lundström, S. 1980. *Ovids Metamorphosen und die Politik des Kaisers.* Uppsala.

Lyne, R.O.A.M. 1989. *Words and the Poet: Characteristic Techniques of Style in Vergil's "Aeneid."* Oxford.

Macan, R. 1908. *Herodotus: The Seventh, Eighth, and Ninth Books.* Vol. 1, part 2. London.

MacArthur, E. J. 1990. *Extravagant Narratives: Closure and Dynamics in the Epistolary Form.* Princeton.

Macherey, P. 1978. *A Theory of Literary Production.* Trans. G. Wall. London.

McKeown, J. C. 1987. *Ovid, Amores.* Vol. 1. Liverpool.

Macleod, C. W. 1973. "Catullus 116." *CQ*, n.s. 23:304–9. Reprinted in *Collected Essays* (Oxford, 1983), 181–86.

———, ed. 1982. *Iliad 24*. Cambridge.

Maehler, H., ed. 1970. *Bacchylidis, Carmina cum fragmentis*. Leipzig.

Manuwald, B. 1979. *Cassius Dio und Augustus (Paligenesia xiv)*. Wiesbaden.

———. 1980. *Der Aufbau der lukrezischen Kulturentstehungslehre*. Mainz.

March, J. R. 1987. *The Creative Poet: Studies on the Treatment of Myths in Greek Poetry*. BICS, suppl. 49. London.

———. 1991–93. "Sophocles' *Ajax*: The Death and Burial of a Hero." *BICS* 38:1–36.

Marcovaldi, G. 1969. *I romanzi greci*. Rome.

Marg, W., ed. 1982a. *Herodot: Eine Auswahl aus der neueren Forschung*. Darmstadt.

———. 1982b. "'Selbstsicherheit' bei Herodot." In Marg 1982a, 290–301.

Martin, R. P. 1989. *The Language of Heroes: Speech and Performance in the Iliad*. Ithaca, N.Y. and London.

Martin, T. 1978. "The Beginnings and Endings in the Leatherstocking Tales." *Nineteenth Century Fiction* 33:69–87.

Martin V. 1990. *Mary Reilly*. New York.

Martin, W. 1986. *Recent Theories of Narrative*. Ithaca, N.Y.

Martina, M. 1981. "*Aedes Herculis Musarum*." *DArch* 3:49–68.

Martindale, C. 1993. *Professing Latin*. Inaugural lecture, Bristol.

Masters, J. M. 1992. *Poetry and Civil War in Lucan's "Bellum Civile."* Cambridge.

Matte Blanco, I. 1978. *The Unconscious as Infinite Sets: An Essay in Bi-Logic*. London.

Meier, C. 1987. "Historical Answers to Historical Questions: The Origins of History in Ancient Greece." In Boedeker 1987, 41–57.

Meuss, H. 1899. "Tyche bei den attischen Tragikern." *Programm, Königliches Gymnasium zu Hirschberg* 3–17.

Meyer, E. 1899. *Forschungen zur alten Geschichte* 2: 217–18. Halle. Reprinted in Marg 1982a, 679–80.

Meyer, H. 1894. "Apollonios von Rhodos und der Schluss der *Odyssee*." *Hermes* 29:478–79.

Meyer N. 1974. *The Seven-Per-Cent Solution*. New York.

Michelini, A. N. 1987. *Euripides and the Tragic Tradition*. Madison, Wis.

Mikalson, J. D. 1986. "Zeus the Father and Heracles the Son in Tragedy." *TAPhA* 116:89–98.

Miller, D. A. 1981. *Narrative and Its Discontents: Problems of Closure in the Traditional Novel*. Princeton.

Miller, J. F. 1991. *Ovid's Elegiac Festivals*. Frankfurt.

Miller, J. H. 1978. "The Problematic of Ending in Narrative." *Nineteenth Century Fiction* 33:3–7.

Mingazzini, P. 1925. "Le rappresentazioni vascolari del mito dell'apoteosi di Herakles." *MAL*, ser. 6, 1.6:413–90.

Mink, L. 1987. *Historical Understanding*. Eds. B. Fay, E. Golob, and R. Vann. Ithaca, N.Y.

Mitchell, R. N. 1991. "Miasma, Mimesis, and Scapegoating in Euripides' *Hippolytus*." *ClAnt* 10:97–122.

Mitchell-Boyask, R. N. 1996. "*Sine fine*: Vergil's Masterplot." *AJPh* 117:289–307.

Moles, J. L. 1988. *Plutarch: Life of Cicero.* Warminster.

Molinié, G. 1982. *Du roman grec au roman baroque.* Toulouse.

Molyneux, J. H., ed. 1993. *Literary Responses to Civil Discord.* Nottingham.

Momigliano, A. 1958. "The Place of Herodotus in the History of Historiography." *History* 43:1–13. Reprinted in *Studies in Historiography* (London, 1966), 127–42.

Montandon, A., ed. 1984. *Le Point final.* Clermont-Ferrand.

Mooney, G. W., ed. 1912. Apollonius of Rhodes, *Argonautica.* London.

Morgan, J. 1989a. "A Sense of the Ending: The Conclusion of Heliodorus' *Aithiopika.*" *TAPhA* 119:299–320.

———, trans. 1989b. Heliodorus, *An Ethiopian Story.* In B. P. Reardon, ed., *Collected Ancient Greek Novels,* 349–588. Berkeley.

———. 1989c. "The Story of Knemon in Heliodoros' *Aithiopika.*" *JHS* 119:99–113.

Morson, G. S. 1987. *Hidden in Plain View: Narrative and Creative Potentials in "War and Peace."* Stanford.

———. 1993. "For the Time Being: Sideshadowing, Criticism, and the Russian Countertradition." In N. Easterlin and B. Riebling, eds., *After Poststructuralism: Interdisciplinarity and Literary Theory,* 203–31. Evanston, Ill.

———. 1994. *Narrative and Freedom: The Shadows of Time.* New Haven, Conn.

Mortimer, A. K. 1985. *La Clôture narrative.* Paris.

Mossman, J. M. 1988. "Tragedy and Epic in Plutarch's *Alexander.*" *JHS* 108:83–93. Reprinted in Scardigli 1995, 209–28.

———. 1991. "Plutarch's Use of Statues." In Flower and Toher 1991, 98–119.

———, ed. 1997. *Plutarch and His Intellectual World: Essays on Plutarch.* London.

Most, G. 1989. "The Stranger's Stratagem: Self-Disclosure and Self-Sufficiency in Greek Culture." *JHS* 109:114–33.

Motto, A. L., and J. R. Clark. 1969. "*Ise Dais*: The Honor of Achilles." *Arethusa* 2:109–25.

Moulthrop, S. 1991. "Reading from the Map: Order and Coherence in a New Medium." In Delany and Landow 1991, 119–32.

Moulton, C. 1973. "Ovid as Anti-Augustan: *Met.* 15.843–79." *CW* 67:4–7.

Moxon, I. S., J. D. Smart, and A. J. Woodman, eds. 1986. *Past Perspectives, Studies in Greek and Roman Historical Writing.* Cambridge.

Müller, C. W. 1976. "Chariton von Aphrodisias und die Theorie des Romans in der Antike." *A&A* 22:115–36.

Müller, G. 1959. *Die Darstellung der Kinetik bei Lukrez.* Berlin.

———. 1975. "Die fehlende Theologie im Lukreztext." In *Monumentum Chiloniense,* Festschrift for E. Burck, 277–95. Amsterdam.

———. 1978. "Die Finalia der sechs Bücher des Lukrez." In *Lucrèce,* Entretiens Hardt sur l'antiquité classique 24, 197–221. Geneva.

Munson, R. 1983. "Transitions in Herodotus: An Analysis Based Principally on the First Book." Diss., University of Pennsylvania.

Murnaghan, S. 1989. "Trials of the Hero in Sophocles' *Ajax.*" In M. M. MacKenzie and C. Roueché, eds., *Images of Authority,* 171–93. Cambridge.

Murray, G. 1946. "Heracles, 'The Best of Men'." In *Greek Studies,* 106–26. Oxford.

Murray, O. 1987. "Herodotus and Oral History." In H. Sancisi-Weerdenburg and A. Kuhrt, eds., *Achaemenid History II: The Greek Sources*, 93–115. Leiden.

Mylonas, G. E. 1961. *Eleusis and the Eleusinian Mysteries*. Princeton.

Nagle, B. R. 1982–83. "Open-Ended Closure in *Aeneid* 2." *CW* 76:257–63.

Nagler, M. N. 1980. "Entretiens avec Tiresias." *CW* 74:89–107.

Nagy, G. 1974. *Comparative Studies in Greek and Indic Metre*. Cambridge, Mass.

———. 1979. *The Best of the Achaeans: Concepts of the Hero in Archaic Greek Poetry*. Baltimore.

Napolitano, F. 1983–84. "Leucippe nel romanzo di Achille Tazio." *AFLN* 26:85–101.

Nicolai, W. 1990. *Euripides Dramen mit rettendem Deus ex machina*. Heidelberg.

Nicolet, C. 1991. *Space, Geography, and Politics in the Early Roman Empire*. Ann Arbor.

Nisbet, R.G.M., and M. Hubbard. 1970. *A Commentary on Horace "Odes," Book One*. Oxford.

Norwood, G. 1920. *Greek Tragedy*. Boston.

———. 1954. *Essays on Euripidean Drama*. Berkeley.

Nuttall, A. D. 1992. *Openings*. Oxford.

O'Higgins, D. 1990. "Sappho's Splintered Tongue: Silence in Sappho 31 and Catullus 51." *AJPh* 111:156–67.

Oliensis, E. S. 1991a. "The Construction of Horatian Decorum." Diss., Harvard.

———. 1991b. "Canidia, Canicula, and the Decorum of Horace's Odes." *Arethusa* 24:107–38.

Olubas, B. 1992. "Rewriting the Past: Exploration and Discovery in *The Transit of Venus*." *Australian Literary Studies* 15:155–64.

Ong, W. 1982. *Orality and Literacy: The Technologizing of the Word*. London.

Oswald, R. 1993. *Das Ende der Odyssee. Studien zu Strukturen epischen Gestaltens*. Graz.

Otis, B. 1970. *Ovid as an Epic Poet*. 2d ed. Cambridge.

Paduano, G. 1972. *Studi su Apollonio Rodio*. Rome.

Panofsky, E. 1955. "*Et in Arcadia Ego*: Poussin and the Elegiac Tradition." In *Meaning in the Visual Arts*, 295–320. Garden City, N.Y.

Papangelis, T. D. 1987. *Propertius: A Hellenistic Poet of Love and Death*. Cambridge.

Paratore, E. 1986. "Gli atteggiamenti politici di Properzio." In G. Cantanzaro and F. Santucci, eds., *Bimillenario della morte di Properzio, Atti del convegno internazionale di studi properziani*, 75–94. Assisi.

Parker, D. 1969. "The Ovidian Coda." *Arion* 8:80–97.

Parker, P. A. 1979. *Inescapable Romance, Studies in the Poetics of a Mode*. Princeton.

Parmentier, L. 1959. "Introduction." In L. Parmentier and H. Grégoire, eds., *Euripide III*, 3–19. Paris.

Parry, A. 1964. "The Language of Achilles." Reprinted in G. S. Kirk, ed., *The Language and Background of Homer*. Cambridge. Originally published in *TAPhA* 87[1956]:1–7.

Parsons, P. 1977. "Callimachus: Victoria Berenices." *ZPE* 2:1–50.

Pasoli, Elio. 1982. *Tre poeti latini espressionisti: Properzio, Persio, Giovenale*. Rome.

Patterson, L. 1993. "Making Identities in Fifteenth-Century England: Henry V and John Lydgate." In J. N. Cox and L. J. Reynolds, eds., *New Historical Literary Study: Essays on Reproducing Texts, Representing History*, 69–107. Princeton.

Peden, R. 1987. "Endings in Catullus." In Whitby, Hardie, and Whitby 1987, 95–103.

Pelliccia, H. 1992. "Sappho 16, Gorgias' *Helen*, and the Preface to Herodotus' *Histories*." *YClS* 29:63–84.

Pelling, C.B.R. 1973. "Plutarch, *Alexander and Caesar*: Two New Fragments?" *CQ*, n.s. 23:343–44.

———. 1986. "Synkrisis in Plutarch's *Lives*." In *Miscellanea Plutarchea*, 83–96. Ferrara.

———. 1988. *Plutarch: Life of Antony*. Cambridge.

———. 1989. "Plutarch: Roman Heroes and Greek Culture." In Griffin and Barnes 1989, 199–232.

———. 1990. "Truth and Fiction in Plutarch's *Lives*." In Russell 1990, 19–52.

———. 1996. "Caesar's Fall." In Mossman 1996, 215–31.

Peradotto, J. 1986. "Prophecy Degree Zero: Teiresias and the End of the *Odyssey*." In B. Gentili and G. Paioni, eds., *Oralità: Cultura letteratura discorso*, 429–59. Rome.

———. 1990. *Man in the Middle Voice: Name and Narration in the "Odyssey."* Princeton.

Perkell, C. 1989. *The Poet's Truth: A Study of the Poet in Virgil's Georgics*. Berkeley.

Perry, B. E. 1930. "Chariton and His Romance from a Literary-Historical Point of View." *AJPh* 51:93–134.

Pfeiffer, R. 1934. *Die neuen διηγήσεις zu Kallimachosgedichten*, *SBAW* 10. Munich.

———. 1953. Callimachus, *Hymni et epigrammata*. Oxford.

Pinter, H. 1979. *Betrayal*. New York.

Platter, C. 1994. "Heracles, Deianeira, and Nessus: Reverse Chronology and Human Knowledge in Bacchylides 16." *AJPh* 115:337–349.

Plepits, K., ed. and trans. 1980. Achilles Tatios, *Leukippe und Klitophon*. Stuttgart.

Pohlenz, M. 1937. *Herodot: Der erste Geschichtschreiber des Abendlandes*. Leipzig.

Pomeroy, A. J. 1991. *The Appropriate Comment, Death Notices in Ancient Historians*. Frankfurt.

Porte, D. 1985. "L'Idée romaine et la métamorphose." In J. M. Frécaut and D. Porte, eds., *Journées ovidiennes de Parménie: Actes du Colloque sur Ovide*. Collection *Latomus* 149. Brussels.

Powell, A., ed. 1992. *Roman Poetry and Propaganda in the Age of Augustus*. Bristol.

Powell, J. E. 1939. *The History of Herodotus*. Cambridge.

Powell, J. U. 1926. *Collectanea Alexandrina*. Oxford.

Price, S. 1984. *Rituals and Power: The Roman Imperial Cult in Asia Minor*. Cambridge.

Quinn, K. 1982. "The Poet and His Audience in the Augustan Age." *ANRW* 2.30.1:75–180.

Quint, D. 1989. "Repetition and Ideology in the *Aeneid*." *MD* 23:9–54.

———. 1993. *Epic and Empire: Politics and Generic Form from Virgil to Milton*. Princeton.

Rabe, H., ed. 1913. *Hermogenis Opera*. Leipzig.

Race, W. H. 1979. "The End of *Olympia* 2: Pindar and the *Vulgus*." *CSCA* 12:251–67.

———. 1989. "Elements of Style in Pindaric Break-Offs." *AJPh* 110:189–209. (= Race 1990: 41–57.)

————. 1990. *Style and Rhetoric in Pindar's Odes.* Atlanta.

Rackcinska, M. 1971. "Chariton, représentant le plus éminent de la première phase du roman grec." In *Acta Conventus XI Eirene,* 597–603. Warsaw.

Rainwater, C., and W. J. Scheick. 1983a. "'Some Godlike Grammar': An Introduction to the Writings of Hazzard, Ozick, and Redmon." *TSLL* 25:181–211.

————. 1983b. An Interview with Shirley Hazzard (Summer 1982). *TSLL* 25: 213–21.

Rawson, E. 1986. "Cassius and Brutus: The Memory of the Liberators." In Moxon, Smart, and Woodman 1986, 101–19.

Reardon, B. 1971. *Courants littéraires grecs des I, II, et III siècles après J.C.* Paris.

————, ed. 1989. *Collected Ancient Greek Novels.* Berkeley.

Redfield, J. M. 1975. *Nature and Culture in the "Iliad."* Chicago.

————. 1979. "The Proem of the *Iliad*: Homer's Art." *CPh* 74:95–110.

Reeve, M. D. 1984. "Tibullus 2.6." *Phoenix* 38:235–39.

Reid, J. S., ed. 1885. *M. Tulli Ciceronis Academica.* London.

Renger, C. 1985. *Aeneas und Turnus, Analyse einer Feindschaft.* Frankfurt am Main.

Rhys, J. 1966. *Wide Sargasso Sea.* New York.

Rich, J. W. 1989. "Dio on Augustus." In Cameron 1989, 86–110.

Richardson, L. 1976. *Propertius: Elegies I–IV.* Norman, Okla.

————. 1977. "Hercules Musarum and the Porticus Philippi in Rome." *AJA* 81:355–61.

Richardson, N. J. 1974. *The Homeric Hymn to Demeter.* Oxford.

Richlin, A. 1992. "Julia's Jokes, Galla Placidia, and the Roman Use of Women as Political Icons." In B. Garlick, S. Dixon, and P. Allen, eds., *Stereotypes of Women in Power,* 65–91. New York.

Richter, D. H. 1974. *Fable's End: Completeness and Closure in Rhetorical Fiction.* Chicago.

Ricoeur, P. 1983. *Temps et récit I.* Paris.

————. 1984. *Temps et récit II: La configuration dans le récit de fiction.* Paris.

Rissman, L. 1983. *Love as War: Homeric Allusions in the Poetry of Sappho.* Beiträge zur klassischen Philologie 157. Königstein.

Roberts, D. H. 1987. "Parting Words: Final Lines in Sophocles and Euripides." *CQ,* n.s. 37:51–64.

————. 1988. "Sophoclean Endings: Another Story." *Arethusa* 21:177–96.

————. 1992. "Outside the Drama: The Limits of Tragedy in Aristotle's *Poetics.*" In A. O. Rorty, ed., *Essays on Aristotle's "Poetics,"* 133–53. Princeton.

————. 1993. "The Frustrated Mourner: Strategies of Closure in Greek Tragedy." In R. Rosen and J. Farrell, eds., *Nomodeiktes: Greek Studies in Honor of Martin Ostwald,* 573–87. Ann Arbor.

Robinson, P. 1988. "A Deconstructive Postscript: Reading Libretti and Misreading Opera." In A. Groos and R. Parker, eds., *Reading Opera,* 328–46. Princeton.

Romberg, B. 1962. *Studies in the Narrative Technique of the First-Person Novel.* Lund.

Romilly, J. de. 1980. "Le Refus du suicide dans l'*Héraclès* d'Euripide." *Archaiognosia* 1:1–10.

Rommel, H. 1923. *Die naturwissenschaftlich-paradoxographischen Excurse bei Philostratos, Heliodoros und Achilleus Tatios.* Stuttgart.

Rosati, G. 1979. "L'esistenza letteraria: Ovidio e l'autocoscienza della poesia." *MD* 2:101–36.

Rösler, W. 1975. "Ein Gedicht und sein Publikum: Überlegungen zu Sappho Fr. 44 Lobel-Page." *Hermes* 103:278–85.

Ross, D. O. 1987. *Virgil's Elements: Physics and Poetry in the Georgics.* Princeton.

Rossi, L. E. 1968. "La fine alessandrina dell'*Odissea* e lo ζῆλος Ὁμηρικός di Apollonio Rodio." *RFIC* 96:151–63.

Roth, P. 1993. *Operation Shylock.* New York.

Rowe, J. A. 1988. *Equivocal Endings in Classic American Novels.* Cambridge.

Rubino, C. A. 1993. "Opening up the Classical Past: Bakhtin, Aristotle, Literature, Life." *Arethusa* 26:141–57.

Rudd, N., ed. 1993. *Horace.* London.

Ruiz Montero, C. 1988. *La estructura de la novela griega.* Salamanca.

Russell, D. A. 1963. "Plutarch's *Life* of Coriolanus." *JRS* 53:21–28. Reprinted in Scardigli 1995, 357–72.

———. 1973. *Plutarch.* London.

———, ed. 1990. *Antonine Literature.* Oxford.

Rutherford, I. C. 1992. "Two Heroic Prosodia: A Study of Pindar *Pa.* XIV–XV." *ZPE* 92:59–70.

———. 1997. *Pindar's Paeans: A Reading of the Fragments with a Survey of the Genre.* Oxford.

Rutherford, R. B. 1982. "Tragic Form and Feeling in the *Iliad.*" *JHS* 102:145–60.

Ruthven, K. K. 1990. *Ezra Pound as Literary Critic.* London.

Saïd, E. 1975. *Beginnings: Intention and Method.* New York.

Salat, P. 1984. "La Fin de l'Éneide." In Montandon 1984, 11–18.

Santirocco, M. 1984. "The Poetics of Closure: Horace *Odes* III 17–28." *Ramus* 13:74–91.

Scanlon, T. 1987. *Spes frustrata: A Reading of Sallust.* Heidelberg.

Scardigli, B., ed. 1995. *Essays on Plutarch's "Lives."* Oxford.

Schadewaldt, W. 1982. "Herodot als erster Historiker." In Marg 1982a, 109–21. (Excerpted from "Die Anfänge der Geschichtsschreibung bei den Griechen," in E. Zinn, ed., *Hellas und Hesperien: Gesammelte Schriften zur Antike und zur neueren Literatur*, 395–416 [Zürich, 1960].)

Scheid, J., and J. Svenbro. 1994. *Le Métier de Zeus.* Paris.

Schein, S. L. 1984. *The Mortal Hero: An Introduction to Homer's "Iliad."* Berkeley.

Schiesaro, A. 1994. "The Palingenesis of the *De rerum natura.*" *PCPhS* 40:81–117.

Schissel von Fleschenberg, O. 1909. *Die Rahmenerzählung in den ephesischen Geschichten des Xenophon von Ephesus.* Innsbruck.

Schmeling, G. 1991. "The *Satyricon*: The Sense of an Ending." *RhM* 134:352–77.

Schmid, W. 1934. *Die Griechische Literatur in der Zeit der Attischen Hegemonie von dem Eingreifen der Sophistik.* In Schmid and Stählin, 1934, pt. 1, vol. 2.

Schmid, W., and O. Stählin. 1934. *Geschichte der Griechischen Literatur.* Munich.

Schmidt, E. A. 1991. *Ovids poetische Menschenwelt: Die Metamorphosen als Metapher und Symphonie.* SHAW 1991:2. Heidelberg.

Schmidt, H. J. 1992. *How Dramas End: Essays on the German Sturm und Drang.* Ann Arbor.

Schmiel, R. C. 1993. Review of Stanley 1993. *BMCR* 4.6.2.

Schmitzer, U. 1990. *Zeitgeschichte in Ovids Metamorphosen: Mythologische Dichtung unter politischem Anspruch.* Stuttgart.

Schor, N. 1987. "Dreaming Dissymmetry: Barthes, Foucault, and Sexual Difference." In A. Jardine and P. Smith, eds., *Men in Feminism*, 98–110. London.

Schrijvers, P. H. 1970. *Horror ac Divina Voluptas: Études sur la poétique et la poésie de Lucrèce.* Amsterdam.

———. 1973. "Comment terminer une ode?" *Mnemosyne* 26:140–59.

Schwinge, E. R. 1991. "Homerische Epen und Erzählforschung." In J. Latacz, ed., *200 Jahre Homer-Forschung*, 482–512. Stuttgart and Leipzig.

Scobie, A. 1973. *More Essays on the Ancient Romance and Its Heritage.* Meisenheim.

Scodel, R. 1982. "The Achaean Wall and the Myth of Destruction." *HSCPh* 86:33–50.

———. 1984. "The Irony of Fate in Bacchylides 17." *Hermes* 112:137–43.

Scott, Sir Walter. 1926. *The Talisman.* New York.

Seaford, R. 1989. "Homeric and Tragic Sacrifice." *TAPhA* 119:87–95.

———. 1994. *Reciprocity and Ritual: Homer and Tragedy in the Developing City-State.* Oxford.

Sedelmeier-Stöckl, D. 1958. "Studien zur Erzählungstechnik des Achilles Tatius." Diss., Vienna.

Segal, C. 1969. "Myth and Philosophy in the *Metamorphoses*: Ovid's Augustanism and the Augustan Conclusion of Book XV." *AJPh* 90:257–92.

———. 1971. *The Theme of the Mutilation of the Corpse in the "Iliad."* *Mnemosyne*, suppl. 17. Leiden.

———. 1985. "Messages to the Underworld: An Analysis of Poetic Immortality in Pindar." *AJPh* 106:199–212.

———. 1986. "Greek Tragedy: Writing, Truth, and the Representation of the Self." In *Interpreting Greek Tragedy: Myth, Poetry, Text*, 75–109. Ithaca, N.Y.

———. 1990. *Lucretius on Death and Anxiety.* Princeton.

Sellick, R. 1990. "'Some Godlike Grammar': The Narrator in *The Transit of Venus*" In A. Brissenden, ed., *Aspects of Australian Fiction*, 87–96.

Shaw, G. B. 1965. *The Complete Plays.* London.

Shelton, J.-A. 1979. "Structural Unity and the Meaning of Euripides' *Herakles*." *Eranos* 77:101–10.

Sheppard, J. T. 1916. "The Formal Beauty of the *Hercules Furens*." *CQ* 10:72–79.

Silk, M. S. 1985. "Heracles and Greek Tragedy." *G&R* 32:1–22.

Simon, C. 1969. *La Bataille de Pharsale.* Paris.

Skutsch, O. 1968. *Studia Enniana.* London.

———, ed. 1985. *The Annals of Quintus Ennius.* Oxford.

Slater, N. W. 1990. *Reading Petronius.* Baltimore.

Slatkin, L. 1988. "Les Amis mortels, à propos des insultes dans les combats de l'*Iliade*." *L'Écrit du temps* 19:119–32.

———. 1991. *The Power of Thetis: Allusion and Interpretation in the "Iliad."* Berkeley.

Smith, B. H. 1968. *Poetic Closure: A Study of How Poems End.* Chicago.

Smith, M. F., ed. 1992. Lucretius, *De rerum natura.* Rev. ed. Cambridge, Mass.

Snell, B., and H. Maehler, eds. 1987–89. *Pindar, Carmina cum fragmentis.* 2 vols. Leipzig.

Snyder, J. M. 1980. *Puns and Poetry in Lucretius' "De rerum natura."* Amsterdam.

Solodow, J. B. 1988. *The World of Ovid's "Metamorphoses."* Chapel Hill.

Söring, J., ed. 1990. *Die Kunst zu Enden.* Frankfurt am Main.

Sourvinou-Inwood, C. 1981. "To Die and Enter the House of Hades: Homer, Before and After." In J. Whaley, ed., *Mirrors of Mortality: Studies in the Social History of Death,* 15–39. London.

Stadter, P. A. 1975. "Plutarch's Comparison of Pericles and Fabius Maximus." *GRBS* 16:77–85. Reprinted in Scardigli 1995, 155–64.

———. 1983–84. "Searching for Themistocles." *CJ* 79:356–63.

———. 1988. "The Proems of Plutarch's *Lives.*" *ICS* 13:275–95.

———. 1989. *A Commentary on Plutarch's "Pericles."* Chapel Hill.

Stahl, H.-P. 1985. *Propertius: "Love" and "War": Individual and State Under Augustus.* Berkeley.

Stanley, K. 1993. *The Shield of Homer: Narrative Structure in the Iliad.* Princeton.

Stark, I. 1984. "Zur Erzählperspektive im griechischen Liebesroman." *Philologus* 128:256–70.

Statin, J. 1991. "Reading Hypertext: Order and Coherence in a New Medium." In Delany and Landow 1991, 153–69.

Stein, H. 1882. *Herodotus.* Vol. 5: Books 8 and 9. Berlin.

Steiner, G. 1959. *Tolstoy or Dostoevsky: An Essay in the Old Criticism.* New York.

Stengel, K. 1911. *De Lucianii veris historiis.* Berlin.

Stephen, G. M. 1959. "The Coronis." *Scriptorium* 13:3–14.

Stern, J. 1967. "The Imagery of Bacchylides Ode 5." *GRBS* 8:35–43.

Stern, M. R. 1991. *Contexts for Hawthorne: The Marble Faun and the Politics of Openness and Closure in American Literature.* Urbana, Ill.

Stevenson, T. R. 1992. "The Ideal Benefactor and the Father Analogy in Greek and Roman Thought." *CQ* 42:421–36.

Stevick, P. 1967. "The Theory of Fictional Chapters." In P. Stevick, ed., *The Theory of the Novel,* 171–84. New York.

Stinton, T.C.W. 1975. "*Hamartia* in Aristotle and Greek Tragedy." *CQ,* n.s. 25:221–54. Reprinted in Stinton 1990, 143–85.

———. 1986. "The Scope and Limits of Allusion in Greek Tragedy." In M. Cropp, R. E. Fantham, and S. E. Scully, eds., *Greek Tragedy and Its Legacy: Essays Presented to D. J. Conacher,* 67–102. Amsterdam. Reprinted in Stinton 1990, 454–92.

———. 1990. *Collected Papers on Greek Tragedy.* Oxford.

Stoppard, T. 1967. *Rosencrantz and Guildenstern Are Dead.* New York.

———. 1993. *Arcadia.* London.

Stössel, H. A. 1975. *Der letzte Gesang der Odyssee: Eine unitarische Gesamtinterpretation.* Erlangen.

Strasburger, H. 1956. "Herodots Zeitrechnung." *Historia* 5:129–61. Reprinted in Marg 1982a, 688–736.

Suerbaum, W. 1968. *Untersuchungen zur Selbstdarstellung älterer römischer Dichter.* Hildesheim.

Sullivan, J. P. 1976. *Propertius: A Critical Introduction.* Cambridge.

Swain, S. 1989. "Plutarch's Aemilius and Timoleon." *Historia* 38:314–34.

———. 1990. "Plutarchean Synkrisis." *Eranos* 90:101–11.

Syme, R. 1978. *History in Ovid*. Oxford.

——. 1986. *The Augustan Aristocracy*. Oxford.

Szegedy-Maszak, M. 1987. "Teleology in Postmodern Fiction." In M. Galinescu and D. Fokkema, *Exploring Postmodernism*, 41–57. Amsterdam.

Tanizaki, J. 1957. *The Makioka Sisters*. Trans. E. G. Seidensticker. New York.

Taplin, O. P. 1977. *The Stagecraft of Aeschylus*. Oxford.

——. 1983. "Sophocles in His Theatre." In *Sophocle*, Entretiens Hardt sur l'antiquité classique 29, 155–83. Geneva.

——. 1992. *Homeric Soundings: The Shaping of the Iliad*. Oxford.

Tarkow, T. A. 1977. "The Glorification of Athens in Euripides' *Heracles*." *Helios* 5:27–35.

Taylor, N. D. 1984. "An Introduction to Shirley Hazzard's *The Transit of Venus*." *World Literature Written in English* 24:287–95.

Thalmann, W. G. 1984. *Conventions of Form and Thought in Early Greek Hexameter Poetry*. Baltimore.

Thickstun, W. R. 1988. *Visionary Closure in the Modern Novel*. London.

Thiel, H. van. 1971. *Der Eselroman, I Untersuchungen*. Munich.

Thielmann, P. 1882. *Das Verbum dare im Lateinischen*. Leipzig.

Thomas, R. 1983. *The Latin Masks of Ezra Pound*. Ann Arbor.

Thomas, R. F., ed. 1988. Virgil, *Georgics*. 2 vols. Cambridge.

——. 1991a. "The 'Sacrifice' at the End of the *Georgics*, Aristaeus and Vergilian Closure." *CPh* 86:211–18.

——. 1991b. "*Furor* and *furiae* in Virgil." *AJPh* 112:261.

Todorov, T. 1967. *Littérature et signification*. Paris.

Tolman, J. A. 1907. *A Study of the Sepulchral Inscriptions in Buecheler's "Carmina Epigraphica Latina."* Chicago.

Tolstoy, L. 1950. *Anna Karenina*. Trans. C. Garnett. New York.

Torgovnick, M. 1981. *Closure in the Novel*. Princeton.

Toynbee, J.M.C. 1971. *Death and Burial in the Roman World*. London.

Treu, K. 1989. "Der antike Roman und sein Publikum." In H. Kuch, ed., *Der antike Roman: Untersuchungen zur literarischen Kommunikation und Gattungsgeschichte*, 178–97. Berlin.

Turner, V. 1981. "Social Dramas and Stories About Them." In W.J.T. Mitchell, ed., *On Narrative*, 137–64. Chicago.

Usher, S. 1969. *The Historians of Greece and Rome*. London.

——. 1985. "Dionysius of Halicarnassus: The Critical Essays. Vol. 2. Cambridge, Mass.

Van Der Loeff, A. R. 1961. Children on the Oregon Trail. Trans. R. Edwards. London.

Vandiver, E. 1991. *Heroes in Herodotus: The Interaction of Myth and History*. Frankfurt am Main.

van Groningen, B. A. 1953. *In the Grip of the Past: Essay on an Aspect of Greek Thought*. Leiden.

——. 1960. *La Composition littéraire archaïque grecque: Procédés et réalisations*. 2d ed. Amsterdam.

Van Sickle, J. 1980. "The Book-Roll and Some Conventions of the Poetic Book." *Arethusa* 13:5–42.

——. 1981. "Poetics of Opening and Closure in Meleager, Catullus, and Gallus." *CW* 75:65–75.

——. 1984. "Dawn and Dusk as Motifs of Opening and Closure in Heroic and Bucolic Epos (Homer, Apollonius, Theocritus, Virgil)." In *Atti del Convegno mondiale scientifico di studi su Virgilio*, 125–47. Milan.

Venini, P., ed. 1970. *P. Papini Stati Thebaidos, liber undecimus*. Florence.

Verrall, A. W. 1905. *Essays on Four Plays of Euripides*. Cambridge.

Versnel, H. S. 1970. *Triumphus: An Inquiry into the Origin, Development and Meaning of the Roman Triumph*. Leiden.

Vessey, D.W.T.C. 1973. *Statius and the "Thebaid."* Cambridge.

——. 1986. "*Pierius menti calor incidit*: Statius' Epic Style." *ANRW* 2.32.5:2965–3019.

Veyne, P. 1984. *Writing History: Essay on Epistemology*. Trans. M. Moore-Rinvolucri. Middletown, Conn.

Vilborg, E., ed. 1955. *Achilles Tatius, Leucippe and Clitophon*. Stockholm.

Vine, B. 1992. "On the 'Missing' Fourth Stanza of Catullus 51." *HSCPh* 94:251–58.

Vlastos, G. 1991. *Socrates, Ironist and Moral Philosopher*. Ithaca, N.Y.

Vogt-Spina, G., ed. 1990. *Strukturen der Mündlichkeit in der römischen Literatur*. Tübingen.

Volkmann, R. 1885. *Die Rhetorik der Griechen und Römer*. 2d ed. Leipzig.

von Albrecht, M. 1964. *Silius Italicus*. Amsterdam.

von Fritz, K. 1967. *Die griechische Geschichtsschreibung von den Anfängen bis Thykydides*. Berlin.

Vretska, K. 1976. C. Sallustius Crispus, *De Catilinae coniuratione*. Heidelberg.

Waanders, F.M.J. 1983. *The History of τέλος and τελέω in Ancient Greek*. Amsterdam.

Walden, J.W.H. 1894. "Stage-Terms in Heliodorus' *Aethiopica*." *HSCPh* 5:1–43.

Walker, H. J. 1995. *Theseus and Athens*. Oxford.

Wallace-Hadrill, A. 1987. "Time for Augustus: Ovid, Augustus, and the *Fasti*." In Whitby, et al. 1987, 221–30.

——. 1989. Review article of Zanker, "Rome's Cultural Revolution." *JRS* 79:157–64.

Walsh, J. J. 1992. "Syzygy, Theme, and History: A Study in Plutarch's *Philopoemen* and *Flamininus*." *Philologus* 136:208–33.

Waltz, R. 1939. "Autour d'un texte de Sénèque (*Nat. Quaest. 4, praef. 17)*." *REL* 17:292–308.

Warner, R., trans. 1954. Thucydides, *The Peloponnesian War*. Harmondsworth.

Wender, D. 1978. *The Last Scenes of the Odyssey*. Mnemosyne, suppl. 17. Leiden.

Wesseling, B. 1988. "The Audience of the Ancient Novel." *Groningen Colloquia on the Novel* 1:67–79.

West, S. 1989. "Laertes Revisited." *PCPhS* 215:113–43.

Whitby, M., P. Hardie, and M. Whitby, eds. 1987. *Homo Viator: Classical Essays for John Bramble*. Bristol.

White, E. B. 1945. *Stuart Little*. New York.

White, H. 1973. *Metahistory: The Historical Imagination in Nineteenth-Century Europe*. Baltimore.

————. 1978. *Tropics of Discourse: Essays in Cultural Criticism.* Baltimore.

————. 1987. *The Content of the Form.* Baltimore.

White, M. 1969. "Herodotus' Starting Point." *Phoenix* 23:39–48.

White, P. 1988. "Julius Caesar in Augustan Rome." *Phoenix* 42:334–56.

White, R. S. 1985. *Let Wonder Seem Familiar: Endings in Shakespeare's Romance Vision.* London.

Wilamowitz-Moellendorff, U. von. 1893. *Aristoteles und Athen.* Vol. 1. Berlin.

————. 1924. *Hellenistische Dichtung in der Zeit des Kallimachos.* Berlin.

Wilkinson, L. P. 1955. *Ovid Recalled.* Cambridge.

Will, E. 1975. Review of Fehling (1971). *RPh* 49:119–21.

Willson, R. F. 1990. *Shakespeare's Reflexive Endings.* New York.

Wiltshire, S. F. 1989. *Public and Private in Vergil's "Aeneid."* Amherst, Mass.

Winkler, J. J. 1982. "The Mendacity of Kalasiris and the Narrative Strategy of Heliodorus' *Aithiopika.*" *YClS* 27:93–158.

————. 1985. *Auctor & Actor: A Narratological Reading of Apuleius' "Golden Ass."* Berkeley.

————. 1990. *The Constraints of Desire: The Anthropology of Sex and Gender in Ancient Greece.* New York.

Winnett, S. 1990. "Coming Unstrung: Women, Men, Narrative, and Principles of Pleasure." *PMLA* 105:505–18.

Winnington-Ingram, R. P. 1980. *Sophocles: An Interpretation.* Cambridge.

Wiseman, T. P. 1984. "Cybele, Virgil and Augustus." In T. Woodman and D. West, eds., *Poetry and Politics in the Age of Augustus,* 117–28. Cambridge.

————. 1985. *Catullus and His World.* Cambridge.

Wolff, E. 1964. "Das Weib des Masistes." *Hermes* 92:51–58. Rpr. in Marg 1982a, 668–78.

Woodford, S. 1971. "Cults of Heracles in Attica." In D. G. Mitten and J. G. Pedley, eds., *Studies Presented to G.M.A. Hanfmann,* 211–25. Mainz.

Woodman, A. J. 1974. "*Exegi monumentum*: Horace, *Odes* 3.30." In A. J. Woodman and D. West, eds., *Quality and Pleasure in Latin Poetry,* 115–28. Cambridge.

————. 1989. "Tacitus' Obituary of Tiberius." *CQ,* n.s. 39:197–205.

Wyke, M. 1987. "The Elegiac Woman at Rome." *PCPhS* 213 (n.s. 33):153–78.

————. 1989. "Mistress and Metaphor in Augustan Elegy." *Helios* 16:25–43.

Wyss, R. 1931. "Die Komposition von Apollonios' Argonautika." Diss., Zürich.

Yunis, H. 1988. *A New Creed: Fundamental Religious Beliefs in the Athenian Polis and Euripidean Drama.* Hypomnemata 91. Göttingen.

Zanker, P. 1987. *Augustus und die Macht der Bilder.* Munich.

Zeitlin, F. I. 1971. "Petronius as Paradox: Anarchy and Artistic Integrity." *TAPhA* 102:631–84.

————. 1990. "The Poetics of *Eros*: Nature, Art and Imitation in Longus' *Daphnis and Chloe.*" In D. M. Halperin, J. J. Winkler, and F. I. Zeitlin, eds., *Before Sexuality: The Construction of Erotic Experience in the Ancient Greek World,* 417–64. Princeton.

Zetzel, J.E.G. 1983. "Catullus, Ennius, and the Poetics of Allusion." *ICS* 8:251–66.

Ziolkowski, J. E. 1981. *Thucydides and the Tradition of Funeral Speeches at Athens.* New York.

Zumthor, P. 1984. "The Impossible Closure of the Oral Text." *YFS* 67:25–42. Reprinted from *Introduction à la poésie orale* (Paris, 1983).

Index

Achilles Tatius, 219–21, 222, 225–26, 227
Adkins, A. H., 32
Aeschylus
   Eumenides, 104, 227
   Oresteia, 7, 259
   Persians, 96
   Prometheus Bound, 270
aftermath, 90–91, 216, 251–73. *See also* coda;
   epilogue
Agawu, V. K., 21
Ahl, F., 154
Aithiopis, 139
Alcaeus, 45n.9, 56n.34
Alcott, L. M., 253
allusion, 20, 141, 258–59, 261, 263, 268,
   270–71, 272. *See also* closure and allu-
   sion; inclusion; intertextuality
analepsis, 211
anticlosure, 21, 54, 91–92, 107–8, 109, 111,
   221. *See also* aperture; closure, refusal
   of; ending, open; unfinalizability
Antiphanes, 256n.17
Antonius Diogenes, 212, 218
aperture, 4–5, 109
Apollonius of Rhodes, 124
   Argonautica, 20, 114, 139, 159n.74, 212,
   214, 224
aporia, 138, 163, 177
apotheosis, 88, 159, 192–94, 197, 262. *See
   also* deification
Appelfeld, A., 264
Apuleius, 212, 219n.42, 223–24, 226, 227
Aratus
   Phaenomena 1153–54: 125
Archilochus, 48, 54
Aristides, Aelius, 44
Aristophanes, 7
   Acharnians, 96
Aristotle, 49–50, 84, 141, 144, 215, 250
   Poetics, 209, 250, 256n.17
arrival, 50
Arrowsmith, W., 83–84
Atwood, M., 255
Augustan ideology, 141, 165, 185, 192, 207–8
Augustanism, 7, 208

Augustus, 142–44, 164, 168–69, 173–78,
   186–87, 191–99, 202–5
Austen, J., 266
Austen-Leigh, J., 266
authorial control, 9–11, 269
authorial intrusion, 230–32, 257
authorial voice, 64, 181, 211, 213

Bacchylides, 50
   Dithyrambs, 55
   Odes
      3: 46
      5: 55n.31, 259–62, 269
      14: 47
      15: 53
      16: 54
      17: 47–48
Bakhtin, M. M., 108–11, 215
Bandera, C., 8
Barchiesi, A., 7, 149n.42
Barlow, S. A., 91
beginnings, 139, 141. *See also* ending and be-
   ginning
Benjamin, W., 254
Bignone, E., 112
biography, 228
Bockemueller, F., 114, 135
Bollack, J., 124
Bond, G. W., 91n.14, 106
book endings, 120–23, 142, 144n.25. *See also*
   closure, infratextual
boundaries, 9, 147, 183; of the text, 11, 13,
   63, 76, 182–83, 187, 228. *See also*
   segmentation
   transgressed, 67n.12, 69
boundlessness, 147, 154–55, 156. *See also*
   continuity
Bright, D. F., 115
Brontë, C., 267
Brooks, P., 6
Brown, R. D., 121
Bundy, E. L., 53
burial, 31–32, 116, 127–28, 151–53. *See also*
   funerals; lament
Burnett, A. P., 91, 95, 260–61

Callimachus
  Aitia, 194, 205, 211, 224
    fr.112.7–9: 125
  Iambi, 50n.21, 125, 211
Catullus, 12n.39, 20, 198, 232
chance, 94–95
Chariton, 19, 212, 215, 216–17, 224, 226–27
    8.1.4–5: 215
    8.8.15–16: 217
Cicero, 118, 121, 171
circularity, 211, 214–20, 221
Cixous, H., 10
closed and open readings, 5–7
closed and open texts, 4–5, 11–12, 77n.34, 108–9, 210, 213–14
closural allusion. *See* closure, signals of
closure
  and allusion, 21, 141–42, 153, 183n.4, 207n.50. *See also* inclusion
  apocalyptic, 108
  civic, 102–7, 110
  cultural, 5
  deferred, 23, 27–28, 252, 262. *See also* delay
  emphatic, 21, 76, 133
  epic, 111
  epigrammatic, 219, 226
  false, 19, 21, 44, 58–61, 120, 137, 144, 153, 249
  formal, 36, 64–66, 70, 76, 126
  and gender, 9–11, 210
  incomplete, 213
  infratextual, 13, 43, 55–58, 61, 64, 116, 211, 224–26. *See also* segmentation
  ironic, 74, 79, 173
  and knowledge, 80–82, 92
  mystical, 223–24
  novelistic, 108–9, 210–27
  ongoing, 26. *See also* continuity
  paratextual. *See* paratext
  patterns of, 44, 61, 196–97, 230, 233. *See also* ending, tangential; framing devices; inversion; recapitulation; ring composition; summarizing vignette
  and performance, 12
  and politics, 7–9, 191–96, 202–8. *See also* imperial power
  polyvalent, 79–80, 81. *See also* ending, multiple
  premature, 21, 160. *See also* closure, false; ending, premature

  refusal of, 18, 131
  reopened, 252
  ritual, 104, 134, 143–44, 151, 154. *See also* funerals; triumph
  signals of, 21, 33, 44, 48–50, 65, 114–17, 125, 141, 144, 153, 183n.4, 193, 195, 230. *See also* death; departure; funerals; generalization; prayer; reception; return
  social, 126, 129, 131. *See also* commemoration
  supratextual, 212. *See also* linkage
  temporary, 32–33, 39–40
  uses of the term, 3–4, 83, 207–8, 209–10
  See also anticlosure; ending
coda, 118, 184
commemoration, 31–32, 40, 89, 102, 143, 207
Conacher, D. J., 83
consolatory narrative, 215–18, 226
Conte, G. B., 5, 20, 203n.39, 224
continuity, 6, 28, 34, 37, 41, 70, 92
coronis, 190–91, 201
crown, 49–50, 186, 201
Curran, L., 172
Cypria, 24, 25, 28, 37

Dante, A., 252
Darwin, C., 110
Davies, M., 149
death, 46, 60, 85–86, 88, 123, 144, 156, 172, 228–30, 247–49, 254–55, 270–73
  as closing motif, 58, 115–16, 117–18, 218, 230
  completed, 229, 234–35
  of the hero, 29–30, 34–35, 99–101
  See also burial; mortality; posthumous narrative
deification, 176, 192, 196–97, 248
delay, 16–17, 145–46, 148, 161
demystification, 164–65, 179
departure, 114–15, 128–31. *See also* arrival
deus ex machina, 89–90, 102–4, 107, 256
Dewald, C., 115, 237, 251, 263
Dickens, C., 253
didactic, 124–26, 137–38
Diderot, D., 221
Dio Cassius, 237
Dionysius of Halicarnassus, 74n.28
dithyramb (*dithurambos*), 43, 44, 47, 61
Dostoevsky, F., 109
Dunn, F. M., 5, 210, 221

Easterling, P., 130
Eco, U., 212
Effe, B., 219
Eliot, G., 211, 267
Empedocles, 120n.27, 124
ending
    abrupt, 142, 151, 214n.22
    alternative, 139, 141–44, 148–49, 158, 262
    ambiguous, 77–80. *See also* closure, poly-
        valent
    anecdotal, 67–70, 81
    antithetical, 56
    and beginning, 13, 19–20, 70, 125, 150–
        51, 160n.76, 218
    closed, 6, 18, 214. *See also* closed and open
        readings; closed and open texts
    consolatory. *See* consolatory narrative
    effective, 90–91
    external, 115. *See also* framing devices
    fablelike, 217
    formulaic, 64–66. *See also* closure, formal
    gnomic, 64, 69. *See also* gnomai
    and history, 63, 76
    incomplete, 90. *See also* closure, incomplete
    indeterminate, 70. *See also* ending, ambig-
        uous
    internal, 17, 115, 116, 226
    "Lucretian," 131, 133, 138
    multiple, 95, 196–97, 201, 256. *See also*
        ending, alternative
    mythological, 53–55, 61
    open, 6, 78, 124, 134, 138, 155, 195, 213,
        255. *See also* aperture; openness
    overdetermined, 195
    postponed, 255. *See also* closure, deferred
    premature, 9, 85–88, 91, 104, 153. *See also*
        closure, premature
    problematic, 5, 63, 112, 131, 139–40
    proleptic, 216–19. *See also* prolepsis
    provisional, 255
    reconstructed, 90–91, 130
    reflexive, 46–48, 52–53, 57, 60. *See also*
        self-reflexiveness
    tangential, 211, 223, 262
    See also book endings; epilogue; happy end-
        ing
Ennius, 20, 137, 211
    Annales, 140–41, 143, 157, 158, 206–7
envoi. *See* coda
epic, 108–9, 126–29, 213–14
    Latin, 7–10, 16–17, 139–62

Epicureanism, 121–23, 128, 135–38
Epicurus
    Epistle to Menoeceus 126–27: 118
epilogue, 139, 156–58, 211–12, 228, 253–54,
    256, 263, 267. *See also* coda; prolepsis;
    synkrisis
epinician (*epinikion*), 43, 44, 48–49, 51, 52,
    61
epiphany, 88–89, 176, 196. *See also* deus ex
    machina
epiphonema, 116, 120, 134, 137
Erbse, H., 244
essentialism, 4
Euripides, 256
    Alcestis, 170
        1159–63: 118
    Andromache, 118
    Bacchae, 84, 88, 118, 130–31
    Children of Heracles, 89, 102–3
    Cresphontes, fr. 449N: 118–19
    Electra, 86n.7
    Hecuba, 89
    Helen, 118
    Heracles, 83–111, 118
        51–54: 85
        158–64: 96–97
        247–51: 105
        575–82: 86–87
        629–35: 87
        827–32: 93
        1146–52: 88
        1246–48: 101
        1341–46: 95
        1423–26: 110
    Hippolytus, 184–85, 236
    Hypsipyle, 118
    Ion, 85, 103
    Iphigenia at Aulis, 171
    Medea, 84, 89, 102, 103n.39, 214, 236
    Orestes, 89–90, 256
    Suppliant Women, 89, 102–4
explicit, 211, 212–13, 217, 222. *See also incipit*

Faulkner, W., 265
Feeney, D., 203n.39
feminist criticism, 10–11
Foley, H. P., 8, 91
Fowler, D. P., 3–4, 210, 212
Fowles, J., 270
framing devices, 17–18, 46–48, 219–20. *See
    also* paratext

freedom, 109–11
Freud, S., 6, 110, 219
funerals, 85, 126–31, 134, 151, 159, 172
  as closing motifs, 36, 40, 114, 126, 129–31,
    143, 153–54, 189, 213
  See also commemoration; triumph

Gale, M., 19
Galinsky, K., 19
Gardner, J., 264
gender roles, 172–73. *See also* closure and
  gender
generalization, 115–16, 230. *See also* epi-
  phonema; *gnomai*; limitations
Genette, G., 211, 251n.2, 267
Gide A., 17
Girard, R., 7–8, 34n.16
Giraudoux, J., 262
gnomai, 51, 58, 59, 60, 116
Gorgias, 56n.34
Grade, C., 263
Grattius, 126
Griffin, J., 31n.12

Hägg, T., 225
Habinek, T., 5–6
Haire-Sargeant, L., 264
Hamon, P., 210
happy ending, 74, 79, 86–87, 91, 215–16,
  222–23, 227, 255, 270
Hardie, P., 8, 20, 21, 213
Hazzard, S., 267–71
Heliodorus
  Ethiopica, 17, 212–13, 214, 221–23, 225,
    226, 227
  2.35.5: 222
Henderson, J., 16
Herodotus, 62–82, 99, 115, 183n.5, 232, 237
  9.105–7: 66
  9.108–13: 66
  9.114–21: 66–67
  9.122: 67–68, 71–72
heroic code, 29–35
heroic values, 96–101
Hershkowitz, D., 19
Hesiod
  Catalogue of Women, 24n.2, 88n.9, 125
  Theogony, 25, 125
  Works and Days, 45, 124
    826–28: 124
Hinds, S., 197

Historia Apollonii regis Tyrii, 218
Holleman, A.W.J., 192, 203
Homer
  Iliad, 23–42, 99, 109, 114, 126–29, 139,
    213–14, 256
  allusions to, 67, 131, 142–47, 148–49,
    189, 257, 258
  Book 1.280–81: 33
  Book 2.35–40: 28
  Book 9: 98
    318–20: 35
    632–36: 38
  Book 11: 96
  Book 22: 55
  Book 24: 151
    560–64: 41
    592–95: 40
    664–67: 39
    801–4: 126–27
  Odyssey, 21, 94, 99, 109, 139, 143–44,
    210, 213–14, 252–53, 256
  themes in, 32, 114, 145, 147
  Book 8: 24n.2, 50
  Book 11: 260
  Book 23: 19
  Book 24: 152
Homeric Hymns, 125
  Hymn to Demeter, 25, 37
Horace
  Odes, 140n.9, 157, 194, 196, 197, 205–6
    4.15.1–2: 205
  Epistles, 157
Housman, A. E., 163
hymns, 159
hypertext, 11

Ibycus, 47
Immerwahr, H. R., 72
imperial power, 8–9, 72, 81, 106–7, 141,
  147, 164, 186–87, 207–8
incipit, 212
inclusion, 19–20. *See also* allusion
intertextuality, 124–35, 143, 264–65. *See also*
  allusion
inversion, 48, 150–51, 196
Irigaray, L., 10
irony, 220. *See also* closure, ironic

Jacoby, F., 75–77
James, H., 108, 221, 255
Jauss, H. R., 220

Johnson, S., 172
Joyce, J., 179

Kamerbeek, J. C., 83
Kauffman, L. S., 11
Kenney, E. J., 112, 187
Kermode, F., 108, 252
komos, 49
kleos, 26, 31, 127–28
Kraus, C., 18

Lacan, J., 171
Lafaye, G., 187
lament, 130, 155–56, 168, 189, 213
Lanham, R., 11
La Penna, A., 192, 212
Leavitt, D., 211, 266n.54
Lefkowitz, M., 262n.38
limitations, 51–53, 57, 61, 81, 119, 155
limits. *See* boundaries
linkage, 262
literacy. *See* orality and literacy
Livy, 196, 237
Longus
    Daphnis and Chloe, 212, 218–19, 224, 225,
        227
        4.40: 219
Lotman, J., 209
Lucan
    Bellum civile, 16–17, 139–40, 146, 147, 162
        8.871–72: 159
Lucian, 212, 213
Lucretius
    De rerum natura, 19, 112–38, 188–89, 192–93
        1.407–9: 121
        1.1114–17: 120
        2.576–80: 117
        3.612–14: 193
        5.1454–57: 120–21
        6.29–32: 119–20
        6.1247–51: 113
        6.1248–51: 189
        6.1250–51: 115
        6.1282–86: 112–13

Macleod, C. W., 41n.22, 126
Manilius
    Astronomica, 126
        5.734–45: 14
Mann, T., 209
Manzoni, A., 212

marriage, 218
Martial, 187
Martin, J., 114
Martin, V., 264
Martindale, C., 7n.13
Marx, K., 110
Marx Brothers, 251
Masters, J., 16–17
Matte Blanco, I., 215
McGushin, P., 134
Meleager
    Crown (*Anth. Pal.* 12.257): 190
memorial. *See* commemoration
Menippean literature, 221
Meyer, N., 265n.49
Michelini, A. N., 83
Miller, D., 30
mise en abyme, 17–18, 216
modifying vignette, 233
Molinié, G., 212
Mommsen, T., 186
morals. *See* gnomai
Morgan, J., 17–18
Morson, G. S., 109, 111
mortality, 24–26, 37, 41–42, 118, 255
Mortimer, A., 219
Müller, G., 117
Murnaghan, S., 213
Murray, G., 83

narratology, 211
Near Eastern myths, 24n.2, 26
New Criticism, 92, 209
New Historicism, 5, 92, 210
new perspectives, 236–37
Nicander, 126
Norwood, G., 83–84
nostos, 114, 214
novels, ancient, 209–27

openness, 139, 221. *See also* closed and open
        readings; closed and open texts
Oppian, 126
orality and literacy, 12, 210
oral narrative, 77–79, 139
otium, 134–35
Ovid, 14
    Amores, 199, 205
        1.15.23–4: 136
    Ars Amatoria, 199
    Epistulae ex Ponto, 206

Ovid (*cont.*)
  3.1127–28: 186
  Fasti, 140, 181, 188, 196
    4.931–32: 196
    Book 6
      725, 771–72, 795–97: 200
      781–82: 202
      797–98: 203
      811–12: 205
  Heroides, 11
  Ibis, 198, 199
  Metamorphoses, 7, 20, 131, 140, 155, 161,
      197–200, 207–8
    2.647–48: 191
    6.419–21: 183
    8.160–68: 182
    9.266–70: 192
    11.194–96: 183
    Book 15: 157, 181–197, 201
      622–25: 187
      624–25: 190
      626–30: 188–89
      743–44: 189
      807–15: 10
      868–71: 195
      871–72: 194
  Remedia Amoris, 199
  Tristia, 187, 197, 199
    1.7.13–14: 197
    2.549–52: 197

paian, 43, 44, 47–48, 55, 61
parade. *See* procession
parallelism, 211, 215, 217, 221–22,
    224n.63
paratext, 211–13. *See also* coronis; *explicit*;
    incipit; *sphragis*
patriarchy, 173n.16, 179–80
Peden, R., 232
Pelling, C., 247
Peradotto, J., 252n.4
performance, 43, 79. *See also* closure and
    performance
Perkell, C., 5n.4
Perry, B. E., 216
Petrarch, 140, 145n.26
Petronius
  Satyricon, 17, 221
Philodemus, 191
Pindar, 44–61
  fr. 89a: 45

Isthmian Odes
  1: 51
  3: 59
  4: 48, 59
  6: 46
  7.42–51: 51–52
  8: 50
Nemean Odes
  1: 50, 54
  2: 49
  4.93–6: 48
  5: 50
  6: 57
  7: 60–61
  7.61–3: 60
  8.32–4: 56
  8.85–7: 47
  9: 45
  10.89–90: 54
Olympian Odes
  1: 47
  2.95–100: 52–53
  3: 52
  4: 51, 54
  7: 51
  6: 47, 49
  8: 46, 50n.22
  8.86–88: 45
  9: 56
  9.76–79: 54–55
  10: 53
  Olympian 13: 45, 56–58, 257
    43–46: 57
    68–69: 58
    91–92: 58
    112–15: 56
  14: 46, 51
Paians
  II: 45
  IV: 54
  V: 50
  VI: 52
Pythian Odes
  1.75–80: 59
  2: 52
  4: 46, 49
  8.98–100: 46
  9: 49
Plato, 115, 215, 220
Plautus, 196
Pliny, 206

Plutarch
 Lives, 228–50
  Agis, 230
  Alexander, 247–48
  Antony, 229, 230, 234–36
   86.8–9: 234
  Aratus, 239, 245
  Aristides, 232, 243
  Brutus, 243
  Caesar, 228, 229, 230, 248–50
   66.1–3, 12–13: 249
   69: 246
   69.1: 249
  Camillus, 230, 245
  Cato maior, 234, 243
  Cato minor, 229, 245
  Cicero, 234, 235, 243
   49.5–6: 233
  Cimon, 240–41, 242
   19.3–4: 238
  Cleomenes, 230
  Coriolanus, 243
  Crassus, 228, 243
  Demetrius, 235, 243–44
  Demosthenes, 231, 239
  Dion, 231
  Flamininus, 229
  Gracchi, 230, 231
  Lucullus, 239–42
   43.2: 241
  Lycurgus, 230, 234n.23
  Lysander, 232, 233
  Marcellus, 231, 234
  Marius, 245
  Nicias, 239
  Numa, 229
  Otho, 230n.11
  Pelopidas, 230
  Pericles, 239n.36
  Philopoemen, 232–33, 238–39
  Poplicola, 230
  Romulus, 230, 232
  Sertorius, 230
  Solon, 230, 232
  Sulla, 232
  Themistocles, 234
  Theseus, 232, 243
Poe, E. A., 212
Pohlenz, M., 75–77
posthumous narrative, 228–36
Potocky, J., 212

Pound, E., 163–64
prayer, 44–46, 52, 57, 197
priamel, 59–60
procession, 15, 50, 129–30, 154, 159. See also
  funerals; triumph
progress, 110, 122–23
prolepsis, 142–43, 211, 216, 218, 251, 257,
  266–67
 external, 251n.2, 267
prooimion, 49
Propertius, 190, 212
 Book 4, 177–78
  4.6: 176
  4.7: 166, 170, 171, 172–73
  4.11: 163–80
   15–16: 167
   26–27: 166
   35–36: 167
   43–44: 167
   47–48: 167
   55–56: 168
   57–60: 168
   71–72: 169
   101–2: 171
prosodion, 45, 47
Proust, M., 209, 218, 267

Quint, D., 8–9, 15
Quintilian, 179

reader expectations, 28n.8, 87, 215–16, 222
reader response, 69–70, 73, 84, 120, 138,
  269–72
recapitulation, 184, 196, 216
 microcosmic, 19, 146, 152, 161. See also
  mise en abyme
 See also parallelism; repetition
reception, 50, 54, 58, 60n.43, 61
reconciliation, 252
recusatio, 163, 176, 179–80
Redfield, J., 30
refrain, 45
repetition, 6, 150–51, 156, 242. See also delay
retrospective patterning, 223, 254, 261
return, 49, 114–15, 126–28, 189, 213–14,
  252. See also nostos; reception
Rhys, J., 264
Ricoeur, P., 209
ring composition, 67–68, 71, 78, 115, 116–
  17, 119, 148n.39, 155, 157, 169, 241.
  See also circularity

Roberts, D., 216
Ross, D., 5
Rubino, C., 111
Rutherford, I., 190

sacrifice, 5–6, 8
Sallust
   Catiline, 133–35
      61.8–9: 133
   Jugurtha, 237–38
      114: 237
Sappho, 49, 50, 51n.25, 55, 61, 258
Schmeling, G., 17, 221n.49
Schmidt, E. A., 182n.3, 196
Seaford, R., 126
Sedelmeier-Stöck, D., 225
segmentation, 13–15
self-reflexiveness, 16, 46, 125, 137, 182. *See also* thematization
Semonides, *Poem on Women* 114–18: 53
Shakespeare, W., 88, 248
Shaw, B., 265
Silius Italicus
   Punica, 20, 140–41, 151, 158–62
      17.283–86: 160
      17.616–17: 162
      17.653–54: 159
Slatkin, L., 36–37
Smith, B. H., 210, 213, 221, 223, 230, 242, 254
Smith, M. F., 121
social ideology, 169. *See also* closure, social
Solon, 51
Sophocles, 7, 99
   Ajax, 88, 130
      473–80: 99
      1120–25: 104–5
   Electra, 259
   Oedipus at Colonus, 85, 102–3, 227, 236, 257–58
   Oedipus Rex, 21, 109
   Philoctetes, 227, 236, 257
   Trachiniae, 18, 96, 130, 236
sphragis, 46–48, 125–26
Stadter, P., 231n.15
Statius
   Achilleid, 139, 160n.77
   Thebaid, 16, 19, 21, 131, 140, 146, 147, 151–58
      1.32–35: 155
      11.737–39: 152

      11.761: 152
      12.787–88: 154
      12.797–99: 156
      12.797–802: 19
      12.810–19: 156–58
Stendhal, 221
Sterne, L., 221
Stoppard, T., 264
   Arcadia, 271–73
Suetonius, 192
summarizing vignette, 230, 232–33. *See also* modifying vignette
summary, 64. *See also* recapitulation
Swinburne, A., 83
Syme, R., 186, 202, 204
synkrisis, 159, 228, 235, 242–50

Tacitus, 237
Tanizaki, J., 263
Telegony, 252n.5
Tennyson, A., 252
terminal generosity, 237–42
terminating motifs, 65. *See also* closure, signals of
thematization, 16–17, 145
Thomas, R., 5–6
Thucydides, 16, 105, 106–7, 127, 135
   2.41: 110
   2.52.4: 113
Tiberius, 202, 204
time, 28, 108, 140–41, 188, 200, 207–8, 209
Tolstoy, L., 109, 267
Torgovnick, M., 210–11, 221, 223, 262
tragedy, Greek, 118–19, 129–31, 227, 236–37
triumph, 143, 151, 153–54, 158–60, 207–8
Turner, V., 15

unfinalizability, 109–11
unraveling, 136

Valerius Flaccus
   Argonautica, 21, 139
Van Der Loeff, A. R., 263n.42
Vegio, M., 144
Velleius, 195
Vessey, D., 16
Virgil, 14
   Aeneid, 7–10, 19–20, 109, 139–41, 142–51, 197, 256
      allusions to, 152–54, 156–62

Book 1: 116
Book 2: 184, 193
   314–17: 151
Book 3: 19
Book 5: 19
Book 6.74–76: 12
Book 12: 21, 131
   43–46: 150
   932–36: 152
   936–42: 146
   945–47: 151
   948–49: 156
   952: 152, 156
Eclogues, 144–45, 147n.36, 191
Georgics, 5–6, 126, 133, 154, 193, 198, 212
  Book 3: 19, 132–33, 143–44, 200
   559–66: 132

West, M. L., 125
White, H., 65, 75n.30
Wilamowitz, U. von, 71, 76–77
Winkler, J., 17–18, 222
Wolff, E., 68n.17
Woodman, A. J., 194
Woolf, V., 209, 211
Wright, M. R., 124
writing. *See* orality and literacy

Xenophon of Ephesus, 215, 217–18, 224, 226, 227

Yeats, W. B.
  Deirdre, 22

Zeitlin, F. I., 17
Zetzel, J., 20